THE BRIGHTON MENDICITY SOCIETY: LIVES OF THE URBAN POOR

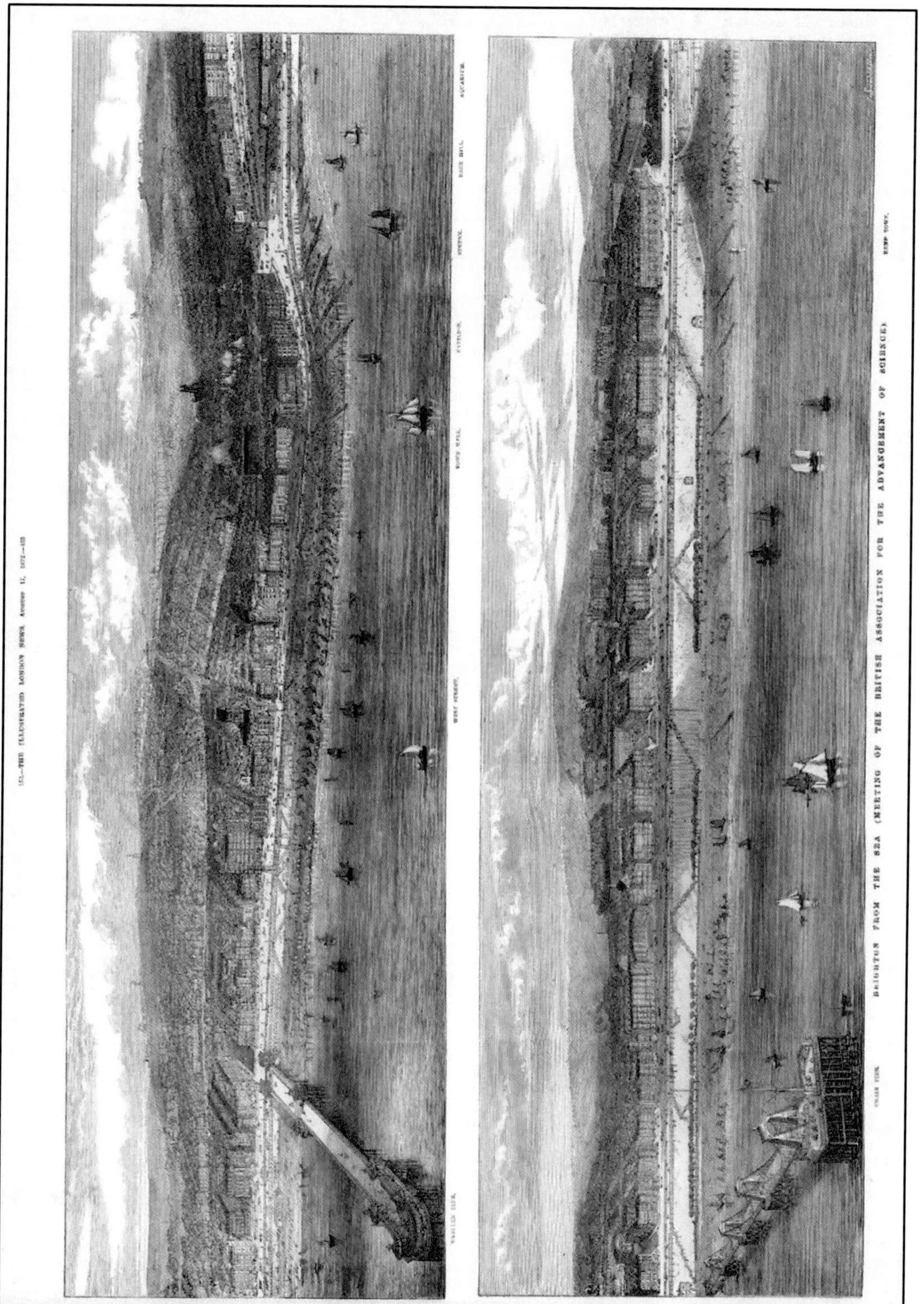

Brighton from the Sea, 1873

THE BRIGHTON MENDICITY SOCIETY: LIVES OF THE URBAN POOR

EDITED BY ANDREW BENNETT

SUSSEX RECORD SOCIETY
VOLUME 102

Published 2022 by
Sussex Record Society
Barbican House
High Street
Lewes
East Sussex BN7 1YE

ISBN 978 0 85445 084 8

Printed by Hobbs the Printers Ltd., Totton, Hampshire

VOLUMES ISSUED BY THE SUSSEX RECORD SOCIETY

Vol. 40 *Chartulary of Lewes Priory (Pt. II), 12th-14th cents.*
Vol. 41 *Transcripts of Sussex Wills up to 1560 Vol. 1 Albourne - Chichester*
Vol. 42 *Transcripts of Sussex Wills up to 1560 Vol. 2 Chiddingly - Horsham*
Vol. 43 *Transcripts of Sussex Wills up to 1560 Vol. 3 Horsted Keynes - Pyecombe*
Vol. 44 *Records of the Barony and Honour of the Rape of Lewes, 1265-1466*
Vol. 45 *Transcripts of Sussex Wills up to 1560 Vol. 4 Racton - Yapton*
Vol. 46 *Chichester Cathedral Chartulary, 13th-16th cents.*
Vol. 47 *Survey of Robertsbridge Manor, 1567-1570*
Vol. 48 *The Town Book of Lewes, 1542-1701*
Vol. 49 *Churchwardens' Presentments, (Pt. I), Archdeaconry of Chichester, 1621-28, 1664-70*
Vol. 50 *Churchwardens' Presentments, (Pt. II), Archdeaconry of Lewes, 1674-1677*
Vol. 51 *Record of Deputations of Gamekeepers, 1781-1928*

Jubilee Volume *Sussex Views from the Burrell Collection*

Vol. 52 *Chapter Acts, Chichester, 1472-1544 (The White Act Book)*
Vol. 53 *The Manor of Etchingham cum Salehurst, 1597-1865*
Vol. 54 *Quarter Sessions Order Book, 1642-1649*
Vol. 55 *Ministers' Accounts of the Manor of Petworth, 1347-1353*
Vol. 56 *Lay Subsidy Rolls, 1524-1525*
Vol. 57 *Custumals of Sussex Manors of the Archbishop of Canterbury, 1285-1330*
Vol. 58 *Chapter Acts, Chichester, 1545-1642*
Vol. 59 *Chartulary of Boxgrove Priory, 12th-14th cents.*
Vol. 60 *Custumals of the Manors of Laughton, Willingdon and Goring, 1292-1338*
Vol. 61 *A Catalogue of Sussex Estate and Tithe Award Maps (Pt. I), 1606-1884*
Vol. 62 *Minutes of the Common Council of the City of Chichester, 1783-1826*
Vol. 63 *The Book of Bartholomew Bolney, 15th cent.*
Vol. 64 *Rye Shipping Records, 1566-1590*
Vol. 65 *Cellarers' Rolls of Battle Abbey, 1275-1513*
Vol. 66 *A Catalogue of Sussex Maps, (Pt. II) 1597-1958*
Vol. 67 *Estate Surveys of the Fitzalan Earls of Arundel, 14th cent.*
Vol. 68 *The Journal of Giles Moore of Horsted Keynes, 1655-1679*
Vol. 69 *The Town Book of Lewes, 1702-1837*
Vol. 70 *The Town Book of Lewes, 1837-1901*
* Vol. 71 *Accounts of the Roberts Family of Boarzell, 1568-1582*
Vol. 72 *Printed Maps of Sussex, 1575-1900*
* Vol. 73 *Correspondence of the Dukes of Richmond and Newcastle, 1724-1750*
Vol. 74 *Sussex Coroners' Inquests, 1485-1558*
* Vol. 75 *The Religious Census of Sussex, 1851*
Vol. 76 *The Fuller Letters, 1728-1755*
Vol. 77 *East Sussex Land Tax, 1785*

In print volumes marked with an asterisk can be obtained from the Sussex Record Society, Barbican House, Lewes, East Sussex, BN7 lYE or through the Society's website: www.sussexrecordsociety.org

CONTENTS

ACKNOWLEDGEMENTS

The cases published here are drawn from the archive of Brighton Mendicity Society held at The Keep, reference: AMS 6930. I am grateful to Jackie Grigg, Chief Executive of Money Advice Plus, successor to the Brighton Mendicity Society, for permission to publish.

I may never have had the idea for this volume without reading Malcolm Pratt's excellent SRS volume Winchelsea Poor Law Records 1790-1841 (vol. 94). With his blessing, I applied the approach that Malcolm used with such good effect for Winchelsea Poor Law records and applied it to the records of the Brighton Mendicity Society. Malcolm has been supportive throughout the lengthy process of researching and writing and I'm grateful to him for sharing his experience.

I am indebted to the council of the Sussex Record Society but in particular Peter Wilkinson and Wendy Walker, who gave me the encouragement needed to start the project, and Roger Pearce and Danae Tankard who have spent countless hours proof-reading and offering valuable advice and constructive criticism. The volume was improved immeasurably as a result of their input.

I regularly encountered words and phrases that initially appeared illegible but the former county archivist of East Sussex, Christopher Whittick, spent many hours enthusiastically helping to decipher the seemingly undecipherable. Christopher's friend Julian Moore also helped with some of the worst examples of bad handwriting.

Ian Hilder supplied some valuable local knowledge relating to William Collingham's final years in Barcombe.

Al Chamberlain and Kirsty Pattrick both helped proof-read parts of the text to ensure they made sense to readers who do not have in-depth knowledge of the 19th Century poor relief system. Emma Coquet and Mike Unwin offered advice and encouragement when momentum was lost.

Past and present colleagues at The Keep have always shown interest in my research and have been tremendously supportive over the last few difficult years. Particular thanks to Tim Evenden for supplying some excellent scanned images.

Thanks to my children Audrey, who helped tidy up the image for the front cover, and Ralph who humoured me tirelessly on lockdown walks around Brighton whilst I recounted some of the tales that appeared on these pages. Lastly, great thanks must go to Sam who, without complaint, got on with the practicalities of life while I got on with this. I simply couldn't have done it without her.

LIST OF ILLUSTRATIONS

Illustrations by kind permission of East Sussex Record Office at The Keep unless otherwise stated.

INTRODUCTION

The reconstituted Brighton Mendicity Society was established in late 1871 to address the growing problem of begging in the town. Its aims were twofold: to relieve beggars directly or put them in contact with other agencies that could, and to check that their claims for relief were not fraudulent. Enquiries were made of every person applying to the charity for financial relief and each enquiry generated a report. This volume comprises transcripts of the earliest surviving reports, which date from January to June 1872, along with further research into the lives of each of the applicants.

There were two usual routes to obtaining relief. The majority of people who approached the charity were referred to as wayfarers: they sought basic sustenance and were usually relieved with bread. Names of people relieved in this way are not recorded but the annual report for 1872, which does not survive but was published in summary in the *Brighton Gazette*,[1] states that 1630 wayfarers received bread and 271 people had cases investigated.[2] The annual report of 1877 shows the huge rise in people using the charity: 4056 adults and 73 children were each given a pound of bread and half a pound of bread respectively and 614 cases were investigated by the charity's agent.[3]

People whose application was deemed worthy of enquiry by the charity were often referred by a third person who gave the pauper an investigation ticket. This document would act as an introduction and allow the charity's agent to conduct some enquiries before deciding on whether to assist the person or not. In most of these cases people were applying for small grants hence the more rigorous approach to checking of credentials.

Some people made a single application and never contacted the charity again, others made numerous applications over many years; but in both instances applicants were assigned a number which remained unique to them. Consequently, some applications provide an insight into a person's life of over the course of decades. Every application included a report which was made by the charity's agent, William Collingham. He recorded details such as names and address of the applicants, what they did for a living, how much rent they paid, how much they usually earned in a week, how many dependants they had, previous addresses and place of birth. After recording this data, which was tabulated on the form, he asked the applicant to make a brief statement about

[1] Brighton Gazette, 21 November 1872.
[2] This figure seems questionable as 200 people had been investigated between January and June alone.
[3] ESRO: PAR 277/7/2/3/34.

the reasons they were asking for relief and then interviewed them to find out a little of their history and the nature of the relief they were seeking. Each report is signed off by Collingham and one of the senior officials, who would record whether the committee agreed to give or refuse relief.

Decisions were usually based on the perception of the applicant's propensity to alcohol, their previous record with the police, if they were deemed to be idle or industrious and whether they were given a good character reference by a person of standing. A successful application could certainly not be relied upon even for those with a seemingly worthy case. Mrs G Waite Vernon (applicant 185) approached the society in May 1872 with the heart-rending appeal 'I have not got one penny in the world. What to do I don't know. If I go to London I cannot stand the noise of the streets' but was deemed ineligible for relief.

BRIGHTON IN THE LATE NINETEENTH CENTURY

The opening of the London to Brighton railway on 21 September 1841 stimulated a huge shift in the physical and economic growth of the town. For some years Brighton's popularity as a resort had been on the wane and its prosperity and population were both declining (Musgrave 1970: Chapter 5). The railway brought with it large numbers of visitors who were abandoning rival resorts in favour of better-connected Brighton and by 1872 Brighton had several attractions that would have appealed to wealthy visitors. First and foremost amongst these was the Royal Pavilion, described in *Page's Handbook to Brighton and Its Vicinity, c. 1871* thus, 'What the Alhambra is to the Spaniard, the Brighton Pavilion is to the Brightonian, a relic of past regal splendour; with this difference, however, that, while the former palace has long since been left to fall to ruins, the latter is not only kept in good repair, but is utilised in such a way as to afford interest and pleasure to the casual visitor, as well as to the habitual resident in Brighton.'[4] The Chain Pier, which stood to the south of New Steine, was opened in 1823 but declined in popularity when Eugenius Birch's more fashionable West Pier was opened in 1866. Birch also designed Brighton Aquarium which was opened in 1872 and contained a small theatre as well as the largest display tank in the world at that time.

The arrival of wealthy visitors, some of whom would stay for an entire season, led to an increase in the resident population who found seasonal employment in the service industries which emerged to cater to their needs. Census returns from 1861 record that the majority of local women gave their occupation as wives or mothers (10,166) but women in service came second (7,294) and textiles

[4] ESRO: AMS 6850/1/22.

was the third most popular profession cited by women (5,316).[5] These figures are reflected in the occupations of the women that applied to the Mendicity Society in 1872 who were commonly employed as charwomen, ironers and dressmakers. Women's fourth most popular response to the occupation section of the census was 'person of rank or property' (1,471). This last group appears in the records of the Mendicity Society as the voices of the upper and middle classes who were contacting the charity out of distrust or benevolent concern for the beggars they encountered in their localities. Men's employment on the 1861 census is far more evenly distributed among the trades but 3,796 were engaged in work in 'art and mechanic productions': double that of any other profession. Probably the largest employer of men practicing these trades would have been the railway works situated to the north of Brighton station.

By the 1870s Brighton had seen three decades of rapid growth. Census abstracts record population figures of 46, 634 in 1841; 65,569 in 1851; 77,693 in 1861 and 90,011 in 1871 (Carder 1990). The two later census returns also record the growth in the rate of homes: 12,727 in 1861 and 16,284 in 1871. The majority of these new dwellings were terraced houses built to the north and north east of the town centre in North Laine and the area once known as Hilly Laine but now generally referred to as Hanover. These dwellings offered housing to both working class and middle-class residents and, for those that could afford it, provided a much-needed alternative to the overcrowded and insanitary slums in the streets off Carlton Hill and Edward Street where the very poorest inhabitants of Brighton lived. These streets, where many of the applicants to the Mendicity Society hailed from, will be examined in greater detail elsewhere in this introduction.

Infrastructure grew to meet the needs of the expanding population of residents and visitors. The Sussex County Hospital welcomed its first patient in 1828 but was expanded in 1839 and again in 1841. The hospital was funded by patrons who were each entitled to put forward the names of people they felt worthy of medical assistance: the larger their contribution the more names they were entitled to propose.[6] For example, the statute and rule book of 1865 states that subscribers of one guinea per annum were allowed to recommend four out-patients annually whereas subscribers of 20 guineas could recommend limitless patients provided that they did not have more than two in-patients and 10 out-patients at one time. New in-patients were admitted every Wednesday and were asked to supply the name of someone who would give security in case of their removal to another institution or their burial; in some cases, the recommender

[5] GB Historical GIS / University of Portsmouth, Brighton Inc/RegD through time, Industry Statistics, Persons aged 20 and over by Sex and 1861 Occupational Order, *A Vision of Britain Through Time.*

[6] ESRO: HB 23/3.

and supplier of security were one and the same. Emergency cases were admitted without the need of a recommendation and costs appear to have been covered by the hospital. The hospital admitted in-patients suffering from infectious diseases at any time during the week and there were strict procedures regarding their care to minimise the risks to staff and other patients.

Although there were outbreaks of cholera throughout the nineteenth century Brighton did not see the public health emergencies of larger towns and cities that occurred elsewhere during the period but both Dr George Samuel Jenks' report of 1842[7] and Dr Edward Cresy's report of 1849[8] noted that poorly drained cesspools were having an extremely detrimental effect on residents' health. Jenks noted that 'Owing to the imperfect and insufficient drainage of the town, the inhabitants are compelled to have recourse to numerous cesspools... and to save the inconvenience of frequently emptying them, they dig below the hard coombe rock until they come to the shingles, where all the liquid filth drains away. The consequence is inevitable; the springs in the lower part of the town must be contaminated.' Cresy felt the problem lay in the gases omitted by the contaminated water, 'The causes of sickness may be traced in the quantity of sulphurated hydrogen which arises from the excrementitious matters retained in the several cesspools throughout the town. This deadly poison pervades all the narrow breathing places which are found at the backs of continued rows of buildings and where there are windows so situated as to admit it to the overcrowded apartments.' As a result of these papers and subsequent reports by local medical officers of health, the authorities invested in the sewerage system during the 1850s and 1860s, but it was not until Sir John Hawkshaw's scheme of 1871-1874 that a truly satisfactory system was established. Hawkshaw built a sewer that ran from Hove Street in the east to Portobello, near to Telscombe Cliffs, in the west which intercepted the existing drainage that would otherwise have emptied into the sea on Brighton beach. The contamination of the water supply not only led to an overhaul of Brighton's sewerage system but also the provision of drinking water to the town. In July 1872 Brighton Corporation purchased the Constant Service Water Company under the terms of the Brighton Corporation Waterworks Act which, at that point, was supplying 18,000 homes in Brighton, Falmer, Preston, Patcham, Hangleton, Ovingdean and Rottingdean (Carder 1990).

The improvements to the sewerage and water systems in 1871-1872 and the creation of the Mendicity Society in 1872 may seem coincidental but they arose from changes to local government administration. In 1869 the Royal Sanitary

[7] The Keep: Reference Room pamphlet BHSB628JEN.1.
[8] The Keep: Reference Room Brighton pamphlet box 14.

Commission was established to consider management of public health. As a result of their findings the Local Government Board Act transferred responsibility for sanitation and public health from the Board of Health to the Local Government Board in 1871. The Local Government Board also subsumed the Poor Law Board which was responsible for the provision of poor relief and a separate section on this subject appears below. In tandem with the Local Government Board Act the Public Health Act of 1872 set up local sanitary authorities which employed local medical officers of health. They were responsible for monitoring public health, reporting on what they found and making suggestions for improvements: their reports give a vivid picture of conditions in Brighton's slums during that period.[9] The reports are considered in more detail elsewhere in the introduction.

The town's mentally ill were cared for at the Sussex County Lunatic Asylum in Haywards Heath. The hospital opened on 25 July 1859 and was originally co-funded by East Sussex and West Sussex. However, in the 1890s East Sussex and West Sussex dissolved their partnership and set up new facilities at Hellingly and Graylingwell respectively, leaving Haywards Heath to be solely administered by Brighton Borough. The annual report of 1872 stated that there were 664 patients comprising 287 men and 377 women, though the hospital had capacity for 792.[10] During the year 88 men and 125 women were admitted and 97 men and 56 women were discharged. It is noteworthy how many of the patients were from outside the county but had been transferred to Sussex under contract from other counties: 60 of the recently discharged men were returned to Hanwell Asylum in Middlesex and 53 people were admitted from Kent Asylum at Maidstone.

Many of the Mendicity Society applicants that had spells in the asylum came from Brighton Workhouse. Although there appears to be no documentation that defines the process of transfer in a step-by-step manner the surviving patient reception documents give a good idea of the procedure involved.[11] Each patient's reception papers contained sections which were to be completed by representatives of different local authorities: the workhouse surgeon, usually David Nichols, would sign a statement summarising the patient's name and occupation, their symptoms and the date of his or her examination; the Justice of the Peace, usually Arthur Bigge, would sign, authorising the removal of the patient from Brighton to the asylum; the costs for the removal would have been covered by the Brighton relieving officer, usually William Brimble Smith, and

[9] ESRO: DB/E/1.
[10] ESRO: HC 2/2.
[11] ESRO: HC 24.

printed receipts for covering those costs appear on the back of the document. The form, which also contains a statement regarding the patient's age, previous address, next of kin and cause of insanity was sent to Dr S W D Williams, the asylum's medical superintendent. If the patient was ever considered well enough to be discharged by the committee of visitors, the clerk would sign-off the paperwork and attach it to the admission papers to close the case. James Gardner's *Sweet Bells Jangled Out of Tune* provides a comprehensive history of the institution.

Aside from the records of these medical institutions the other large set of records which provided useful insight into the lives of the mendicants were the reports of the Police Courts published in local newspapers. Until 1972 the English court system was split into three tiers: Assize Courts which dealt with the most serious crimes and whose function was transferred to Crown Courts; Quarter Sessions, which were abolished in 1972, dealt with lesser criminal cases and civil administration; Petty Sessions, or Police Courts as they were sometimes known, were replaced by Magistrates' Courts and dealt with petty crime. The *Brighton Gazette*, *Brighton Guardian* and *Brighton Examiner* all reported the proceedings of the Police Court in some detail and, as so many Mendicity Society applicants passed through the courts, they are a rich biographical source. Hard copy and microfilms of these newspapers are available at The Keep but a growing number have been digitised by the British Newspaper Archive.

The chief constable's report of 14 June 1871, which is summarised in the minutes of the Watch Committee of Brighton Borough Council, records that for a town with a population of approximately 90,000 people there was one chief constable; two superintendents; three inspectors; three detectives; four sergeants and 88 constables.[12] The town was split into 35 night-beats and 19 day-beats. The police station was then situated in the town hall along with holding cells and the magistrates' court room. One of the constables enumerated in the report of 1871 was William Collingham. He resigned his position on 20 December 1871 having been appointed the role of agent for the nascent Mendicity Society.[13] Collingham's initials appear on almost all of the applications made to the charity. A brief biography of Collingham appears later in the introduction.

Although Brighton could not have been described as a 'military town' there was a military presence during the later 19th century. The 1st Sussex Rifles and 1st Sussex Artillery Volunteers occupied drill halls in Gloucester Road and Church Street and cavalry units were housed at Preston Barracks on the Lewes Road.

[12] ESRO: DB/B/12/5.
[13] ESRO: SPA/3/17/1.

Documents recording the make-up of units are not held locally so it has not been possible to give figures of troops that were stationed in Brighton but parish registers of churches in Preston attest to the significant number of troops marrying or having children with local women. Regimental bands of cavalry or artillery units stationed at Preston Barracks often played concerts on the West Pier or in the Pavilion grounds for visitors and residents alike. However, despite the pomp of the military bands Brighton's star was waning by the end of the nineteenth century. Lewis Melville's *Brighton: its history, its follies and its fashions* published in 1909 lamented, 'Brighton is interesting only in its past. As Bath has become the home of the half-pay officer, so Brighton has developed into the Cockney's paradise, the Mecca of the stock-broker and the chorus girl. The glory indeed has departed.'

POOR RELIEF IN THE LATE NINETEENTH CENTURY

The Poor Law Amendment Act of 1834 was designed to reduce the financial burden of caring for the poor and standardise practices across the country. The Act established a governing body known as the Poor Law Commission whose primary task was to group the country's roughly 15,000 parishes into new administrative units called Poor Law Unions. Each of these unions was run by an elected Board of Guardians.[14] As a Local Act parish, Brighton was exempt from forming a union and it operated its own workhouse independently but, like every other administrative area, it raised funds by means of a local poor rate which was levied upon local property owners. However, just like parish unions, Brighton was expected to reduce payments to paupers living in their own homes (often referred to as outdoor relief) and instead make them receive indoor relief at the workhouse.

Most people that contacted the Mendicity Society had, or would have, spent time in the workhouse. These institutions provided beds for the unemployed, the sick and those too elderly or infirm to work. Conditions were deliberately unpleasant and were intended to deter people from entering unless they had no other option: parents were separated from children, husbands were separated from wives and the able bodied were expected to carry out menial work. James Gardner's *A History of Brighton Workhouses* (Gardner (2012)) gives a detailed

[14] These administrative areas have a continued existence in the boundaries of registration districts. In 1872 the Board comprised William Baker; Samuel Bastick; Edwin Booth; Alfred Buckwell; Edmundus Burn; Henry Carr; William Challen; Thomas Chandler; William Cornish; John Craven; Octavius Fox; Edward Fussell; Daniel Greenin; James Hall; John Hawkins; William Hudson; William Lucas; Joseph Lugard; William Onions; Richard Patching; William Payne; Richard Pearce; Thomas Phillips; William Pierson; Henry Saunders (Boyces Square); Henry Saunders (Buckingham Road); George Sinnock; Henry Stevens; William Tankard and William Thompson, ESRO: AMS 6432/7/1.

description of life in the institution, which had previously been situated at Church Hill but new premises on Elm Grove were opened in 1867.

Anyone wishing to gain admission to the workhouse would be interviewed by the relieving officer or the clerk acting on behalf of the Board of Guardians. If the official felt they were a suitable case for indoor relief an admission order was signed by the relieving officer and formal admission was granted by the Board at the next weekly meeting. The order was then valid for six days. The admission procedure involved handing in clothes, bathing and being issued with a workhouse uniform before men, women and children were split up and sent to the appropriate part of the building. Whilst living at the workhouse people were free to discharge themselves as long as they gave reasonable notice to the authorities. Failure to gain permission before leaving the premises could result in a charge of the theft of the uniform (Gardner 2012). Unfortunately, no administrative records from Brighton Workhouse survive from the 19th Century so it is impossible to say how fluid the population of the institution was. The only insight into the movement into and out of workhouses in this volume is the case of Caroline Skinner (applicant 74) who was admitted to Hastings Workhouse 45 times between 8 July 1877 and 15 February 1899. Her stays varied in length between two nights and almost three months, but the majority lasted between three and four weeks.

Outdoor relief had always been a contentious issue as local rate payers often resented the allocation of funds to people who some may have perceived as lazy or profligate. In 1844 the Poor Law Commission took the view that the outdoor relief bill had not been reduced sufficiently so passed the Outdoor Relief Prohibitory Order which banned outdoor relief to able-bodied men and women in almost all circumstances. Following scandals and bad publicity the Poor Law Commission was dissolved in 1847 and the Poor Law Board was created in its place. In 1852 the Board attempted to address the continued problem of outdoor relief which many considered was still proving too expensive to maintain. Its Outdoor Relief Regulation Order included restrictions on giving relief to the sick, elderly and widowed and was unpopular with local Boards of Guardians who felt their autonomy was being undermined.

The administration of poor relief was changed again in 1871 when the Poor Law Board was replaced by the Local Government Board. The new body, which arose from a statement by the president of the Poor Law Board, George Goschen, had a broader remit covering public health, sanitation and the local government responsibilities of the Home Secretary and the Privy Council. Goschen's Minute, as it was known, theorised that the rise of paupers in certain areas of London was directly attributable to the rise in charitable giving in those locations (Harris

2007). He argued that indiscriminate outdoor relief perpetuated demand from more claimants rather than resolving the problems of the existing population. Goschen wanted to establish a clearer delineation between those who may receive financial help from the Poor Law and those who could gain relief from charities. He felt it was the Poor Law's responsibility to prevent people falling into destitution and charity's place to assist those who were merely poor. He was also keen to ensure that no one who was receiving poor relief from the authorities should also gain from charitable aid and it was from this idea regarding the division of responsibility for these two groups that the Charity Organisation Society was established in 1869 (more on the formation of the Mendicity Society and Charity Organisation Society can be found below). In 1871 the Local Government Board issued a circular influenced by Goschen's suggestions which stated that the distribution of outdoor relief to single able-bodied men and women, to women whose husbands had deserted them for less than twelve months, and to able-bodied widows with only a single dependent child should be prohibited: outdoor relief should only be given to applicants after they had been visited by a relieving officer and should be granted for no more than three months. This policy resulted in a reduction of 268,000 people receiving outdoor relief between 1871 and 1880 (Harris 2007).

The impossible position that abandoned women were put in as a result of this policy may account in a minor way for the larger number of female applicants to the charity (126 women to 74 men): Elizabeth Pavey (applicant 65), Mary Goble (applicant 95), Margaret Murray (applicant 105), Ann Simmons (applicant 143) and a French woman named Le Bas were all deserted by their husbands. Both Goble and Murray had been assaulted by their husbands but were reluctant to see them imprisoned due to the adverse effect that would have on the household finances. David Englander describes the dilemma faced by abandoned women who, with the cuts to relief, needed to work but bore the sole responsibility of their children, 'Neither the central authority nor local boards of guardians could agree on a uniform policy towards women. The former thought that relief policy should underpin the integrity of the family; the latter emphasized the rights of the child and the tolerance of the ratepayer… Outdoor relief, when granted, had to be minimal so as not to offend ratepayer sensibilities. Confusion reigned.' (Englander 1998).

HISTORY OF THE BRIGHTON MENDICITY SOCIETY

The words mendicant and mendicity are rarely used now and they were already slipping into obscurity in the 19th Century. The terms describe beggars and the act of begging but the Brighton Mendicity Society, which was formed in late

1871 and is the focus of this volume, had changed its name to the Charity Organisation Society within a matter of months.

An earlier Mendicity Society was established in Brighton in 1824 to deal with the growing number of beggars that were operating in the town.[15] This charity was run from premises at 108 Church Street and appears to have been a fairly small operation with limited means and a low profile. In January 1850 a man named J J Brinton wrote to the editor of the *Brighton Gazette* accusing too many people of 'indiscriminate almsgiving' which he felt was fuelling the problem of begging on the streets of Brighton.[16] He went on to claim, 'A lazy, lying, saucy mendicant importunes lustily for assistance; to excite our pity he exhibits a cauterized limb, which generally is pretended to have been burnt at sea, or occasioned by fire damp in a coal mine, but which really has been 'dressed up' for the purpose by the use of some well-known ingredients from the chemist's shop. We believe his story, sympathise with him in his sufferings, undraw our purse strings, drop our mite into his soft attenuated hand, unused to manual labour, and go on our way leaving the bare-faced hypocrite 'laughing in his sleeve' at our credulity and moreover at liberty to victimise others in the same way.' Brinton finished his tirade by stating that 'A good Mendicity Society in Brighton would be a capital check to these mendicants and I anticipate shortly to hear of one being established.' The editor of the *Brighton Gazette* replied that Brinton appeared to be in ignorance of the fact that Brighton already had a functioning Mendicity Society but concurred that the public should desist from giving money directly to beggars. The work of this earlier Mendicity Society does not appear to have been regularly reported by local press which perhaps accounts for Brinton's ignorance and the general lack of knowledge about its aims.

The presence of street beggars and the effect they were having on the public consciousness is well illustrated in an article published in the *Brighton Gazette* in February 1851.[17] It highlighted not only the prevalence of begging but also the tactics used by beggars to elicit maximum sympathy from passers-by. 'One point was omitted to be noticed on Monday and that was the horribly cruel way in which infants are made use of by the professed beggars for the purpose of exciting commiseration. It is not a long while ago that a woman was brought before the Bench on a charge of vagrancy with a child in her arms having sores on its limbs, which it was too evident and well ascertained had been caused by the inhuman mother by burning; and for months past a woman has been about the town with an infant of a few months old strapped on to a musical instrument

[15] Brighton Guardian, 25 May 1871.
[16] Brighton Gazette, 17 January 1850.
[17] Brighton Gazette, 27 February 1851.

and exposed for hours to all the inclemencies of the weather. And let the would-be-charitable reflect that it is by promiscuous alms-giving that these horrible cruelties are encouraged.'

The early incarnation of the Mendicity Society seems to have been run in much the same way as it was in the period examined in this volume. In 1825 the *Brighton Gazette* ran a short editorial piece on the charity stating, 'This society is well calculated both to discover the silent sufferer of penury and to repress the daring effrontery of the sturdy beggar.'[18] The office was run using a system whereby those in need of relief could be presented with a ticket. When the recipient presented the ticket at the charity's office they would be investigated and given assistance if they were considered deserving.

By 1871 begging had clearly become so prevalent in Brighton that the clergy and representatives of other bodies concerned with the welfare of the poor felt that it was time to reinvigorate the old charity in line with the changes to local government described in the previous section. This idea was first discussed at a meeting of the Watch Committee of Brighton Borough Council on 22 February 1871.[19] The newspaper report stated that the committee invited a deputation consisting of Dr John Hannah, vicar of Brighton, John Deverell, Douglas Fox, Robert Johnson, Thomas F Chilver and William Henty to discuss how to deal with the problem. The article went on to state that societies with similar aims had been established in Hampstead and Blackheath which had reduced the number of mendicants by a proportion of 10 to one. The recent rise in the number of local beggars was, they thought, attributable to the increased ease with which people could obtain pedlars' licences. It was felt that this was the result of a misunderstanding by the police who were granting licenses to anyone who could gain lodging for a single night: it was not explained what they felt the correct procedure should have been.

Later in March 1871 William Henty of the nascent Mendicity Society wrote to the Board of Guardians suggesting that they put forward two representatives to sit on the committee and William Challen and William Samuel Tankard were nominated.[20] The same report mentions the success that authorities in Hampshire had enjoyed with a similar scheme and suggests that Hampshire's success may result in increased numbers of beggars coming to Brighton. At a meeting of the Guardians in April 1871 William Challen presented the idea that the Mendicity Society would operate by distributing tickets to various residents

[18] Brighton Gazette, 13 January 1825.
[19] ESRO: DB/B/12/5.
[20] Brighton Gazette, 30 March 1871.

of the town who, in turn, would give them to beggars they encountered.[21] It is unclear why Challen described this as a novel idea as it followed the model which had been used by the Mendicity Society since the 1820s: it is possible that the old system had lapsed or differed in a subtle way not described by the report. Challen explained that the recipient of the ticket would be able to approach the Mendicity Society who would then assess which applicants were deserving of relief. This system, it was felt, would have the dual effect of giving assistance to those in real need of relief and be a means of 'getting rid of a great number of the resident beggars in the town who were continually following the gentry about.'

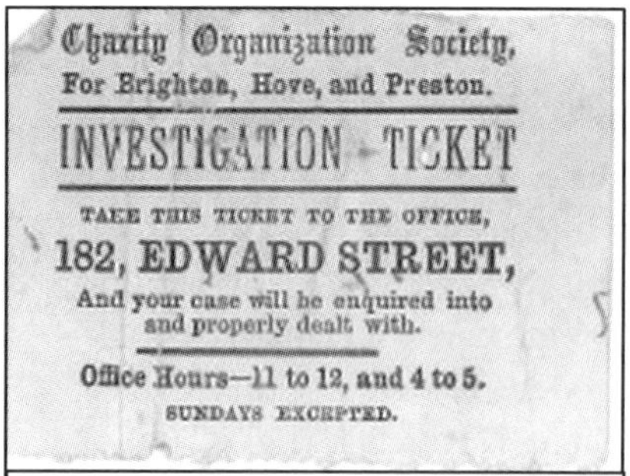
Charity Organization Society,
For Brighton, Hove, and Preston.
INVESTIGATION TICKET
TAKE THIS TICKET TO THE OFFICE,
182, EDWARD STREET,
And your case will be enquired into and properly dealt with.
Office Hours—11 to 12, and 4 to 5.
SUNDAYS EXCEPTED.

Charity Organisation Society investigation ticket, AMS 6930/6/179

The ticketing scheme had been adopted by a number of similar fledgling societies in order to regulate and administer relief of the poor in their districts. This system encouraged parish District Visitors, members of the Mendicity Society and members of the public to give tickets to people that they noticed begging in the street or, as was also common at the time, door-to-door begging. If the pauper approached the charity their case would be assessed and, where appropriate, relief would be given either in the form of food, a small grant, a ticket for the Sussex County Hospital or a referral to another organisation. A meeting of May 1871 reported in the *Brighton Herald* gave a good summary of the perceived benefits of the ticketing system: 'The Society would place tickets of relief in the hands of all families in the town, whether subscribers or not, who will accept them, and the almsgiver, when solicited for relief, by bestowing them instead of alms, will thus have saved his money and be enabled to apply it through the hands and the investigations of the Society in a way to effect a certainty of charitable relief upon the really helpless and deserving to the exclusion of the imposter. This is the truest charity, which always labours in its vocation, and does not flatter itself by a momentary feeling of satisfaction for duty done by the mere dropping of a penny or a sixpence into the hands of a beggar.'[22] The report went on to argue that the suppression of almsgiving would put an end to begging and cited Dorset as a county where such measures were having the desired effect.

[21] Brighton Gazette, 6 April 1871.
[22] Brighton Gazette, 25 May 1871.

At a committee meeting on the suppression of mendicity held on 23 May 1871 at the National School, Church Street, a draft report was read aloud voicing concern that Brighton's ability to deal with the problem of street begging was limited due to its status as a municipal borough.[23] The committee also felt that any efforts they made to address the problem would count for nothing if the surrounding local authorities were not taking similar steps to monitor the movement of itinerant workers or habitual beggars: 'In deciding on the best plan suited to Brighton, to protect itself against the growing evil of mendicancy, it is found that the position and circumstances of the town as a Municipal Borough restrict its organisation within narrow limits. Until the County itself takes action, no effective movement can be made here for helping the onward progress of the honest wayfarer, by tickets addressed to or from neighbouring Unions, as in Hampshire; or for any relief outside its own boundaries, to be administered by the police or otherwise.' The report went on to consider the relationship between the Mendicity Society and the other agencies in Brighton that helped relieve the needs of the town's poorest residents. They had no wish to displace any of the existing institutions whose primary function was to deal with the deserving poor; merely expand the scale of the Mendicity Society that had been running in Brighton since 1824. The new incarnation of the charity would be run along the lines of a similar body established in Bristol. William Henty stated that the Bristol Association, 'co-operated with other societies and when the case of an individual was investigated care was taken to provide for the necessities of his case and, if needful, to introduce him to another society'.

A public meeting was convened at the Town Hall on 14 June 1871 by the Mayor of Brighton, Alderman Richard Webb.[24] He stated that vagrancy was the most important issue facing Brighton and the rest of the county and that the problem had 'increased to such an extent as to be hardly bearable'. He went on to state that the charity's real purpose should be to decrease vagrancy and assist the deserving poor. The Vicar of Brighton, Archdeacon John Hannah, remarked that he thought there were 'four classes of mendicants to be dealt with whom he would characterise as the fluctuating and the resident poor, each class being subdivided into the necessitous and deserving and into the imposing and worthless. There was the honest wayfarer and the man who purposely journeyed from place to place for a living; there were the resident poor reduced by sickness and calamity to sore distress and there were those who recklessly and heedlessly brought all their misery upon themselves. His desire was to afford relief and assistance to the really deserving and to punish those who made a mere trade of mendicancy.' Next to speak was Alderman John Cordy

[23] Brighton Guardian, 25 May 1871.
[24] Brighton Gazette, 15 June 1871.

Burrows who had been mayor in 1857 and 1858 and would become mayor again later in 1871. Burrows referred to the fact that when Edward Cresy made an official inspection of the town for the Board of Health in 1849 he calculated that there were approximately 1,600 vagrants living in Brighton.[25] Burrows wondered how much this figure would have increased now that the population had grown to 80,000 or 90,000. He credited the town council for adopting the Common Lodging House Act, which gave them a regulatory role over all tramps' lodging-houses and similar establishments. Burrows described the appalling conditions to be found in some of these lodging houses: 'in four bedrooms 80 or 90 persons were found, and in another room where one man was lying dead, 18 other people were living'.

The committee decided upon the name the Mendicity Society for Brighton, Hove and Preston at a meeting on 30 June 1871.[26] It stated that its objects were: to repress mendicity in its various forms, including street begging, begging letters and false petitions; to investigate thoroughly the cases of all poor persons coming before the society; to relieve cases of urgent necessity and to bring existing local charities and the poor law authorities into co-operation with one another. The *Brighton Gazette* of 16 November 1871 carried an advertisement for the posts of charity agent and collector. The agent's position came with a weekly wage of 30 shillings, the collector's job was paid on commission. The successful applicant for the role of charity agent was William Collingham whose career is discussed in detail elsewhere in the introduction.

The charity's first annual report stated that in March 1872 it had become affiliated with the Charity Organisation Society of London and that consequently it proposed to change its name to the Charity Organisation Association for Brighton, Hove and Preston.[27] The Charity Organisation Society (COS), discussed in brief earlier in this introduction, was formed following the reading of a paper by the Unitarian minister and social reformer Henry Solly entitled, 'How to deal with the Unemployed Poor of London and with its 'Roughs' and Criminal Classes' at a meeting of the Society of Arts in London on 22 June 1868 (Bosanquet 1914). Having heard Solly's paper 'The London Association for the Prevention of Pauperism and Crime' was created by a committee of influential men including Solly; the art critic John Ruskin; former chair of the Board of Directors of Convict Prisons for Ireland, Sir Walter Crofton; and former Governor of the Straits Settlements, General Sir William Orfeur Cavenagh: in due course this organisation adopted the title The Charity

[25] Census abstracts give the population of Brighton in 1851 as 65,569.

[26] Brighton Gazette, 6 July 1871.

[27] Brighton Gazette, 21 November 1872.

Organisation Society.[28] Sir Orfeur Cavenagh, as he usually styled himself, is not known to have had any previous links to Brighton but his comments and signature appear on Brighton Mendicity Society application forms from 1 January to 15 March 1872. This suggests that although the committee members of Brighton Mendicity Society did not create a formal link to the Charity Organisation Society until they affiliated in March 1872, they must have had the intention of doing so very early in the charity's development.[29] Cavenagh's comments were perhaps intended as an indication of how applications would have been dealt with by the society's head office and therefore as a marker for the local administrators to follow.

The aims of the newly-badged charity were broadly the same as its predecessor but were worded in the following way in the annual report of November 1872: '1st – to afford every charitable agency in the district means of inter-communication, with a view to prevent the abuse of charity by undeserving persons or those sufficiently relieved; 2nd – to secure investigation, through both paid and voluntary agency, of the cases of all poor persons coming before it, with the ultimate object of referring them to the proper quarter for relief; 3rd – to repress mendicity; 4th – to afford relief where no other sources are available, as far as possible on definite principles.'[30]

This annual report covers the same period as the applications transcribed in this volume and gives the following statistics: dismissed as not requiring relief, 4; ineligible, 54; undeserving, 43; giving false addresses, 5; referred to parish authorities, 36; referred to district agencies, 4; referred to private persons, 15; referred to charitable institutions, 9; referred to other districts, 3; assisted by grants, 44; assisted by loans, 1; assisted by employment, 1; assisted by hospital letters, 14. Total, 233
Wayfarers relieved with bread, 1384
Grand total, 1617

The annual report of 1872 does not give any indication of the financial state of the charity in its first year of existence. However, the annual report of November 1873 published in the *Brighton Herald* does give a fairly detailed breakdown of the charity's income and outgoings.[31] Mr Maclauchlan Brandreth, the charity's

[28] The Straits Settlements now make up Malaysia and Singapore.

[29] The two earliest application forms in the series transcribed in this volume carry the following header, 'Society for Organising Charitable Relief and Repressing Mendicity, 15 Buckingham Street, Strand, WC'. Later forms are headed Brighton Mendicity Society and Charity Organisation Society for Brighton, Hove and Preston.

[30] Brighton Gazette, 21 November 1872.

[31] Brighton Herald, 29 November 1873.

honorary solicitor, stated that subscriptions and donations amounted to £372 which, with an existing balance of £168 4s 6d, gave an overall total of £540 4s 6d. The debit side showed that £85 16s 7d (which included £24 1s 8d for bread) had been given as grants, and other expenses amounted to £266 18s 8d, making a total outlay of £352 15s 3d and leaving a balance of £187 9s 3d. It is impossible to know exactly what criteria were applied by charity officials when deciding whether to relieve people or not, but it is difficult not to be reminded of the contemporaneous alternative to the acronym COS, 'Cringe or Starve' when seeing this figure (Englander 1998). Possibly the most noteworthy example of the charity's parsimony appears in Kate Green's (applicant 61) request for assistance to help pay for her three-year-old son's burial in February 1872: she was advised to ask her husband's employer for the money.

A letter from Robert Johnson, the Charity Organisation Committee's secretary, was read at a meeting of the Watch Committee on 6 January 1873. The letter sought to create closer ties between the charity and the committee and invited a member to sit on the council of the COS, but the committee minute book contains the statement 'This committee does not consider it consistent with their duty to appoint one of their member to be a member of the Society'.[32]

CARLTON HILL IN THE 1870S

The reconstituted Brighton Mendicity Society started dealing with applications from paupers in January 1872. The majority of the people with recourse to the Mendicity Society lived in the area immediately to the east of the Royal Pavilion, between Edward Street and Carlton Hill. This area, which was served by St John the Evangelist, was developed in the early years of the 19th Century and was the most densely populated part of Brighton.[33] A second concentration of slum housing was situated between Eastern Road and Upper St James's Street and was served by All Souls, Eastern Road. These parishes appear to have administered a broad range of small charities to help serve the poor living within their boundaries, but anyone needing longer term care would have to look to the workhouse.

The application papers contain numerous examples of people whom the Mendicity Society recommended to the workhouse authorities but who did not wish to go. James Whitehead, a 70-year-old labourer (applicant 27); Sarah Wells,

[32] ESRO: DB/B/12/5.

[33] The earliest document relating to this area held at ESRO is a letter from Atkinson and Wildes, Chancery Lane, to Thomas Attree, solicitor, Brighton, regarding the property of a Mr Gardner on the west side of Thomas Street. The letter dates from 21 June 1815 but refers to a conveyance of 24-25 October 1806, ESRO, AMS 7100/1815/6-21.

a 74-year-old needlewoman (applicant 38) and Charlotte Colbran, a 68-year-old nurse (applicant 99) were amongst those who refused the workhouse, instead hoping to gain outdoor relief from the Guardians.[34] It is worth noting that many applicants to the Mendicity Society had been in receipt of outdoor relief from the Guardians and this is often referred to in the papers as 'parish relief'. The funds they received were allocated not by the ecclesiastical parish but by the Guardians of the Parish of Brighton or Brighton Board of Guardians as they were more commonly known. The annual report of the incumbent of St John's, Carlton Hill, in 1870 described those unwilling to enter the workhouse in unflattering terms, 'It is pretty well proved that the real poor – those that are truly in want of the necessaries of life, and for whom every human heart must bleed, *never* beg in in the streets. They either go to the workhouse; or, if they linger on without accepting the 'test' of the Union, from motives of family affection or pride, they do so silently in their lodgings, and, as we know too often, remain there starving until help comes too late. They will not endure to join the dishonest trade of the professional beggar; but in any case – the fact is proved – that from some motive or other, such persons have never yet been found among the number of street mendicants.'[35]

However, the workhouse and Board of Guardians represent only part of the complex web of organisations which aimed to relieve those who found themselves in abject poverty. Many parishes ran an array of small charities each of which had its own specific remit: the parish of St John, Carlton Hill, Brighton, had a coal club, a children's shoe and clothing fund, a sick and lying-in linen society and a blanket lending society. This parish also provided treat days for school children and penny dinners for the very poorest people in the area.[36] 'We found that an Irish stew might be provided on a large scale at a very moderate expense and after a few trials it appeared that the meal was greatly appreciated and evidently supplied popular want. The dinners commenced on the 1st of January 1870 and ended on the 6th of April; during which period 5,234 dinners were served at the charge of one penny each. A liberal supply of bread was given with each plate and each person was served with what might be called a satisfying meal. These dinners re-opened in the year in which we are now writing [1871] and were continued three times a week from January 13th to March 10th; during which interval 9,238 dinners were served at a total cost of £81 10 4d.'[37]

[34] The Guardians sometimes felt that giving outdoor relief, a regular subsistence grant which would enable people to remain in private accommodation, was more suitable or cost effective than placing them in the workhouse.

[35] ESRO: PAR 277/7/2/1a/32.

[36] ESRO: PAR 277/7/2/1a/32.

[37] Brighton Guardian, 17 May 1871.

Amongst the most popular of these charities were the parish schools. St John the Evangelist was consecrated on 28 January 1840 and its first incumbent Reverend Spencer Rodney Drummond, vicar of St John's between 1843 and 1861, founded St John's schools in 1847.[38] These became huge institutions which, by 1870, taught 830 children.[39] Drummond's successor, the Reverend Aaron Augustus Morgan, took over the running of the parish in February 1862.[40] Morgan was a controversial character: during his incumbency attendance at St John's declined and, in March 1874, he and the curate Reverend John Moore Fincher resigned their positions. However, it was during Morgan's incumbency, in 1872, that St John's was promoted from being a district to becoming a parish in its own right.

St John's annual report of 1872 states that funds had been found to appoint a second curate but no one suitable or willing came forth.[41] The parish employed two scripture readers, Daniel Toye and G R Luff, who were tasked with visiting those in the parish who, due to sickness or infirmity, were unable to attend church in person. While scripture readers took care of parishioners' souls, District Visitors acted on behalf of parish charities and they appear to have had more practical responsibilities. There are numerous references to the work of District Visitors in the reports transcribed in this volume. The work of these volunteers was described thus in the 1872 annual report of St John, Carlton Hill, 'Theirs is also work attended with much difficulty and mortification. They have to knock at strange houses, and oftentimes to endure strange welcomes. The poor are naturally suspicious and are slow to believe that a stranger can call upon them with disinterested motives. Hence the modest tap at their door is sometimes answered by an abrupt enquiry 'What's your business?' or by the announcement clamorously, often petulantly vociferated, 'Ain't got nothin' for you today' as though the visit were one in which the obligation lay on the part of the visitor… These repulses, though not frequent, are at any rate such as District Visitors are exposed to and render their work irksome and disheartening; but none of these things have quenched the zeal or relaxed the energy of those who work in St John's.' District Visitors' duties appear to have covered both pastoral and financial responsibilities: as well as ministering to the sick and acting as a conduit between the poor and charitable aid they also collected weekly subscriptions from these families. The report stated that in 1872, 'they have, by their personal exertions, succeeded in inducing the poor to lay by for profitable uses the large sum of £325 11s 5d, a considerable portion of which might

[38] Brighton Gazette, 14 November 1861.
[39] Brighton Guardian, 17 May 1871.
[40] Brighton Gazette, 20 February 1862.
[41] History of Brighton, Churches 2 (Smith's Cuttings), The Keep, BH600430.

otherwise have been frittered away, or have been transferred to the till of the publican.'[42]

The poor standard of living and the wayward lifestyles of the residents of Carlton Hill, Edward Street and their environs appear to have been a source of fascination for local journalists of the period. In 1866 *The Brighton Examiner* published a number of eye-witness accounts describing particular streets and areas in Brighton. Best known of these is the account of a night on the casual ward of Brighton Workhouse, then situated at Church Hill.[43] However, an investigative journalist who styled himself 'The Original Dogberry' published an article describing some of his perambulations about town including one piece entitled, 'Edward Street on a Sunday Eve'.[44] He contrasts the glitter and glare of North Street and the well-to-do pleasure seekers of West Cliff on earlier expeditions with the crowds of Edward Street and their partiality for beer shops. He stated, 'As I mixed with the throng, every now and then I met groups of navvies attired in the blue Guernsey and fancy necktie which constitute their 'best', standing at the corners, outside the doors of the beer shops a little too early for them to become comfortably inebriated. But in an hour or two the fun will have become fast and furious and the ear will be greeted on every side with the most discordant noises.' He describes further encounters with men and women who were, 'by their coarse features and aspen-like motion, clearly shown to be helpless devotees at the shrine of Bacchus.' Towards the end of his walk he claims to witness a woman ejecting her young daughter from their house, striking her around the head and shouting, 'I've rigg'd ye out, ain't I? Get out wid ye, ye lazy – ', further comments led the journalist to infer that the daughter was being forced into a life of prostitution by her mother.

One of the most notorious streets in this area was Derby Place. Ten of the applicants to the Mendicity Society were living there at the time of their application and many more had lived there in the past or would do so in the future. This was probably, in part, due to the numerous common lodging houses situated on Derby Place: these were establishments where people could rent beds or rooms for very short periods of time.[45]

In February 1851 the *Brighton Gazette* reported on a meeting of magistrates who were discussing the problem of begging and alms-giving in Brighton. They

[42] Ibid.
[43] Brighton Examiner, 18 December 1866.
[44] Brighton Examiner, 18 September 1866.
[45] In 1872 numbers 11 and 20 Derby Place were being used as lodging houses and there is reference to another establishment called Regan's Lodging House which we know from the 1871 census was situated at 41-42 Derby Place.

stated that about 5,000 vagrants passed through Brighton yearly and that at the last count there were somewhere between 50 and 60 tramps' lodging houses in Brighton.[46] The article went on to describe the conditions in an average lodging house, 'men, women and children mingled together, going from one bed to another, and the children trained up in the art and mystery of begging and thieving from their infancy'. They were considered 'receptacles for burglars, thieves, pick-pockets, vagrants, and persons of the most profligate character, all of whom mingled together in the most horrible way.'

Eighteen years later the *Brighton Gazette* published a report which assessed the levels of poverty within the parish of St John the Evangelist.[47] The report stated that there were '13 common, – or what may really be termed, tramps' lodging houses with public kitchens attached. The largest of them contains 50 single and 12 double beds offering accommodation for 74 persons. Then also there are 21 beer shops and 10 public houses and gin shops – the very bane of society. In the three worst streets and courts, Derby Place, Chesterfield Street and Thomas Street there are about 150 houses, most of them occupied by three families in each house, and a great many of them living and sleeping in one room. In these three streets there are nine common lodging houses open at all times to receive professional beggars, thieves, prostitutes and the very dregs of society. There are, besides, a number of houses let out in rooms to women of abandoned character. These streets contain a population of nearly 2,000 souls, very few of whom attend any place of worship.'

A parish report of 1870 referred to the houses in this area as hovels inhabited by people such as street musicians, hawkers and beggars who lived in the most precarious way.[48] It described the average diet of the local resident as consisting of bread, tea, dripping, varied occasionally with the addition of winkles gathered from the shoreline and sheep's trotters. An article entitled *Low Life At Brighton* containing much of the same copy and undoubtedly by the same author appeared in the Brighton Guardian in May 1871.[49] Both pieces contain the following passage which describes some of the characters a visitor to the area may have encountered:

'From this district emerge daily street musicians who make their way to the Parade to earn an uncertain livelihood by the harp, the violin, the banjo or the bones. From hence issues the Irishman with his grey hose and shillelagh; the nautical man or, ancient mariner, with his sails and windmills; the acrobat with

[46] Brighton Gazette, 27 February 1851.
[47] Brighton Gazette, 27 May 1869.
[48] History of Brighton, Churches 2 (Smith's Cuttings), The Keep, BH600430.
[49] Brighton Guardian, 17 May 1871.

his inverted and victimised children; the blind man with his dog and begging box; the quivering woman, shaking like aspen, with real or accommodated palsy; the syncopated man, deprived of more than half his outward humanity, creeping like a snail along the ground with his wooden propellers to the precincts of benevolence; the dislocated mendicant with his 'disjecta membra' [scattered fragments] scarcely retained in their normal position by bands braces and scaffolding – the blind woman, supported by her colleague who never ceases to cry throughout the whole day, 'Please to give a a'penny to a poo' blind!'. These classes, though perhaps most interesting to the visitor, are not the only ones to be found in the district. They might furnish the comic part of the sketch; street Arabs, beggars, drunken men and women, and those whose career is lower than even these would fill up its darker shades. But though little is known from general observation of this district, the public is kept pretty well acquainted with its condition.'

The census of 1871 backs up the reports produced in the previous two years. It shows that common lodging houses were situated at 11, 20-21, 38, and 41-42 Derby Place, which had 18, 26, 30, and 47 residents respectively.[50] Derby Place was also the focus of the town missionary, Reverend J J Jones, during his address at the first annual meeting of the Chapel Street Ragged School Mission in about 1872.[51] Jones stated that the majority of the children who attended the ragged school came from Derby Place and his description was designed to both satisfy people's curiosity about the area and promote a general interest in the residents' welfare. He stated that there were about 50 dwellings and two or three of these had been knocked together to form three common lodging houses which were run by Mr Leicester, Mrs Middleton and an Irishman named Regan.[52] Jones noted that although of a poor standard he was pleased to report that none of these houses had cellars as was common in similar housing in London. He observed:

'The first room as you enter the passage would be occupied by four post bedsteads; this sort are, I suppose, cheaper than any other sort. A four-post bedstead, such as one often sees, can be bought for 2s 6d. Considering the price you must not look for minor details as sacking, curtains etc. All that is required is that the party who sleeps should be lifted above the floor and if that can be accomplished, all are satisfied. A table 2s, and two or three chairs. One of them is preserved in such a state that a visitor can sit on a rope-bottomed chair or on the

50 1871 Census: Supt Registrar's District 77, Sub District 2B, Enumeration District 7.

51 History of Brighton, Churches 2 (Smith's Cuttings), The Keep, BH600430.

52 Regan's lodging house was 41-42 Derby Place. Thomas Regan was born in Ireland in about 1825. 47 people were enumerated at this address in 1871 including eight members of his family and Caroline Tester (applicant 129) who applied to the charity whilst resident at the address.

edge of a thin bedstead and with their apron wipe a chair, with a plank nailed across that has just served as a table for baby, for a visitor to sit on. This, with a shovel, one pot or kettle, with a brown paper lid, constitute the whole of the furniture of a room. The walls reviewed occasionally with cuts from the *Police News*, now and then with pictures from the *British Workman* and *Band of Hope Review*. Bad as this condition would be thought where human beings have to live [sic], sometimes there is even more wretchedness, not even pretence of a bed; a man or a family of children on a heap of rags in a dark corner of a room and an old publican's can which cooks all they eat and drink. How it's done is a mystery: a stiff piece of board for a shovel, no proper plastered wall to divide the room from the next door so that a neighbour's foul chimney often causes the smoke to come through the wall and in the bitter winter some of them have to keep their door wide open to let the smoke that comes like this through the partition. Rags and other things often are called in requisition as a stop gap to make things more bearable. It was a room such as this I found a woman one day, utterly unconscious, and after sending my wife with nourishment, towards evening a man came in with one arm and after speaking to him of the desperate condition of his wife he said that he could not help it – that he sold hot roast chestnuts and all he could take was from 8d to a shilling a day: the profits would be only 2½d and out of that what could he do? They offered me the House but who's going in the Workhouse? Quick was his answer. At number 4 in the street is a notorious drunkard with six children, one of whom, a girl of 15, has been taken to the school for girls in Egremont Place, where she will be trained as a servant.'

The address goes on to describe the destitution of some of the inhabitants and Jones puts much of the blame for their condition at the door of the local pubs Peison's beershop, the Golden Boot, the Little Globe, the Helmet and the Town Hall Inn.[53]

The preponderance of poor-quality housing was addressed by some organisations and during the early 1850s the Brighton District Association for Improving the Dwellings of the Industrious Classes financed the building of the Model Lodging House, Church Street.[54] The idea for this organisation was first raised at meeting held at Brighton in December 1848 which was chaired by Sir Ralph Howard MP, who was also the chairman of the Metropolitan Association for Improving the Dwellings of the Industrious Classes.[55] A provisional committee was set up in January 1849 and the Brighton association was formed

[53] History of Brighton, Churches 2 (Smith's Cuttings), The Keep, BH600430.
[54] ESRO: AMS 6432/1/94.
[55] Brighton Gazette, 28 December 1848.

at a meeting in April 1851.[56] The building was erected in about 1852 and was designed to contain accommodation for fifteen families in sets of three rooms each with a separate scullery and water closet.[57]

The poor standard of housing in Derby Place referred to by the Reverend J J Jones would have taken a terrible toll on the health of their inhabitants and Medical Officer of Health quarterly reports produced for Brighton Borough Council during this period describe in detail the numbers of deaths and their various causes. The reports also set the results in context, giving details of weather conditions and any other environmental factors that might have accounted for unexpectedly high or low numbers of deaths in any given quarter. The extremely cold weather of November and December 1871 had caused a rise in fatalities from respiratory conditions and nationally prompted a rise in deaths from smallpox though no deaths from this disease occurred in Brighton during that quarter.[58] The reports also set the figures for Brighton in a national context: smallpox had caused 6,380 deaths in England and Wales between October and December 1871 against 4,612 in the preceding quarter. The first quarterly report of 1872 states that the extraordinarily cold weather of the preceding quarter broke on 13 December 1871 and was followed by a higher than average seasonal temperature which lasted into January 1872. Although this had a generally positive effect on the mortality rate the proportion of deaths of children under five was particularly high at 40.1% of the 568 deaths registered in Brighton between January and the end of March 1872.[59]

As well as giving grand totals of deaths the figures given in the Medical Officer of Health's reports are broken up by each sub-registration district. The slum housing in the Carlton Hill area lay in the St Peter's sub-district which, it is important to consider when looking at these figures, also included Brighton Workhouse and the hospital. The first quarterly report of 1872 shows the overall population of Brighton as 91,684. St Peter's sub-district accounted for 55,043 people or 60% of the town's population but it produced 74% of all births and 74% of all deaths registered in the same period. 16.4% of all deaths occurred in public institutions such as the workhouse or hospitals.

The second quarter of 1872 saw a fall in the number of registered deaths to 409: 32.3% of these were children under five and 14% of all deaths occurred at the workhouse or in hospital. Streets are occasionally named in the reports but the majority of statistics measure births and deaths by the district in which they

[56] Brighton Gazette, 3 April 1851.
[57] Brighton Gazette, 18 December 1851.
[58] ESRO: DB/E/1/1.
[59] ESRO: DB/E/1/1.

occurred. The second quarter of 1872 records three deaths resulting from scarlatina at Bedford Buildings, which was the address of several applicants to the Mendicity Society. In the same report the previously mentioned Model Lodging House on Church Street was the site of a death from typhoid. Two deaths from smallpox were recorded in this quarter at the workhouse. The report for the third quarter of 1872 shows 484 registered deaths in Brighton with 36.6% of those being infants under one year. The reason for such a high mortality rate in the very young appears to be an outbreak of diarrhoea which killed 108 people in Brighton during the quarter. That number included 100 children under five of which 87 were infants under one. The last quarter of 1872 enjoyed unusually high temperatures which had a positive effect on the welfare of Brighton's inhabitants with 451 deaths registered for the whole town, which was a reduction of 49 from the same quarter in 1871. These figures include the deaths from smallpox of a three-month-old girl and a 26-year-old milkman at Brighton Workhouse; 16 deaths from scarlatina (all of which occurred in St Peter's sub-district); 16 died from diarrhoea and whooping cough killed six. Diseases of the respiratory organs caused 136 deaths in this quarter and diseases of this nature were consistently the most common cause of death.[60]

By 1877 the Carlton Hill area was considered to be such a threat to public wellbeing that the Medical Officer of Health, Dr Richard Patrick Burke Taafe, recommended its clearance in 1877. An outbreak of typhoid fever in the Little St James Street area during the late 1880s spurred local politicians into action and demolition work commenced in the early 1890s.

THE APPLICANTS

Of the 200 people that applied to the Mendicity Society, and its successor the Charity Organisation Society between January and June 1872, 126 were women and 74 were men. The reason for such a large discrepancy is unclear but probably rests on a few different factors: the longer life expectancy of women means there are more applications from widows than widowers; applicants may have thought that approaches from wives would be looked upon more favourably than those from husbands and it is possible that women acted as household treasurers more regularly than the men. As we have seen, policy changes in the early 1870s made it more difficult for women to claim outdoor relief, making them more reliant on charitable giving (Englander 1998).

There was no stipulation in the charity's rules that an applicant had to have lived in Brighton for a certain amount of time so the geographical spread of

[60] ESRO: DB/E/1/1.

people's birthplaces is wide: 50 were born in Brighton, Hove or Portslade (25%); 51 were born elsewhere in Sussex (25.5%); 70 were born in the United Kingdom but out of the county (35%); 18 born abroad (Ireland, Hungary, Germany, USA and Italy) (9%) and 11 did not give a place of birth place or a place of birth could not be determined (5.5%). Religion did not appear to be a matter for consideration either. The majority of the applicants were probably Church of England but there are reasonable numbers of Catholics and other non-conformists though the Brighton Hebrew Philanthropic Society took care of the needs of Jewish paupers.[61]

Many of the applicants lived in close proximity and we have evidence that some of the applicants knew each other but it seems highly likely there are more instances that are not made apparent in the records. George Platt (applicant 3) was enumerated at 7 Gloucester Terrace on the 1871 census where he lodged with Caroline Tucker (applicant 39) who approached the charity on 26 January 1872. Hannah Danes (applicant 97) and Louisa Mills (applicant 98), both living at 12 St Nicholas Road applied on 8 March 1872. Edward Murray (applicant 105) was recorded as living with a widow named McCarthy. There are enough coincidences in the lives of Murray and Catherine McCarthy (see application 80) to assume that this is the same woman. Many of the applicants moved between a limited number of lodging houses and again it seems likely that word of the charity's work was passed amongst this transient population. Albert Draycot (applicant 195) applied to the charity on 7 June 1872 when he was living at the lodging house at 2 Thomas Street. Edmund Walters (applicant 197), also resident at 2 Thomas Street, applied on 12 June and received help so it seems probable that the two men knew each other or at least spoke about the application.

Catherine Brickley (applicant 116) and Mary Brickley (applicant 156) applied to the charity in March and April 1872. The relationship between them is unclear but they both had run-ins with a woman named Catherine Coleman who lived in the same neighbourhood. The long-running feud between the Brickleys and Coleman illustrates a recurrent theme that runs throughout the applications – that of domestic violence. The majority of these cases were perpetrated by husbands against wives but there are a number of instances of women assaulting other women. Mary Shaw (applicant 40) assaulted a woman named Margaret O'Connor with a lemonade bottle causing a serious cut for which she was sentenced to a month's hard labour. Shaw was also found brawling with her husband at The Level. When asked whether he knew anything of the parties the Chief Constable, George White, said 'there was about six of one and half a dozen of the other' but Shaw's husband was found to be the aggressor. Ann Nicholls

[61] ESRO: AMS 6924.

(applicant 94) and Elizabeth Webb taunted and assaulted each other for over ten years in the 1890s and 1900s. The most extreme cases of domestic violence directed by husbands at wives occurs in Mary Goble's application (application 95). Her husband, James Goble, committed a number of misdemeanours before finally abandoning his wife in August 1872. His father, also James Goble, appeared in court following an appalling attack on his wife, Jemima Goble, ten days after she had given birth. Eliza Clark (applicant 154) endured a similarly violent marriage. Her husband George Clark had a long history of mental illness and during one of his episodes broke Eliza's arm.

George Clark was one of 13 applicants (or their dependants) who were patients at the county asylum at Haywards Heath. From a modern perspective it seems hardly surprising that such a high proportion of people were experiencing psychiatric problems: they were malnourished, had little or no hope of escaping penury, lived in substandard accommodation and often succumbed to alcoholism. They were admitted with a wide range of conditions from senile dementia to melancholia, but mania was the most common form of mental illness mentioned as a reason for treatment. One of the most extreme examples of manic behaviour amongst the applicants appears in Catherine Brickley's (applicant 116) reception papers. She was admitted to the county asylum on 11 September 1879 and spent long spells there until her death in 1913. The supposed cause of her illness was alcohol and David Richards, the workhouse surgeon, stated that whilst previously resident in his establishment she was 'very violent and dangerous to herself and others – breaks windows and furniture, bites, refuses food – is sleepless and requires constant restraint.' Many of the other patients were displaying violent behaviour and this seems congruent with the asylum's admission policy at this point. Samuel Duckworth Williams, who was appointed Superintendent in 1870, instigated a policy of returning harmless and chronic cases to workhouses or back into private care (Gardner 1999: 217). Presumably this policy also influenced decisions regarding the types of patients being admitted to the hospital.

During the nineteenth century emigration societies were established across the country to help poorer people fund resettlement to the colonies. Between 12 April and 18 April 1872 five applications (137, 139, 140, 143 and 145) were made to the charity in order to raise funds for help emigrating to Canada so it seems likely that these applicants either knew each other or at least had mutual friends. Sydney Berry (applicant 137) and George Lidgold (applicant 139) both worked for the London Brighton and South Coast Railway Company and sailed to Canada on the SS Scotland on 30 April 1872: Lidgold with assistance from the Juvenile Emigration Society. All the applicants seeking to emigrate in these papers had Canada as their destination, but the USA, Australia and New

Zealand were also popular. Richard Grey, husband of Ann Grey (applicant 124), had been promised funding from the Juvenile Emigration Society for his son and daughter whilst the rest of the family joined the Sussex Emigration Club No 1. There appears to be little literature on the subject of emigration societies but Timothy Hatton's *Emigration from the UK in 1870-1913: Quantity and Quality* suggests that emigrants to the Antipodes were more skilled than those to Canada. Interestingly the Charity Organisation Society turned down an appeal by Harriet Reeves (applicant 16) in 1904 for the two pounds seven shillings it would cost her to join her son in the USA and therefore rid themselves of somebody who was viewed as a persistent beggar. She made her first application in 1872 and was always refused relief on grounds of having a 'bad character'.

Many other mendicants, especially those that were known to the charity over a long period of time, used aliases in an attempt to fool the committee that they were making a fresh claim. One applicant who seemed particularly adept at creating this subterfuge was Hannah or Ann Nicholls (applicant 94). She used the surnames Eldridge, Mitchell, Whitting, Stringer, Harley and Hill when she approached people, hoping that the charity would not realise they all related to the same woman. The most common style of begging during this period appears to have been door-to-door visits which would have attracted less police attention than the street begging we are more familiar with in the 21st century. This system allowed poor people to find regular patrons, but it also meant that they were more likely to be found out if they relied on the same people: often paupers would give inconsistent stories or benefactors would talk to their friends who had relieved the same people using different names. The Mendicity Society and later the Charity Organisation Society appear to have been quite willing to press charges against people they felt were transgressing. For the period covered by this volume there is no evidence that the charity took any of their applicants to court. However, they often encouraged their contacts to prosecute anyone they deemed to be asking for money fraudulently or who begged persistently. Few people seemed keen to pursue legal action if they found out that the story that had been given to them was false.

WILLIAM COLLINGHAM

William Collingham deserves special attention as his handwriting forms the greatest part of the papers examined in this volume. Collingham was the society's agent whose job it was to visit applicants, record their testimony and report his findings to committee members. He was a former policeman so ideally suited to the job of agent: he knew how to make enquiries within the communities he worked amongst and was probably familiar with many of the people who made claims.

William Collingham, son of Frances and William Collingham, labourer, was baptised in Piddinghoe on 25 August 1844.[62] Frances Collingham died in 1845 but William Collingham senior and his family continued to live in Piddinghoe where they were enumerated in 1851.[63] William Collingham junior had moved to Brighton by 1861 where he was enumerated at 37 Elder Street. This was the home of James Wenham, dairyman, and Collingham was employed as his servant.[64] He joined Brighton police force on 9 April 1864 but was reprimanded by the Chief Constable on 20 June 1864.[65] His police record contains the following entry for that date, 'Thomas Tutt, 47 Blackman Street reports he was standing at the bottom of Cheapside about 10.40 talking to his wife and a young woman and a man named Martin. PC Collingham came up and made use of an insulting expression by telling his wife [presumably Tutt's wife] if she wanted her maidenhead taken he would take it if she went on The Level.'

Collingham married Catherine Triggs at St Nicholas, Brighton, on 6 August 1865.[66] On 15 May 1867 he was promoted to second class constable and on the 27 October 1869, he was promoted to first class. Collingham received a commendation from George White, chief constable on 20 February 1871 for his actions two days earlier, 'This man deserves great credit for the manner he got up a case against two men named Cox and Stoner for stealing 3 sacks of coals on the 18th Feb 71'. A few weeks after this incident the couple were enumerated at 34 Dinapore Street where they lived with their son William and lodger, Richard Collingham, a fishmonger born in Firle. Collingham was again praised on 16 November 1871, 'This constable is deserving of great credit in apprehending a girl named Jarrold who had been obtaining goods under false pretences for the last three months. There were about 8 cases against her, she was convicted on two. Sentenced to 6 months.' He resigned from the police on 20 December 1871 when he was appointed agent to the Mendicity Society but was sworn in as a special constable on 27 December 1871.[67]

William Collingham remained with the Mendicity Society and its later incarnations for the rest of his working life. In 1881 he was enumerated at the

62 ESRO: PAR 444/1/2/1.

63 Death of Frances Collingham Q2 1845 Lewes 7 291.

64 It is not known if this family were related to Frances and John Wenham who applied to the Mendicity Society in May 1872 (applicant 176).

65 ESRO: SPA/3/17/1.

66 ESRO: PAR 255/1/39.

67 ESRO: Watch Committee minutes DB/B 12/5.

charity's offices at 182 Edward Street with his wife and children and was still living there 10 years later. By 1901 he had moved to Woodland Cottage, Barcombe.[68] William Collingham died, aged 62, at the Sussex County Hospital, Brighton, on 22 March 1908 leaving £682 9 shillings 10 pence to Catherine and his sons William and George.[69] He was buried at Barcombe on 26 March 1908.[70] His headstone carried the following inscription 'In ever loving memory of my beloved husband William Collingham, born at Piddinghoe, Sussex, died 22nd March 1908, aged 62 years. 37 years agent to the Brighton Charity Organisation Charity Society, gone but not forgotten, the time is short. O weep not for him, tis unkindness to weep, his weary frame is but fallen asleep, no more fatigue and endurance he knows, o weep not, o break not his gentle repose. Also of Catherine Collingham, wife of the above who departed this life 8 Dec 1916 aged 73 years – at rest'.[71] The following note on Collingham's burial was published in the Barcombe parish magazine, ''His loss will be deeply felt by many both in Barcombe and Brighton, where he had many friends and no enemies'.[72]

The Charity Organisation Society's annual report of 1908 included the following obituary, 'It is with deep regret we record the death of William Collingham in March last. For thirty-seven years, ever since its foundation, in fact, he had been agent for our Society; he was very well known by all classes in our town and universally liked and respected, but only those who were privileged to work with him know how entirely he deserved that liking and respect. Integrity was perhaps the distinguishing feature of his strong and fine nature, not confined to its narrow sense of honesty in material things, but taken in the wider sense of giving to each his due, unmoved by any other consideration. During the greater part of his life he had worked on a system now superseded, and it is no small proof of his ability that he was ready to grasp new ideas and willing to work them out. In him the Society lose a servant who cannot be replaced, and the poor a kind, wise friend.[73]

THE RECORDS

The charity's archive consists of all the usual series one would expect to find in a collection of this type: constitution and rules, minutes, annual reports and

[68] Woodland Cottage, Barcombe was described in the Land Valuation Survey Fieldbook (TNA: IR58/12562) as 'a cottage, garden & paddock of 1a.2r. (formerly occupied by Mrs Collingham) owned by Lord Monkbretton - freehold'.

[69] England and Wales National Probate Calendar (index of wills and administrations).

[70] ESRO: PAR 235/1/5/2.

[71] Thanks to Ian Hilder for this transcription.

[72] ESRO: PAR 235/7/4/42.

[73] ESRO: AMS 6930/4/1.

correspondence. Particular to the Mendicity Society, and later the Charity Organisation Society, are the applications for relief made to the charity by paupers living in Brighton. This volume examines the first 200 applications to the charity made between January and June 1872. This is the only extant series of application papers: an insignificant number of later applications survive but they do not form a coherent series so have not been included in this volume.

It is unknown whether the forms completed by William Collingham were written whilst at the home of the applicant or at the charity's office. It is also unclear whether he completed the form whilst conducting the interview or wrote it later from notes taken. His writing is generally good but the sense is sometimes made unclear by the lack of punctuation so I have introduced punctuation for clarity where necessary.

Application forms are often accompanied by correspondence with people that had put the applicant in touch with the charity and in some cases examples of begging letters survive. The handwriting in these letters is hugely variable but in most cases it has been possible to transcribe almost everything. The only person whose letters contained large tracts that were illegible was Caroline Miles (applicant 92a). Miles was a prolific writer of begging letters; her handwriting is frequently illegible and she often over-writes in order to save paper which makes reading more difficult still. However, the letters are fairly repetitive and cover much of the same subject matter, so it is possible to piece together her tale by reading them all.

In order to create as comprehensive biography as possible for each of the applicants I used a variety of additional sources. Local newspapers were important for their detailed coverage of the proceedings of the Police Court, the Coroner's Court and their inclusion of reports regarding the charity's formation. Original copies are held at The Keep but many of the Brighton newspapers for this period have been digitised by the British Newspaper Archive and this searchable website proved to be a very valuable resource. East Sussex and Brighton and Hove parish records held at The Keep verified places and dates of births, marriages and burial.

The large number of applicants with mental health conditions meant that I had regular need to consult the archive of the county asylum at Haywards Heath. Excellent work by volunteers has made this a far easier task than it used be as all 19th century admissions have been individually listed on The Keep's catalogue. Less comprehensive but similar work has simplified searching for admissions to the Sussex County Hospital. Treatment of some of the patients was recorded in detail by the hospital's surgeons and their casebooks, which provide detailed descriptions of the patient's condition and their circumstances, have also been listed by volunteers.

I found Ancestry indispensable for census returns; emigration records and baptisms, marriages and burials relating to applicants who spent time in different parts of the country. FreeBMD was also useful to double-check names and dates of civil registration of births, marriages and deaths or to provide information on people who could not be found in other sources. Each of these sources was invaluable in its own right but they provided an even richer insight into people's lives when used in aggregation.

LIST OF CASES

CASE	DETAILS
1	William Homewood (also given as Holmwood), 32, labourer, 36 Thomas Street, Brighton
2	James Ridley, 77, plasterer, 10 Wellington Villas, Brighton
3	George Platt, 35, handchair man, 12 Upper Russell Street, Brighton
4	Albin Andrews, 36, painter, 39 Edward Street, Brighton
5	Henry James, 41, labourer, 39 Thomas Street, Brighton
6	Francis Russell, 56, hawker, 32 Thomas Street, Brighton
7	Ellen Hammond, 24, wife of a Painter, 37 Mount Pleasant, Brighton
8	Reuben Gibbs, 66, carpenter, 54 Cavendish Street, Brighton
9	Mary Herriott, 65, charwoman, 30 Washington Street, Brighton
10	Henry Collier, 54, hawker, 15 Camelford Street, Brighton
11	George Meads, 44, hawker, 37 Derby Place, Brighton
12	Lucy Miles, 32, wife of a labourer, 47 Hanover Terrace, Brighton
13	Hannah Shirley, 75, charwoman, 9 George Street Gardens, Brighton
14	Benjamin Goldsmith, 26, labourer, 31 William Street, Brighton
15	Ellen Small, 43, charwoman, 2 Steel Buildings, Gloucester Road, Brighton
16	Harriett Reeves, 29, wife of a labourer, 19 John Street, Brighton
17	Hanna Gaynor, 40, hawker, 33 Thomas Street, Brighton
18	Mary Jupp, 34, wife of a labourer, 11 Essex Place, Brighton
19	Susannah Burstow, 35, wife of a plasterer, 2 Kingsbury Road, Brighton
20	Mary Marshall, 63, charwoman, 12 Chesterfield Street, Brighton
21	Frances Sampson, 21, wife of a waterman, 17 Little St James Street, Brighton
22	Francis Healey, 19, labourer, 11 Derby Place, Brighton
23	Charles Linsted, 27, servant, Running Horse, King Street, Brighton
24	John Meads, 52, labourer, 97 Hanover Street, Brighton
25	Caroline Taylor, 38, wife of a flyman, 46 Baker Street, Brighton
26	Ann Rogers (also given as Rodgers), 52, needlewoman, 7 Nelson Place, Brighton
27	James Whitehead, 70, labourer, 32 Essex Street, Brighton
28	Sarah Hilton, 52, hawker, 35 William Street, Brighton
29	Richard Redman, 45, labourer, 18 St Martins Place, Brighton
30	Ellen Mckieg [also given as Ellen Mckiege], 48, hawker, 10 Derby Place, Brighton
31	George Marchant, 50, fisherman, 2 Saunders Court, Brighton
32	Julia Donally, 59, charwoman, 4 Little St James Street, Brighton
33	Maria Spears, 45, charwoman, 11 Cheltenham Place, Brighton
34	William Mitchell, 54, labourer, 28 Viaduct Terrace, Brighton
35	Ann Kirby, 48, wife of a flyman, 6 Hereford Street, Brighton
36	Matilda Sharp, 36, wife of a labourer, 5 Essex Cottages, Brighton

37	John Richardson, 64, painter, 15 Derby Place, Brighton
38	Sarah Wells, 74, needlewoman, 10 Oxford Place, Brighton
39	Caroline Tucker, 48, dressmaker, 30 Mount Zion Place, Brighton
40	Mary Shaw, 50, fish seller, 50 Hereford Street, Brighton
41	Mary Nash, 73, nurse, 9 Park Crescent Terrace, Brighton
42	Henry Gladman, 32, labourer on the railway, 39 New England Street, Brighton
43	Susan Cole, 39, wife of a labourer, 14 Viaduct Terrace, Brighton
44	Caroline Dewey, 67, charwoman, 19 Regent Hill, Brighton
45	Elizabeth Peabody or Elizabeth Jones, 57, hawker, 16 Freehold Terrace, Preston
46	Sarah Foster, 67, wife of a bricklayer, 36 Paradise Street, Brighton
47	Thomas Martin, 30, labourer, 39 Quebec Street, Brighton
48	Elizabeth West, 38, wife of a shoemaker, 10 Spa Street, Brighton
49	Emma Meyer, 34, dressmaker, Egremont Street, Brighton
50	Elizabeth Tullet, 62, wife of a sawyer, 24 Richmond Buildings, Brighton
51	Harriett Whitfield, 38, wife of a plasterer, 8 Viaduct Terrace, Brighton
52	Eliza Maynard, 23, ironer, 32 Sun Street, Brighton
53	Fanny Bird, 9, 63 Hereford Street, Brighton
54	Thomas Jeffery, 33, cabinet maker, 6 Little St James Street, Brighton
55	Henry Roberts, 29, French polisher, 1 Upper Bedford Street, Brighton
56	Christian Remm, 29, cabinet maker, no address
57	Mary Plumley, 78, no occupation, 5 Inverness Road, Brighton
58	Alice Nash, 9, 3 St James Gardens, Brighton
59	Thomas Turner, 65, carpenter, 39 Over Street, Brighton
60	Mary Keymer, alias Mary Mitchell, 25, hawker, 19 Hereford Street, Brighton
61	Kate Green, 25, wife of a labourer, 28 Hereford Street, Brighton
62	Catherine Ford, 41, wife of a labourer, 5 Inverness Road, Brighton
63	John Taylor, 37, fishmonger, 12 Bedford Buildings, Brighton
64	Elizabeth Streeter, 41, wife of a painter, 5 Ship Street Gardens, Brighton
65	Elizabeth Pavey, 39, laundress, 33 Sun Street, Brighton
66	Harriett Still, 47, charwoman, 14 York Road, Brighton
67	Sarah Leonard, 44, wife of a porter, 14 Leicester Street, Brighton
68	Fernard Pauwels or Powell, 23, wife of a musician, 49 Meeting House Lane, Brighton
69	Elizabeth Avery, 45, servant, 1 Sugars Court, Upper Bedford Street, Brighton
70	Susan Reeves, 33, wife of a labourer, 27 Apollo Terrace, Brighton
71	Francis Lakey, 52, tailor, 17 Carlton Street, Brighton
72	Alfred Soughton, 31, baker, 4 Elder Street, Brighton
73	Matilda Curtiss, 57, tailoress, 9 Nelson Place, Brighton
74	Caroline Skinner, 32, needlewoman, 29 Edward Street, Brighton
75	Henry Shaw, 53, 10 College Place, Brighton
76	Mary Howick, 40, charwoman, 16 Brigden Street, Brighton

77	Eliza Page, 30, washerwoman, 58 Carlton Row, Brighton
78	Jane Alce, 35, wife of a labourer, 23 Hereford Street, Brighton
79	James Stevens, 82, drover, 8 Somerset Street, Brighton
80	William Mccarthy, 60, labourer, 79 Egremont Street, Brighton
81	Jane Parker, 39, wife of a labourer, 7 Bread Street, Brighton
82	William Lewry, 72, labourer, 16 Park Crescent Road, Brighton
83	Catherine Batts, 20, washer, 30 Quebec Street, Brighton
84	Maria Carter, 57, needlewoman, 13 Mount Street, Brighton
85	Sarah Bertie, 63, Needlewoman, 28 Carlton Street, Brighton
86	William Meager (also given as Meagher), 62, hawker, 3 Lavender Street, Brighton
87	Ellen Hilton, 24, wife of a chair bottomer, 38 Thomas Street, Brighton
88	John Butland, 11, 26 Nelson Row, Brighton
89	William Stone, 81, hawker, 24 Thomas Street, Brighton
90	Frederick Goldsmith, 49, porter, 27 George Street Gardens, Brighton
91	Charlotte Leigh, 47, no occupation, 22 Crown Street, Brighton
92A	Caroline Miles, 27, dressmaker, 23 Scotland Street, Brighton
92B	Elizabeth Floate, 39, charwoman, 11 Model Lodging House, Church Street, Brighton
93	Anna Booty, 38, charwoman, 18 Marine View, Brighton
94	Ann Nicholls, 29, charwoman, 44 Cumberland Place, Brighton
95	Mary Goble, 22, wife of a labourer, 5 Grosvenor Street, Brighton
96	Mary Mannel, 70, needlewoman, 34 Crown Street, Brighton
97	Hannah Danes, 49, nurse, 12 St Nicholas Road, Brighton
98	Louisa Mills, 53, nurse, 12 St Nicholas Road, Brighton
99	Charlotte Colbran, 68, nurse, 13 Marlborough Street, Brighton
100	Elizabeth Wright, 28, washerwoman, 3 Jersey Street, Brighton
101	Jane Patching, 64, washerwoman, 19 Providence Place, Brighton
102	Joseph Birnbaum (also given as Bernbaum and Bernbam), 50, musician, 43 Cavendish Street, Brighton
103	Martha Hewitt, 35, wife of a shoemaker, 13 Riding School Lane, Brighton
104	John Reading, 43, hawker, 5 Egremont Street, Brighton
105	Margaret Murray, 29, hawker, 84 Spa Street, Brighton
106	Fanny Lewis, 30, wife of a hawker, 11 Derby Place, Brighton
107	Margaret Harrington, 64, washerwoman, 3 Essex Place, Brighton
108	Orpha Moppett, 43, washerwoman, 31 Hereford Street, Brighton
109	Frances Hemsley, 55, charwoman, 7 Ivory Place, Brighton
110	Amelia Rigg, 32, no occupation recorded, 72 Islingword Road, Brighton
111	Harriett Napper, 47, washerwoman, 10 Scotland Street, Brighton
112	Joseph Rossi, 75, hawker, 36 Cumberland Place, Brighton
113	James Etheridge, 33, waterman, 21 Essex Street, Brighton
114	John Cooper, 52, labourer, Bakers Bottom, Brighton

115	Sarah Bennett, 63, cook, 3 Over Street, Brighton
116	Catherine Brickley, 23, hawker, 37 Cumberland Place, Brighton
117	Thomas Mitchell, 30, clerk, 75 Shrubland Road, Hackney, London
118	Marian Flowers, age not given, occupation not given, 30 Southampton Street, Reading, Berkshire
119	Ellen Smith, age not given, occupation not given, 3 Queens Road, Hornsey, London
120	William North, about 35, labourer, 22 Eastern Road, Brighton
121	Jane Saunders, 39, dressmaker, 21 High Street, Brighton
122	Ann Jones, 37, charwoman, 37 Mary Magdalene Street, Brighton
123	James Cooper, 41, labourer, 22 Aberdeen Road, Brighton
124	Ann Grey, 38, charwoman, 13 Little St James Street, Brighton
125	Frank Kent, 50, fisherman, 24 Cambridge Street, Brighton
126	Samuel Burton Palmer, 73, coal agent, 13 Toronto Terrace, Brighton
126	John Clarke of London
128	George Bassett, 43, fisherman, 29 Dorset Street, Brighton
129	Caroline Tester, 48, ironer, Regan's Lodging House, Brighton
130	Mary Purser, 36, hawker, 47 Chesterfield Street, Brighton
131	Richard Pockney (also given as Pocknee), 74, no occupation, 9 Nelson Street, Brighton
132	Mary Rivers, 58, bonnet maker, 13 Jubilee Street, Brighton
133	Ellen Bishop, 26, wife of a labourer, 42 Elder Street, Brighton
134	William Staplehurst, 65, labourer, 28 Cobden Road, Brighton
135	German Buxton, 37, railway labourer, 51 Jersey Street, Brighton
136	Elizabeth Camfield, 74, hawker, Wellington Inn, [Thomas Street], Brighton
137	Sydney Berry, 17, railway labourer, 72 Upper Lewes Road, Brighton
138	Rose Simmonds, 14, daughter of a carpenter, 28 Southampton Street, Brighton
139	George Lidgold, 35, railway labourer, 9 Stanley Street, Brighton
140	Mary Kennett, 52, laundress, 27 Quebec Street, Brighton
141	James Avyes, 34, labourer, 3 Cumberland Place, Brighton
142	Elizabeth Callaghan [also given as Callagan], 45, hawker, 23 Cavendish Street, Brighton
143	Ann Simmonds, 42, washer, 21 St Martin's Place, Brighton
144	Henry White, 37, hawker, 43 Chesterfield Street, Brighton
145	John Hill, 26, labourer, 10 Shuters Gardens, Brighton
146	Thomas Sullivan, 52, hawker, 38 Thomas Street, Brighton
147	Elizabeth Wells, 66, 22 Meeting House Lane, Brighton
148	Emma Ellyatt (also given as Emma Elliott), 50, wife of a handchair man, 69 Albion Street, Brighton
149	Jane Richards, 22, charwoman, 81 Carlton Hill, Brighton
150	Mary Mitchell, 38, wife of a labourer, 90 Spa Street, Brighton

151	Charles Powell, 37, shoemaker, 10 Nelson Place, Brighton
152	Mary Maw, 57, wife of a railway company engine driver, 27 Boston Street, Brighton
153	Mrs [Fanny Foster] Cary, [52], 173 Lewes Road, Brighton
154	Eliza Clark, 40, washerwoman, 32 Southampton Street, Brighton
155	Ellen Moore, 17, servant, 10 Edward Street, Brighton
156	Mary Brickley, 60, charwoman, 3 Sugars Court, Upper Bedford Street, Brighton
157	Ann Hills, 34, washerwoman, 45 Hereford Street, Brighton
158	Eliza Cumming (also given as Cummins), 42, washerwoman, 9 Quebec Street, Brighton
159	Charles Butler, 54, hawker, 100 Hanover Terrace, Brighton
160	Mary Marchant, 46, wife of a waterman, 23 Blucher Place, Brighton
161	Thomas Simon, 25 Cumberland Place, Brighton
162	Robert Seifort, 39, musician, 3 Laurel Row, Brighton
163	Catherine Hollister, 45, no occupation, 24 York Road, Brighton
164	Lucy Bruce, 48, dressmaker, London
165	Thomas Keen, 56, hawker, 11 Derby Place, Brighton
166	John Thomas, 64, no occupation, 31 Derby Place, Brighton
167	Sarah Terry, 46, washerwoman, 21 Grosvenor Street, Brighton
168	Charlotte Cecil, 56, needlewoman, 3 Derby Place, Brighton
169	Mary Ann Moore, 66, governess, 25 Norfolk Road, Brighton
170	Ellen Knight, 24, ironer, 27 George Street Gardens, Brighton
171	James Norris, 52, handchair man, 9 Park Crescent Road, Brighton
172	Nicholas Gorman, 76, no occupation, 37 Derby Place, Brighton
173	William Carson, 40, labourer, 15 Chesterfield Street, Brighton
174	Esther Botting, 36, wife of a labourer, St Martin's Cottage, Brighton
175	William Butland (also given as Buckland), 36, labourer, 26 Chesterfield Street, Brighton
176	Frances Wenham, 40, wife of a carter, Pyecombe
177	Maria Washington, 32, wife of a bricklayer, 26 Frederick Street, Brighton
178	Caroline Tucker, 47, washer, 11 St Peter's Street, Brighton
179	Lucy Card, 51, charwoman, 22 Holland Street, Brighton
180	Sarah Miller, 59, charwoman, 20 Sun Street, Brighton
181	Julia Bray, 24, charwoman, 41 Wood Street, Brighton
182	Jane Mander, 36, needlewoman, 12 Derby Place, Brighton
183	Maria Skinner, 31, wife of a gardener, 8 Kew Street, Brighton
184	William Marcutt, age and occupation not known, previously of 2 Sudeley Place, Brighton
185	Mrs G Waite Vernon, age not recorded, professor of piano and singing, 16 Bedford Street, Brighton
186	Emily Wells, 26, ironer, 3 Carlton Place, Brighton

187	Caroline Deighton, no age given, ironer, 21 Circus Street, Brighton
188	Margaret Johnson, 51, needlewoman, 54 Hereford Street, Brighton
189	Unknown French woman thought to be called Le Bas
190	Elizabeth King, 30, no occupation, 84 George Street, Hove
191	Esther Wilson, 43, nurse, 12 Upper North Street, Brighton
192	Barbara Cook, wife of a clerk, 56 Clarence Square, Brighton
193	William Saxby, 25, chair bottomer, 11 Whichelo Place, Brighton
194	Archibald Stevens, 38, carter, 47 Spa Street, Brighton
195	Albert Draycot, 30, shoemaker, 2 Thomas Street, Brighton
196	James Davies, 76, no occupation, 58 Gloucester Road, Brighton
197	Edmund Walters, 17, labourer, 2 Thomas Street, Brighton
198	Alice Sams, 37, mattress maker, 50 Spring Gardens, Brighton
199	Frederick Pepper, 65, no occupation, 78 Hanover Street, Brighton
200	Ellen Sparks Or Sparkes, 41, wife of a railway labourer, 29 St Mary Magdalene Street, Brighton

BIBLIOGRAPHY

Bosanquet, Helen. 1914. *Social work in London, 1869 to 1912: a history of the Charity organisation society* (J. Murray)

Carder, Timothy. 1990. *Encyclopaedia of Brighton* (Lewes: East Sussex County Council)

Englander, David. 1998. *Poverty and Poor Law Reform in Nineteenth-Century Britain, 1834-1914: From Chadwick to Booth* (Routledge)

Gardner, James. 1999. Sweet Bells Jangled Out Of Tune (Brighton, James Gardner)

——2012. *A History of the Brighton Workhouses* (Brighton, James Gardner)

Harris, Bernard. 2007. 'Charity and poor relief in England and Wales, circa 1750-1914,' in Harris, Bridgen (eds) *Charity and Mutual Aid in Europe and North America since 1800* (Routledge)

Musgrave, Clifford. 1970. *Life in Brighton: From the Earliest Times to the Present* (Faber)

THE CASES

1 WILLIAM HOMEWOOD (ALSO GIVEN AS HOLMWOOD), 32, LABOURER, 36 THOMAS STREET, BRIGHTON

William Homewood applied to the Mendicity Society after an accident that occurred whilst in the employ of a Mr Chappell.[74] *Homewood was born in Hadlow, Kent, in 1841 and was enumerated on the 1871 census at a lodging house in Maidstone where he lived with his wife Caroline and four children and was employed as a butcher.*[75] *By the time of his application to the Mendicity Society on 1 January 1872 he was employed as a labourer and living at 36 Thomas Street, Brighton, where he paid 3s 6d rent per week. He had lived at this address with his wife and four children for four months but had previously lived in Essex Street, Brighton. William Homewood died in July 1872.*

1 January 1872
Statement: Wants to go in the hospital. Wants to get a basket for his wife to hawk fish.
Report: I have known this man for this two years he is a hard-working man but is very much given to drink. I bought two baskets by order of the committee which I gave three shillings for and she was very thankful for them.
Approved, Orfeur Cavenagh

10 January 1873
Further information: since this case was before the committee 12 months ago applicant has lost her husband and after that she went into the country hop picking and saved up a few pounds and with the assistance of a few friends she took a small grocers shop in Richmond Street where she remained for three months and then failed in business and left a week ago. Since that she has taken a small house, 31 Little St James Street, and she has also taken out a licence and got a little stock of fancy articles to try and get her living by hawking. WC [William Collingham]
Referred to private person, R P Hooper chairman

Letter written by Caroline Homewood of 31 Little St James Street, Brighton [to Mrs Smith of 11 Arundel Terrace], 18 January 1873
My Lady, I hope that you will pardon me for writing this note to you. I are the poor woman who picked up your purse or case. I don't know which it was for I ran after you as fast as I could my lady. My husband died in July leaving me with four small children to provide for and now I have not got any work to do.

[74] Probably John Thomas Chappell, builder of Hove.
[75] William Homewood birth registered Q1 1841 Malling 5 332.

My lady I should be so thankful if you could help me in giving me some work. I can do any work in a house. So now I must conclude and remain your most humble servant, Caroline Homewood

25 January 1873
Mr Sharp the collector received this letter from David Smith esq, 11 Arundel Terrace who would like to know something of the case.
Report of case as previously ascertained – to be sent to Mr Smith. George D Ryder, chairman

2 JAMES RIDLEY, 77, PLASTERER, 10 WELLINGTON VILLAS, BRIGHTON

James Ridley was born in Lindfield, West Sussex, in about 1795. By the time of his application he had been living with his wife, Chessell, at 10 Wellington Villas for 12 months and had been in Brighton for 50 years. Old age had forced him to give up plastering in 1870: he had previously worked for Mr George Lynn, builder.

3 January 1872
Statement of applicant: He wants to get a little assistance as the money from the parish (5s per week) is not quite enough to live on.
Report: I have made enquiries respecting James Ridley of 10 Wellington Villas and find he is living rent free and instead of him having five shillings a week from the parish it comes to nearly seven shillings a week.
Referred to poor law, Orfeur Cavenagh

3 GEORGE PLATT, 35, HANDCHAIR MAN, 12 UPPER RUSSELL STREET, BRIGHTON

George Platt was born in Bow, Middlesex, in about 1836 but was resident in Brighton by July 1862 when he appeared at the Magistrates' Court for stealing two bottles of sherry and a bottle of brandy from a truck owned by Findlaters and Co parked at Montpelier Terrace.[76] *Although married he was enumerated on the 1871 census at 7 Gloucester Terrace where he lodged with Caroline Tucker [applicant 39 who approached the charity on 26 January 1872] but at some point between the taking of the census on 2 April 1871 and his application to the charity he moved to 2 Queen Street. He lived at this address with his wife, Louisa, and son, George, but was evicted on 3 January 1872. On the following day Platt found lodgings at 12 Upper Russell Street before making his application to the Mendicity Society. His case was sent to the society by Lady Huntingfield*

[76] Brighton Gazette, Thursday 10 July 1862.

of 35 Regency Square, who was a patron of the charity. By the time of the census in March 1891 Platt was shown to be resident at Brighton Workhouse.

4 January 1872
Statement: Wants to get some money to get their things as the party where they did lodge has kept their things.
Report: I have made enquiries respecting Leweaser [Louisa] Platt and find her and the husband have been hired furnished rooms, getting in debt and then changing their lodgings and their things. They say the landlady has kept for rent is only a small box [sic]. When I visited the home I found the room very comfortable. They was frying bacon. The man is a strong, able man and the woman looks strong enough for any kind of work.
Dismissed, ineligible. NB report should be made to Lady Huntingfield

Letter from Louisa Platt, 39 Church Street, to the Reverend Charles Chilver, 27 Upper Brunswick, Place, Hove, Friday [26 February 1875]
Dear Reverend Sir, I am very sorry to trouble you again but owing to the winter being so severe my husband has not been able to do anything for this three days it has left us quite without food and firing. The children are better but they are still very poorly. I am to keep them in the warm. I am really in great need or I would not trouble you. Trusting this will meet with your assistance. I beg to remain your humble servant, Louisa Platt

Letter from the Reverend Charles Chilver, 27 Upper Brunswick, Place, Hove, to the Mendicity Society, 26 February 1875
My dear sir, I do not know what to do in the case of this Mrs Platt who has just been to my house with the enclosed note. She came to me only 10 days ago pleading the illness of her children and I gave her an order for coals and some bread and milk tickets. I have relieved her before at my home when she came on a similar errand and I have also visited their home when I saw the husband who seems to be continually out of work. What can be done on this case? Will you take this case up or advise me in any way? Believe me, faithfully yours, Charles S Chilver

1 March 1875
With respect to the annexed letters I find that the husband still draws a handchair although hand chairmen earn very little with their chairs at this season of the year respectable, industrious men have no difficulty in obtaining employment to clean boots, knives and windows at gentlemen's houses in the morning but Platt belongs to a class of men that prefer to walk out with a servant girl and smoke a cigar to work. He has an illegitimate child for which he has to pay 2s 6d per week towards its maintenance. The two children who have

been ill are now getting better, the family left their lodgings at 39 Church Street on Saturday last £1 13s in debt and are said to have removed into the neighbourhood of Russell Street. WC [William Collingham]
Undeserving: report to be forwarded to Mr Chilver,[77] R P Hooper

4 ALBIN ANDREWS, 36, PAINTER, 39 EDWARD STREET, BRIGHTON

Albin Andrews' father was Richard Andrews, Mayor of Southampton between 1849 and 1851 and again in 1856.[78] Following his death on 28 March 1859 Richard Andrews' effects were valued at under £10,000.[79]

Albin Andrews was born in Southampton in about 1836 but appears to have moved to Winchester by 1859 when he captained a cricket team at the Antelope Ground, Southampton, against his brother Arthur Andrews of Southampton.[80] Arthur Andrews's team won by 86 runs. On New Year's Eve 1859 Albin Andrews donated a guinea to the Winchester Volunteer Rifle Corps towards the formation of a band.[81]

He appears on the 1861 census at 12 St James Terrace, Winchester, where he lived with his wife Alice Lovell Andrews (née White) and their four-month-old son, also named Albin. He was, according to numerous advertisements in the Hampshire Chronicle in 1860, an agent for the North British Fire and Life Insurance Company and the same publication carries numerous references to Andrews throughout the 1860s. In February 1862 he donated ten shillings to the Hartley Colliery disaster relief fund.[82] A year later he donated ten shillings to the Royal Marriage Fund.[83] In August 1863 his daughter Margaret Alice died in Winchester aged 18 months.[84] In October of that year he stood in local government elections for St Maurice ward in Winchester: the Hampshire Chronicle reported, 'Mr Councillor Spencer, in a very brief speech, proposed Mr Albin Andrews as a candidate for the ward (great cheering). Mr Andrews had sprung from an excellent parent, and it would do the burgesses [a] great honour if they placed him in the council (hear and much excitement)'.[85] The birth of another daughter at 3 St Peter's Street, Winchester, was advertised in the Hampshire Chronicle in November 1863.[86] In May 1864 Andrews brought charges against a Mr M Gillo, furniture remover, whom Andrews

[77] Charles Samuel Chilver was curate at St Nicholas, Brighton in 1875, *Crockfords Clerical Directory*.
[78] https://www.southampton.gov.uk/Images/Southampton-Mayors-1217-2014_tcm63-363508.pdf.
[79] England and Wales National Probate Calendar (index of wills and administrations).
[80] Hampshire Chronicle, 23 July 1859.
[81] Hampshire Chronicle, 31 December 1859.
[82] Hampshire Chronicle, 22 February 1862.
[83] Hampshire Chronicle, 21 February 1863.
[84] Hampshire Chronicle, 29 August 1863.
[85] Hampshire Chronicle, 17 October 1863.
[86] Hampshire Chronicle, 14 November 1863 England and Wales National Probate Calendar (index of wills and administrations).

accused of verbally abusing him.[87] *The magistrate hearing the case encouraged the two men to settle out of court.*

In May 1864 Andrews stood a wager for £10 with Mr Jones, a local music seller, whereby Jones would drive from Southampton to Winchester and, on his arrival, Andrews would drive the same route back to Southampton. Jones took a light match-cart and used a horse recently bought for £8 from John Tubb's stud near Winchester: he took just under 40 minutes to complete the twelve miles. Andrews drove a four-wheel trap and used a small white cob which had previously served in the yeomanry. He completed the journey in one hour and one minute.[88]

In July 1864 Andrews donated a guinea to the St Cross restoration fund.[89] *In June 1865 the Hampshire Chronicle carried a notice that the partnership between Andrews and John Knights, a veterinary surgeon, was to be dissolved by mutual consent.*[90] *A subsidiary notice stated that Knights was to continue the business and all accounts were to be sent to Mr Collins, solicitor.*

Andrews arrived in Brighton from Portslade in November 1871. At the time of his application he was living at the Globe Inn, 39 Edward Street, where he paid 2s 4d per week for his lodgings. He had been employed as a painter with Brighton Corporation before being laid off three weeks earlier but he returned to Hampshire for the lavish funeral of his brother Alderman Arthur Andrews in October 1872.[91] *In April 1875 Andrews, now back in Winchester, was accused by his wife of 'putting her in bodily fear by his drunkenness and violent conduct. She said that for six weeks he had used threats towards her, saying that he would sell everything, and she was in fear of her life. He was bound over, himself in £20 and two sureties of £10 each, to keep the peace for six months. Being unprepared with bondsmen he went below to the cells.'*[92]

Andrews appears on the 1881 census employed as a clerk and lodging at 36 Albert Street, Southampton, but he was back in Brighton by November 1883 when he applied to the Charity Organisation Society for a second time. He was admitted to the Sussex County Lunatic Asylum with what was termed epileptic dementia on 13 July 1887.[93] *He had previously been resident at Brighton Workhouse where he was examined by the surgeon Douglas McKissock Ross who considered Andrews' speech irrational and incoherent and his behaviour a danger to others. This observation was corroborated by the workhouse attendant William Davis, who informed McKissock that Andrews had recently barricaded himself in the dormitory where he took a 'chamber utensil' to throw at one of the inmates: he stood behind the door for four hours. On arrival at the asylum he was seen by the deputy medical superintendent, Edward Walker, who considered Andrews to be in delicate health*

[87] Hampshire Chronicle, 14 May 1864.
[88] Hampshire Chronicle, 2 July 1864.
[89] Hampshire Chronicle, 16 July 1864.
[90] Hampshire Chronicle, 24 June 1865.
[91] Hampshire Chronicle, 19 October 1872.
[92] Hampshire Advertiser, 24 April 1875.
[93] ESRO: HC 24/5333.

and noted that his memory was so impaired that he did not know whether it was summer or winter. Andrews's medical record states that he died at 8.45am on 3 September 1889. He was buried at the asylum's cemetery on 6 September.[94]

4 January 1872
Statement: wants a little assistance until he gets work.
Report: I made enquiries respecting Albin Andrews and find all his friends are very respectable. His father was mayor at Southampton. Mr Ridley, North Street, has assisted him several times. Mr Mills, Bond Street, has assisted him several times and paid his lodgings a long time. I have known him a long time and during that time his habits have been very intemperate. It's a low public house where he lodges.
Dismissed, undeserving, Orfeur Cavenagh

12 November 1883
Report: Andrews applied at the office Monday for some temporary relief. He came from London on Wednesday last in search of employment and is now at work for the Corporation but will receive no wages till Friday evening meanwhile he is quite destitute. WC [William Collingham]
Grant of 3 shillings, Thomas W Holland

5 HENRY JAMES, 41, LABOURER, 39 THOMAS STREET, BRIGHTON

At the time of his application to the Mendicity Society Henry James was living upstairs at 39 Thomas Street with his wife, Elizabeth, and their three children. He was born in Southampton in about 1831 and came to Brighton from Ringmer in about 1869. James had been at this address in Thomas Street for the duration of his time in Brighton and paid three shillings per week rent. He had been employed as a labourer by Mr Hardwick of Hangleton but had been out of work for a month.

5 January 1872
Statement: wants some assistance until he gets work
Report: I have made enquiries respecting Henry James [and] find he has been out of work three weeks and when he was in full [time] work and earning over a pound a week he was getting in debt and at the same time his wife was known to go out begging. His home is in a destitute state.
Referred to parish, Orfeur Cavenagh. NB warning to woman re: persistent begging

[94] ESRO: HC 11/2.

6 FRANCIS RUSSELL, 56, HAWKER, 32 THOMAS STREET, BRIGHTON

Francis Russell was born in Dublin in about 1816. He moved to Brighton in about 1870 and for the nine months preceding his application had lived with his wife Margaret and their six children in two rooms at 32 Thomas Street where they paid rent of four shillings per week. Before this they had lodged at 12 Thomas Street and the three youngest children attended Chesterfield Street school. The family all hawked goods and made an income of 12 shillings per week but were six shillings in arrears. Their case was put forward to the charity by Mrs Turner.

6 January 1872
Statement: Francis Russell would not have come only the lady sent him: a little assistance would be very agreeable
Report: I made enquiries respecting Francis Russell and their home is in a passable state and Russell and his wife are both industrious persons. They have got the three youngest children at home and the eldest daughter. The other two are away in service.
Ineligible, Orfeur Cavenagh

29 November 1872
Further information: the secretary received the annexed letter from Mr Weston who afterwards called at the office on the same subject. When I called on Mr Breach he told me that he acted as he did because he knew the family to be very distressed and unable to earn a living from having no goods to offer. The husband too is very near-sighted and under these circumstances he was sure that the magistrates would not convict. The home is in a very destitute state but the wife says if she had a license and a little wool she could get a living. They have four children at home with them.
Referred to parish. Alexander Hamilton, Chairman

7 ELLEN HAMMOND, 24, WIFE OF A PAINTER, 37 MOUNT PLEASANT, BRIGHTON

Ellen Hammond, her husband Peter, 26, and their two children, Charles and Louisa, lived at 37 Mount Pleasant for which they paid five shillings per week. Her husband had previously worked as a house painter with a Mr Carter of St George's Road but had been out work for seven weeks. Ellen Hammond was born in Newick in about 1848 and moved to Brighton when she was four. The family's case was put forward by Mrs Fox.

Only one Peter Hammond could be found in Brighton on the 1871 census and two references appear in the Brighton Guardian that relate to a man of this name. The ages given in census returns and newspaper reports are inconsistent but within a year or two of each other so it seems likely that they relate to the same man. The Brighton Gazette of

26 January 1860 reported the hearing of William Coulstock, landlord of the Unicorn Inn, North Street, who was charged with serving minors. Peter Hammond was one of the underage drinkers and deposed, 'I am 13 years old. On Sunday evening about 5 o'clock, I went with four other boys into the Unicorn tap room, and about half past six, four or five more came in and we stopped till about half nine. I think we had three pots of ale, some gin and water and some gin and cloves. The first two pots of ale were brought in by the landlord.' The magistrate, Mr Bigge, asked who paid for the drinks, 'We clubbed round sir. Most of us were smoking. I was but I did not like it much. I spent 11d and lent my mate, James Potter, 3d.' William Coulstock was found guilty and fined £5. Local press also reported a Peter Hammond, aged 20, being charged five shillings for being drunk and disorderly in Edward Street.[95]

6 January 1872
Statement: Ellen Hammond wants a little assistance till her husband gets work. [She] would not have gone to Mrs Fox only she heard the lady was very good to the poor.
Report: I made enquiries respecting Mrs Hammond and find she goes out to work two or three days a week and the husband has been out of work for this last seven weeks. I have known this man for this last ten years and when he is in work his habits are very intemperate.
Referred to Poor Law, Orfeur Cavenagh

8 REUBEN GIBBS, 66, CARPENTER, 54 CAVENDISH STREET, BRIGHTON

Reuben Gibbs was a carpenter who had been working for Mr Bravery of Edward Street but had been out of work for two months after falling sick. He was born in Bishopstone in about 1808 but had moved to Clapham, Surrey, by July 1835 where he married Emma Bastwick of Nottingham. The couple were still living in Clapham in 1851 but by 1871 had moved to 69 High Street, Brighton, where they lived with their 11-year-old grandson, James. Mr Weston, of 33 Western Road, Hove, made the committee of the Mendicity Society aware of Gibbs who had been living at 18 Camelford Street before taking lodgings at 54 Cavendish Street. They paid rent of 2s 6d per week for their room and had no arrears. The couple expressed a wish to return to London but the 1881 census shows their grandson, James, living with them at 18 High Street, Brighton, where James is described as a photographer.

8 January 1872
Statement: Reuben Gibbs – I have known Mr Weston a long time and went to him for a little assistance as I am short of work. I should like some assistance to get to London where I think I could get work.

[95] Brighton Gazette, 7 December 1865.

Report: I made enquiries respecting Reuben Gibbs and find his home in a passable state. The wife refuses to go to London. This man has been getting his living by carrying parcels at the railway station and holding horses and carrying parcels [on] market day.
Further inquiry, Orfeur Cavenagh. Ineligible, Orfeur Cavenagh. Referred back to Mr Weston by committee

9 MARY HERRIOTT, 65, CHARWOMAN, 30 WASHINGTON STREET, BRIGHTON

Daniel Hack alerted the Mendicity Society to Mary Herriott. Hack was a successful Quaker businessman with premises on Trafalgar Street and was clearly familiar with Mary Herriott, who was born in Plumpton in about 1807 but had been living in Brighton for some time, though not the 40 years she claimed on the application form. She was enumerated on the 1851 census at Gilwell House, Waltham, where her husband Benjamin and eldest son William were employed as grooms. By 1861 the family had moved to the livery stables on Dyke Road where her husband and sons were employed as stablemen and in 1871 Mary, now a widow, was living at 3 Old Shoreham Road with her younger son, Henry. By January 1872 she was working as a charwoman for Mrs Reynolds at 3 Clifton Hill and was earning two shillings per week but found herself four shillings in debt with 1s 2d rent to pay per week for her room at 30 Washington Street. She was buried at Bear Road cemetery, Brighton, on 2 February 1876.[96]

9 January 1872
Statement: I wants a little assistance till I gets work. The reason I went to Mr Hack was they have relieved me before.
Report: I made enquiries respecting Mary Herriott and find she is a widow having parish relief and goes out to work on three days a week. Her home is in a passable state. I have seen Mrs Reynolds and find she is a very respectable woman.
Ineligible, Orfeur Cavenagh

10 HENRY COLLIER, 54, HAWKER, 15 CAMELFORD STREET, BRIGHTON

The Mendicity Society was first made aware of the Collier family by Lawrence Peel of Sussex Square. Henry Collier, a hawker, was living at 15 Camelford Street with his 26-year-old wife, Mary or Mary Ann, where they had been staying for three months. Their case was presented to the charity again in October 1877 by Sarah Austen (born c1804), an annuitant of 8 Palmeira Square, Hove. Another elderly annuitant, Emma Holland

[96] ESRO: BH/L/3/1/5 - Woodvale Cemetery burial plot ZBW 49.

(born c. 1813) of 11 Vernon Terrace, took up their cause in November 1882. By December 1905 Henry Collier had died but the case of Mary Collier, now 61, and her five children, aged between 20 and 39, was taken up by the Howard Charity.[97] Mary Collier had been resident at various addresses at Oxford Court near London Road between at least 1877 and the time of the last report at the behest of Mr Billett in October 1922.

9 January 1872
Report: I made enquiries respecting this family and find carriages are often driving up to the house, no doubt to relieve them. The man is of intemperate habits and they strongly deny having any relief from anyone in the town.

10 February 1875
This case was dismissed by the committee as undeserving in January 1872 in consequence of the wife who sells hassocks being a notorious beggar and for some time her licence was stopped but on her promising not to use it for begging purposes it was renewed for a time.[98] No complaints were made but lately she has gone back to her old practices. The family now live at 20 Oxford Court. The wife broke her arm 11 weeks ago for which she is an out-patient at the hospital. She has two children living and her husband requests assistance to enable him to take out a hawker's licence to sell hassocks. WC [William Collingham]
Undeserving, R P Hooper

Letter written by A Henstridge to B Johnson 23 October 1877
Dear Sir, could you kindly find out any particulars of Mrs Collier, 19 Oxford Court, Oxford Street, London Road for Mrs Austen. She has for several years been begging in one form or another but Mrs Austen thinks possibly she may not be one of the most deserving and would be glad of any particulars with which you could furnish her as to her bona fides. I remain, dear sir, yours truly,
A Henstridge

[24 October 1877]
Mrs Austen requests a report of this case. Collier gets his living by making hassocks and by running after the Brighton Harriers.[99] His wife, who still sells hassocks, had a very bad confinement three weeks ago and is now in a very weak state. The home is in a dirty and destitute condition. The Reverend P Fletcher has relieved the family during the last three weeks and recommends that Mrs Collier should be assisted for another fortnight.

[97] The Howard Charity was established by the local philanthropist John Howard to assist the aged, sick, crippled and widows with young children. Its inauguration was recorded in the *Brighton Gazette* of 25 November 1905.

[98] Hassocks are clumps of rough grass or turf used for heating.

[99] Brighton Harriers were a local fox hunting meet.

WC [William Collingham]
Report favourable

29 July 1879
Mrs Austen requests another report of this case. On enquiring I find that her husband was ill [for] three weeks suffering from an injury to his shoulder but he resumed work last week. His wife still sells hassocks. She has now four children. The house is in a dirty and destitute state. WC [William Collingham]
Report to Mrs Austen, R P Hooper

20 October 1881
Mrs Collier was sent by Mr Dene and applied at the office on Wednesday for relief for her husband from the Jubilee and Accident Fund.[100] A week ago last Saturday he fell from a horse at Portslade and injured his back and ribs for which he is attended by the dispensary doctor and is not likely to be able to work for a fortnight. No complaints have been made about the wife since 1875. She now has five children. A son aged ten is ill in bed suffering from an injury to his head by being blown down in the late gale. WC [William Collingham]
Grant of 5 shillings, R P Hooper

31 October 1881
Collier requests relief for one more week by which time he hopes to be able to work. He has received a little help from Mr Dewe. WC [William Collingham]

Letter written from 11 Vernon Terrace, Brighton, 2 November 1882
Miss Holland would be very much obliged to the secretary of the Charity Organisation Society if he could furnish her with some particulars of a family of the name of Collier residing at 18 Oxford Court.
She has been in the habit of relieving them for some time and she much wishes to know whether they are respectable people in their ways and what help they have.

3 November 1882
Report: Miss Holland of 11 Vernon Terrace requests a report of this case. Collier still runs after the Brighton Harriers. His wife who is in ill health still sells hassocks. The family seem to have improved lately. Their home is in a destitute condition.

[100] The Jubilee and Accident Fund was set up to mark the jubilee of the reign of King George III on 25 October 1809. It gave relief to residents of Brighton and Hove who suffered injuries on land or at sea. During the 1870s many of that charity's committee members, including Marriage Wallis, Daniel Hack and W D Savage, were involved with the administration of the Mendicity Society (The Keep BHBox6/41).

WC [William Collingham]
Report to Miss Holland, R P Hooper

Letter written from 11 Vernon Terrace, Brighton, 26 July [1887]
Miss Holland would be very much obliged for some information about a family of the name of Collier residing at 18 Oxford Court. She has known them a good many years buying hassocks and shell work and so on from the woman who seemed always having babies and really very poor. Now she sends her boy weekly to say how ill she is and Miss Holland really does not know what resources they may have and how to help them in the best way. There is evidently no scruple about asking on their part. Can the husband do anything and does he? She is glad to find money for them if it can be properly directed but she is not able to go about herself.

27 July 1887
Report: Miss Holland of 11 Vernon Terrace requests another report of this case. Collier continues to run after the Harriers during the winter and in the summer he makes hassocks. His wife had a bad miscarriage seven weeks ago and is now in a very weak condition. They have six children dependant on them and seem greatly in need of help.
Report to Miss Holland, R P Hooper

2 May 1888
Report: Collier applied to the office on Tuesday for assistance to get his wife nourishing food. She had another miscarriage three months ago and is now confined to her bed suffering from an internal complaint. Applicant continues to make hassocks. They have five children dependant on them and appear miserably poor. WC [William Collingham] Grant of 5 shillings and refer to parish

Letter from the Secretary, Howard Charity, 8 December 1905
Re: Collier, 1 Oxford Court, application number 44
We have known something of this family ever since 1872 but have had no enquiries about them at our office since 1887. They have always been in a more or less destitute condition. Mrs Collier has gone about selling hassocks since 1872. Her three married daughters are in poor circumstances and not in a position to help her. The son, Richard, has been ill 12 months and has decided to go into the Union [workhouse] but is now pounding the streets with the 'unemployed'. The daughter, Rose, is not fit for service but does a little charring. The family are untidy people and also weak-minded but their character as to sobriety is satisfactory and they are doubtless in needy circumstances. Our

committee must recommend the case for relief but think it should be left to the Guardians.
F Williamson, Hon Sec

6 December 1905
Statement: work has been very quiet for several months. Therefore, Mrs Corney kindly brought my case under the notice of the Howard [charity] and I hope I shall not lose my parish my relief.[101]
Report made using the text of the letter of 8 December 1905. Howard Charity not advised to offer relief

Notes written 9 October 1922 – 15 January 1923
Mr Russell reports that Mrs Collier is a widow and very poor – he gave her 2s 6d worth of coal; known to Miss Ambrose – a hassock maker, a great beggar; 3s 6d pension from Howard Charity; not having relief from the Guardians; not requiring relief; reference verbally to Mrs Billett; reference verbally to Mrs Russell.

11 GEORGE MEADS, 44, HAWKER, 37 DERBY PLACE, BRIGHTON

George Meads's case was sent to the Mendicity Society by Mrs La Vauchy of 2 Manchester Street. Meads was born in London in about 1828 but moved to Brighton in about 1870. He and his wife Mary, who was also a hawker, and their five children aged between 1 and 13 had lived in two rooms on the top floor of 37 Derby Place since 1871. At the time of the application the Meads were earning 12 shillings a week and paying 3s 6d in rent. They were a few shillings in arrears.

9 January 1872
Statement: George Meads would like a little assistance till he gets better.
Report: I made enquiries respecting this family find the husband is receiving parish relief. The woman goes out hawking and the oldest boy goes to work. Further information respecting this case – the man does not receive parish relief now he is better and will be able to go our hawking in a few days if the weather is fine. The wife is sick from a cold and sore throat. The Reverend Mangan says this is a very deserving case. He has relieved them on two or three occasions. Mr Toye the scripture reader says they are a very deserving family.[102] The home is in a passable state.

101 Mrs Corney was listed at 28 Stanford Avenue in *Towner's Directory, 1902*.
102 Daniel Toye is listed as the scripture reader at St John the Evangelist, Carlton Hill in the church's annual report of 1869 (PAR 277/7/2/2). In 1871 he was enumerated at 28 Upper St James Street where

Relieved by grant, Orfeur Cavenagh.
NB five shillings

12 LUCY MILES, 32, WIFE OF A LABOURER, 47 HANOVER TERRACE, BRIGHTON

Lucy Miles, née Hart, was born in Newick in about 1840. She and her husband David, a labourer, paid 3 shillings a week for their two rooms at 47 Hanover Terrace, which they shared with their five children aged between 2 and 11.[103] *They had been at this address for three months but had only been in Brighton since about September 1871 before applying to the charity. David Miles had been working for a Mr Hunt but had run up arrears of ten shillings in the six weeks he had not been working.*

9 January 1872
Statement: Lucy Miles saw the bill outside and would be glad of a little assistance until my husband gets work.
Report: I made enquiries respecting Lucy Miles and find the home in a most destitute state. They have no bed, only a bag of straw to lay on and the children lay on a few rags in one corner of the room. Although they are poor the children are kept clean. They have not been to school for this last three months not being able to pay for them. I have seen Mr Hunt and the only work he will have for him will be help unload[ing] a vessel. Mr Hooper gave me a shilling [and] with that I bought some bread and they were very thankful for it and strongly recommended them to go in the union [workhouse].
Relieved by grant [of] 10 shillings and woman will be made to obtain a lying-in ticket, Orfeur Cavenagh[104]

13 HANNAH SHIRLEY, 75, CHARWOMAN, 9 GEORGE STREET GARDENS, BRIGHTON

Hannah Shirley was one of the oldest, and ultimately the longest-lived, applicants to the Mendicity Society. Her exact year of birth is difficult to establish because she gave inconsistent ages to census enumerators and charity clerks but we know that she was born Hannah Ford at Stoke Ash, Suffolk, between 1797 and 1801.

he lived with his wife Elizabeth, daughter Ann and a young servant. He was 57 years old and described as a retired builder.

103 Lucy Hart marriage to David Miles registered Q2 1859 Lewes 2b 224.

104 This is probably a reference to the Brighton and Hove Lying-In Institution, 76 West Street, which offered free medical attention to women in the latter stages of pregnancy, Treacher's Almanac 1872, Reference Room, The Keep.

Hannah Shirley moved to Brighton between 1835 and 1837 and, according to census returns and applications to the charity, lived at various addresses in Carlton Street, Grosvenor Street, Cumberland Place and Lennox Street. She married Charles Shirley of Ovingdean, but the date and location of the wedding is not known. At the time of her first contact with the charity she was living in one room at 9 George Street Gardens, for which she paid 2 shillings per week rent. She had given up work in October or November 1871 due to old age and her case was sent to the Mendicity Society by Mrs Hack, wife of Daniel Hack, the Quaker businessman and grocer.

Hannah Shirley's daughter Charlotte Shirley was, according to the census and hospital records, born in Brighton in about 1835. The admission register states that Charlotte was admitted to the Sussex County Hospital on 27 July 1870 having been ill for five months with what they termed uterine dementia.[105] *She was recommended for treatment by William Norris Dampier, curate, and was discharged on 28 September 1870.*[106] *Whilst convalescing, Charlotte Shirley was seen by Dr Henry Moon and his case notes state that her malady was in fact a case of vaginitis having been 'overworked, suffering from chest attacks'.*[107] *Moon went on to state that he found Charlotte Shirley 'excitable and untrustworthy'. The clerk of the Mendicity Society described Charlotte Shirley as 'weak of mind' and suggested she was something of a burden to her mother but she married John Silvester, a widower, at St John, Carlton Hill, on 9 March 1875.*[108]

The 1891 census shows Hannah Shirley living at 49 Mount Pleasant, next door to her grandson, John Augustus Shirley. She was buried at Bear Road cemetery, Brighton, on 4 August 1891 aged at least 90 years old.[109] *The Woodvale Cemetery burial register shows that an unnamed person paid 10 shillings towards the cost of her burial which allowed them to place a memorial tablet on her grave.*

10 January 1872
Statement: Hannah Shirley wants a little assistance as the money she gets from the parish is not quite enough to live on.
Report: I have made enquiries respecting Hannah Shirley. Her home is very comfortable. I have seen Mrs Cook and find she [Hannah Shirley] is a respectable woman but is now too old for work.
Referred to poor law, Orfeur Cavenagh

3 April 1873
Statement: Hannah Shirley wants assistance to enable her to get some furniture to furnish a room.

105 ESRO: HB 35/3/1870-3963.
106 William Norris Dampier was curate of St John's, Carlton Hill, ESRO, PAR 267/5/1/5.
107 ESRO: HB 62/22 ff396.
108 ESRO: PAR 267/1/3/1.
109 ESRO: BH/L/3/1/8 - Woodvale Cemetery burial plot ZLK 79.

Report: This person went to Mr Ryder begging on Thursday and told a tale about her having taken a small house and that she was greatly in want of a few things to enable her to let one room furnished so that she might be able to clear nearly her rent. Since the case was before the committee nearly 15 months ago applicant has kept her grown up daughter [Charlotte Shirley], a dress maker, who for some time has been unable to work through nervous debility and was formerly in the workhouse asylum and has an illegitimate son aged 11 living with her at her mother's. I have no doubt that applicant receives a great deal of charity for she is constantly going about begging. Mr Beal informs me that he has known her for several years as a persevering applicant for relief. WC [William Collingham]
Ineligible, R P Hooper

8 May 1874
This woman is continually going about begging and telling a pitiful tale of distress about her poor dear daughter. Although her daughter is said to be of weak mind she is in the habit of staying away from home and sleeping with a man named [John] Silvester, a widower, St John's Place, and takes to his children the greater portion of the bread which the Guardians allow her mother, who begged of Mr Hayes and Mr Brandreth a short time ago and in addition to her begging of Mrs Bright she begged of a lady who gave her a sixpence in the Pavilion grounds on Thursday and on Friday.[110] I saw her go to Mr Hack's in Trafalgar Street begging where she received some tea and sugar. In my opinion if the Guardians were acquainted with these facts they would take her outdoor relief (4s 3d) into consideration. WC [William Collingham]
Undeserving: to be reported to Mrs Bright and Guardians, R P Hooper

7 May 1880
Miss Jackson, 13 Pavilion Parade, requests a report of this case. When the case was reported to the Guardians six years ago they stopped Mrs Shirley's outdoor relief but lately they have allowed her 2 shillings in goods and a 1 shilling in cash weekly on account of her age. Miss Jackson allows her 5 shillings a month and a friend 4 shillings a month besides which she receives a great deal of charity but I have had no complaints about her begging for some considerable time. WC [William Collingham]
Report to Miss Jackson, R P Hooper

7 October 1890
Mrs Christie of 57 Montpelier Road requests a report of this case. Miss Shirley now resides at 7 Mount Pleasant. The Guardians allow her 2 shillings 6 pence

[110] Sarah Bright, wife of Edward Bright, goldsmith, 19 Goldsmid Road, Hove.

per week and the Earl of Munster 10 shillings a month besides which several friends assist her occasionally. She is now 97 years of age, keeps a very tidy home and we have not had any complaints of her begging for a very long time past.
George Collingham
Report to Mrs Christie, Thomas W Holland

14 BENJAMIN GOLDSMITH, 26, LABOURER, 31 WILLIAM STREET, BRIGHTON

Despite his long life and peripatetic existence Benjamin Goldsmith appears never to have moved beyond the boundary of Sussex. He was the son of Thomas and Sarah Goldsmith and was born in Waldron in 1846. By 1861 he was working as an agricultural labourer at Blackham Court Farm, Withyham. He married Mary Ann Freeman in Lewes in the December quarter of 1867 and by 1871 the couple had moved to 59 John Street, Brighton, with their one-year-old daughter Anne who was born in Eastbourne.

Benjamin Goldsmith's case was forwarded to the Mendicity Society by Mr Davies of 51 Dyke Road. Goldsmith and his family were living in one upstairs room at 31 William Street, for which they paid 3s 6d per week. He had been working as a labourer for Mr Chappell of Hove but had been out of work for six weeks and had run up arrears of 15 shillings.

Anne Goldsmith died in the June quarter of 1872 aged two and Mary Ann Goldsmith died in Brighton in the March quarter of 1876 but Benjamin remarried in the June quarter of June 1877. The 1881 census enumerates him, his wife Louisa Goldsmith (née Smith) and their infant daughter at Keymer where he was working as a journeyman baker. The following two census returns show that he remained in this profession: by 1891 he was living at 1 St James Court, Brighton, with Louisa and their son, James, who was 10. In 1901 the family had moved to 29 Hanover Terrace, Brighton. Benjamin died in Brighton in the March quarter of 1924, aged 78.

10 January 1872
Statement: Benjamin Goldsmith wants a little assistance till he gets work.
Report: I have made enquiries respecting Benjamin Goldsmith and find his home in a passable state. I have seen Mrs Seymour and find they have relieved them several times and they kept coming till they got tired of them. I have seen Mr James, town missionary, and he says he is a very sober man. This man and his brother has [have] now both got work and would be glad of a little assistance to help them over the week.
Further inquiry - referred to Poor Law, Orfeur Cavenagh. 2s 8d mentioned to be expended in the purchase of bread. NB the result of the reference to the Poor Law to be continued and reported hereafter

15 ELLEN SMALL, 43, CHARWOMAN, 2 STEEL BUILDINGS, GLOUCESTER ROAD, BRIGHTON

Ellen Small appears to have been beset by accidents which hampered her ability to make her own way in life. She was born in Brighton in about 1829 and lived with her mother, Mary Small, a greengrocer, at 8 Cranbourne Street until at least 1851. She was enumerated in the 1861 census as an 'invalid' living with her brother and his family at 14 Orange Row.

Her case was sent to the Mendicity Society by Mrs Goulty of 2 Sussex Square when she was two weeks' rent (6 shillings) in arrears. Small's last employment had been as a charwoman with Mrs Strong of 21 Cannon Place, 10 years previously. However, a broken kneecap appears to have made working impossible and it may be this injury that rendered her an 'invalid' on the 1861 census. She had been receiving 2s 6d per week from the parish during an illness but the form does not state the nature or the duration of the illness.

Small was admitted to the Sussex County Hospital on 27 June 1889 with a fractured arm, having been knocked over in North Street. At this time she was living at 11 Essex Place which, in January 1872, had been the home of the Jupp family.[111] *No census record could be found for 1891 but she seems to have used variations of her name: Ellen, Eleanor and Helena were all used at different periods of her life so it is possible that she had used another variant at this point. She was buried at Bear Road cemetery on 23 August 1895.*[112]

11 January 1872
Statement: the lady told me when I wanted any assistance I was to go to her because I attends Union Street Chapel.[113]
Report: I made enquiries respecting Ellen Small and find she keeps her brother's house which is in a passable state and occasionally goes out to work. Her brother is a shoemaker and sometimes goes out bird catching. I have seen Miss Goulty and they have been continually relieving of her.
Dismissed, ineligible, Orfeur Cavenagh

14 January 1873
Further information: this person brought a ticket to the office on Tuesday afternoon which was given to her by Mr Christie of 4 Compton Terrace who says that applicant has been in the habit of calling on him about twice a week for assistance. Upon visiting the home I found it in a dirty and destitute state. The brother still goes bird catching and occasionally he does a little shoe making. I have no doubt that applicant receives a great deal of charity from different persons. I have frequently seen her about at different parts of the town. Mr Beal

[111] Mendicity Society applicant 18.

[112] ESRO: BH/L/3/1/9 - Woodvale Cemetery burial plot ZBE 9.

[113] The Union Street Chapel, or Union Chapel, was a nonconformist place of worship in central Brighton.

has known applicant to be in the habit of receiving charity for several years. WC [William Collingham]
Ineligible, report sent to Mr Christie, R P Hooper

19 January 1876
Report: Miss Tugwell of 7 Clifton Terrace has been in the habit of relieving this woman but before doing so again Miss T requests a report of the case. The woman, who is known by the name of tea leaves, still keeps her brother's house. She is frequently begging in the Montpelier district. The police have had a great deal of trouble with her and she has been twice convicted for begging. WC [William Collingham]
Undeserving. To be reported to Miss Tugwell, R P Hooper

3 July 1889
Report: This person now of 11 Essex Place was sent by a ticket and applied at the office on Tuesday for relief from the Jubilee Accident Fund. According to her statement two young men knocked her down in North Street on Friday last and fractured her left arm for which she is an out-patient at the hospital. She came out of the Union [workhouse] two months ago. The previous reports will show that she has been a troublesome beggar for many years. Under these circumstances the case seems a fit one for the Poor Law authorities to deal with. WC [William Collingham]
Ineligible, Thomas W Holland

16 HARRIETT REEVES, 29, WIFE OF A LABOURER, 19 JOHN STREET, BRIGHTON

Harriett Reeves, née Tabbenor, had an unhappy relationship with the Mendicity Society which lasted for 34 years. She was born in Marylebone, Middlesex, in 1843, and the birth of her illegitimate son Robert Edward Tabbenor was recorded in Croydon in October 1867.[114] *She arrived in Brighton in 1869 with Robert and her husband John, who was born in Rusper in 1837.*[115] *At the time of her first application the family rented one room at 19 John Street, for which they paid two shillings per week rent. They were three shillings in arrears and John had been out of work for three months due to his employer's shortage of work.*

On 22 January 1877 Harriett Reeves appeared before magistrates on a charge of being drunk in St James Street on a Sunday night. The Brighton Guardian reported that she was discharged with a caution as this was her first appearance before the Bench.[116] *However,*

[114] Robert Edward Tabbenor birth registered Q4 1867 Croydon 2a 204.
[115] Harriett Tabbenor marriage to John Reavis registered Q4 1876 Brighton 2b 438.
[116] Brighton Guardian, 24 January 1877.

the Mendicity Society's agent commented that when apprehended she was working as a prostitute and was so violent that it took three constables to hold her down. By March 1881 John and Harriett Reeves had moved back to her native London but had clearly fallen on hard times again as they applied for relief at the St Pancras Committee of the Society for Organising Charitable Relief and Repressing Mendicity. The move to London could not have paid dividends as the Reeves were back in Brighton by March 1886.

John Reeves died on 17 November 1903 and his death may have prompted Robert Tabbenor's invitation to his mother to emigrate to the USA in October 1904. Tabbenor had a chequered past: on 12 November 1879 he was admitted to the Royal Philanthropic Society School, Redhill, Surrey.[117] *By March 1887 he was serving a prison sentence, though it is not known what for. He arrived in America in 1903 and settled at Philadelphia where he married a local woman named Mitilda (sic) and found employment as a fireman. He became naturalised on 13 April 1917.*[118] *Reeves and Tabbenor both approached the Mendicity Society for funds to aid Reeves' passage to the USA. Despite the appealing prospect of unburdening themselves of Harriett Reeves, they declined to offer financial support.*

11 January 1872
Statement: Harriett Reeves wants a little assistance till my husband gets work.
Report: I made enquiries respecting this family and their home is in a most destitute state. The only furniture in the room is a mattress to lay on and an old counterpin to cover over them. I have known this man for this last two years and he never seems to have any regular work or to be anxious to get work.
Referred to Poor Law, Orfeur Cavenagh

Letter written by R Patching on behalf of St Johns, 23 February 1877
Gentlemen, please state whether the cases named below are deserving of relief from the Brighton Jubilee and Accident Fund and oblige, R Patching
Harriett Reeves, 13 Spa Street, accident to wrist; Edward Bailey, 57 Egremont Street, injured eye; Thomas Boyes, 14 Claremont Row, sprained ankle; William Divall, 33 Queens Place, injured arm;
Emily Windsor, 42 Carlton Row, injured arm

26 February 1877
Reeves, who still jobs about, went on to work last week for the Corporation. His wife, who is now a prostitute, was locked up a month ago for being drunk and disorderly. She was very violent and it took three constables to hold her and this will probably account for her injured wrist. WC [William Collingham]
Undeserving. Report to Mrs Patching, R P Hooper

[117] Surrey History Centre: 2271/10/18.

[118] Naturalisation petitions East Pennsylvania 1795-1930 M1522, Roll 133, petition numbers 23501-23750.

24 November 1879
Reeves, now of 17 Whichelo Place, applied at the office on Saturday for some assistance. He has been out of work for three weeks. His wife has been ill in bed a month suffering from inflammation of the lungs. The son is at Redhill reformatory. Home is in a destitute state. WC [William Collingham]
Referred to parish, A Holland

Letter from the St Pancras (South) Committee of the Society for Organising Charitable Relief and Repressing Mendicity, 11 March 1881
Re: John Reeves a labourer, a wife and one child – homeless
Sir, the above has applied for assistance and states that he formerly lived at 13 Spa Street, Brighton, for two years and left 10 months ago. He refers us to Mrs Howell of 8 Egremont Place, Brighton, and Mrs Brown of 5 Richmond Place, Brighton. Kindly cause the usual enquiries to be made as to character etc [and] report in due course. Yours faithfully, George Gibson, Hon Secretary per Charity Committee

12 March 1881
The St Pancras Committee request a report of this case. Mrs Howell of 8 Egremont Place and Mrs Brown formerly of 5 Richmond Place now of 23 Upper Rock Gardens state that they employed the wife for upwards of two years as charwoman and always found her willing and trustworthy. The husband is a lazy drinking man and lived for a long time on his wife's prostitution. WC [William Collingham]
Report to St Pancras Committee, R P Hooper

5 March 1886
Mrs Reeves, now of 55 Sloane Street, was sent by Mr CJA Rumbold and applied at the office on Thursday for some assistance. Her husband is at work for the relief committee earning 10s 6d per week. Applicant sells oranges and they are not in any urgent need of help. WC [William Collingham]
Ineligible GDT[119] 6 March 1886

28 March 1887
Reeves, now of 21 Nelson Place, applied at the office on Monday for a dispensary letter. He has recently gone out with a shoe black box and with regard to his health there does not appear to be much the matter with him. His wife is on the streets. Their son is in prison and they are considered utterly

119 Initials difficult to read but probably GDT which would match with G D Turnbull who sat on the council of the Charity Organisation Society during the 1880s.

unworthy of encouragement. WC [William Collingham]
Undeserving, JPH [or JDH]

Letter written by R J Burdon of 18 York Place, Brighton, 23 March 1888
Dear Sir, I should be much obliged if you would enquire into the cases of the following persons who have all been applying for relief and would let me know how many of them are really deserving: Reeves, 15 Woburn Place; Mills, 19 Woburn Place; Vickers, 22 Woburn Place; Gibbs, 10 Nelson Place; Moore, 35 Nelson Place. With many apologies for troubling you so repeatedly. I remain yours very truly, R J Burdon

26 March 1888
The Reverend R J Burdon of St Peters requests a report of this case.[120] Reeves now resides at 15 Woburn Place and jobs about as a labourer. His wife is in ill health. They have not improved since my last report and seem very poor. WC [William Collingham]
Report to Mr Burdon, R P Hooper

24 January 1889
Reeves applied at the office on Wednesday for assistance to tide him over until he can obtain employment. He has had no constant work during the last five weeks and at present he has none in view. His wife is in delicate health. Their home is in a destitute condition and they have not improved since my last report. WC [William Collingham]
Referred to parish, R P Hooper

9 February 1889
Reeves applied at the office on Friday for relief from the Jubilee Accident Fund. On Thursday when he was standing in Edward Street a horse kicked him and fractured a rib for which he is an out-patient at the hospital but with regard to his character he has been a drinking man and has generally lived on his wife's prostitution. WC [William Collingham]
Referred to parish, R P Hooper

7 June 1890
Mrs Reeves, now of 50 William Street, applied at the office this morning for an out-patient's letter to the Sussex County Hospital. Recently she has gone out washing and according to her statement she has injured her breast with the handle of a wringing machine. Her husband jobs about with bathing machines

[120] The Reverend R J Burdon appears in *Pike's Directory* of 1888 as a clergyman of St Nicholas, Brighton.

and the previous reports will show that they have long been most unfavourably known to the society.
A letter granted, A F Bond[121]

12 October 1904
Statement: My son Robert Edward Tabbenor has been out in Philadelphia two years where he offers me a house. For particulars see his letter appended and I can manage to get my outfit by selling a few things but have no means to pay my passage money which would cost £2 7s.
Report: The previous reports show that the applicant has been a woman of exceedingly bad character since 26 February 1877. In Riding School Lane she kept a disorderly house which was full of disreputable people and she has only been in her present situation two months. Mrs Claxton took her without a reference and on several occasions she has returned home the worse for liquor. Since her son left Redhill Reformatory the police have a large number of convictions recorded against him and therefore the statement about work in Philadelphia for his mother can hardly be relied upon. WC [William Collingham]

14 October 1904
Unassisted on grounds of character, VAB[122]

3 November 1904
Mrs Reeves called at the office this afternoon to ask the committee to reconsider their decision and handed in the annexed letter offering her work, a good home and the regular wages in Philadelphia, USA. WC [William Collingham]

4 November 1904
Previous decision confirmed.
VAB

Letter written by the Reverend Gerard Mottram Hutton, St Mary's Vicarage, Brighton, 15 December 1905
Dear Sirs, Re: emigration of Mrs Reeves, 13 Carlton Place
The above-named woman living in St Mary's parish, a householder, is anxious to emigrate to the United States. She has a son, born out of wedlock, by name Robert Edward Tabbenor, who declares his willingness to keep her and to pay

121 The Charity Organisation Society annual report of 1883 records a Major General Bond as a member of the council and the *Page's Directory* of that dates shows a Major General A F Bond living at 1 Ventnor Villas.
122 Possibly the Reverend Vicar Armstrong Boyle, vicar of Portslade, and vice chariman of the Charity Organisation Society.

for her passage out. At present he has sent £1 only towards the passage but he promises to send more. Have you an office in Philadelphia and if so can you find out anything about R E Tabbenor and can you advise as to the likelihood of the authorities allowing Mrs Reeves to enter the States if Tabbenor sends the full £6 required? Mrs Reeves does not bear a good name at all. In fact I am told that when she was living in Riding School Lane she might have had proceedings taken against her for keeping a disorderly house. I have told her son this but he still declares his willingness to have her and (if he can keep her) he will be ridding Brighton of a woman who is bound to come upon the rates sooner or later and who might perhaps become a better character with someone to look after her. A great deal depends on Tabbenor's character. Yours faithfully, Gerard Mottram Hutton

16 December 1905
Letter from the Reverend GM Hutton of St Mary's vicarage asking to have enquiries made in Philadelphia regarding applicant's son. The previous report states that he was formerly in Redhill Reformatory. Since he left there the police have a large number of convictions recorded against him. His mother walked the streets for many years besides which she has kept disorderly houses and has been a hard drinker therefore she appears a fit subject for the parish to deal with. WC [William Collingham]

19 December 1905
Reported to G M Hutton

Letter from M E Heathcote to the Reverend Gerrard Hutton, 19 December 1905
Re: Harriet Reeves
Dear Mr Hutton, the above has been unfavourably known to our society since 1872. Last October she made to us the same application she is making to you, and we were so dissatisfied with the letters of the son that we refused to have anything to do with it. The said son was formerly in Redhill Reformatory, and since he left the police have a large number of convictions recorded against him. Mrs Reeves lived by vice for many years, besides which she has kept disorderly houses, and has been a hard drinker. We could not at all recommend you take up the case. Faithfully yours, M E Heathcote

Letter written by M A Crawford, almoner, regarding Harriett Reeves, 61, 13 Carlton Place, 22 January 1906
Dear Miss Heathcote, the Dr wants this patient to have some new teeth for which she states she cannot afford to pay. She tells me she usually goes out to service but has not been out for the past four months: as the lady she lived with went away she tells me she is however going back to the same situation on Feb

12th and could then pay towards cost of teeth. I believe she is known to you and did not wish at first to apply to COS as she said Mr Cunningham [William Collingham] gave her a bad character some time ago – yet when she found I could do nothing else for her she said she would like to come and see what you could do for her. I am afraid it is not a very promising case. Yours truly, M A Crawford

23 January 1906
Mrs Reeves was sent by the hospital almoner and applied at the office this morning for a set of new teeth. She has recently done a little charring and the previous reports show that she has always had an exceedingly bad character. WC [William Collingham]

Letter to the Charity Organisation Society from Harriett Reeves, January 1906
Dear sir, I hope you will excuse my writing to you and troubling you in this matter, but owing to the bad character which Mr Cunynghame [Collingham] and his son have unjustly given me I consider I have been debarred from having a fresh set of teeth which some lady at the hospital considered I required. I had to go from the hospital to the Charity Organisation, that was quite a month ago and have not heard anything further. You will see for yourself by the following list that I am not the bad woman Mr Cunynghame [Collingham] has tried to make me out to be. Below are a few of the names of the people I have worked for.

Laundry work: Mrs Williams, Bakers Bottom; Mrs Clifford, Southover Street; Mrs Matthews, Queens Park; Mrs Gole [sic], Carlton Hill; Mrs Rodgers, 17 Gloster Place; Mrs Dench, 32 John Street; Mrs Baker, Bakers Bottom; Mrs Rosall, Elm Grove; Mrs Matthews, 55 Preston Road; Mrs Clackston, 12 Regency Square – four month in service; Mrs Medhurst, 15 Belgrave Place – five months service and should have back there but owing to an injured knee a month ago have not been able to do so and have also worked for Mrs West, Barnet, Griggs, Hutchins, Thomas, Worsley, Brown and several others and could supply their addresses if required. There are a few of my lodgers' names on whom Mr Cunynhame [Collingham] stated I have been living: Mrs Wells, one year; Owl, three years; Harman, two and a half years; Patching, nine months; Gardner, six months; Everett, one year; Heather, three months; Ray, ten months; Holmes, one year. If you would kindly lay these facts before the committee, it would help to clear my character as Mr Cunynghame [Collingham] told the clergyman of this district that I have always been living on the prostitution of other women. Hoping you can excuse my troubling you, I remain yours respectfully, Mrs H Reeves, 13 Carlton Place, Brighton

24 February 1906
Letter from Mrs Reeves complaining that the agent and his son George have given her a bad character, WC [William Collingham]

27 February 1906
Recorded NVC[123]

17 HANNA GAYNOR, 40, HAWKER, 33 THOMAS STREET, BRIGHTON

Hanna, or Johanna, Gaynor was known to Brighton police long before the Mendicity Society was aware of her. She was born in Bristol in about 1832 and arrived at Brighton in about 1844. In November 1867 she was fined five shillings for being drunk and disorderly on Trafalgar Lane.[124] *Five months later she went before magistrates again, this time charged with the more serious crime of theft: on 1 April 1868 Gaynor was arrested for being drunk and disorderly on Trafalgar Street and when she was taken in for questioning by PC Dowison she was found to have two pairs of boots on her person.*[125] *Gaynor had entered the premises of John Stevens, bootmaker, at 90 Trafalgar Street but gave inconsistent stories about how she came to have the boots. The chief witness was Elizabeth Stevens, daughter of the prosecutor, and she stated that Gaynor had looked at the boots but did not pay the 5s 6d required. Gaynor maintained that Elizabeth Stevens had allowed her to take the boots on approval but agreed to plead guilty 'for the sake of her children'. Mr Bigge, the magistrate, refused to accept the plea and committed the prisoner for trial at Quarter Sessions. On 14 July 1868 Johanna Gaynor was charged with larceny and sentenced to three months' hard labour.*[126]

In April 1871 Gaynor, her husband Thomas, a labourer born in Tipperary, and their five children were enumerated at 5 Essex Place. She was charged with being drunk and disorderly on Edward Street on 23 October 1871 and was ordered to pay five shillings plus costs or face seven days' hard labour.[127] *By January 1872, when the family's case was presented to the charity by Mr Davis of 51 Dyke Road, they had moved to 33 Thomas Street. Thomas Gaynor had been out of work for six months and Johanna was hawking, but her income was not meeting the cost of the 3s 6d per week rent they were paying for their room and they were two weeks in arrears. By 1881 the Gaynors and their children were living at 17 Egremont Street with three other families. By the time of Johanna Gaynor's third application in November 1883 she stated that she had separated from her husband, but they appear to have been reunited again by the time of the next application*

123 Probably Mr N V Combe, vice chariman of the Charity Organisation Society.
124 Brighton Gazette, 14 November 1867.
125 Brighton Gazette, 2 April 1868.
126 Criminal Registers 1791-1892, class HO 27, piece 151, page 130.
127 Brighton Guardian, 25 October 1871.

in February 1885. Both individuals appear on the 1891 census in Brighton Workhouse. Thomas Gaynor died in late 1892 and Johanna Gaynor died in the June quarter of 1899.

11 January 1872
Statement: Hanna Gaynor wants a little assistance to get some stock for a start.
Report: I made enquiries respecting this family and find them very destitute. The woman says if she could get a hundred herrings she could get their living. The man is anything but an industrious man. He never has any regular work. The woman has been convicted for felony.
Referred to poor law, Orfeur Cavenagh. NB the applicant is known to have received an order for the workhouse

Letter written by Johanna Gaynor, 33 Little St James Street, c. 1875
My dear madam, please to excuse the great liberty I take in addressing you only having heard of your great charity I can assure you it is out of severe want I trouble you. I had been suffering from pleurisy since Christmas and have not been out to earn anything for myself. I am really dying of want. I am expecting my confinement every day which makes me much worse my dear madam. If it did lay in your power to bestow a little of your charity on me I should be very grateful. My husband is at work for the parish and all he gets is seven shillings a week. I have to pay 3s 6d a week for rent which I could not. The landlord told me if I did not give him a little money this week I must leave. I have not means to give him anything [and] I shall be thrown out in the street. I am afraid to die. That is the reason I troubled you I hope my dear madam you will forgive me for troubling you. Wishing to remain your humble and patient servant, Johanna Gaynor

30 March 1875
Mrs Robinson requests a report of this case. I find the wife was confined on Friday last. Although the husband has been receiving only 1s a week from the parish he will have extras in consequence of his wife's confinement for a fortnight. In fact the case is being very well attended to by the relieving officer.
WC [William Collingham]
To be reported to Mrs Robinson, R P Hooper

17 November 1883
Report: Mrs Gaynor applied at the office this morning for a dispensary letter. Applicant is now separated from her husband and supports herself and youngest child by selling flowers. She is a low drunken woman, well known to the police and seems to be in a bad state of health. WC [William Collingham]
Referred to parish, R P Hooper

Letter from B Ellis, 19 Chichester Place, Brighton, 26 February [1885]
Dear Sir, thank you for your note of this morning. I am sorry to trouble you again but Mrs Gaynor, 62 Egremont Street, has just applied for relief. Will you kindly enquire into the case. Yours faithfully, B Ellis

27 February 1885
Mrs Ellis of 19 Chichester Place requests a report of this case. Gaynor and his wife, who now reside at 68 Egremont Street, get their living by selling flowers. They have one child dependent on them and have greatly improved since the case was before the committee in November 1883. WC [William Collingham]
Report to Mrs Ellis, R P Hooper

Letter from Miss Ridding, 2 Denmark Terrace, 21 May [1885]
Miss Ridding has this morning been asked to relieve a woman who has called on her under the name Mrs Gaynor who states she lives at 62 Egremont Place and has broken her arm by a brewer's dray having knocked her down. Sent is a card of a solicitor, a Mr Trevor Pollard, 7 Prince Albert Street, who, she says, 'has taken up her case' do the Charity Organisation Society know anything of her?[128]

22 May 1885
Miss Ridding of 2 Denmark Terrace requests a report of this case. Gaynor now resides at 62 Egremont Street and still [sells] flowers. His wife was knocked down in Tidy Street a night ago by a dray belonging to Mr Hemsley, brewer, of 2[9] Edward Street when her right arm was broken and she is now a patient at the hospital.[129] She has recently been very much addicted to drink and has an order for the workhouse in [her] possession. WC [William Collingham]
Report to Miss Ridding, R P Hooper

18 MARY JUPP, 34, WIFE OF A LABOURER, 11 ESSEX PLACE, BRIGHTON

Mary Jupp, née Brown, was born in Brighton in 1838 and lived at 11 Essex Place with her husband George and their daughters: Ellen, 12; Mary 5 and Elizabeth, 3.[130] *George Jupp had been labouring for a Mr Charman of Robert Street but had been out of work for two months and by January 12th found himself 3s 9d in debt: exactly one week's rent.*

[128] A photograph of Trevor Pollard, solicitor, is held by ESRO as AMS 6878/1/1.

[129] H Hemsley ran the Painters Arms, 29 Edward Street; S Hemsley ran the Grand Duke of Baden, 67 Edward Street. There is no record of Mrs Gaynor's admittance to the hospital at this date, suggesting she was treated as an out-patient.

[130] Mary A Brown marriage to George Jupp registered Q1 1866 Brighton 2b 293.

12 January 1872
Statement: I was out with the children and a lady gave me the ticket.
Report: I made enquiries respecting this family and find they have one son who goes to work. The wife goes out two or three days a week. The oldest girl goes out minding children and gets a few half pence. The man occasionally gets a day's work. The home is in a passable state.
Ineligible, Orfeur Cavenagh

19 SUSANNAH BURSTOW, 35, WIFE OF A PLASTERER, 2 KINGSBURY ROAD, BRIGHTON

The Burstows' case was sent to the Mendicity Society by the Quaker businessman, Daniel Hack. Susannah Peters married Henry Burstow in Spring 1863.[131] *When she applied to the charity in January 1872 Henry Burstow had been employed as a plasterer by Mr Walker of Cliftonville but had been out of work for five months due to cold weather. By the standards of the other applicants Burstow had the potential to earn a very respectable wage and this was reflected in the higher standard of living the family appears to have enjoyed: they paid eight shillings a week for a house just off London Road and some distance from the slums of Carlton Hill where the majority of the other applicants lived.*

12 January 1872
Statement: I have not got anything for my children to eat. My husband has been out of [work] since Chris[tmas].
Report: I made enquiries respecting Henry Burstow and find he is a plasterer and did work for Mr Walker, builder, Cliftonville and there was earning 25s a week and in the summer when in full work a plasterer gets 6s a day besides over time. He belongs to the plasterers' band and also belongs to the volunteers. His home is very tidily furnished. The man is [a] strong looking man but the woman looks as if she does not get enough to eat. They had not food in the house: Mr Hack kindly gave me 5s with that I bought bread and butter, tea, sugar etc which they was thankful for. The wife has a sister in business in the Western Road and has helped them several times.
Ineligible, Orfeur Cavenagh

[131] Susannah Peters marriage to Henry Burstow registered Q2 1863 Brighton 2b 390.

20 MARY MARSHALL, 63, CHARWOMAN, 12 CHESTERFIELD STREET, BRIGHTON

Mary Marshall, née Morris, was born in Reigate, Surrey, in about 1809 and married William Marshall at St Mary's church, Reigate, on 4 July 1841.[132] *William Marshall's death was registered at Reigate in late 1853 and Mary Marshall claimed to have been living in Brighton since about 1851 though it is quite likely she moved south after her husband's death.*[133] *Mary Marshall had been out of work for three weeks and was 3s 6d, or two weeks' rent, in debt when her case was forwarded to the Mendicity Society by Annie Neild of 3 College Road.*

12 January 1872
Statement: Mary Marshall wants a little assistance till she gets work.
Report: I have made enquiries respecting Mary Marshall and find she is a widow and did go out hawking when she had no work. She has a daughter about 30 who is in the infirmary. Her home is in a passable state.
Grant of 5s authorised by payment of – money provided a licence will be issued, Orfeur Cavenagh.
5 shillings given by a member of the committee

14 January 1873
Further information: applicant called at the office this morning and stated that her old licence had ran out and that she had no means to renew it and is therefore unable to get her living and she hopes the committee will take a favourable view of her case. WC [William Collingham]
Grant of 5s for a licence, R P Hooper

4 September 1874
This person who supports herself by doing a little charring and by hawking ornaments for fire stoves applied at the office on Friday for a little temporary assistance. Applicant is suffering from rheumatic gout in her right hand and for the class of persons to which she belongs I believe her to be very respectable. WC [William Collingham]
Grant of 5 shillings, GDR, chairman

20 January 1875
This woman, who has saved up 3s, applied at the office on Wednesday for 2s to enable her to renew her licence which will cost 5s. WC [William Collingham]
Grant of 2 shillings for licence, R P Hooper

[132] Mary's surname is also registered as Morris on the same entry.
[133] Death of William Marshall registered in Q4 1853 Reigate 2a 65.

21 FRANCES SAMPSON, 21, WIFE OF A WATERMAN, 17 LITTLE ST JAMES STREET, BRIGHTON

In her application to the Mendicity Society, Frances Sampson claimed to have been born in Brighton but census returns show that she was born Frances Ann Lewery in Cuckfield in about 1851. She stated that she had been living in Brighton for eight years and civil registration records show that she married Thomas Sampson in Hove in the September quarter of 1869. Sampson was a waterman and was born in Brighton in about 1845. He is enumerated on the 1861 census, aged 15, at 16 Derby Place living with Thomas Harman, fisherman. A twenty-year-old fisherman named Thomas Sampson was charged in July 1867 with having broken and entered the shop of John Pointing on the Chain Pier, stealing jewellery and other goods to the value of £60. Witnesses stated that Sampson and his fellow defendant, Thomas Best,[134] were drinking at a beer-house in Edward Street until 11.30pm and others stated that the pair had been dealing with some of the stolen items on the day after the robbery. Sampson was sentenced to 18 months' hard labour.[135]

Thomas and Frances Sampson and their infant children, James and Anne, had been renting their single room at 17 Little St James Street since about June 1871. Mrs Bovill of 3 Lower Rock Gardens had forwarded the family's case as Thomas Sampson had not been able to work for Mr Trott due to the poor conditions at sea. The couple owed 1s 6d which equated to a week's rent.

Thomas Sampson died in July 1874. Frances Sampson married Nathaniel Pumphrey, a fisherman, on 27 December 1875 at St Peter's, Brighton.[136] She died in Brighton in October 1909.

13 January 1872
Statement: the lady has always assisted me before when I wanted a little relief.
Report: I made enquiries respecting Frances Sampson and find her home in a passable state. Her husband has not been earning anything for this last two weeks on account of the weather but he has gone to sea today.
Dismissed, ineligible, Orfeur Cavenagh

26 April 1872
Mrs Sampson came to the office on Friday sent by Miss Bovill, 3 Lower Rock Gardens, and stated her husband had only earnt one shilling and eight pence during the week and that her two children was suffering with the whooping cough. I made enquiries and found her statement was correct and informed Miss Bovill the result of my enquiry and she has relieved them.
Previous dismissal confirmed, R P Hooper, chairman

[134] Thomas Best was admitted to St Francis Asylum on 7 August 1876. His mental disorder was described as 'dipsomania', ESRO HC 24/2993.

[135] Brighton Gazette, 25 July 1867.

[136] ESRO: PAR 277/1/3/3.

22 FRANCIS HEALEY, 19, LABOURER, 11 DERBY PLACE, BRIGHTON

Francis Healey was born in Brynmawr, Breconshire on 18 September 1854. He came to Brighton from Tulse Hill, London, in June 1871 and took lodgings at 11 Derby Place for which he paid 1s 9d per week. Healey described himself as a labourer but was noticed begging on Marine Parade by the novelist Edward Campbell Tainsh.[137] *He first applied to the Mendicity Society on 15 January 1872 asking for help to gain an apprenticeship with a tailor, and for a second time on 20 January 1873 when he was treated as an out-patient at the Sussex County Hospital. His final application to the charity on 4 November 1874 asked for funds to help complete his apprenticeship: the tailor, Mr Shelley of 28 Clifton Hill, and Mr Tainsh both spoke highly of Healey and enquired whether funds might be made available to buy him a prosthetic leg.*

Healey married Mary Anne Payne of Dudley, Worcestershire, in Brighton in the September quarter of 1874. The marriage is not recorded in any of the Church of England registers, suggesting it took place at a non-conformist chapel. The 1881 census shows Healey as a tailor living with his wife and two children at Broad Green, Croydon. By 1891 the family, now with four children, had moved to 27 Crossfield Road, Cleator, Cumberland, where he was employed as a Conservative registration agent.

Healey, also known as Frank Healey, died on 22 December 1894 and, according to the funeral notice, was buried at Cleator Moor. The notice stated 'he was well known as the Conservative agent for the Barnard Castle division, to which post he was elected June last. Mr Healey, who was only forty years of age, had worked hard in the Conservative cause from the time of his early manhood. Trained for the priesthood, he was well-educated, and proved himself a platform speaker of some power. The main part of his work has been done in the last fourteen years and principally in the southern counties. It was only in 1889 that he came north, into Cumberland, and joined the staff of a local paper. The Conservative cause can lay claim to very few such men of the calibre of the late Mr Healey. His death will be mourned by friend and opponent alike.'[138]

15 January 1872
Statement: Francis Healey would like to be prenticed to a tailor
Report: this is the young man with only one leg, that used to go begging on the Marine Parade. Mr Tainsh will make further enquiries respecting this young man. I write in accord to maintenance being approved for one week pending enquiries
Further information respecting this case: I have seen Mr Tainsh he has kept him since this case went before the committee at the expense of five shillings and three pence per week. Since that he has been put prentice to a tailor and is

[137] Edward Campbell Tainsh (1835-1919) was born in London but, by 1868, was a professor of literature in Brighton. He published St Alice (1867), Mr Johnston's School (1867), Crowned (1868), One Maiden Only (1870) and The Christian Hypothesis (posthumously published in 1922).

[138] Daily Gazette for Middlesbrough, 24 December 1894.

serving a month on trial which is nearly completed, then there is no doubt he will go on at his apprenticeship which the expense for that will be ten pounds. A friend of Mr Tainsh will give five pounds, Mr Tainsh has two pounds what he got from Healey's friends. His wages to start with will be 2s 6d per week, Mr Tainsh's friend will give 2s 6d per week for the first six months, Mr Shelley, tailor 28 Clifton Hill is where Healey is working.
Relieved by grant, £1 10s half the balance

Letter written by Edward Tainsh, 5 Abbey Road, Brighton, 12 June 1872
Dear Sir, I am sorry to have been so long in writing you. But matters have not long been settled, and since, I have been unusually busy and very poorly. First I must thank you as representing the Mendicity Society for the £1 10s towards the expenses of the boy Healey. The boy now stands apprenticed to Mr Shelley, tailor, of 28 Clifton Hill. His expenses for board and lodging before I could place him were about £3. This I paid. His premium was £10. Of this you paid £1.10s; a friend of mine – Miss Smith of Kilburn - £5, and the boy's friends at Norwood £2. I paid the remainder. The Norwood friends also sent some clothes and Miss Smith added money on account of which Mr Shelley undertook to give Healey 5s a week to begin with, so making him able to live from the first.
These, I believe, are the facts. Believe me dear sir, yours very truly, Edward Tainsh

20 January 1873
This young man has conducted himself extremely well while he has been with Mr Shelley. He is now laid up and an out-patient at the hospital but no doubt he will be able to work in a few days. His wages being only 7s a week he was unable to save anything and therefore requests the committee to assist him with a small grant. WC [William Collingham]
Conditional grant of 10s

4 November 1874
Applicant will complete his apprenticeship in April next and is anxious to learn the cutting part of the business for which Mr Tainsh and his friends will undertake to provide the necessary expense. To succeed in this part of the business it is desirable that he should have an artificial leg which will cost 10 or 12 Guineas for which purpose Mr Tainsh strongly recommends the case to the favourable consideration of the committee, adding that having already done so much for the young man, he hopes that the committee will raise the necessary amount without calling upon him unless an unexpected difficulty should occur. Mr Shelley speaks very highly of applicant's character and conduct and cordially joins in the recommendation. WC [William Collingham]
Grant of 5s

10 February 1876
This man was never able to raise any money for his artificial leg. About 12 months ago he got married and is now living in Croydon. His wife was recently confined. Mrs Winans of Chichester Terrace forwarded £2 to the office towards paying for the leg and as the man has not succeeded in getting anything towards the expense Mrs Winans said through her butler that the Society had better send him a Post Office Order for the £2.[139] WC [William Collingham]
The £2 given by Mrs Winans to be forwarded to Francis Healey by P[ost] O[ffice] Order in accordance with her request

Letter written by Edward Tainsh, 5 Abbey Road, Brighton, Wednesday, 11 November [1874]
Dear Sir, thank you for your note. I am very glad that the committee of the Charity Organisation Society are kindly willing to help Frances Healey to an artificial leg; but I am afraid that a grant of £2 will leave him more to do in getting the remainder than he will easily manage. The cost of the leg will be £10 or £12. The suggestion did not arise with me and all that I have been able to do for him has been directed towards his advancement in his estate and the holding him together during a very difficult period of his life and in which as I think he has behaved excellently. The last thing that I have arranged for him is that he shall learn cutting out. I am of opinion that if the committee were disposed to increase the amount of their grant they would be putting to a good use the resources at their disposal. Believe me, yours truly, Edward Tainsh

Letter written by Francis Healy, 1 Hunters Terrace, Croydon, Surrey, 14 February 1876
Dear Sir, I have received your Post Office Order value two pounds and accept my thanks for the same. I remain yours faithfully, Francis Healy

23 CHARLES LINSTED, 27, SERVANT, RUNNING HORSE, KING STREET, BRIGHTON

Charles Linsted was born in Finningham, Suffolk, and had been living in Brighton since about August 1871. His previous address was listed as the Globe, Edward Street. Prior to his move to Brighton Linsted had been working for a Mr Fox of 26 Bruton Street, Mayfair, London, and living in a lodging house at 27 Thomas Street, Westminster, but had been out of work for nine months following the death of his employer. He owed one week's rent of 2s 4d.

[139] Mrs Anne Marie Winans, 36 Chichester Terrace.

15 January 1872
Statement: Charles Linsted wants assistance to get back to London where he can get work.
Report: I have known this man for the last three months, he has had no regular work. He did lodge at a public house in Edward Street. He is a strong able man able to walk to London. I have seen Mr Wingfield, he has relieved him several times.
Dismissed as ineligible, Orfeur Cavenagh

24 JOHN MEADS, 52, LABOURER, 97 HANOVER STREET, BRIGHTON

The Mendicity Society's agent, William Collingham, had encountered John Meads in January 1859 when Collingham was employed as a police constable. Meads, whom the Brighton Gazette described as 'a rough looking fellow,' had been charged with stealing a glass tumbler from the Hare and Hounds, London Road. The landlord's wife, Elizabeth Gorringe, stated that she had seen Meads loitering near the pub and had noticed a large number of glasses missing since before Christmas. Collingham had taken Meads into custody the previous day after finding him drunk and begging on Francis Street. Collingham had seen Meads trying to dispose of the glass but Meads tried to claim the glass was his and that he intended to sell it to buy bread. He was sentenced to two months' hard labour.[140]

Meads had been in trouble with the police in November 1858 when he was charged with stealing five fowls, worth 15 shillings, from Frederick Hallett at Lindfield and subsequently assaulting PC William Vidler at East Grinstead. He was sentenced to seven months' hard labour.[141]

At the time of his application to the Mendicity Society John Meads was living with his wife Caroline and 17-year-old daughter Rosetta.[142] *He was born in Burgess Hill in about 1820 but had been living in Brighton for 30 years. Meads had been working for Mr Marshall at the drainage works and despite having been out of work for three weeks owed no rent. The family's case was forwarded to the charity by Daniel Hack of Trafalgar Street.*

16 January 1872
Statement: John Meads has been sick for three weeks and went to Mr Hack for a little assistance.
Report: I have made enquiries respecting John Meads. His home is in a passable state. He is brother to the Meads at St Johns Common. His habits are very intemperate. I had this man in custody six or seven years ago for being drunk

140 Brighton Gazette, 12 January 1865.
141 Brighton Gazette, 6 January 1859.
142 Caroline Britcher marriage to John Meads registered Q2 1850 Ticehurst 7 733. Their daughter Rosetta's birth registered Q1 1855 Tonbridge 2a 359.

and begging in London Road. He was sentenced to two months' imprisonment with hard labour. Mr Beal also knows this man as a constant visitor.
Dismissed as ineligible, Orfeur Cavenagh

25 CAROLINE TAYLOR, 38, WIFE OF A FLYMAN, 46 BAKER STREET, BRIGHTON

The Taylor family rented the entire house at 46 Baker Street for which they paid the considerable sum of eight shillings per week. They were from Lindfield but had lived at this address for 14 years and were still living there at the time of their second application for relief in December 1873. In January 1872 Caroline Taylor's husband, David, had been prevented from working for Mr Vann through illness for three months and had run up arrears of £4 10s. Their case had been forwarded to the Mendicity Society by H A Barclay of Lewes Crescent.

16 January 1872
Statement: my husband has been sick for three months but now he is at work. I want to get some assistance to take my blind boy to Guys Hospital. What I want is my railway expenses.
Report: I made enquiries respecting Caroline Taylor and find her statement is false. I have seen Mr Hollman, the cab inspector at the railway station, and he knows the man has been at work regular and also the railway police. The home is very well furnished, they have got the whole house and let furnished apartments, but they have no lodgers now. The Reverend T Cook has given Mrs Taylor five shillings to get the boy some clothes.[143] Mrs Taylor's friends are people well to do in the town.
Undeserving, Orfeur Cavenagh

Letter from Mrs Cohen, 14 Adelaide Crescent, Hove, 2 December 1873
Mrs Cohen requests a report of Mrs Taylor, 46 Baker Street, London Road, Brighton

4 December 1873
Mrs Cohen sent the annexed letter to Mr Beal who handed it over to this society and on enquiry I find the husband, who is a little given to drink, still drives a fly at the railway. The wife does a little cooking. The son Joseph, who is blind, was admitted into the Blind Asylum in Eastern Road in March 1872. The fee payable is £2 10s, a quarter in advance, towards which Miss Glyn pays £1 and Mrs Taylor collects the remainder in doing which she is very apt to mention about her husband and being given to drink and that she has worked hard to get him a

[143] The Reverend Thomas Cooke was perpetual curate of St Peter, Brighton, between 1824 and 1873.

comfortable home but the comfortable home was got for a single sister whom an old gentleman was going to keep and educate but a short time afterwards he saw her with another man in consequence of which he had no more to do with her. WC [William Collingham]
To be reported to Mrs Cohen, R P Hooper

26 ANN ROGERS (ALSO GIVEN AS RODGERS), 52, NEEDLEWOMAN, 7 NELSON PLACE, BRIGHTON

Ann Rogers was born in Findon in 1820. In 1861 she was enumerated at 45 Spring Gardens, Brighton, with her husband John Rogers, a shoemaker from Tipperary. Her profession is given as shoe binder. By the time of her application to the Mendicity Society on 18th January 1872 Ann Rogers was living with her husband in one room at 7 Nelson Place, Brighton, where she was paying 1s 3d per week rent. She was five shillings in arrears when her details were passed to the charity by the Reverend Neil Crispin, priest of St Joseph's, Elm Grove. By 1881 her husband had died and Rogers was living at 12 Eastern Road, Brighton.

18 January 1872
Statement: Ann Rogers wants a little assistance till trade is better when her husband, who is a shoemaker and is in the Workhouse, can come out and obtain work.
Report: I have made enquiries respecting Ann Rodgers and find her home in a most destitute state. Her husband is in the Workhouse. Mr Powers, 2 Atlingworth Street, pays for a girl at the Catholic Schools, Bristol Road, for them. Mr Oliver knows she is a very poor woman and thinks if we relieve her this week she would be as bad off the next.
Referred to the Poor Law, Orfeur Cavenagh

13 December 1872
Further information: This person brought a ticket to the office on Thursday afternoon and stated that she wanted a little temporary relief. Upon enquiry I find she has been working for a second-hand clothes dealer living in Marine Gardens but she has not had but very little to do lately her husband is still in the Workhouse. The home is in a destitute state. WC [William Collingham]
Referred to parish authorities, R P Hooper

27 JAMES WHITEHEAD, 70, LABOURER, 32 ESSEX STREET, BRIGHTON

James Whitehead told the Mendicity Society that he had been living in Brighton for 27 years at the time of his first application to the charity in January 1872 but census returns suggest that he came to Brighton at some point before 30 March 1851, when he was enumerated at 63 Nottingham Street, and after the birth of his daughter, Caroline, in Bristol in about 1849. Each census between 1851 and 1871 records a different birthplace for Whitehead: Preston, Lancashire; Woodbridge, Suffolk and Prescot, Lancashire, respectively. These census returns suggest he led a fairly peripatetic existence until he settled in Brighton as his first three children were born in Bath, West Bromwich and Bristol. However, once in Brighton the family remained at 32 Essex Street between about 1856 and at least June 1872. They paid four shillings per week rent and were £1 in arrears at the time of the initial application.

The report of 9 March 1877 notes that the woman with whom James Whitehead had been living in 1872 was not his wife. However, this woman, named Caroline, seems to be the same person that was enumerated with James Whitehead on every census between 1851 and 1871.

18 January 1872
Statement: James Whitehead wants a little assistance to get some timber to make some picture frames with.
Report: I have made enquiries respecting James Whitehead and find his home in a comfortable state. Mr Cotterill gave him a good character.[144] He gets six shillings a week there besides extras and also goes window cleaning [and] carpet beating. His son gets two shillings and his breakfast at 111 Marine Parade. He has also a grown up daughter who is a dressmaker and lives at home with them.
Dismissed, ineligible, Orfeur Cavenagh

10 June 1872
Further information respecting this case: I find applicant left Mr Cotterill's employment about three weeks ago through a dispute with one of the servants. About a week ago he had a distress for rent when Mr Hayward, broker, lent him the money required (£2 14s 0d) for a fortnight on the security of his furniture. The time for payment expires on the 20th of this month. I advised him to get a loan sufficient to pay off the broker's claim and get a little stock of wood. He applied to the parish a fortnight ago but refused to go into the house.
Ineligible, R P Hooper, chairman

9 March 1877
This man applied at the office on Friday for five shillings to enable him to take out a hawker's licence to sell combs and cutlery. The person he lived with in 1872 was not his wife. They quarrelled and separated some time ago. Since then applicant has been in the workhouse. He now resides in a tramps lodging house.

[144] The Reverend G Cotterill was employed as an assistant master at Brighton College and was enumerated on the 1871 census at 5-6 Arlington Villas.

I have lately seen him associate and drink with the lowest characters in Edward Street and I feel sure that if he had a licence he would use it as a cloak for begging. WC [William Collingham]
Undeserving, F H Appach

26 March 1877
Mrs Morgan of 14 Wellington Road Villas, who has relieved this man on several occasions, requests a report of the case. WC [William Collingham]
To be reported to Mr Morgan, R P Hooper

28 SARAH HILTON, 52, HAWKER, 35 WILLIAM STREET, BRIGHTON

Census returns show that Sarah Hilton was born in Somerset in about 1820. She had moved to Brighton from Shoreham in about 1871 with her 70-year-old husband, George Hilton, a bricklayer who had been laid off by Mr Garrett five months previously.[145] *George Hilton was born in Steyning and had previously been married to Sophia Slaughter who died in Brighton in the March quarter of 1864. He married Sarah in the December quarter of 1865. The couple's case was forwarded to the charity by the Reverend Neil Crispin of 137 Elm Grove.*[146] *They paid three shillings per week rent for their room and were two weeks in arrears.*

18 January 1872
Statement: Sarah Hilton Wants a little assistance till her husband gets work.
Report: I have made enquiries respecting Sarah Hilton: her home is in a passable state. Her husband has been sick for ten weeks, he was knocked down by a cab at the top of North Road. The cabman drove off and he does not know who the cabman was. Mr Garrett gave him a good character but says he is too old for work. The wife goes out hawking lace. Miss Mohun says the wife is an industrious person.[147]
Grant of 3 shillings per week for two weeks pending reference to Poor Law or other local agency,
Orfeur Cavenagh
Outdoor relief refused on the [*illegible*] of his not being a resident householder admittance to the workhouse has been offered and refused the woman states that she has now obtained work,
Orfeur Cavenagh

[145] T and W Garrett had premises at of 57 Middle Street and also employed Richard Redman, applicant 29.
[146] The Reverend Neil Crispin was the incumbent of St Joseph's Catholic church, Elm Grove.
[147] Miss Mohun lived at 8 Dorset Gardens.

2 January 1874
Mrs Hilton applied at the office on Friday for assistance to enable her to renew her licence which ran out on Tuesday last. Since this case was before the committee nearly two years ago the husband has been unable to earn anything. The wife does a little washing and charring and sometimes hawks a few trifling articles. Her stock in trade generally consists of a cabbage net, a toasting fork and a yard or two of crochery work. The relieving officer, to whom they and their family are well known, states that they have been removed home to Arundel where they belong once or twice, if not three times.
WC [William Collingham]
Undeserving, R P Hooper

26 February 1875
This old couple now live at 29 Spa Street. Their circumstances are much the same as they were 13 months ago and Mrs Robinson requests a report of the case. WC [William Collingham]
To be reported unfavourably to Mrs Robinson, R P Hooper

29 RICHARD REDMAN, 45, LABOURER, 18 ST MARTINS PLACE, BRIGHTON

Richard Redman had been working for Mr Garrett of 57 Middle Street but was laid off in December 1871 due to shortage of work. He was confident of finding employment with Mr John Thomas Chappell at Cliftonville as William Homewood had done earlier in the month but was £1 in arrears and was paying 5s 6d per week rent for the house he shared with his wife, Clara (née Collieson), and eight children. [148] *Redman fathered four children with Clara and eight with his first wife, Maria (née Unwins), who died in 1867. Redman was born in Cuckfield in about 1827 but had been living in Brighton since at least 1841 when he was enumerated at Marshall's Row.*

18 January 1872
Statement: Richard Redman wants a little assistance till he gets work. There is no doubt I shall get work on at [sic] Mr Chappell's Cliftonville in course of a week or two.
Report: I made enquiries respecting Richard Redman and find his home in a destitute state. I have seen Mr Garrett and he gave him a good character. He has been to the parish authorities and declined to go in the workhouse.
Referred for further begging to the clergyman of the district, Orfeur Cavenagh.
The applicant and his son have obtained work, Orfeur Cavenagh

[148] Mendicity Society applicant 1.

30 ELLEN MCKIEG [ALSO GIVEN AS ELLEN MCKIEGE], 48, HAWKER, 10 DERBY PLACE, BRIGHTON

Little is known of Ellen McKieg's life before her application to the Mendicity Society. She was born in London in about 1824 but had been resident in Brighton since about 1866: she told the Mendicty Society that she had lived first at 36 Derby Place and then, from 1869, in a single room at 10 Derby Place. However, she was enumerated on the 1871 census living in the lodging house at 11 Derby Place where she earned her living as a licensed pedler.

At the time of her application McKieg was clearly very unwell and in no position to pay her 2s 6d rent or the two weeks' worth of arrears. She was a widow and dependent on her son for financial support. Miss Bovill of 3 Lower Rock Gardens forwarded the case to the charity but her death was registered in the March quarter of 1872.[149]

The son's name has not been established but the surname McKieg has appeared in only two other Brighton records: a William McKieg was married in Brighton in December 1869[150] *and a man of the same name was admitted to the Sussex County Hospital on 31 July 1872 suffering from syphilis.*[151]

18 January 1872
Statement: Ellen McKeig wants a little assistance because she does not want to go in the workhouse.
Report: I have known this woman for this last five years. She used to go hawking lace. She was a very industrious woman but is too ill to get out of bed. She is in deep consumption. Her livelihood entirely depends on her son who goes hawking shell boxes.
Grant made by private liberality for immediate relief. Further enquiries, Orfeur Cavenagh
The matter has been brought under the consideration of the parochial authorities and temporary relief presented by them. Orfeur Cavenagh

31 GEORGE MARCHANT, 50, FISHERMAN, 2 SAUNDERS COURT, BRIGHTON[152]

Two men named George Marchant applied to the Mendicity Society in the first six months of 1872 but it is not known whether they were directly related.[153] *Marchant is thought to*

149 Death of Ellen McKeig (sic) registered Q3 1872 Brighton 2b 141.
150 William Thomas McKeig (sic) marriage registered Q4 1869 Brighton 2b 433.
151 ESRO: HB 35/3/1872-3756.
152 Saunders Court is almost certainly a reference to Saunders Buildings: a courtyard situated at the rear of 3 Black Lion Street.
153 The other man named George Marchant was baptised at St Nicholas on 7 December 1823 (PAR 255/1/2/4). He worked as a fisherman, married a woman named Mary and applied to the Mendicity Society on 29 April 1872 (case 160).

have been baptised at St Nicholas, Brighton, on 21 September 1821.[154] *On 18 June 1834 a 13-year-old boy named George Marchant was admitted to the Sussex County Hospital with a comminuted fracture of the thigh: he was cured and discharged on 3 September 1834.*[155] *In 1851 a 29-year-old man named George Marchant was enumerated lodging at 36 King Street, Brighton. In 1861 a 40-year-old man by this name was enumerated at sea, working as the master of the 'Topsy'.*

By the time of his application to the Mendicity Society in January 1872 George Marchant had been working for George Priest of Middle Street, but had been out of work for two months. He had lived with his wife, Mary, and their three children at Saunders Buildings since about 1865. They paid rent of 3s 6d per week but were nine shillings in arrears when their case was forwarded to the charity by Mrs Pedlar of 30 Brunswick Square. On 16 March 1872 a 50-year-old man named George Marchant was charged with being drunk and disorderly in Black Lion Street, Brighton: he was fined five shillings plus costs or faced seven days' imprisonment.[156]

The death of a 66 year-old-man named George Marchant was registered in Brighton in the December quarter of 1887.

19 January 1872
Statement: George Marchant wants a little assistance. When the weather gets finer he can go to sea.
Report: I have made inquiries respecting George Marchant and find their home in a passable state. He has not been to sea for several weeks on account of the weather. His wife broke her arm some time ago and she is not able to work. The son goes to sea occasionally. They lost one child twelve months ago and one two months ago.
Further inquiry, Orfeur Cavenagh. Given from 20 to 25 shillings per week, of intemperate habits.[157]
Dismissed as ineligible

32 JULIA DONALLY, 59, CHARWOMAN, 4 LITTLE ST JAMES STREET, BRIGHTON

Like Sarah Hilton, Julia Donally's case was forwarded to the charity by the Reverend Neil Crispin of 137 Elm Grove, priest of St Joseph's church.[158] *Donally was born in Dublin but had come via Shoreham to Brighton where she had been since about January 1871. She had been working at Preston Barracks where she had been previously employed but, due to*

[154] ESRO: PAR 255/1/2/3.
[155] ESRO: HB 35/1/1834-411.
[156] Brighton Guardian, 20 March 1872.
[157] This entry is unclear, but it is thought that the 20 to 25 shillings referred to was given by Mrs Pedlar who forwarded Marchant's name to the charity.
[158] Applicant 28.

sickness, had been out of work for a month. She rented one room at 4 Little St James Street for which she paid 6d per week rent. She was 2s 6d in arrears.

19 January 1872
Statement: Julia Donally wants a little assistance till she gets work.
Report: I have made enquiries respecting Julia Donally and find her home in a destitute state. She has been getting her livelihood by selling fruit and charring at the barracks. She would like to go to Colchester where she has a daughter.
Further investigation, Orfeur Cavenagh. It has been ascertained that the applicant has two daughters living in Little St James Street, a fact previously concealed. Dismissed as ineligible, Orfeur Cavenagh

33 MARIA SPEARS, 45, CHARWOMAN, 11 CHELTENHAM PLACE, BRIGHTON

Maria Spears was born in Oxford but had been in Brighton for about 30 years at the time of her application to the Mendicity Society. She had been out of work for two weeks but was 30 shillings in debt and was paying 1s 6d for her single room at 11 Cheltenham Place. She claimed to have been living at this address for seven years but a 45-year-old woman by this name, also born in Oxford, was enumerated on the 1871 as a domestic servant at Oak Hall, Keymer.

23 January 1872
Statement: Maria Spears wants a little assistance till she gets work for I have to support my mother [sic].
Report: I have made enquiries respecting Maria Spears and find her house in a passable state. They have not paid any rent since the 25th of July. They have applied to the parish for relief and refused to go in the workhouse. This woman has a mother aged 76 to support.
3 shillings allowed for support for the current week pending the submission of the case for the consideration of the local district agency, Orfeur Cavenagh

34 WILLIAM MITCHELL, 54, LABOURER, 28 VIADUCT TERRACE, BRIGHTON

At the time of his first application to the Mendicity Society William Mitchell had been out of work for three weeks and was 17 shillings in arrears. He had been working for Mr Drury of Lewes Road but had been laid off due to lack of work. Mitchell was born in Balcombe but had lived in Brighton for 21 years. At the time of his application he had been living at Viaduct Terrace for six months with his wife, Dinah, and four children who were aged between 13 and 20.[159] *Dinah Mitchell was described as having kings evil, or scrofula, on*

[159] Dinah Hallett marriage to William Mitchell registered Q2 1858 Brighton 2b 300.

the census of 1871. The case was forwarded to the charity by S Cowell of North Street.[160]

24 January 1872
Statement: William Mitchell wants 3 shillings to get his furniture back. The landlord sold him out for not keeping the rent paid up.
Report: I have made enquiries respecting William Mitchell and find the house belongs to Mr Collwell, Pelham Square, and, he finding he could not get the rents of several houses, employed Mr Trangmar, Queens Road, as an agent and he put distress in [sic], the oldest son has got work today.[161] The home is in a destitute state. Mr Drury gave him a good character. I advanced the three shillings which he was very thankful for.
Further consideration, Orfeur Cavenagh. Grant of 3 shillings sanctioned, Orfeur Cavenagh

3 February 1873
Further information: applicant called at office this afternoon and stated that he was anxious to get suitable clothes for his two daughters that they might take situations. Upon enquiring I find the husband is at work three days a week for the parish and that his eldest son is earning 16s per week. The Reverend Mr Mansell, 36 London Road, recommends the case and suggests that should the committee make a grant he would undertake to see that it was properly laid out. WC [William Collingham]
Deferred, R P Hooper

7 February 1873
Upon further enquiry I find that the youngest daughter goes to nurse children in North Road for which she gets 3d a day and her board. She goes home to sleep and attends an evening school. I advised the father to let her stay where she is at present to which he is agreeable. With respect to the other girl I find she was in a situation in the London Road which she left to be an ironer but, finding that she could not stand that kind of work, she is very willing to return to service and Captain Cuthbert has seen her late mistress who will report further on the case.[162]
Clothes (boots excepted) granted.
Report to Captain Cuthbert, R P Hooper

21 February 1873
Further information: on Tuesday applicant applied to the Guardians for a pair of

[160] This was probably Samuel Cowell, grocer and tea dealer of 143 and 145 North Street.
[161] F T Colwell, builder and undertaker of 19 Pelham Square.
[162] Captain J R Cuthbert of 18 Portland Place.

boots for his daughter which were granted him and I bought some flannel, calico, print and linsey. Total cost 12s 3½d. I took the things to 91 London Road and made arrangements for the girl to go into her situation on Thursday morning

24 February 1873
Mrs Banbury called at the office and stated that the girl Mitchell had given notice to her on account of Mrs Banbury refusing to allow her to go home to sleep. WC [William Collingham]

35 ANN KIRBY, 48, WIFE OF A FLYMAN, 6 HEREFORD STREET, BRIGHTON

Ann Kirby, née Lemman, was born in Horsted Keynes but, at the time of her first application to the Mendicity Society, had been living in Brighton for 25 years. She had been living at 6 Hereford Street with her 60-year-old husband Charles, a flyman, where they occupied two rooms, since about 1870.[163] *Charles Kirby was born in Gravesend, Kent, and in July 1867 a 50-year-old fly driver of this name was charged with receiving half a bushel of stolen oats from Stephen Darvell.*[164] *Charles Kirby had been short of work for about two years and the couple found themselves five shillings in debt and paying two shillings per week rent. Their case was sent by Annie Neild of 3 College Road and Ann Kirby gave Mr Dubbin of 55 St James Street as a reference.*

25 January 1872
Statement: Ann Kirby wants a little assistance. If it was only the rent paid it would be acceptable.
Report: I have made enquiries respecting Ann Kirby and find the home in a destitute state. This woman is a cripple and has been for this last twelve months, before that she used to look after furnished houses [and] live rent free and get eight or ten shillings a week. The husband, at the same time, had a fly of his own. His habits are intemperate. Mrs Neild believes the woman to be a very deserving person for relief.
Referred to Poor Law, Orfeur Cavenagh

Letter from Mrs M Kennedy (per Frances How) of 6 Marine Terrace, Brighton, to Mr Johnson, 2 January 1873
Sir, a person named Mrs Kirby of 53 Church Street comes to me occasionally for relief which I give her from time to time as I know her to be much afflicted and I have not found her encroaching. Twice lately a man has come purporting to be from her and saying she is ill in bed and not able to come. I shall be obliged if

[163] Ann Lemman marriage to Charles Kirby registered Q1 1857 Brighton 2b 218.
[164] Brighton Gazette, 25 July 1867.

you will ascertain the truth of this statement and let me know the result as I am not able to go out. I am sir yours faithfully, Mrs M Kennedy

3 January 1873
Further information: since this case was before the committee nearly twelve months ago, the wife has obtained a hawker's licence and has been in the habit of sitting in the Dyke Road with a basket of small fancy goods. She says that Mrs Kennedy has been in the habit of assisting her for some time but being unable herself to call on Mrs Kennedy she sent her husband. WC [William Collingham]
Case to be reported to Mrs Kennedy, R P Hooper

15 June 1874
Report: Mrs Bright requests a report of this case. On enquiry I find that Mrs Kirby still continues to sit with her basket in the Dyke Road and no doubt gets a great deal given to her. Her husband, who has always been a man of lazy and intemperate habits, has lately been in ill health but is now getting better. WC [William Collingham]
To be reported to Mrs Bright, R P Hooper

4 February 1875
Captain Morris requested that this case should be brought before the committee in the hope that they will grant a little temporary assistance. Her husband died a month ago since which time she has not been able to go out with her basket but she intends to start today. Her present address is 53 Church Street. WC [William Collingham]
Grant of 5 shillings, R P Hooper

11 September 1875
Mrs Kirby applied at the office on Friday for assistance to enable her to visit a relative in Gravesend for the benefit of her health. Mrs K is in delicate health and thinks the change would do her good. The fare to Gravesend and back would cost about 13 shillings. WC [William Collingham]
John [?] Elphick; In Eligible [sic], C A Baines, Chairman

10 March 1876
Ann Kirby of 8 Vine Place, case sent by A J Larking esq
Report: Mr A J Larking of 18 Clifton Terrace recommends this case to the society as one deserving of assistance. Mrs Kirby has not been able to go out with her basket for the last four months. The Guardians allow her relief at the rate of 2s 6d a week besides which she gets a little charity.
WC [William Collingham]
Ineligible, R P Hooper

36 MATILDA SHARP, 36, WIFE OF A LABOURER, 5 ESSEX COTTAGES, BRIGHTON

Matilda Traynor and George Sharp married in 1858.[165] *At the time of their application to the Mendicity Society in January 1872 Sharp had been labouring for Mr Saxby of Upper St James Street but he had not worked for three weeks and had been out of work for seven of the last twelve months.*[166] *They lived with their five children aged between twelve and seven months' old and paid 3s 3d rent per week for the house but were £1 5s in arrears. Their case was forwarded by G D Ryder esq.*

25 January 1872
Statement: Matilda Sharp wants a little assistance till her husband gets work.
Report: I have made enquiries respecting George Sharp. The house is in a destitute state. Mr Saxby said he could not depend on him as his habits was intemperate.
Referred to Poor Law, Orfeur Cavenagh. NB result of the reference to the relieving officer to be reported at next meeting

37 JOHN RICHARDSON, 64, PAINTER, 15 DERBY PLACE, BRIGHTON

John Richardson's case was forwarded to the charity by the Reverend Aaron Augustus Morgan, vicar of St John's, Carlton Hill. Richardson was born in Birmingham but had been living in Brighton since about 1866. He occupied one room at 15 Derby Place for which he paid two shillings per week rent and had been at this address for six months. Before this he had been resident at Brighton Workhouse and he returned to the workhouse at some point between January 1872 and the time of Richardson's second application in May 1873.

25 January 1872
Statement: John Richardson wants to get 5 shillings for to get a licence. He was taken to the police office on Tuesday for not having one.
Report: I have made enquiries respecting John Richardson and find he has been getting his living by painting apartments cards and going about the town at the different lodging houses and selling them. I have known this man for this last five years. He is a sober industrious man.
Grant of five shillings, Orfeur Cavenagh
Conditional grant of 2s 6d sanctioned for the purchase of food etc in addition to aid per private individuals, Orfeur Cavenagh. NB The agent will see that the licence will be procured

165 Matilda Traynor marriage to George Sharp registered Q2 1858 Brighton 2b 312.
166 Mr Saxby was almost certainly the father of William Saxby, applicant 193.

Further information respecting this case: Mr Ryder called at the office yesterday and stated a Miss Rose Champ called on him and stated this man was in great distress. I called at his lodgings and found him in about the same state as he has been in for this last four years. The home is in a passable state. I think now he has a licence he can get a passable living.

7 May 1873
This man who has been in the workhouse all the winter came out on Tuesday. He now wants 5s to enable him to take out a new licence so that he may be able to carry on his regular occupation: painting and selling apartment cards. WC [William Collingham]
Referred to parish, G D R, Chairman

38 SARAH WELLS, 74, NEEDLEWOMAN, 10 OXFORD PLACE, BRIGHTON

Sarah Wells was born in Wandsworth but had come to Brighton in about 1855. She had been living at Oxford Place since September 1871 where she paid 1s 6d per week rent for her upstairs room. She was 4s 6d in arrears having been short of work for two months.

26 January 1872
Statement: Sarah Wells wants a little assistance for two or three weeks till she gets work.
Report: I have made enquiries respecting Sarah Wells and find she gets her living mending umbrellas and doing a little needle work. The home is in a passable state. She has applied to the parish and refused an order for the workhouse.
Grant of 3s as temporary relief. Further enquiry, Orfeur Cavenagh

39 CAROLINE TUCKER, 48, DRESSMAKER, 30 MOUNT ZION PLACE, BRIGHTON

Caroline Tucker was enumerated on the 1851 census at 105 Upper North Street with her husband, William Tucker, a 26-year-old classics and mathematics master and her one-year-old son, also named William.[167] *She was born in Brighton and appears on the 1871 census as a widow living at 7 Gloucester Terrace with her daughter and their lodger George Platt who applied to the charity for relief on 4 January 1872 (applicant 3). When Caroline Tucker applied to the Mendicity Society she was working as a dressmaker and living with her daughter, Caroline, and son, William. She paid 3s 6d per week rent for two*

[167] This couple appear to be no relation to the couple also named William and Caroline Tucker that applied to the Mendicity Society on 18 May 1872, case 178.

rooms and was up to date with payments. Her case was forwarded to the charity by Mrs Walker of Furze Hill House, Hove.

26 January 1872
Statement: Caroline Tucker would be thankful for a little assistance till work is better if it was only nine shillings to pay her bread bill. She would be very thankful.
Report: I have made enquiries respecting Caroline Tucker and find she and her daughter get their living dress making. Mrs Walker gave them a good character and says they are very industrious persons only work is very slack at the present time. She has relieved them several times. The son is travelling with a theatrical company, the home is in a comfortable state.
Ineligible, Orfeur Cavenagh. NB result of inquiry to be communicated to Mrs Walker

40 MARY SHAW, 50, FISH SELLER, 50 HEREFORD STREET, BRIGHTON

Mary Shaw was born in Ireland and had been living in Brighton for eight years by the time of her first application to the Mendicity Society in January 1872. She had two children from a previous marriage but in 1872 lived with her husband, William, and daughter, Mary. The family paid 1s 6d per week rent for their single room and were six shillings in arrears.

Mary married William Shaw in 1867[168] *but in March 1868 the couple appeared in court when Mary accused William of assault.*[169] *Mary had been living apart from William for some time when he saw her walking along Grand Parade. They exchanged words and he continued to follow her to the station and then on to the Level where he tore the bonnet from her head and assaulted her. Constable Alfred Clifford stated that he had seen the couple brawling on the ground. George White, the Chief Constable, when asked whether he knew anything of the parties, said he thought 'there was about six of one and half a dozen of the other' and that 'the defendant had caught a Tartar in his second wife'. William Shaw was considered to be the aggressor and was fined five shillings and costs or 10 days' hard labour.*

The Brighton Gazette recorded Mary Shaw's appearance at the county bench at Hove on 14 December 1868.[170] *She was charged with stealing four flannel shirts and a pair of cotton drawers from Preston Barracks. From the evidence of Esther Dockerell of 29 St Martin's Place it appeared that Shaw offered the items for sale about a month previously. Shaw stated that she was authorised to sell them on behalf of the 4th Dragoon Guards and Dockerell paid five shillings before handing them over to Detective Mann. Sergeant Baldry*

[168] Mary Jane Barnes marriage to William Shaw registered Q1 1867 Brighton 2b 283.
[169] Brighton Gazette, 12 March 1868.
[170] Brighton Gazette, 17 December 1868.

of the 4th Dragoons identified the articles as coming from his regiment. Shaw, who was described as vendor of nuts and oranges, was found guilty and sentenced to three months' hard labour.

Mary Shaw was in trouble with the police again in August 1872 when she was charged with stealing a purse containing £1 4s from Esther Simmonds.[171] *Simmonds did not attend the hearing so Shaw was discharged but she was in court again in September following an altercation with her neighbour, Theresa Burns.*[172] *The women had fallen out and recently Mary Shaw had been causing a disturbance in front of Burns' house, threatening to 'limb' her and occasionally striking her. A witness stated both women were given to quarrelling and that she did not know which was the worst of the two. Mr White, the Chief Constable, referred to Shaw as the 'worst woman in Brighton.' She was bound over in the sum of £10 with a surety for the same amount to keep the peace for three months.*

In January 1877 Mary Shaw made a complaint against John Marchant, a greengrocer of Edward Street, who was charged with assaulting 'an old Irish woman.' At the Police Court hearing Shaw stated that Marchant had tried to sell her diseased potatoes. When she discovered the misdemeanour, an altercation ensued which resulted in Shaw pelting Marchant with the vegetables in his shop. The bench took the view that the complainant was more at fault than the defendant and the case was dismissed.[173]

Shaw was in trouble again in August 1881 when she met a woman named Margaret O'Connor on Egremont Place.[174] *Shaw threw a potato at O'Connor, missing her but striking the baby she was carrying. Two hours later, also on Egremont Place, Shaw saw O'Connor again and this time assaulted her with a lemonade bottle which was broken by the force of the blow to O'Connor's head. She bled profusely and the house surgeon at the Sussex County Hospital told her that she was lucky to have survived. Shaw was sentenced to a month's hard labour.*

At the time of her last application to the charity in June 1896, Shaw had been out of Brighton Workhouse for five weeks and was living at 10 Bedford Buildings.

27 January 1872
Statement: Mary Shaw wants a little assistance for a few weeks till work gets better.
Report: I have made enquiries respecting Mary Shaw and find she does not live with her husband. She gets her living selling fish and oranges. The girl goes to the Catholic school, Bristol Road. The home is in a destitute state. This woman has applied to the parish and refused to go in the workhouse. This family are well known to the Police Court through their intemperate habits and other offences.
Dismissed as undeserving, Orfeur Cavenagh

171 Brighton Guardian, 21 August 1872.
172 Brighton Guardian, 30 September 1872.
173 Brighton Guardian, 3 January 1877.
174 Brighton Herald, 3 September 1881.

Letter written by Elizabeth Robertson of 9 Belgrave Terrace, Brighton, sent to Colonel Barlow of the Charity Organisation Society, 3 February 1884
Dear Sir, will you kindly enquire into the case of a Mrs Shaw, 17 Mount Pleasant. The woman accosts me continually, asking for assistance; she talks much to the cabmen and appears very idle and I greatly doubt if she is a deserving person. With kind regards I am sincerely yours, Elizabeth Robertson

4 February 1884
Mrs Robertson of 9 Belgrave Terrace requests a report of this case. Mrs Shaw, who has lost her husband, now resides at 17 Mount Pleasant and supports herself by selling flowers. She is said to be of somewhat weak mind. Nothing has been known against her character for several years and she appears very poor. WC [William Collingham]
Report to Mrs Robertson, A F Bond

6 June 1896
This person took her discharge from the Union five weeks ago and has since supported herself by selling matches but her old certificate has expired and she has no means to renew it. She has no friends in a position to assist her and is recommended as a quiet, decent woman. WC [William Collingham]
Ineligible, M H E Sherard, approved J W Kirby

41 MARY NASH, 73, NURSE, 9 PARK CRESCENT TERRACE, BRIGHTON

The Mendicity Society was informed of Mary Nash's plight by Cordy Burrows, the prominent councillor and former mayor of Brighton. She was born in Abingdon, Berkshire, in about 1799 and is enumerated on both the 1841 and 1851 census living in Henley on Thames with her husband James Nash, an attorney. She moved to Brighton in about 1857 and is shown on the 1861 census as widowed and employed as proprietor of 21 Clifton Terrace where she lived with her daughter Clara.

By 2 April 1871 Mary Nash was living at 27 St Mary Magdalene Street where she was recorded as being out of employment. On her application to the Mendicity Society in January 1872 she had been nursing a Mr Shaw of North Road but ill health had prevented her from continuing with that type of work. Nash lived alone paying three shillings per week rent and owing two weeks rent to her landlord. She died in Brighton in 1878.

30 January 1872
Statement: Mary Nash wants a little assistance as she would like to open a small shop.
Report: After personal investigation the committee considers that the applicant is a deserving object of charity. For many years she had charge of a gentleman's

house and upon the house being sold she for some time kept a lodging house and afterwards maintained herself by going out as a nurse. She has however lately suffered from rheumatic fever and is consequently now unfit for night nursing and has difficulty in obtaining a livelihood by taking needlework. She is still fit to take charge of an empty house.
Relieved by private liberality. Reference to her made to Poor Law and district local agency

42 HENRY GLADMAN, 32, LABOURER ON THE RAILWAY, 39 NEW ENGLAND STREET, BRIGHTON

Henry Gladman was born in Laughton in about 1840 but came to Brighton via Framfield at the end of 1871. He had found employment as a railway labourer and was earning three shillings per day as a starting wage.[175] *After working for only just over a month he suffered an eye injury and he was sent to the Mendicity Society by the matron at the eye hospital. By the time of his application he had been out of work for seven weeks and was having difficulty supporting his wife Emily and their infant daughter, Edith.*[176] *No further applications were made to the charity so it appears that Gladman managed to get back to work soon after his case was considered. However, on 8 May 1872 he was admitted to the Sussex County Hospital with a crushed toe.*[177] *He was considered cured when he was discharged on 15 May 1872.*

Gladman's career on the railways continued for the rest of his working life. By 1877 he was employed as a striker and was earning 3s 8d per day and he was still shown to be working at the railway works in 1901 when he was described on the census as a smith's hammer man.[178] *He died in 1907.*

30 January 1872
Statement: Henry Gladman wants a little assistance for a short time till his eye gets better. Mr Patching has allowed him 2s 6d a week for four weeks but cannot continue it any longer.
Report: I have made enquiries respecting Henry Gladman and find he was working for the railway company breaking up an old boiler and a piece flew and hit him in the eye. He was working for the company five years ago and was discharged when they shortened hands. At that time he belonged to the Insurance and Provident Society and in case of accident he would receive 30 shillings a week and he has not been back for the company long enough to get

175 UK Railway Employment Book RAIL414; Piece 763.
176 Emily Sharp marriage to Henry Gladman registered Q4 1866 Brighton 2b 336.
177 ESRO: HB 35/3/1872/2232.
178 UK Railway Employment Book RAIL414; Piece 764.

relief.[179] The men collected a few shillings for him at Christmas. The house is in a passable state.
Present 1 Feb 1872: J Deverell, Honourable G D Ryder, F J Rumbold. The committee considered this case as one eligible for assistance - ordered an allowance of 3s per week for a fortnight and soup tickets daily for the same time

43 SUSAN COLE, 39, WIFE OF A LABOURER, 14 VIADUCT TERRACE, BRIGHTON

James Cole, Susan Cole's husband, had been employed as a labourer by Mr Legg of Patcham but had been out work for seven weeks. They lived with their three children aged between three months and nine years old in one room, for which they paid three shillings per week rent. Susan Cole was born in Cornwall but had moved to Brighton in about 1865. The family's case was forwarded to the charity by the landowner Clifford Borrer. They were six shillings in arrears.

1 February 1872
Statement: Susan Cole would be thankful for a little assistance. She believes her husband will have work next week.
Report: I have made enquiries respecting this family and find they have a home in a destitute state. The man believes he will have work to go to next week at Mr Legg's, Patcham. The wife goes to laundry work but since her confinement she has not been able to work.
3s allowed for a week and 6d for a quart of [missing] per day and Collingham to report the case to the district clergy, JD[180]

44 CAROLINE DEWEY, 67, CHARWOMAN, 19 REGENT HILL, BRIGHTON

The Reverend John Benjamin Figgis of the Countess of Huntingdon's Church on North Street forwarded the case of Caroline Dewey to the Mendicity Society. Dewey had been working as a charwoman but, despite having been out of work for a month, had not fallen behind with her rent payments. She was born in Portsea, Hampshire, but had been in Brighton since about 1842. She was enumerated on the 1871 boarding at 3 Lime Street describing herself as a laundress. Ten years later she was enumerated at Brighton Workhouse. Her death was registered in Brighton in April 1882.

179 No record could be found of an organisation by this exact title but it may be a referernce to the Brighton and Sussex Mutual Provident Society for Life Insurance situated at 11 Prince Albert Street. By 1872 the society had shortened its name to the Brighton and Sussex Mutual Provident Society.

180 Signature probably that of John Deverell whose name appears in the list of Charity Organisation Society council members in the annual report of 1877.

1 February 1872
Statement: Caroline Dewey wants a little assistance till she gets work.
Report: I made enquiries regarding this woman and find she lives with a niece who is an ironer. This woman does a little needle work and occasionally gets a day's work. She has been to the parish and refused to go in the workhouse. The home is in a passable state.
Collingham to apply to Mr Morris or relieving officer and meanwhile if no parochial assistance obtained to allow her 3s for a week JD

45 ELIZABETH PEABODY OR ELIZABETH JONES, 57, HAWKER, 16 FREEHOLD TERRACE, PRESTON

What we know about Elizabeth Peabody and the man she referred to as her husband, Richard Peabody, is limited as they do not obviously appear on census returns of the period. From the information given on the Mendicity Society's form we know that they seem to have led a fairly peripatetic existence. We also know that the woman who applied to the charity in February 1872 was almost certainly called Elizabeth Jones, the woman referred to in Richard Peabody's application of December 1878.

Elizabeth Jones was born in Yarmouth, Hampshire, but had been living with Richard Peabody, who was working in Seaford as a labourer for a Mr Nye until being laid off in January 1872. The couple had been living in Brighton for only two days before her case was forwarded by Mrs Stevens of 50 Montpelier Road.

Two months before Richard Peabody's application in December 1878 the couple had both appeared at Lewes police court for being drunk and disorderly. Peabody was sentenced to 14 days' hard labour for using foul language and continuing to cause a disturbance after being remonstrated with by tradesmen on Cliffe High Street. Elizabeth Jones, who was reported as living with Peabody, was also charged with being drunk and fined nine shillings.[181]

1 February 1872
Statement: Elizabeth Peabody wants a little assistance till her husband gets work.
Report: I made enquiries respecting Elizabeth Peabody and find she gets her living hawking lace. Her husband is a labourer and has got work when he likes to go to it. They are both of very intemperate habits. The home is in a passable state. I cautioned this woman if she was found begging again she would be brought before the magistrates.
Undeserving, JD

[181] Sussex Advertiser, 8 October 1878.

30 December 1878
This man, while drunk, applied at the office on Saturday afternoon for assistance to tide him over till the Lewes Discharged Prisoners Aid Society do something for him.[182] According to his statement, when returning from harvesting this year he got too much drink at Lewes and was sentenced to 14 days' imprisonment and on the third day a warder pushed him down and broke his right leg. He now walks on crutches and gets his living by begging. He came from Lewes seven weeks ago and is lodging at 37 Derby Place.[183] He is a single man but lives with a woman named Jones who made an application in February 1872 when it was dismissed as undeserving. WC [William Collingham]
Undeserving, R P Hooper

17 November 1879
Peabody applied at the office on Saturday for some assistance to tide him over till he can obtain light employment. The Discharged Prisoners Aid Society granted him 1s a day for 12 months. Applicant is now able to take a situation either as night watchman or to do any light work. He still lives with the woman Jones. The home is in a destitute state. WC [William Collingham]
Undeserving, reference to parish, R P Hooper

46 SARAH FOSTER, 67, WIFE OF A BRICKLAYER, 36 PARADISE STREET, BRIGHTON

Sarah Thomas was born in Porstlade in about 1805 and married Francis Foster of Henfield at St Nicholas church, Brighton, on 2 November 1829.[184] Francis Foster was admitted to the Sussex County Hospital on 30 November 1836 following an accident that resulted in him fracturing a patella.[185] He was discharged after eight days. The couple were enumerated at 52 Chesterfield Street on the census returns of both 1851 and 1861 but moved to 36 Paradise Street two months before their application to the Mendicity Society. They paid four shillings per week rent for the whole house but were nine shillings in arrears. They remained at that address until at least 3 April 1881 when they were enumerated for a final time, Sarah dying in the December quarter of 1888 and Francis in the December quarter of 1882.

[182] By 1872 there were 34 small Discharged Prisoners' Aid Societies in Britain. They provided food, shelter, clothing and advice on finding work to people recently discharged from prison. This work is carried out by the National Association for the Care and Rehabilitation of Offenders (NACRO), Colonel G. D. Turner, 'Aid For Prisoners on Discharge', *The Police Journal: Theory, Practice and Principles, 3:1 (1930).*

[183] 37 Derby Place had also been home to George Meads, applicant 11, in 1872.

[184] ESRO: PAR 255/1/3/6.

[185] ESRO: HB 35/1/1836-832

2 February 1872
Statement: Sarah Foster wants a little assistance for her daughter who is sick. She thinks if she could get a little nourishment for her she would soon get better.
Report: I have made enquiries respecting Sarah Foster and find her house in a destitute state. Miss Mahon gave her a good character. Her daughter is not able to work. There are two grown up sons at home, one has work. Instead of the husband having only six shillings a week he has been earning at an average [of] over sixteen shillings a week and in the summer his wages is twenty four shillings a week.
Ineligible, JD

47 THOMAS MARTIN, 30, LABOURER, 39 QUEBEC STREET, BRIGHTON

The Reverend Neil Crispin, priest of St Joseph's Catholic church on Elm Grove, forwarded Thomas Martin's case to the Mendicity Society. Census returns for 1851, 1861 and 1871 show Martin's father, also Thomas Martin, as a library porter: the report on his son made in February 1872 reveals that Thomas Martin senior was an employee of Thomas Page, stationer, bookseller and librarian of 173 North Street. Thomas Martin junior also worked for the firm in 1861 but by 1871 had become a porter at Brighton station.

Thomas Martin junior was born in Brighton and had been living on Quebec Street for four years. He stated that he was unmarried and had been working for Mrs Huggett of 41 Holland Street, Brighton, but had been out of work for four months due to sickness. However, he was enumerated on the 1871 census living at 41 Holland Street with his wife, Jane Martin, and his sixteen-year-old stepson David Huggett.[186] *He named Mr Rymer of Bristol Road as a reference.*[187]

2 February 1872
Statement: Thomas Martin wants a little assistance till he gets work.
Report: I have made enquiries respecting Thomas Martin and find he is living with his father who works for Mr Page, North Street. His wages is a pound a week. His wife does not enjoy good health. A younger brother is working at the cemetery. The home is in a destitute state. Mr Rymer seems to have forgotten this man. He says if he had a pair of boots to wear he believes he could soon get work.
Allowed 3s for an old pair of shoes to enable him to get work, JD

[186] Jane Ann Harris marriage to Thomas James Martin registered Q4 1861 Brighton 2b 382.
[187] The Reverend Canon Rymer, Catholic Chapel House, Bristol Road.

48 ELIZABETH WEST, 38, WIFE OF A SHOEMAKER, 10 SPA STREET, BRIGHTON

Elizabeth West (née Breach) and her husband Thomas West were in contact with the Mendicity Society and the charity's subsequent incarnations over the course of 34 years. Over this period the couple approached the charity seven times: the first two applications were made by Elizabeth but all subsequent contact was with her husband. Thomas West, shoemaker, was born in Arundel in about 1830 and Elizabeth Breach in Arlington in about 1832. Elizabeth moved to Brighton in about 1849 and the couple were married on 25 August 1850 at St Nicholas' church, Brighton.[188] *The 1861 census enumerates the West family at 8 Spa Street, Brighton, where they lived with their three children, niece, Mary Breach, and another family member, George Breach. The family living at 9 Spa Street was almost certainly that of Thomas West's brother, Henry West, who was also born in Arundel.*

By 1871 Thomas and Elizabeth West had moved to 10 Spa Street but were still next door to Henry West and his family. At the time of the West's first approach to the Mendicity Society in February 1872 they had six children aged between 21 and six months. They were paying 3s 6d rent per week for the entire house but were £2 in arrears.

Thomas West applied to the Brighton and Jubilee Accident Fund in October 1880 and June 1892 following work-related accidents but appears to have made a full recovery on both occasions.[189] *West rented a workshop at 55 Sloane Street between about 1885 and 1892. The family were living at 20 Carlton Hill by August 1885, had moved to 39 Hereford Street by 1892 and by the time of the application in May 1906, Thomas West, now a widower, had moved to 9 Pilgrims Cottages, Leicester Street.*[190] *William Collingham, the charity agent who was still working in 1906, recorded which of West's children were still living and how many children they each had. Matilda Price, 46, a widow, had four children; Frederick had seven; Sarah Chapman had seven; Henry, four, and Alice Sargent, also four. Caroline, Thomas, William and Louisa had all pre-deceased him.*

West was enumerated on the 1911 census living at 3 Circus Court with his daughter Sarah Chapman and her family and was described as 'helpless'. He died in July 1911 aged about 81.

3 February 1872

Statement: Elizabeth West wants a little assistance as the money her husband gets is not enough to keep so large a family.

Report: I made enquiries respecting this family and find the husband has plenty of work but says he wants about a pound's worth of leather to give him a start.

[188] ESRO: PAR 255/1/3/22.

[189] The form filled out by the hospital orderly states 18 July 1892 but the charity's notes and other correspondence regarding the matter suggest the date was, in reality, 18 June 1892. Brighton and Jubilee Accident Fund was also known as The Jubilee and Accident Fund.

[190] Elizabeth West died in April 1902.

The wife goes out to work. She is of intemperate habits, they are well known to the parish, the home is in a passable state.
Dismissed, ineligible
R P Hooper

Ticket issued by the Sussex County Hospital to the Honorary Secretary of the Brighton and Jubilee Accident Fund, 14 October 1880
I hereby certify that Thomas West of 59 John Street, Brighton, has sustained an injury by accident in suffering from abscess of right hand and is incapable of following his usual occupation. Edward W Witten, surgeon

15 October 1880
West, now of 59 John Street, was sent by Mr Jones, town missionary, and applied at the office on Thursday for relief from the Jubilee and Accident Fund.[191] Applicant, who has been ill [for] three weeks suffering from a poisoned finger was formerly a drinking man but during the last three years has been a total abstainer. His wife is a low drunken woman. They have three children dependent on them. Their home is in a destitute condition. WC [William Collingham]
Grant of 5s per week for two weeks, R P Hooper

16 May 1883
Mrs West applied at the office on Wednesday for an out-patient's letter to the Sussex County Hospital for her daughter Alice age 10 who is poorly [and] said to be suffering from consumption. WC [William Collingham]
Granted, R P Hooper, chairman

14 August 1885
Mrs West applied at the office on Thursday for an out-patient's letter to the Sussex County Hospital. The husband now has a small workshop in Sloane Street and appears to have a decent connection. According to applicant's statement she has been poorly for several weeks but judging by appearances this does not seem to be the case. WC [William Collingham]
Ineligible, R P Hooper

Letter sent by Miss Adams of 19 St George's Terrace, Brighton, 23 October [1889]
Miss Adams begs to recommend as an object worthy of charity Thomas West, cobbler, at work in 55a Sloane Street – Miss Adams has known Mr West a long

[191] John James Jones, missionary, was listed in *Pike's Directory of Brighton, 1888*, living at 67 Cobden Road, Brighton.

time he has a large family and some orphan grandchildren to support and some assistance to provide leather for repairing would be a great help to him.

25 October 1887
West was sent by Adams, 19 St George's Terrace and applied at the office on Monday for 10s worth of material for boot repairing. He still rents the workshop in Sloane Street. The parish give him 5s worth of work a week and for several years he has struggled hard for his family but his wife is a great trouble to him and some of the grown up children are also a heavy drag on him consequently he is always in distress. WC [William Collingham]
Ineligible, A F Bond

Letter sent by Miss Adams of 19 St George's Terrace, Brighton, 2 December [1889]
Miss Adams would be glad to recommend John West, cobbler, who is working in Sloane Street – number 55. A little help in the way of leather to mend a large stack of old boots and shoes would seem very acceptable.

2 December 1889
West was sent by Miss Adams, 19 St George's Terrace, and applied at the office on Monday for 10s worth of materials for boot repairing. His circumstances are the same as they were two years ago and the previous reports will show that the family are always in a chronic state of destitution.
WC [William Collingham] Ineligible, R P Hooper

27 December 1889
West applied at the office on Friday for £1 to enable him to purchase materials for boot repairing. His circumstances are the same as they were a month ago and I would suggest that he be referred to the Benevolent Loan Fund.
WC [William Collingham]

Letter sent by W D Savage JP of Ellerslie, 23 Freshfield Road, Brighton, 17 June 1892[192]
Sir, Thomas West, shoemaker, of 54½ Sloane Street having strained his arm, so as to be unable to work, stands much in need of temporary aid – he is an industrious hard working man and I hope that he may get something from the Jubilee Fund as a temporary aid. I am sir yours, W D Savage

Ticket issued by the Sussex County Hospital to the Honorary Secretary of the Brighton and Jubilee Accident Fund, 18 July [June] 1892
I hereby certify that Thomas West of 39 Hereford Street, Brighton, has sustained

[192] William Dawson Savage, JP and chemist.

an injury by accident in a sprain of the shoulder which has partially disabled him from his usual occupation. O R Prankerd.[193]

17 June 1892
West was sent by W D Savage esq JP and applied at the office on Friday for relief from the Jubilee Accident Fund. He continues to repair boots but a fortnight ago he strained his right arm for which he is attended by Dr Prankerd and is partially unable to follow his usual occupation. His wife is still addicted to drink but applicant continues to bear a good character and is considered quite deserving of temporary relief. WC [William Collingham]
2s 6d per week for two weeks, R P Hooper

1 July 1892
West applied at the office on Friday for relief for one more week. His arm is much better and he is expecting to be in full employ again in the course of a few days.
2s 6d, R P Hooper

16 May 1906
Statement: In consequence of my age I need a few comforts that I cannot obtain and should be glad if the Howard Charity can assist me.
Report: The applicant's late wife was a low, drunken woman. Some of the children have been troublesome especially the son Frederick and at one time the father was inclined to drink but since 1877 he has been a total abstainer. For many years the Guardians gave him 5s a month of work a week from the union besides the 3s outdoor relief allowed him and then he managed very well but since the end of last summer he has not been able to work on account of his age. His rent is as stated and the committee allow him 2s per week. He receives the 10s from the poor box at Christmas besides which he is generally given Bates Charity and the references recommend him as a respectable, worthy old man.[194]
WC [William Collingham]

Letter written to the Honourable Secretary of the Howard Charity, 18 May 1906
Re: West, Thomas, 84, widower
Dear Sir, we have made inquiries concerning above and find that at one time he was addicted to drink but since 1877 he has been a total abstainer. His late wife was a drunkard and some of the children have been troublesome. For many years the Guardians gave 5s worth of work a week from the union besides 3s

[193] Orlando Reeves Prankerd, surgeon.

[194] Bates Charity was administered by Brighton Corpration. It distributed bread, meat and coal to the poorest residents, ESRO CHC/9/2/26).

outdoor relief but since the end of last summer he has been unable to work on account of his age. His rent is 3s a week and the committee allow him 2s per week; also he receives 10s from the poor box at Christmas and is generally given Bates Charity. His references describe him as a worthy and respectable old man but we do not consider him in need of further relief. Yours faithfully, A Woodhead, Hon Sec
I note this 3s allowed by the committee weekly seems to have been concealed from you

49 EMMA MEYER, 34, DRESSMAKER, EGREMONT STREET, BRIGHTON

Although Emma Meyer was born in Brighton she had only returned from Germany the week before her application to the Mendicity Society. No record of her could be found on census returns, suggesting that her name was recorded incorrectly by William Collingham.

Statement: if I had clothes I could obtain work
Report: Mr Deverell gave me five shillings which was laid out on food, lodgings and clothes. Mrs Hayes gave her a shawl all of which she was very thankful for and says there is no doubt she will soon get work having clothes fit to go and ask for it.
Relieved from private sources, R P Hooper

50 ELIZABETH TULLET, 62, WIFE OF A SAWYER, 24 RICHMOND BUILDINGS, BRIGHTON

Elizabeth Tullet (née Holloway) was born in Chatham, Kent, but stated on her application to the Mendicity Society that she had been living in Brighton for 57 years. She married William Tullet, a sawyer, at St Nicholas, Brighton, on 13 June 1830. The couple and their sons James and Edward had been living at 24 Richmond Buildings for three years and prior to that had lived at 5 Richmond Buildings. Their case was forwarded to the charity by Mr Bollen of Western Road and they supplied the name of Mr Harris of Richmond Place as a reference. William Tullet had been out of work for three years following an accident. They paid weekly rent of 1s 6d for their single upstairs room and were nine shillings in arrears.

The younger son, Edward, who was born in about 1835, was charged with stealing two ewes from Manor House Farm, Brighton in July 1866. The hearing at Brighton magistrates' court stated that on 12 April Frederick Francis Hallett's sheep were safe in a fold at the back of the hospital but by the following morning two ewes were missing. Mr Alce, Hallett's shepherd, observed blood and entrails in the fold and in a ditch 300 yards away he found the carcasses of two sheep which, like the rest of the flock, were marked with an E. On the evening of the 12th Tullet and his friend Thomas Stevens asked a butcher named Pledge of Carlton Street whether he wished to buy two sheep.[195] *Pledge declined so Stevens and Tullet approached a jobbing butcher named Funnell of 35 William Street. Tullet mentioned that the sheep were 'coming on the cross,' by which he meant they were stolen, and consequently Funnell reported them to the police as he had previously been charged with receiving stolen goods and did not wish the police to think he was in the habit of doing so. Both men were found guilty of killing with intention of stealing the carcase: Stevens was sentenced to 18 months' hard labour, Tullet to 12 months' hard labour.*[196]

3 February 1872
Statement: Elizabeth Tullet would be thankful for a little assistance.
Report: I have made enquiries respecting this family and find the man goes selling sawdust the woman is too old for work. They have two grown up sons but do not live at home. One of them is well known to the police having been convicted for sheep stealing. Mr Harris has relieved them several times. They have an order for the workhouse. The home is in a destitute state.
Referred to Poor Law, R P Hooper

51 HARRIETT WHITFIELD, 38, WIFE OF A PLASTERER, 8 VIADUCT TERRACE, BRIGHTON

William Collingham, the Mendicity Society's agent, recorded Harriett and James Whitfield's surname as Witfell and their address as 17 Viaduct Terrace. However, they were both enumerated on the 1871 census at 8 Viaduct Terrace along with their seven-year-old daughter Mary Ann as Whitfield. Their case was sent to the charity by Sarah Bright of 19 Goldsmid Road, Hove, and she provided Mrs Mitchell of Carlton Row as a reference.[197] *James Whitfield had been employed by Mr Martin of Albion Street but had been out of work for five weeks. The couple paid 3s 6d per week for their two rooms and were 6 shillings in arrears.*

5 February 1872
Statement: Harriett Witfell wants a little assistance till her husband gets work.
Report: I have made enquiries respecting this family and find the man has been out of work [for] five weeks. The wife goes to laundry work, the oldest boy has no use of his right hand. The children attend York Road school. I referred the man to the parish authorities for work. The home is in a passable state.
Referred to parish authorities who are offering work at 2s 6d per diem, R P Hooper

[195] Probably George Pledge, of 19 Carlton Hill, described as a greengrocer in *Page's Directory of 1874*.
[196] Brighton Gazette, 19 July 1866.
[197] Sarah Bright was married to Edward Bright, goldsmith.

52 ELIZA MAYNARD, 23, IRONER, 32 SUN STREET, BRIGHTON

Eliza Maynard had been working for Mrs Willard of Albion Hill and had been earning four shillings per week in that employment, but she was paying two shillings per week rent and was five shillings in arrears.[198] *She rented a single room, which she shared with her three-year-old son, George, and one-year-old daughter, Emma. Maynard was born in Lincolnshire and came to Brighton via Norwood in the summer of 1871. The case was forwarded to the charity by Thomas Allen of 19 St Aubyns, Hove.*

5 February 1872
Statement: Eliza Maynard would be thankful for a little assistance as work is so short at the present time.
Report: I made enquiries respecting Eliza Maynard and find she is a widow with two children. She gets her living at laundry work. The home is in a destitute state. Mrs Willard gave her a good character.
Temporary relief given pending further enquiries, R P Hooper

Further information respecting Eliza Maynard: I have seen Mr Meeres, 6 St George's Place, the clergyman of that district, and he will attend the case.
Referred to clergyman of district, R P Hooper

53 FANNY BIRD, 9, 63 HEREFORD STREET, BRIGHTON

Fanny Bird's mother, Mary Bird, was born in Brighton in 1835. Mary Bird was a dressmaker and had been earning two shillings per week but found herself six shillings in arrears on the weekly rent payments of 1s 6d. At the time of her application to the charity she had been living with her daughter in a basement flat for five weeks. Prior to that they lived at 26 Upper Bedford Street.

Mary Bird stated that she was a widow on both the Mendicity Society form and the 1871 census, when she was living at 5 Sloane Street with her daughter. However, no record of her marriage could be found and a woman of corresponding age by the name of Mary Ann Bird was enumerated on the census returns of 1841 and 1861 at 116 Edward Street living with her father, Charles Bird, a grocer.[199]
By 1881 Mary Bird was resident at Brighton Workhouse but Fanny Eliza Bird, who was 19 in 1881, was working as a servant for a photographer of 15 Kings Road named Bernard Le Grave. The death of a woman named Mary Bird was recorded in January 1890.

5 February 1872
Statement: Fanny Bird wants a little assistance as her mother is so short of work.

[198] Mrs Willard was probably the wife of George Willard, a pork butcher of 139 Albion Hill.
[199] Death of Charles Bird registered Q1 1863 Brighton 2b 145.

Report: I have made inquiries respecting this woman and find she is [a] cripple. She does a little needle work. The home is in a most destitute state. Mr Ellis has relieved her several times. She has applied to the parish and refused to go in the workhouse.
Relieved with 2s 6d to be expended by the charity agent who is to report further on the case, R P Hooper

Further information respecting Mary Bird: I went to Mr Snowden Smith's and find he is out of town. I then went to his curate and he promised to attend to it at once.
Referred to clergyman of district, R P Hooper

54 THOMAS JEFFERY, 33, CABINET MAKER, 6 LITTLE ST JAMES STREET, BRIGHTON

Thomas Jeffery, his wife Eliza and their seven children had been living at 6 Little St James Street for three years at the time of his application to the Mendicity Society; previously they had been resident at 34 North Gardens. They paid weekly rent of 3s 6d for the house but were 30 shillings in arrears as he had been short of work for five weeks. Jeffery's employer, a Mr Fieldus of Queens Road gave him a good reference.[200] *His case was sent to the charity by a Mr Young of 36 Sussex Square who, on the same day, forwarded the case of Henry Roberts, applicant 55.*

Thomas Jeffery was born in Mayfield in about 1839 but had been living in Brighton for 28 years. He was enumerated on the 1851 census at 1 Mulberry Square, North Street, where he lived with his uncle, Robert Jeffery, also a cabinet maker.[201] *Jeffery married Eliza Goldsmith of Laughton at St Nicholas, Brighton, on 2 March 1862.*[202]

The couple, their five sons and one daughter, were enumerated on the 1881 census still living at 6 Little St James Street. By 1901 Thomas and Eliza Jeffery were living at 32 Park Place. By this time Jeffery was 63 years of age and was described as 'unable to follow occupation'.

7 February 1872
Statement: Thomas Jeffery wants a little assistance till he gets work.
Report: I have made enquiries respecting Thomas Jeffery and find his wages would be about a pound a week in the summer. At this time of the year he works for shops and they do not pay but a very low price. Mr Fieldus gave him a good character. He received 12 shillings last night for work done. The wife

[200] John Fieldus and Son, furniture dealer, 131-132 Queens Road, Brighton.
[201] Mulberry Square is listed in *Taylor's Directory, 1854* as being small houses situated at 146 North Street.
[202] ESRO: PAR 255/1/3/35.

does not earn anything on account of so large a family. The home is in a passable state.
Referred to poor law for report, R P Hooper. Answer returned, unknown to parish authorities. Case referred to parish authorities, R P Hooper

55 HENRY ROBERTS, 29, FRENCH POLISHER, 1 UPPER BEDFORD STREET, BRIGHTON

Henry Roberts was born in Brighton and was enumerated on the 1861 census working as a whitesmith at 68 Hereford Street, where he lived with his parents. His father, also Henry Roberts, was born in South America. Henry Roberts the younger married Amelia Tugwell at St Nicholas church on 12 April 1862. The couple had been living at 1 Upper Bedford Street since about 1869.

This case was forwarded to the Mendicity Society by Mr Young of 36 Sussex Square who, on the same day, forwarded the case of applicant 54, Thomas Jeffery. Henry Roberts had been working for a Mr Brown of Jew Street but, due to shortage of work, had only been earning five shillings per week for the previous month. Amelia Roberts worked as a dressmaker but her income during this period, if any, is not recorded. The family paid 3s 9d for the whole house but had arrears of 25 shillings.

Amelia Roberts died in the March quarter of 1882 aged 39.

7 February 1872
Statement: Henry Roberts wants a little assistance till he gets work.
Report: I have made enquiries respecting Henry Roberts and find he was sick for four weeks but now is able to work and in the summer his wages would be about 30 shillings a week and then he is often out drinking about till 12 o'clock at night. The wife does a little dressmaking. The home is in a passable state.
Ineligible, R P Hooper

56 CHRISTIAN REMM, 29, CABINET MAKER, NO ADDRESS

Christian Remm was born in Prussia in about 1843. He had travelled from Manchester and arrived in Brighton on the day of his application. Previously he had been working for a Mr Bailey of Ankerds Lane, Manchester. He had been out of work for six weeks and gave the reason for leaving his last job as 'could not agree' with his former employer. Remm does not obviously appear on any census returns but a man by this name, apparently born in about 1837, travelled from London to Sidney arriving in Australia on 13 November 1882.[203]

[203] New South Wales, Australia unassisted immigrant passenger lists, 1826-1922.

7 February 1872
Statement: Christian Remm wants his fare to London. He is not able to walk. He has been sick two days. The reason he says he left his work at Manchester was because they were Jewish and could not agree. Since he left Manchester he has been to Scotland in search of work.
Report: this man says if [he] could get to London he could get his passage home by the Prussian ambassador. After I had questioned this man and told him has case would go before the committee tomorrow he said I need not trouble about that – he would try and get to London.
Withdrawn by applicant, R P Hooper

57 MARY PLUMLEY, 78, NO OCCUPATION, 5 INVERNESS ROAD, BRIGHTON

Mary Plumley was born in Pevensey on 9 July 1793 and baptised at the parish church on 9 April 1794.[204] *She was enumerated at Pevensey on the census of 1851 living with her brother Thomas Plumley and daughter, whose name was listed as Iza Plumley but in most documentation is given as Catherine or Catherine Iza Plumley. Plumley stated on the application form that she had been resident in Brighton for 20 years and by 1861 she was living at 1 Back of Lewes Road, now Park Crescent Place, with Catherine. On the census returns of 1851 and 1861 Plumley described herself as unmarried but she changed her condition to widow on the 1871 census and on the Mendicity Society's application form.*

The case of Mary Plumley was forwarded to the charity by the Reverend Thomas Cook, vicar of St Peter's, Brighton. The family paid rent of 5s 6d per week and were one week in arrears. She is enumerated at this address on the 1871 census with her daughter Catherine Iza Ford, son-in-law Joseph Ford, and their two children. Catherine Ford made a separate application to the charity two days later.[205]

8 February 1872
Statement: Mary Plumley want assistance for herself and her son-in-law and wife and two children to get to Bath where they believe they could live much cheaper than they can here.
Report: from enquiries made I find the son-in-law works for the town authorities and his wages is 15 shillings a week.
Dismissed, ineligible, undeserving, R P Hooper

204 ESRO: PAR 443/1/1/2.
205 See application 62.

58 ALICE NASH, 9, 3 ST JAMES GARDENS, BRIGHTON

Alice Nash was the youngest child of Louisa or Emma Louisa Nash, a 38-year-old widow who was born in Plymouth in about 1834. Nothing is known of Louisa Nash's first husband but she married for a second time at St Luke's, Brighton, on 18 April 1892 to George Harris, a pedlar of 28 Southampton Street.[206] *The entry in the marriage register gives her father's name as William James Patey and the baptism of a Emma Louisa Russell Patey was recorded at the New Tabernacle or the Norley Chapel, Plymouth, on 8 May 1835.*[207]

Alice Nash stated on the application form that she, her mother and three older brothers had been living in Brighton for seven years and had been at their present address for two months; their previous address had been 20 Apollo Terrace. The family paid 2s 6d per week rent for their two upstairs rooms and were up to date with the payments. The family's case had been forwarded to the Mendicity Society by Marriage Wallis, the Quaker businessman.

Between Nash's first and second application to the charity she was charged with stealing flannel from Catherine Skuse, who kept a second-hand shop in the Lanes. The Brighton Guardian reported that Nash visited the shop to sell an old shirt but left taking with her a piece of blue flannel that Skuse had been working on. It was proved that Nash sold this material for 6d to Mrs Amelia Jones whose husband kept a shop in Edward Street. Nash told Mrs Jones that she had been given the flannel by a dressmaker for whom she had been working but when apprehended by PC Roser said that she found the flannel dragging at the bottom of her dress when she left Skuse's shop and, being in want of money, sold it. She was found guilty and sentenced to six weeks' hard labour.[208]

Emma Nash made several applications for relief: by 26 September 1872 the family were staying at the Royal Standard boarding house on Edward Street and by 12 February 1892 she gave her address as 28 Southampton Street – the address of George Harris whom she married the following month.

8 February 1872
Report: Alice Nash wants a little assistance till her brothers get their wages tomorrow.
Statement: I have made enquiries respecting this family and find there are four children. One is out of employ, the other two sons work at the telegraph office. Their wages is 12 shillings a week. Mr Lewis, St James' Street, has relieved them several times. The woman strongly denies having sent her child to anyone besides Marriage Wallis esq. Mr Gravely spoke to me this morning and said the child came to his shop yesterday with the same excuse. The home is in a destitute state.

206 ESRO: PAR 268/1/3/1.
207 Ancestry.com England, select births and christenings 1538-1975.
208 Brighton Guardian, 17 July 1872.

Relieved with a quarter of bread, R P Hooper. This case has been investigated by the agent and it appears that it has been frequently relieved by various persons and the case generally is unfavourably reported on, R P Hooper

26 September 1872
I have made enquiries respecting this person and find she took a begging letter to Mrs Cohen a fortnight ago and the letter was mislaid and then applicant called again on Wednesday but Mrs Cohen, not liking to relieve without knowing something about her, she sent the letter for investigation but when [I] informed Miss Cohen of Mrs Nash's character she said she could not think of doing anything for her and she wished me to tell her never to come near the house again, but if anything could be done for the son who is ill she would be very pleased to assist in the matters. Upon enquiry I find Mrs Nash came out of Lewes prison on Thursday 5th September where she had been sent for six weeks for stealing a piece of flannel and as soon as she came out she began to sell the clothes off her son's bed to get drink with. I am informed that ladies and gentlemen are in the habit of relieving her with clothes and food and no sooner than she gets them she sells them for drink. The eldest son works for a laundress, his wages are 10s per week; Charles, who is sick, the telegraph company allows 5s per week; Thomas, his wages are 5s per week: total £1. In my opinion it would be a good thing for the family if the sons could be put into some comfortable lodgings and the girl into some training school then let the mother to be her chance. The home is in a destitute state. WC [William Collingham]
Miss Cohen to receive a copy of this report. The daughter was further inquired about and the police informed as to Mrs Nash. GDR [George Dudley Ryder]

12 February 1892
Mrs Nash applied at the office on Thursday in the name of Harris for 7s for her husband to trade with as a fish hawker. In October 1872, the committee took up the case of the daughter Alice and sent her to the Girls' Industrial Home in Egremont Place.[209] Since then applicant has cohabited with a man named Harris who is recovering from an attack of influenza. They are both addicted to drink and her sons have recently been trying to get her into a home for inebriates but without success.
WC [William Collingham]
Undeserving, R P Hooper

[209] The Industrial Home for Girls, Egremont Place, was established in 1854. It could accommodate 30 poor or orphaned girls between the ages of seven and 14. They were given training in needlework, cooking, housework and laundry work in readiness for a future in domestic service, Industrial Home for Girls, Brighton, Sussex (childrenshomes.org.uk).

28 March 1893
This couple were married at St Luke's church free last Easter Monday and for further particulars see case number 7725. WC [William Collingham]

59 THOMAS TURNER, 65, CARPENTER, 39 OVER STREET, BRIGHTON

Thomas Smidley Turner, his wife Martha and their extended family including children, grandchildren and Martha's sister Eliza Jackson were enumerated on the 1851 census at 2 Elm Tree Cottages, North Street, Brighton. He was born in Deptford and his profession was given as journeyman carpenter. He and Martha (née Jackson), a dressmaker, were married at St Mary, Islington, on 23 May 1828. The couple's eldest children were born in Newington and Brixton but their third child, John, was born in Brighton 12 years previously suggesting that the family arrived in Brighton at some point before 1839.

By 1861 the Turners and their daughter's family, the Betteridges, had moved to 39 Over Street, Brighton, and they were living at this address when they applied to the Mendicity Society for relief. The application form does not record how much rent they paid, how much Thomas Turner earned or if they were in debt, but does state that their case was forwarded to the charity by a Mrs A M Gardiner of 4 Brunswick Square.

The census of 1881 shows most of the family including Martha, who is recorded as an upholsterer and a married woman, still living at 39 Over Street. A carpenter named Thomas Turner, aged 78, was enumerated at the workhouse on the 1881 census. This man's age is not consistent with Turner's, but the other details suggest it is the same man. His death was recorded in the December quarter of 1882.

8 February 1872
Report: I made enquiries respecting this family and find the man is a carpenter and the money he gets he spends on drink. The wife and her daughter are upholsterers and also the wife's sister. The wife has been sick [for] five weeks. The home is in a passable state.
Collingham is desired to inform Mrs Gardener of the circumstances of the case and report at next committee meeting, R P Hooper. Further information respecting this case: I saw Mrs Gardener and informed her [of] the result of the case and she had found out that they were not a deserving party.
Dismissed, undeserving, Orfeur Cavanagh

60 MARY KEYMER, ALIAS MARY MITCHELL, 25, HAWKER, 19 HEREFORD STREET, BRIGHTON

Mary Mitchell, or Keymer, was born in Portslade in about 1847 but stated that she had been living in Brighton for three years when her case was forwarded to the charity by Mrs Jason Smith. Mary and her husband William, who was born in Crawley in about 1843, were enumerated on the 1871 census at 19 Hereford Street where they lived with their three children Harriett, William and Alice.[210] *William was born in Newhaven in 1869 but both his sisters were born in Brighton. The report of 9 February 1872 states that William Mitchell was recently charged with stealing fowls at Ovingdean but no record of this could be found in local press.*

William Mitchell was a labourer who had been working for a Mr Baker of St George's Road. He had been short of work for three weeks but was still earning three shillings per week, which was one shilling short of their weekly rent. It is not stated why Mary Mitchell used the name of Keymer but it was almost certainly an attempt to divert attention from her husband's forthcoming court appearance.

The family were enumerated at 7 Reculver Road, Deptford, on the 1881 census where William was still employed as a labourer. The youngest children were born in Brighton in about 1874 and Bermondsey in about 1877.

9 February 1872
Statement: Mary Keymer wants a little assistance till her husband gets work.
Report: I have made enquiries respecting this woman's statement and find it's false. Instead of the name being Keymer it's Mitchell and instead of her husband being out of work he is at work for Mr Marshall at the drainage works. He is out on bail for fowl stealing at Ovingdean and committed to take his trial at the assizes. The house is in a passable state.
Dismissed, undeserving, R P Hooper. Woman subsequently appeared, admitted her falsehood and begged pardon – cautioned and disciplined, R P Hooper

61 KATE GREEN, 25, WIFE OF A LABOURER, 28 HEREFORD STREET, BRIGHTON

According to information supplied on their application form, the Green family had been living in Brighton for five years and had previously lived at 11 Bedford Buildings. Kate, or Kitty, Green (née Simmons) was born in Rodmell in about 1847 and her husband Reuben was born in Seaford at some point between 1832 and 1841 (he gave various ages on different census returns and on the marriage register): the couple were married in Seaford on 25 August 1866.[211] *A 29-year-old labourer named Reuben Green appeared before magistrates in Seaford in October 1866, charged with absenting himself from the service of his master, Thomas Woodhams. The magistrate reluctantly sentenced him to one month's imprisonment: the suggestion being that the law was an unpopular one.*[212] *It is also worth noting that a 25-year-old man from Seaford by the name of Reuben Green*

[210] Mary Ann Billing marriage to William Mitchell registered Q4 1867 Brighton 2b 366.
[211] ESRO: PAR 480/1/3/2.
[212] Sussex Advertiser, 10 October 1866.

crewed on a vessel called the Marseilles of Newhaven between 1 July 1868 and 30 July 1869, although Green never seems to have referred to himself as a mariner.[213]

Kate Green's application to the Mendicity Society was forwarded by Annie Neild of 3 College Road when the family were 30 shillings in arrears on their weekly rent of 3s 6d for the entire house at 28 Hereford Street. Reuben Green was employed as a labourer by a Mr William Hills, market gardener of 11 Montague Place, and was earning 15 shillings per week but he could not cover the full cost of his son's burial. The child was enumerated on the 1871 census as Reuben Green and was two years old in April 1871. By 1881 Reuben and Kate Green had four children, the eldest were born in Brighton but the two younger children were born in Beddingham suggesting that the family lived there between about 1876 and 1880. By 1891 they had moved to 35 Cowper Street, Hove, and they were still resident in the street in 1901 when they lived at 70 Cowper Street.

9 February 1872
Statement: Kate Green wants a little assistance to help bury her child on Sunday. She has a pound to pay on Sunday and the other 2s 6d a week.
Report: I have made enquiries respecting this woman's statement and find it's correct. I have seen Mrs Hill to know if her husband would let them have a few shillings and they pay back a shilling a week. She will ask her husband to do so. The home is in a destitute state.
Dismissed, ineligible, R P Hooper

Letter written by Mrs Basden, 21 The Drive, Hove, addressed to Colonel Barlow, secretary of the Charity Organisation Society, 28 July 1893[214]
Mrs Basden presents her compliments to Colonel Barlow and begs to recommend the bearer Mrs Green, 35 Cowper Street, Hove, for assistance towards purchasing a glass eye the charge for which will be (Mrs Basden thinks) one guinea. Some 10s towards which have been already provided. Mrs Basden has known Mrs Green for the last four years and can, with confidence, recommend her as a very respectable and deserving person.

1 August 1893
Mrs Green, now of 35 Cowper Street, Hove, was sent by Mrs Basden, 21 The Drive, and applied at the office on Monday for assistance to enable her purchase a glass eye at a cost of 15s towards which 10s has been promised thus leaving 5s to be raised. For several years past she has gone out charring till three months ago when she lost her right eye. Her husband is employed on the road in the neighbourhood of Patcham with wages at 18s per week. They have two children

213 ESRO: RSS/1/443-449.
214 Mrs Basden's husband, Major General Basden, sat on the council of the Mendicity Society.

dependent on them and are recommended as quite industrious people. WC [William Collingham]
Grant of 5s, R P Hooper

2 August 1893
Invoice issued by T Rowley and Son, 128 St James Street, Brighton for one glass eye: 15s. Paid 4 August 1893

62 CATHERINE FORD, 41, WIFE OF A LABOURER, 5 INVERNESS ROAD, BRIGHTON

Catherine Ford (née Plumley) was the daughter of Mary Plumley, applicant number 57. She was born in Pevensey and married Joseph Ford on the 13 May 1867 at St Nicholas, Brighton.[215] *The couple lived with their two young children at 6 Hanover Terrace before moving to Inverness Road in about 1870. Joseph Ford was employed as a labourer by the surveyor's department of the borough council for which he was paid 15 shillings per week. The couple paid 5s 6d per week rent for the whole house and were one week in arrears. Ford's case was forwarded to the Mendicity Society by A Stocking of 11 Denmark Terrace.*

10 February 1872
Statement: Catherine Ford wants a little assistance as the money her husband gets is not enough to keep them.
Report: this is the same family that wished to be sent to Bath on Thursday. The mother lives with them and receives three shillings a week from Pevensey.
Dismissed, undeserving, R P Hooper

63 JOHN TAYLOR, 37, FISHMONGER, 12 BEDFORD BUILDINGS, BRIGHTON

The Taylor family made several applications to the Mendicity Society and the charity's subsequent incarnations between 1872 and 1887. At the time of John Taylor's first application he was employed as a fishmonger and worked for Mr Haylar of Prince Albert Street, Brighton. He was born in Brighton and lived with his wife Elizabeth and six-year-old son Thomas at 12 Bedford Buildings, Upper Bedford Street, where they paid rent of 5s 6d per week but were 30 shillings in arrears on payments. In the first instance their case was forwarded to the charity by Mrs Haslewood of 13 Chichester Terrace, Brighton, the same address given for a Mrs Dymoke who forwarded the details of applicant 64 to the charity.[216]

[215] ESRO: PAR 255/1/3/41b.
[216] Mrs Haslewood is listed in directories at this address but there is no mention of Mrs Dymoke.

The family's case was taken up by Laurence Peel in 1878 when they were living at 3 Somerset Street.[217] *He showed continued interest in the Taylors and enquired about them again 1879 when they lived at 50 Sloane Street.*

10 February 1872
Statement: John Taylor wants a little assistance till he gets able to work.
Report: I have made enquiries respecting this man and find he has been sick [for] three months. Mr Haylar gave him a good character. There is no doubt this man has consumption. He has applied to the parish authorities and refused to go in the workhouse. His wife is not able to earn anything. She has no use of the left hand. The home is in a passable state.
Consideration deferred pending further enquiry into the result of the reference to the poor law authorities, Orfeur Cavenagh. Referred to poor law – outdoor relief has been granted, Orfeur Cavenagh

Letter written by Laurence Peel, 32 Sussex Square, to Robert Johnson, Charity Organisation Society, 5 November 1878
Dear Sir, I shall feel obliged of your reporting to me respecting Mrs Taylor, 3 Somerset Street, who has applied for assistance informing me why, with a husband and two children she should be in the state of destitution in which she is described as being. Should not the parish afford them some relief? Mrs Taylor is unable to work and her husband (though willing) unable to obtain employment. Ever truly yours, Laurence Peel

6 November 1878
Report: Mr Laurence Peel requests a report of this case. Taylor, who suffers from bronchitis, jobs about cleaning windows, beating carpets and attending sales. He is said to be somewhat given to drink. His wife, who looks after unfurnished houses, suffers from rheumatism and has scarcely any use of her hands. She bears a good character. Their son has been earning 6s a week as an errand boy but he now endeavouring to obtain a situation as page boy. They have a daughter aged six who attends St Mark's School. When the case was referred to the Guardians in February 1872 the family received out door relief for nine weeks and Taylor was afterwards granted full work for a fortnight since which time he has not troubled the parish. As a rule jobbing painters earn more money than labouring men. The case of the wife seems a fit one for a District Visitor to assist but the district in which the family reside is a poor one.[218] WC [William Collingham]

[217] Laurence Peel was a life member of the Mendicity Society.
[218] District visitors acted on behalf of the parish: ministering to the sick; collecting subscriptions to parish charities and ensuring that they had access to the relief to which they were entitled.

To be reported to Mr Laurence Peel, R P Hooper

Letter written by Laurence Peel, 32 Sussex Square, to Robert Johnson, Charity Organisation Society, 11 November 1878
Dear Sir, in reply to your letter may I request you to employ the enclosed sovereign in the manner you may consider best calculated to afford relief. Yours gratefully, Laurence Peel

11 November 1878
Report: on the receipt of the Society's report Mr Laurence Peel forwarded a sovereign to the office to be given to Mrs Taylor in the manner the committee consider best calculated to afford her relief.
WC [William Collingham]
5s a week in hand for four weeks to be forwarded to Mrs Taylor from the money sent by Mr L Peel, JWH

Letter written by Laurence Peel, 32 Sussex Square, to the agent of the Charity Organisation Society,
21 December 1879
Mr Laurence Peel will thank the agent of the Charity Organisation Society to report to him upon the case of Mr and Mrs Taylor living at 50 Sloane Street near Kemp Town station who have applied to him for assistance and have been represented to him by the lady through whom the application has been made – as persisting from cold and hunger

22 December 1879
Report: Mr Laurence Peel requests a report of this case. The husband has been ill [for] seven weeks suffering from pleurisy. The wife is still in delicate health. Their son earns 6s a week, the family receive parish relief at the rate of 6s 8d per week and they also get a little help from the district. WC [William Collingham]
Ineligible, report to L Peel, R P Hooper

29 April 1887
Report: Taylor, now of 74 Princes Road, sent to the office on Thursday for temporary relief to enable him to get nourishing food. He has been poorly [for] seven weeks suffering from pleurisy for which he is attended by the dispensary doctor and seems in a very weak condition. His wife has been confined to her bed during the last four years. Their son is in the army, the daughter looks after the home and they appear very poor. WC [William Collingham]
Grant of 5s. Referred to parish, R P Hooper

64 ELIZABETH STREETER, 41, WIFE OF A PAINTER, 5 SHIP STREET GARDENS, BRIGHTON

The Streeter family's case was forwarded to the Mendicity Society by J Hamblin of the Queens Hotel Brighton. Elizabeth Streeter (née Sifleet) was born in Newick and she married William Streeter of Cuckfield at St Nicholas, Brighton, on 6 July 1856 when both were resident at 3 Fleet Street, but they had been living with their five children aged between five and 14 at 5 Ship Street Gardens since about 1863.[219] *They paid seven shillings per week rent for the entire house and were not in arrears. William Streeter had been employed as a painter by Mr Lockyer of King Street where he earned 7s 6d per week but had been short of work for six weeks. Their 14-year-old son, Alfred, was employed as a clerk by Mr Richards of 144 Western Road and was paid 3s 6d per week, whilst 10-year-old Frank was paid 2s 6d for working as an errand boy for Mr Dollman of Western Road. When all three were fully employed they earned a total of 13s 6d per week. The family were still resident at 5 Ship Street Gardens in 1882.*

10 February 1872
Statement: Elizabeth Streeter wants a little assistance till her husband gets work.
Report: I have made enquiries respecting this woman's statement and find it is false. Instead of her husband having only three days' work he was at work the whole week. His wages last week came to £1 5s 6d besides the boys' 6s. Mr Lockyer gave him a good character and says he will have plenty of work for him. The home is in a passable state.
Dismissed as undeserving, Orfeur Cavenagh. General result of enquiry to be communicated to Mr Hamblin. The woman to be cautioned

Letter from the Reverend J B Figgis of 26 Clifton Road, Brighton, to Colonel Barlow, Charity Organisation Society, 22 November 1882[220]
Dear Colonel Barlow, the bearer – Mrs Streeter, 5 Ship Street Gardens – is a poor woman whose blind daughter some of my people visited till she died. She now has a son very ill, she tells me, and she comes asking a little firing. My funds for the poor are £10 overdrawn and I thought you might be able to put her on your list for coals. A little help in kind would I think be well bestowed. Believe me dear Colonel Barlow, sincerely yours J B Figgis

24 November 1882
Mrs Streeter was sent by the Reverend J B Figgis and applied at the office on Thursday for some assistance but on my recognizing her as the person who applied to the society in February 1872. She declined to answer questions and

[219] ESRO: PAR 255/1/3/28.
[220] John Benjamin Figgis, minister of Countess of Huntingdon's chapel.

when I called at her house in the evening she refused to let me see her house.
WC [William Collingham]
Report to Mr Figgis, R P Hooper

30 January 1883
Report: Mrs Dymoke of 13 Chichester Terrace called at the office at the end of last week and stated that she had seen Mrs Streeter sitting on the Old Steine apparently sinking through want of food. Mrs D gave her temporary relief and requests a report of the case. I find that Streeter is now earning £1 a week. There are two sons at home. One earns 17s a week and the other is in ill health so that the present weekly income of the family for four persons to live on is £1 17s 0d.
WC [William Collingham]
Report to Mrs Dymoke, R P Hooper

65 ELIZABETH PAVEY, 39, LAUNDRESS, 33 SUN STREET, BRIGHTON

Elizabeth Pavey (née Russen) was born in Romsey, Hampshire in about 1839. She married James Pavey, a shoemaker born in Wilton, Wiltshire, at Holy Trinity, Southampton, on 8 November 1858.[221]

The Paveys were enumerated at Newington, Surrey, on the 1861 census but are thought to have moved to Brighton six months before Elizabeth's application to the Mendicity Society in February 1872. Elizabeth earned 1s 9d per week as a laundress but James Pavey had been short of work for two months. They paid weekly rent of 1s 3d for their upstairs room at Sun Street where the couple and their four children had lived for a month: previously they had rented a room at 7 Chesterfield Street.

James died in Brighton in the June quarter of 1878;[222] *Elizabeth was buried at Bear Road cemetery on 21 April 1908.*[223]

12 February 1872
Statement: Elizabeth Pavey wants a little assistance till she hears from her husband, who left home two months ago in search of work.
Report: I have made enquiries respecting this woman and find her home in a most destitute state. Her husband deserted her about two months ago. She then went in the workhouse for five weeks and when the parish authorities were going to send them home she refused to go and left the house. I am informed the husband could have plenty of work at Mr Whittakers and that he has had one three-month imprisonment for deserting his wife and family before.

[221] Ancestry.com England, select marriages 1538-1973.
[222] Death of James Pavey registered Q2 1878 Brighton 2b 141.
[223] ESRO: BH/L/3/1/5 - Woodvale Cemetery burial plot ZBI 90.

A loaf of bread and a quart of soup to be allowed only for seven days pending further enquiries,
Orfeur Cavenagh

This woman has not heard anything of her husband yet. I have seen Mr Meeres, 6 St George's Place, the clergyman of that district and he will call and see her. The mother's name is Fanny Russen [who lives at] Banning Street, Romsey. She receives parish relief at Romsey.
Referred to poor law, Orfeur Cavenagh

66 HARRIETT STILL, 47, CHARWOMAN, 14 YORK ROAD, BRIGHTON

Mrs Kemp of 88 London Road forwarded the Still's case to the Mendicity Society. Harriett Still, her husband Henry and their three children aged between one and 12 years old, had been living in one room at 14 York Road for 12 weeks. They paid 1s 9d rent per week and were 1s 6d in arrears. Previously they had lived at 4 Elder Street and had been resident in the parish for five years. Harriett Still was born in Lindfield but had been living in Brighton for five years when she applied for relief. She was earning 4s 6d as a charwoman and her husband, Henry Charles Still, was earning four shillings per week making skewers for butchers. He was born in Brighton in about 1813.

On the 1881 census the couple were enumerated at 49 Cumberland Place: Harriett was still employed as a charwoman but Henry Still was described as an invalid and deaf. This census return shows the couple living with their children aged between four and 14 years old who were born in Brighton and Cuckfield meaning that, if the enumerator had not made a mistake, Henry Still's youngest child was born when he was about 64.

12 February 1872
Statement: Harriett Still wants a little assistance till work gets better.
Report: I have made enquiries respecting this family and find the man gets his living making skewers for butchers, the wife occasionally gets a day's work. Mrs Kemp gave them a good character. She has relieved them several times and believes that if they had a half crown's worth of wood to give them a start they would be able to get their living. The home is in a destitute state.
Relieved by grant of 2s 6d for the purchase of skewer wood, Orfeur Cavenagh

67 SARAH LEONARD, 44, WIFE OF A PORTER, 14 LEICESTER STREET, BRIGHTON

Sarah Leonard, née Godley, had a 30-year association with the Mendicity Society and its successor body the Charity Organisation Society. She was born in Brighton in about 1828 and married David Leonard, who was a year older, on 19 October 1844 at St Nicholas,

Brighton. The marriage register states that Sarah was living at 14 Rock Street and David, a sailor, was living at 191 Edward Street.[224]

In September 1860, a 34-year old man named David Leonard was charged with stealing two sixpences from Charles Vanderhoff of 1 Dorset Street whilst both men were drinking at the Three Kings beer shop on Edward Street.[225] *Vanderhoff alleged that Leonard had put his hand into his waistcoat pocket and stolen the money. PC Worger took the accused into custody but on checking him found no money. Leonard was remanded until the following day but at the hearing PC Worger stated that Vanderhoff was drunk and that both men were convicted thieves. A witness named Richard Eaves of 38 Cumberland Place stated that he did not see Leonard's hand go into Vanderhoff's pocket and the case was dismissed.*

David and Sarah Leonard and their four children were enumerated on the 1871 census at 8½ Park Place, Brighton: David was employed as a porter and Sarah was a charwoman. By February of 1872 they had moved to 14 Leicester Street where they paid rent of 3s 6d per week for the entire house and were not in arrears. The family's case was forwarded to the charity by Mr Hayes of Belgrave Place and he was the first of many benefactors to express an interest in the Leonards over the next thirty years. In June 1872 Sarah Leonard's case for relief was forwarded to the charity by Dr Buchanan of Egremont Lodge, Egremont Place, but this was the last contact until November 1880.

The application for relief submitted in March 1882 refers to David Leonard's admittance to the Sussex County Hospital. The hospital's admission register corroborates this claim: he was admitted on 15 February 1882 suffering from acute pneumonia and was recommended by F Chambers of 45 Egremont Place.[226] *Leonard was attended to by Dr Moore and his casebook records that Leonard, still employed as a porter, was admitted on 21 February [sic] 'complaining of a bad cough and weakness of his heart. For 32 years he has been a porter and is used to carrying heavy weights. Has had a cough for six days and doesn't know how he caught it. Family history good. He has a rather anxious expression on his face and his conjunctivae are slightly jaundiced, raised temperature of 101 degrees and perspires freely'.*[227] *He was discharged on 14 March 1882.*

By 1891 David, who was still working as a porter aged 69, and Sarah Leonard were living at 11 Lodge Buildings, St James Street. David Leonard died in the March quarter of 1894 and Sarah Leonard applied to the Charity Organisation Society 13 months after his death when she was living at 5 Mount Pleasant.[228] *She remained at that address until at least November 1900 when a report on her was prepared for Mrs Lucy Penney. The report listed all of her children and their status: Daniel, 58, was an army pensioner; James, 56, a labourer with a large family; Alfred, 40, a jobbing porter separated from his wife; William, a 38-year old widower, was a labourer with two children; George, 36, was a painter with five children and Emma Wells, 32, was married to a labourer and had seven*

224 ESRO: PAR 255/1/3/16.
225 Brighton Gazette, 27 September 1860.
226 ESRO: HB 35/4/1882/199.
227 ESRO: HB 62/31 p186.
228 Death of David Leonard registered Q1 1894 Brighton 2b 170.

children. Sarah Leonard was enumerated in 1901 living at 5 Mount Pleasant with her sons Alfred and William and granddaughter Anna. She died late July or early August 1904 aged 82 and was buried at Bear Road cemetery on 3 August 1904.[229]

12 February 1872
Statement: if the committee will look over it this time she will never send out begging letters again.
Report: I have made enquiries respecting this family and find the man is a porter and goes about with commercial travellers, he is of intemperate habits. The son is a painter but has had no regular work lately. This woman has been cautioned by the police for sending begging letters about before. The house is in a passable state.
The woman and boy to be recommended to appear at the office on Thursday, Orfeur Cavenagh.
Mrs Leonard and her son will attend the committee on Thursday, duly cautioned, Orfeur Cavenagh.

15 June 1872
Dr Buchanan called at the office this morning and stated that he had been in the habit of assisting Mrs Godley, 20 Henry Street, but that lately he had lost sight of her until this morning and to his surprise she declared that she had not received anything from him during the interval although her daughter Mrs Leonard had called about three times and asked for, and obtained, relief on her behalf. Mrs Godley was entirely ignorant of her daughter's applications to Dr Buchanan and never received a farthing of what she got from him. Should the committee wish to take action in the matter Dr Buchanan promised to give his assistance.
WC [William Collingham]
Referred for further enquiry from Dr Buchanan, R P Hooper

17 June 1872
Further information respecting this case: Dr Buchanan states he cannot recollect the date that Mrs Leonard applied to him. He also states that he does not see that we could go on with this case without calling the mother to give evidence against the daughter to which he objects. I ordered Mrs Leonard to attend the committee today so that she might be cautioned again.
To be cautioned, R P Hooper, chairman

18 November 1880
A Miss Tugwell, 7 Clifton Terrace, called at the office on Wednesday stated that Mrs Leonard had applied to her for assistance but before relieving her Miss T

229 ESRO: BH/L/3/1/10 Woodvale Cemetery burial plot ZDH 34.

requests a report of the case. Leonard jobs about as a porter and is still very much given to drink. His wife receives a great deal of charity. They have no children dependent on them and do not appear to be in distress. WC [William Collingham]
Undeserving, to be reported to Miss Tugwell, Hayter Johnson

Letter written by Miss Carpenter of 45 Brunswick Square, Hove, sent to Mr R Johnson of the Mendicity Society, 24 March 1881
Miss Carpenter will be much obliged to the secretary if he will cause enquiry to be made respecting a family of the name of Leonard, 14 Leicester Street up Rock Gardens. Mrs Leonard has been in the habit of applying for assistance on the score of poverty and that of having to provide for a very delicate daughter.

25 March 1881
Miss Carpenter, 45 Brunswick Square, requests a report of this case. The daughter Emma is not in delicate health. She is a troublesome girl, will not stay in service and has lately gone out ironing three days a week. WC [William Collingham]
Undeserving, report to Miss Carpenter, R P Hooper

9 March 1882
Mr H Dering requests a report of this case. The husband has been an in-patient at the hospital a fortnight said to be suffering from inflammation of the lungs. His wife lives principally by begging. WC [William Collingham]
To be reported to Mr Dering, R P Hooper

15 March 1882
Mrs Leonard applied at the office on Wednesday for assistance to enable her to get her husband nourishing food. He left the hospital last week but is still weak and not able to work. WC [William Collingham]
Undeserving, Thomas W Holland

Undated begging letter from Sarah Leonard, 14 Leicester Street, c1883
With my humble duty to you and I am in great trouble about my rent on account of my husband not being able to work for several weeks which causes me to be in arrears with my rent and unless I can get a little money to pay I am afraid I shall be distressed or turned out of my house. The lady belonging to this card has kindly granted me the favour in returning me the card to see if I could get a friend to help me I should be truly thankful with a little help. Your humble servant, Sarah Leonard

Letter from Elizabeth C Vincent, 51 Egremont Place, to the Mendicity Society, 17 April 1883
Dear Madam, Mrs Leonard of 14 Leicester Street, Edward Street asked me to write to you. She is at the present time in great need of help as this winter has been unusually trying to her. Her husband is quite unable to do hard work since his serious illness last spring; inflammation of the lungs. She has been obliged to pawn all she could to buy food and now really needs the clothing. I believe her to be very steady and if you could assist her to redeem the pledges she would be truly grateful.
I am District Visitor in Leicester Street and have known Mrs Leonard for years. I am going from Brighton tomorrow for a time or would have gladly answered any enquiries. Trusting you will excuse me troubling you. I remain yours respectfully, Elizabeth C Vincent

Letter from Mrs J G Barclay, Exton House, Second Avenue, West Brighton, 17 April [1883]
Mrs J G Barclay will be much obliged if you will see about the enclosed case for her and if necessary give some help from her. Will you let her [Mrs Barclay] know about this case before the end of this week as she is leaving Brighton.

18 April 1883
Mrs Barclay of Exton House, Second Avenue requests a report of this case. The husband still jobs about as a porter. His wife, who earns a trifle by washing, has clothes and other articles in pledge for 17s but as they have only themselves to provide for. In my opinion they ought to be able to manage without charitable assistance. WC [William Collingham]
Report to Mrs Barclay, G D Turnbull 19/4/83

Letter from Mrs Tindal Robertson, 9 Belgrave Terrace, Brighton, to the Mendicity Society, 20 January 1885
Mrs Tindall-Robertson will feel obliged if the secretary will kindly forward her reports of the following cases, viz Mrs Leonard, 14 Leicester Street and William Measor, 57 Cavendish Street

21 January 1885
Mrs Tindall-Robertson requests a report of this case. The husband still jobs about as a porter. His wife is constantly out begging and they do not appear to be in distress. WC [William Collingham]
Report to Mrs Tindall-Robertson, F Y Toms R[oyal] N[avy]

23 September 1886
The Reverend J Halliwell requests a report of this case.[230] Leonard now resides at 10 Park Place and continues to job about as a porter. His wife still goes out begging and they are considered quite unworthy of encouragement. WC [William Collingham]
Report to Mr Halliwell, R P Hooper

Letter from Mrs D Garnett, Furze Hill Lodge, Hove, to the Mendicity Society, 22 November 1887
Dear Sir, will you kindly tell me if Mrs Leonard, 10 Park Place, is respectable and deserving of help. She did not really beg from me so I should not like her to know of these enquiries. Yours truly, D Garnett

23 November 1887
Miss Garnett of Furze Hill Lodge requests a report of this case. Leonard and his wife still reside at 10 Park Place and have not improved since my last report. WC [William Collingham]
Report to Miss Garnett

Letter from Mrs Gay, 5 Percival Terrace, Brighton, to the Mendicity Society, 13 December [1887]
Mrs Gay will feel obliged if Mr Collingham will see about the enclosed. The name is Mrs Leonard and [Mr] Leonard possibly 10 Park Place. She has just called and brought us the enclosed which she wanted back but Mrs Gay has detained it as she understands such papers are illegal. The tradesman who gave it had better be spoken to about it.

14 December 1887
Mrs Gay of 5 Percival Terrace provided the annexed recommendation to the office on Tuesday and requests a report of the case. The recommendation was given to Mrs Leonard's married son last year, consequently both families then used it for begging purposes and this year they have commenced again with the date cut off. WC [William Collingham]
Report to Mrs Gay, R P Hooper

Testimonial written for Sarah Leonard's son by Miss T F Holland and forwarded to the Charity Organisation Society by Mrs Gay of 5 Percival Terrace, c. 1887
Sir, having known the bearer for some time and he having worked for me this last year I can recommend him as a sober and honest man and I should employ [him] if I had sufficient work. Miss T F Holland, 104 Church Street, Brighton

[230] The Reverend John E Halliwell, vicar of St Paul's, Brighton.

Stamped by T F Hollands and Sons, painters, glaziers and house decorators, 104 Church Street, Brighton. Endorsed: A lady has given the 6d H E E

Letter from Edward Beves, 117 Church Street, Brighton, to the Mendicity Society, 2 May 1889
Dear Sir, will you be good enough to have enquiry made as to Mrs Leonard, 10 Park Place, who is seeking assistance by means of a letter. Yours truly, Edward Beves

2 May 1889
Mr E Beves of 117 Church Street requests a report of this case. Leonard still goes out with commercial travellers. His wife continues to seek charity and the previous reports will show that she was known to the police as a professional beggar long before their society was established in 1871. George Collingham
Report to Mr Beech, R P Hooper

Letter from C H Peters, 16 York Road, Hove, to the Mendicity Society, 9 January 1891
Dear Sir, will you kindly cause inquiries to be made respecting a Mrs Leonard of 11 Lodge Buildings, Little St James Street. She called at the above address this morning and declared that her husband had been run over on New Year's Day and that they were starving. Please do send me some tickets. I am yours truly, C H Peters

10 January 1891
Mr C H Peters, 16 York Road, Hove, requests a report of this case. The husband slipped down in Edward Street on the 1st of January, fell against a horse and cart, and cut his face for which he is attended by the parish doctor and would be better off in the parish infirmary. His wife still goes out begging and the previous reports will show that they have been most unfavourably known to the Society since the 12th of February 1872. George Collingham

12 January 1891
Mrs Leonard applied at the office on Monday for assistance to enable her to get her husband nourishing food. He is still confined to his bed and as mentioned in the previous report he would be better off in the parish infirmary. George Collingham
Refer to parish, E Eager

6 March 1895
Mrs Napper, Warnham House, Ship Street, requests a report of this case. Mrs Leonard lost her husband 13 months ago. The Guardians allow her 3s per week

and the previous reports will show that she has been known to the society as a troublesome beggar during the past 23 years. George Collingham
Report to Mrs Napper, Thomas W Holland

Letter from Lucy R Penney, for Robert H Penney JP, Highcroft, Dyke Road, Brighton, to Colonel Barlow, the Charity Organistion Society, 19 June 1896
The writer of the enclosed letter often asks for help. I should be glad of any information you can give me about her. Yours sincerely, Lucy R Penney

Letter from Sarah Leonard, 5 Mount Pleasant, Brighton, to Mrs R H Penney, Highcroft, Dyke Road, Brighton, 19 June 1896
Kind Christian friend, this carries my humble duty to you truly hopes this will find you quite well as I can assure you mam I am suffering very much with aches and pains and am very weak indeed. God cannot think how truly thankful to you I am for your very great kindness to me. My son has not any work this week and man as believe [sic] the good Samaritan and I feel you will not be offended with me for asking you to enclose a small order. I shall be very thankful to receive it. I hope you will think I am imposing on you too much [sic] as I am sure it helps me very much indeed. I remain your humble servant, Sarah Leonard

22 June 1896
Mr R H Penney, Highcroft, Dyke Road, forwarded the annexed begging letter to the office on Saturday and requests a report of the case. The writer has been known to this society as a troublesome beggar upwards of 24 years. Her children also beg and the Guardians continue to allow 3s a week outdoor relief besides which they grant her boots occasionally. WC [William Collingham]
Report to Mr Penney, C W Mellor

10 February 1898
The Reverend P T Andrews, vicar of St Johns, sent to the office yesterday to ask whether I had been the cause of Mrs Leonard having her parish relief stopped.[231] Her relief has not been stopped as represented but the Guardians refused to grant her boots last Tuesday and it seems strange that she was ever allowed outdoor relief as the officers and some of the Guardians know that she has been a drinking woman and a troublesome beggar for many years. WC [William Collingham]
ACW[232]

231 The Reverend Percy Thomas Andrews, vicar of St Johns, Carlton Hill.
232 Miss A C Woodhead.

Letter from Jessie Young, 16 Belgrave Place, Brighton, to the Charity Organisation Society, 28 February 1898
Miss Jessie Young presents her compliments to Mr Cunningham [Collingham] and would feel much obliged if he would kindly let her know why it is that Mrs Leonard of 5 Mount Pleasant is no longer, after the 7th of March, to receive parish relief. Miss Young is District Visitor at Mount Pleasant and constantly sees Mrs Leonard who, of course, is much distressed at the prospect of losing the relief but there may be reasons which cause it to be thought desirable.

2 March 1898
Miss Jessie Young, District Visitor, 16 Belgrave Place, would be much obliged if the committee can kindly inform her why Mrs Leonard's parish relief is to be stopped after this week. Her present allowance expires next Tuesday and she can then apply to the Guardians to renew it but as she is a well-known beggar it is doubtful whether they would do so. WC [William Collingham]
Report to Miss Young, C W Mellor

16 December 1899
Miss J E Bell, 48 Marine Parade, requests a report of this case. Mrs Leonard's parish relief was stopped on the 9th of August 1898 since then she has subsisted on charity and as she is too old to earn her own living she would be better off in the workhouse. WC [William Collingham]
Reported verbally On Saturday, M E Heathcote

21 November 1900
This person subsists on charity and the previous reports show that she has been known to the society as a troublesome beggar since Feb 12th 1872. Her children are not in a position to help her as she is too old to earn her own living. She would be far better off in the workhouse. WC [William Collingham]
Reported to Mrs Penney, M E Heathcote

Letter from Sarah Leonard, 5 Mount Pleasant, Brighton, to Mrs R H Penney, Highcroft, Dyke Road, Brighton, 14 February [1902]
Kind Christian friend, I trust that you will not be offended with me for writing to you mam. I am suffering very much with rheumatics and I have lost the sight of one of my eyes which is a great trial for me. I can assure you mam my age is telling on me very much of late which I am seventy-eight years of age mam. I have never taken the liberty to send to you since you sent me word not to send my little grandchildren as you thought it was bringing them up in a very bad way mam. I have missed your kindness very much and I should be most truly thankful if you would kindly send me a little help as I am not able to get so far

through my eyesight being so bad. Trusting mam that you and your dear family are quite well. I remain your humble servant, Sarah Leonard

Letter from Mrs Lucy R Penney, Highcroft, Dyke Road, Brighton, to the Charity Organisation Society, 14 February 1902
I have today received the enclosed letter. I have given Mrs Leonard one of your investigation tickets and shall be glad to hear something about her. Yours sincerely, Lucy R Penney

17 February 1902
Mrs R H Penney forwarded the annexed begging letter to the office on Saturday and requests a report of the case. Mrs Leonard still subsists on charity. The previous reports show that she has been known to the society as a troublesome beggar during the last 30 years and temporary relief would not be likely to do her any permanent good. WC [William Collingham]
Reported to Mrs Penney

Letter from George Beal, 207 Western Road, Brighton, to Colonel Dodd, the Charity Organisation Society, 15 November 1902
Private: Dear Sir, a friend of mine has been helping a Mrs Leonard, 5 Mount Pleasant, do you know anything of her, whether she is worthy of assistance? Your kind reply will oblige, yours truly, George Beal

17 November 1902
Mr G Beal 207 Western Road requests a report of this case. Mrs Leonard still subsists on charity and would be far better off in the Union [workhouse]. Her son, William, lives with her. He is a lazy worthless fellow and does no work. When I see him he is generally considerably the worse for liquor and says he wonders I am not shot. WC [William Collingham]
Report to Mr Beal, C Rashleigh 18/11/02
19 November 1902
Letter to Mr Beal copy appended AM

Letter from A Morris, for the secretary of the Charity Organisation Society to George Beal, 19 November 1902
Dear Sir, re: Sarah Leonard, we have known the above for the last thirty years unfavourably She subsists on charity and would be far better off in the Union [workhouse]. Her son lives with her and is a lazy, worthless fellow and does no work and often is considerably the worse for liquor. Yours faithfully, A Morris

68 FERNARD PAUWELS OR POWELL, 23, WIFE OF A MUSICIAN, 49 MEETING HOUSE LANE, BRIGHTON

Fernard and Jules Pauwels both appear to have been French nationals but had been living in Brighton for nine months at the time of their application to the Mendicity Society. Previously they rented lodgings at 24 Surrey Street but since about July 1871 they had been residents at 49 Meeting House Lane where they claimed to have been paying five shillings per week for a single room. Jules Pauwels, who was born in about 1844, earned four shillings per week but stated that they were 30 shillings in arrears. Fernard Pauwels was heavily pregnant at the time of the application and the birth of a child named Violette Graziella was registered in Brighton in the March quarter of 1872.[233]

A man named Jules Pauwels married Hermance Delettre at Marylebone on 22 February 1873.[234]

13 February 1872
Statement: Fernard Powell wants a little assistance for she expects to be confined in a day or two.
Report: I have made enquiries respecting this woman's statement and find it's false. She and her husband both strongly deny having any relief from anyone in the town. I have seen Mrs Polhill, 17 Brunswick Square. That lady has given the woman linen and wine and has also relieved the husband. I have also seen Lady Finch, 148 Kings Road. That lady has given them linen to the value of about 30s also a ticket for the lying-in institution and engaged a nurse for her in her confinement. Instead of the rent being 5s a week it's only 3s 6d and instead of owing 30s rent it's only about 7s. They keep two dogs, the house is in a passable state.
Dismissed as undeserving, Orfeur Cavenagh

Request from the St Marylebone Charity Organization Committee, 151 Marylebone Road, 17 February 1875
Dear Sir, I shall be obliged by your making inquiries into the case noted at foot, reporting their result to me at your earliest convenience. H Galloway Gill for Honorary Secretary
Case: Jules Pauwels, 18 Dorset Street
Applicant's statement: that he lived at 49 Meeting House Lane, Brighton, for one year and left about six months ago. Applicant is a Frenchman, 30 years of age

18 February 1875
Further information: the St Marylebone Committee requests a report of this case. I find that the man obtained an engagement in a band at Bath and left Brighton

[233] Violette Graziella Pauwels birth registered Q1 1872 Brighton 2b 279.
[234] Jules Pauwels marriage to Hermance Delettre registered Q1 1873 Marylebone 1a 875.

in May 1872 and I am informed that he was in Brighton a few months ago but he did not lodge on this occasion at 49 Meeting House Lane. WC [William Collingham]
To be reported to Marylebone Committee, R P Hooper

69 ELIZABETH AVERY, 45, SERVANT, 1 SUGARS COURT, UPPER BEDFORD STREET, BRIGHTON

Elizabeth Avery (née Noakes) was born in Newhaven in about 1827 and married Thomas Avery at St Nicholas, Brighton, on 10 October 1858.[235] *The entry in the marriage register records Thomas Avery, who was born in Hamsey in about 1810, as a widower. Nothing is known of his first wife but marriages between men called Thomas Avery and Sarah Miller and Jane Hawes took place at Brighton in 1838 and 1839 respectively. Both women appear to have died in 1855.*

The couple's case was forwarded to the Mendicity Society in February 1872 by G Gregory when they were paying 2s 2d per week rent and were four shillings in arrears. Thomas Avery was shown to have no occupation but an income of five shillings per week, Elizabeth Avery's occupation was given as servant but she appears not to have been earning any money at that time.

By July 1874 Thomas and Elizabeth Avery were living at 14 Rock Court and their case was forwarded to the charity by Daniel Hack, a Quaker businessman and life member of the charity. The 1881 census shows the couple living at 35 Essex Place where Elizabeth is described as a charwoman and Thomas is marked as blind but had employment as a cutler. They were still living at 35 Essex Place in March 1885 when the wife of Dr William Tindal Robertson forwarded their case to the charity.[236]

13 February 1872
Statement: Elizabeth Avery wants a little assistance to help support her husband who is blind.
Report: I have made enquiries respecting this man and find he has been blind five years. He used to stand on the Marine Parade with vesuvians and now his legs is [sic] bad.[237] He is not able to get about. He applied to the parish authorities and refused to go in the workhouse. His wife is in service at Mr Kearne's, 5 Lower Rock Gardens. Her wages is [sic] 5s a week. The house is in a destitute state.
Referred to poor law, Orfeur Cavenagh. NB a report of the result of the reference required it being considered by the committee a case deserving of relief. This

235 ESRO: PAR 255/1/3/31.

236 Dr William Tindal Robertson (1825-1889), physician, and MP for Brighton, 1886-1889, who lost his sight in the mid-1870s.

237 Vesuvians were slow burning matches specially designed for lighting cigars.

case went before the Board of Guardians this morning and they gave an order for the house saying the man belongs to Hamsey. NB it appears this man has been returned to his own parish once or twice by the Guardians. No further action needed, Orfeur Cavenagh

14 July 1874
Mrs Avery, who was sent by Mr Hack, applied at the office on Tuesday for some assistance for her husband who she said was ill. On enquiry I find that for several years he worked for Mr English, cutler, North Street, but for the last six or seven years he has been blind since which time he has supported himself by sitting on the Marine Parade near the bottom of Charlotte Street selling small books and cigar lights. For some considerable time he has suffered from a bad leg and a fortnight ago he fell over a pail in the passage which increased the wound and rendered him incapable of getting about. The wife does a little washing. The Guardians disapproving of the system of street begging have given them on several different occasions an order for the house and they now have one in their possession. WC [William Collingham]
Ineligible, to be reported to Mr Hack

15 November 1878
This man who resides at 16 Essex Place, still sits on the Marine Parade. His wife goes out charring and takes in needle work. Nothing is known against their characters. WC [William Collingham]
To be reported to Dr T Robertson, R P Hooper

20 March 1883
Mrs Tindal Robertson requests a report of this case. Avery has been confined to his room during the last six months. His wife earns a trifle by going out charring. The Guardians allow them 3s 6d a week and they receive a little help from friends. WC [William Collingham]
Report to Mrs T Robertson, A F Bond[238]

21 December 1886
Dr Tindal Robertson MP forwarded the annexed begging letter to the office on Monday and requests a report of the case. Mrs Avery lost her husband at the end of last January since which time she has gone out charring and nursing. Nothing is known against her character and she appears to be doing her best to keep out of the workhouse. WC [William Collingham]

238 The Charity Organisation Society annual report of 1883 records a Major General Bond as a member of the council and *Page's Directory* of that dates shows a Major General A F Bond living at 1 Ventnor Villas.

Report to Dr T Robertson, J W Kirby

Begging letter written by Elizabeth Avery and forwarded to the Mendicity Society, 21 December 1886
Dear Sir, I hope you won't think a great liberty of me in writing to you but as I have got no work to do and no parish pay. They have not give me any since my husband has been dead. I have such a hard struggle to getting any food or firing or I would not trouble you but if it is only a small trifle and would get me a little coal. I should be very thankful. I remain your humble servant, Mrs Avery, 35 Essex Place, Brighton
Dr Tindal Robertson will feel much obliged if Colonel Barlow will kindly have the case of Mrs Avery investigated, 9 Belgrave Terrace, Dec 20

70 SUSAN REEVES, 33, WIFE OF A LABOURER, 27 APOLLO TERRACE, BRIGHTON

Susan Reeves stated on her application to the Mendicity Society that she was born in Henfield but the census of 1871 records her place of birth as Fletching. Her husband, Ramoth Reeves, was born in Twineham in about 1840 but no record of their marriage could be found.[239] *A man named Ramoth Reeves married Catherine Barnett in Henfield in the autumn of 1859.*[240] *Ramoth and Catherine Reeves were enumerated on the 1861 census at Brookfield Farm, Woodmancote, where they lived with their eight-month-old son, Richard.*[241]
It is not known when Catherine Reeves died but Ramoth Reeves was enumerated on the 1871 census at 52 Cumberland Place, Brighton, with his new wife Susan. The couple lived with six children: Richard, the son of Catherine, who was now 10; Lucy who was also 10 and born in Surrey, London, suggesting that she was the daughter of Susan Reeves from a previous relationship and four children aged between eight and two years old all of whom were born in Henfield and Lewes. If the younger children were the product of Ramoth and Susan's marriage it suggests that Catherine died in about 1862.

The Reeveses' case was forwarded to the Mendicity Society by T Crunden.[242] *The application form stated that the couple had eight children, the eldest of which, Mary, was in service in London. This daughter was not enumerated with the rest of the family in 1871 so must have been a child from Susan's previous marriage. The family had moved to Brighton in about 1869 and had previously lived at 16 Park Place. They paid four shillings per week for the whole house at 27 Apollo Terrace and were seven shillings in arrears.*

[239] The marriage of a man named Ramoth Reeves to either Ann Head or Mary Ann Pockney was registered at Lewes in 1868, Q3 1868 Lewes 2b 251.
[240] Ramoth Reeves marriage to Catherine Barnett registered Q3 1859 Steyning 2b 338.
[241] Ramoth Reeves was enumerated as Barnett Reeves on the census returns of 1861 and 1871, presumably as a reference to his first wife's family name.
[242] Probably Thomas Crunden, cabinet maker, 21 New Road, Brighton.

Ramoth Reeves was employed by Mr Marshall at the drainage works but had been short of work for three weeks.

Nine days after Susan Reeves's initial approach to the Mendicity Society she appeared before magistrates charged with stealing a shirt and clothes brush, the property of Mrs Gains, at 20 Richmond Hill. Reeves subsequently tried to sell the shirt, which she said she had found, to a Mrs Burchell of Edward Street. She was found guilty and sentenced to two months' hard labour.[243] *Six days later, on 28 February 1872, Susan Reeves again went before the magistrates charged with stealing two books and a basket from Mary Poole of 2 Apollo Terrace. The items had been found by PC Raggett when he searched Reeves's home at 27 Apollo Terrace. She pleaded guilty and said she had been driven to act in the way she did because of distress. One month's hard labour was added to the two months' sentence given to her for the earlier crime.*[244]

In October 1872 Susan Reeves was charged with felony.[245] *The Brighton Guardian report of the hearing stated, 'Susan Reeves, 34, a decent looking woman who has a baby in her arms was charged with stealing a coat, a pair of trousers and two jackets, the property of George Heuser of the Brighton Town Band'. Reeves appears to have broken into Heuser's house on Lennox Street and, after stealing the clothing, which was worth about £2 10s, went to a beer shop on Edward Street where she sold the jacket; the rest of the clothes were found at her house. Reeves admitted the theft but said that she did so under the influence of drink and that usually she was a good wife and mother. The magistrate, Mr Bigge, stated that she had been convicted of similar robberies twice before and that he had 'never known anyone become a thief when drunk who was not so when sober'. She was sentenced to two months' hard labour.*

Susan Reeves applied to the Mendicity Society again in February 1873 by which time the family were living at 26 Chesterfield Street, where they paid five shillings per week rent for the house and were £1 5s in arrears. Their case was taken up by Mrs Trille of 126 Queens Road, Brighton. The next application in February 1874 was made directly by Susan Reeves with no intermediary: the family were living at 6 Nelson Place and were looking for help to move to Sutton, Surrey, where her husband had found work with John Thomas Chappell, who had secured a contract to install drainage at Banstead Asylum.[246]

Susan Reeves died in Wandsworth gaol in the June quarter of 1875.[247] *Ramoth Reeves fell into a well at St Mary's Hospital, Paddington, on 2nd of November 1878 and as result had his left foot amputated. His employers, Messrs Easton and Anderson, bought him an artificial leg and gave him about £15 following the accident but despite this financial aid Reeves was still forced to write to the Mendicity Society in May 1879 asking for help to keep him out of Brighton Workhouse until he could resume work. He appears to have made a good recovery as he was enumerated on the 1881 census at 2 James Watt Place, Erith,*

243 Brighton Guardian, 28 February 1872.
244 Brighton Guardian, 6 March 1872.
245 Brighton Guardian, 4 October 1872.
246 London Metropolitan Archives: MA/D/A3/004/1/1-2.
247 No reference to Reeves's death in prison or the nature of her crime could be found in local press.

Kent, working as a general labourer and living with his wife, Jane Reeves (née Clark), his children Richard, Thomas, Alfred, Minnie and Ruth and his stepson, George Clark. The 1891 census records Reeves, now 52 and a widower for the third time, still employed as a labourer and living at 31 Beadonwell Road, Erith, Kent, with Julia Maldengraft, a 50-year-old laundress born in Kerry, Ireland, but now widowed.

13 February 1872
Statement: Susan Reeves would be thankful for a little assistance till Saturday when she will have her husband's wages.
Report: I have made enquiries respecting this family and find the man is a hard-working man. He has had no regular work lately but is gone on at the drainage works this week. The wife is not able to work. She has been very weak since her last confinement. The Reverend Dr Hannah will pay one month's schooling for the two eldest boys, one has no shoes to go in. The wife says if she had clothes for Lucy she could go to Keymer in service. The home is in a very destitute state. Marriage Wallis gave me a shilling, with that I bought some food for them which they was very thankful for.
Reverend R P Hooper gave me clothes and I gave the boy boots, socks, trousers WC [William Collingham]
Relieved by grant, the girl I find cannot write her own name, Orfeur Cavenagh.
NB a loaf of bread and 2 quarts of soup to be allowed daily for four days, an estimate to be submitted of the cost of supplying the daughter with clothes to enter service and the boy with a pair of shoes. Further inquiries, Orfeur Cavenagh

Letter to Robert Johnson from Susan Reeves, 27 Apollo Terrace, Brighton, c. 1872
To Mr Collingham: Sir I have sent, according to your wish, the list of clothing that is wanted for my little girl [to] go to service and after you have seen what you can do for me I will endeavour to supply the remainder and if you can obtain from my lady any needlework of any kind I will gladly repay you back with sincere thanks for what you and others have done for my family. I cannot feel too grateful. Your humble servant, S Reeves

19 February 1873
This person called on Mrs Trille on Wednesday and stated that she was in arrears with her rent and that the landlord had threatened to put in a distress on Thursday if some of the rent was not forthcoming. She also stated that she had a daughter who wanted a situation and that if she could get a place and borrow a few shillings to prevent her home from being broken up she would be able to manage but Mrs Trille declined to do anything for her until her case had been investigated. Upon enquiry I find her statement respecting the arrears of rent is correct. The husband is working for Mr Aird at the main sewer but since the case

was before the committee 12 months ago applicant has been twice convicted for felony: the first time she was sentenced to three months and the second to two months' imprisonment. WC [William Collingham]
Undeserving GDR [George Dudley Ryder], chairman

Letter from Mrs Tatham, [February 1874][248]
Re: Mrs Reeves, 6 or 7 Nelson Place. This woman has called upon Mrs Tatham asking for help to go and join her husband who is in good work at some distance. Please enquire and report if there is any truth in the statement. Mrs T told her to come here perhaps she has called.

11 February 1874
Mrs Reeves applied at the office on Wednesday for assistance to enable her and her family to remove to Sutton where, according to her statement, her husband is at work digging a well and that after the job is finished he expects to go onto work as a hanger for Mr Chappell, builder, who has got the contract to build a large asylum at Banstead almost close to where her husband is now at work. Although applicant's husband is earning good wages they have a large family and have been obliged lately to keep two homes. On enquiry I find that since my last report nearly 12 months ago Mrs Reeves has managed to keep out of trouble and is, I believe, slightly improved. The railway fare to Sutton for Mrs Reeves and her family would cost about 14s. WC [William Collingham]
Report to Mr Tatham and case to stand over, R P Hooper
Letter from John Adams, Hundred Acres, Sutton, Surrey, 13 February 1874
Sir, I received yours of the 13th this day. Richard Reeves has been working under me 12 months. He is a hard-working man and attends to his work every day since he has been with me. Reeves' wages have been little over £2 5s 0d per week. I am yours faithfully, John Adams, Banstead Common, Sutton, Surrey

17 February 1874
I advise no prosecution in this case but a severe caution as I fear that we should do more harm than good in the first, M Brandreth[249]
Having asked Mrs Reeves when she called on Mr Tatham she declared that she had never called at all adding that she did not know where he lived. Resolved to clear the matter up I took her to Mr Tatham's on Saturday morning when Miss Tatham at once recognised her as the woman who had called and so did two servants who were separately questioned. Notwithstanding this the woman stuck to her story and positively declared that she had never entered the house. Mr Johnson, secretary, received an answer to his letter of enquiry addressed to

[248] Probably the wife of George Tatham, 46 Old Steine, Brighton.
[249] Probably M R Brandreth, solicitor, 63 Middle Street, Brighton.

the foreman of the work on which the husband is engaged to the effect that the man Reeves is a hard-working man and that his wages are at least £2 5s od a week. WC [William Collingham]
Undeserving, case referred to Mr Brandreth for his advice, George D Ryder, chairman

Letter sent by Ramoth Reeves, 33 Eastern Road, Brighton to Mr Chalen, Henfield, 13 May [1879]
Dear Sir, I take the liberty to write these few lines to you to ask you if you if you can help me in any way? I met with a sad accident on the second of November last and lost my leg and sprained my other foot very bad. My leg is nearly well now but my foot is very bad yet and I am not able to work yet. I had a little money when it happened and with a little support from my master have paid my way until the last few weeks and now I don't know what to do. I have three children at Mr Emsley's, Brookside Farm, Henfield, and I cannot pay for them now I have applied to the parish here and they say I belong to Henfield and and [sic] they cannot allow me anything but to go in the house. I do not want to go there yet as I am in hopes in a few weeks I shall be able to go to work. My master has promised to find me a situation as soon as I am able to get about. A little later I have a artificial leg and could go now if my foot was stronger. If you could get the children in a school or or [sic] somewhere for a few weeks I could manage myself and would pay for them when I get to work. If you cannot help me I must go in the workhouse. I remain yours truly, Ramoth Reeves, Brighton. Your answer to this will greatly oblige

21 May 1879
The Reverend R P Hooper brought the accompanying letter to the office on Tuesday and requested a report of the case. Reeves fell down a well at St Mary's Hospital, Paddington, on the 2nd of November last and has since had his left foot amputated. His late employers Messrs Easton and Anderson of 3 Whitehall Place, London, have given him an artificial leg at a cost of £7 7s od and have also sent him about £15 since the accident occurred. He hopes to be able to resume work in the course of two or three weeks. His wife died in Wandsworth gaol nearly four years ago and he is now living with another woman. His three youngest children are at Henfield. The Brighton Guardians have offered him an order for the house. WC [William Collingham]
Report to Mr Hooper, R P Hooper, chairman

71 FRANCIS LAKEY, 52, TAILOR, 17 CARLTON STREET, BRIGHTON

Francis Lakey gave only the scantest details about his family's financial predicament. Lakey did explain that he and his wife, Ann, had been living at their present address for a week and before that were residing at 51 John Street. He also gave his profession as tailor but beyond that no further information was given: the Mendicity Society's agent, William Collingham, recorded 'party refuses to answer any further questions'. The Reverend Robert Poole Hooper, chairman of the Mendicity Society, forwarded the Lakey family's details to the Mendicity Society. Francis Lakey, who was born in Lyme Regis, Dorset, in about 1820, married Ann Williams of Whitechurch at Axminster, Devon, in the September quarter of 1842.[250] *The couple were enumerated in Lyme Regis in 1851 with their three children. By 1861 the family had moved to Brighton and were enumerated at Model Lodging House, Church Street, with their six children, the youngest of whom were born in Brighton in about 1856 and 1860.*

The couple's eldest son, also Francis, appeared before magistrates in June 1859, when he was 14 years old, charged with stealing a silver spoon belonging to Michael Simon Nuremberg, reader at the Synagogue.[251] *Lakey took the spoon to the shop of A Martin, Prince Albert Street, but the young assistant, suspecting it was obtained dishonestly, gave him into custody for which he was commended by the magistrate, Mr Bigge. Lakey was committed for three months' hard labour.*[252]

In May 1872, the Mendicity Society entered negotiations with John Deverell, who acted for Purbrook Industrial School, Cosham, Hampshire, to enquire whether their son George could attend the school.[253] *When his case came before the Bench, representatives of the Mendicity Society intervened in an attempt to get Brighton School Board to send him to an industrial school and to encourage the magistrates to place an order on Francis Lakey to help towards his son's education.*[254] *Lakey stated in court that he could not contribute towards the cost of schooling as he earned only 17 shillings per week, not the 25 shillings quoted in the courtroom. The court settled that Lakey would be sent to the workhouse for a week and from there to Purbrook Industrial School for four years. The magistrate stated that he should not be maintained at the public expense and made an order of two shillings per week. The Brighton Guardian reported '[Francis] Lakey, in the course of some remarks, said he would never be able to pay the money – the subject then dropped.'*

Ann Lakey died in Brighton in the June quarter of 1876.[255] *In 1881 Francis Lakey was enumerated at 7 Nelson Place living with his 11-year-old son Thomas who was born deaf;*

[250] Probably Whitchurch Canonicorum, Dorset.

[251] At this point the Synagogue was situated on Devonshire Place, Brighton.

[252] Brighton Gazette, 16 June 1859.

[253] The correspondence refers to the child as both John and George but although the Lakeys did have a son called John he was born in 1850 so would have been 22 in 1872. John Deverell sat on the council of the Charity Organisation Society (see annual report of 1877) but his links to Purbrook Industrial School are unclear.

[254] Brighton Guardian, 12 June 1872.

[255] Death of Ann Lakey registered Q2 1876 Brighton 2b 134.

a 61-year-old widow named Mary Ann Homewood and her boarder Friend Payne. Lakey died in Brighton and was buried at Bear Road cemetery on 7 July 1885 aged 65.[256]

Letter from Anne A Nockolds, 37 Hova Villas, Hove, 9 February 1872[257]
Sir, on Tuesday last a little boy called at several houses in Hova Villas professing to be sent by a Mrs Mills of Eastern Terrace with a box of books and a note to explain that the books were given by a lady to be sold for the benefit of a distressed tailor's family living at 51 John Street. When your society was mentioned to him he said his mother would not wish to go there for relief as only a twopenny loaf of brown bread would be given her and it would be published that she was in rags so begged I would not take the trouble of writing to you; on consideration however, I have thought it better to do so, not requesting you to enquire into the matter but giving you the option of doing so if you think fit. From what our servant said (we did not see the boy) he must have been too young to have carried the box of books himself, there must have been some grown person with him. I am sir yours respectfully, Anne A Nockolds
Undeserving, R P Hooper

15 February 1872
I have made enquiries respecting this family and find the man is a tailor. He is of intemperate habits. The wife is an invalid and is not able to earn anything. There is a large family, amongst them is two grown up sons who go hawking, one daughter who goes hawking books. There is a boy about eleven years of age who is often out begging, he is known to the Reverend R P Hooper, 29 Cambridge Road, also to Mr Hamblin, Queens Hotel, where he was continually going for relief till Mr Hamblin gave him a mendicity ticket. Since that they have not seen him. He is also known to Mrs Nockolds, 51 Lansdowne Place also to R H Penny esq, 15 Alexandra Villas. I cautioned them if they send this boy begging again the father would be brought before magistrates. The home is in a destitute state. There was three beer cans in the room.
Dismissed as ineligible, Orfeur Cavenagh. NB the boy's parents are perfectly able to support him, they deny having sent him out to beg. He has been duly cautioned

22 May 1872
I have seen Sabina Avard, the housemaid at 92 Kings Road, she states the boy Lakey came here about a week ago and asked to see the two ladies dressed in

[256] ESRO: BH/L/3/1/7 - Woodvale Cemetery burial plot ZCB 72.
[257] Anne Arram Nockolds died unmarried at 37 Hova Villas on 10 August 1890 leaving £455 6s 3d. This amount was later resworn as £4,774 11s 1d.

black that was in the drawing room. Afterwards he stated his father had got a coat he must get home in the morning and that he wanted sixpence to get some trimmings to finish it. He stated Mrs Buchanan, Egremont Lodge, had sent him but the Reverend Mr Davis, 17 Clifton Terrace, being there and knowing him so well they did not give him anything. Mr Davis will be out of town from Friday till Monday but if he could do anything to assist in this case he would be very pleased to do so. Dr Buchanan of Egremont Lodge states if he can do anything to assist or to help get this boy sent away to some school and not to prison he would be very pleased to do so.
Deferred to Saturday pending Mr Brandreth's report. R P Hooper, Chairman

Letter from John Deverell, 10 St George's Road, Belgravia, to Robert Johnson, secretary of the Mendicity Society, 27 May 1872
Dear Sir, in answer to your enquiry as to the boy, the committee are desirous to send [him] to an industrial school. I write to say that I will arrange with Mr Jerram the superintendent for his reception if an order is made by the Brighton Bench on the application of the school board, the only body who are now competent to become responsible for the payment of the boy. I believe the treasury grant is reduced to 3s 6d per week as to boys sent by the school board. If so I conclude the school board would agree to make up the 7d per week for an urgent case such as the one you refer to appears to be. I am of course willing to do anything I can to meet the wishes and wants of the Mendicity Society in which you know I take a deep interest but I must take care not to establish what might prove a precedent injurious to the funds of the school. Perhaps you will be so kind as to consult the school board and then communicate further with me and I on the other hand will confer with the inspector of the industrial school in Parliament Street. In the mean time the poor boy may be sent to the Union under the act of 1866 pro tem.[258] I hope you are all going on prosperously. I often regret I cannot be amongst you. Yours truly John Deverell
PS If you write tomorrow direct to me at Purbrook Park, Cosham, Hants, if on Wednesday as above

Letter from John Deverell, 10 St George's Road, Belgravia, to Robert Johnson, secretary of the Mendicity Society, 31 May 1872
Dear Sir, I have called at the office of the Industrial Schools this day and find that as the Purbrook Industrial School was established before the late regulation came into operation I can receive a boy sent under the Brighton School Board if over 10 years of age at 2s per week being the same sum the town council had consented to pay. If the magistrates decide to send the boy, whose case is reported in the Brighton Daily News received this day from you, please to

[258] The Industrial Schools Act, 1866.

communicate direct with Mr T Jerram directing to him Purbrook Industrial School, Cosham, Hants. I am, dear sir, yours truly John Deverell

Letter from John Griffith, Findon, Worthing, 1 June 1872
Sir, I beg to thank you for sending us timely information about John Lakey. After taking note of the letter I will send it on for other members to read before Tuesday's meeting. The more easy and full the communication between your admirable society and our board the better, I hope, for both. With great respect, yours faithfully,
J Griffith

Letter from John Griffith, Brighton School Board Offices, the Pavilion, 7 June 1872
Dear Sir, our board is anxious to cooperate with your society and has directed our clerk and our officer Mr Bennett to attend on Tuesday next the day to which the case of George Lakey [sic] is now adjourned. On rereading the Industrial Schools and Education Act (CC CXVIII & 14, 12 and LXXV & 27, 28) you will see that while our board is the prison authority and as you state the municipal authorities can no longer pay – it is still open to you or 'any person' (CXVIII.14) to bring the child before two justices. We would willingly pay towards the support of such a child but as the father is (we are informed) in receipt of 25s wages per week on an average you will agree with us on it's being probably his duty to pay. If anything special as to the parents' poverty or great pecuniary trouble owing to present circumstances of illness so makes it the duty of our board to contribute, our clerk has authority to promise our contribution. Again thanking you for the friendliness and help of your communication. I remain yours sincerely,
John Griffith

72 ALFRED SOUGHTON, 31, BAKER, 4 ELDER STREET, BRIGHTON

Alfred Soughton was born in Preston in about 1841 and was enumerated on the census of that year in Rottingdean with his mother, Ann Soughton. Ten years later the family were living in Preston and in 1861 Alfred Soughton, still living in Preston with his parents, was working as a baker. By 1871 Soughton had married and lived at 8 Station Road, Preston, with his wife, Ann, and their four children, who were aged between seven and one.

The family's application in February 1872 states that they had been living in Brighton for 12 months but it must have been a little less than this as they were enumerated in Preston on 2 April 1871. The Soughtons' case had been forwarded to the Mendicity Society by Mrs Moncrief of 13 Goldsmid Road, Hove, when the family were a week in arrears on the rent of two shillings they paid for an upstairs room at 4 Elder Street. Alfred Soughton had been employed by G Carter, baker and pastry cook of 103 London Road, but had been out of work for four months due to sickness. The application form also provides Mr E Ellis, bread and biscuit baker of 62 Edward Street, as a reference. During Soughton's illness he had received six weeks' worth of relief from the parish but had no other means of income.

In May 1872, it became apparent that the Soughton family were trying to emigrate to Canada and by June 1872 were still £1 short of their fare. The application does not record what became of them but Canadian passenger lists show that they sailed on the SS Niger from London via Plymouth to Quebec, leaving London on 12 June and arriving at Quebec on 2 July 1872.[259] *Alfred Soughton's death was recorded in Wentworth, Ontario, on 26 December 1912.*[260]

16 February 1872
Statement: Alfred Soughton wants a little assistance till he gets work.
Report: I have made enquiries respecting this family and find they received parish relief [for] six weeks during sickness and then went into the workhouse for two weeks and left about two weeks ago. I have seen Mr Carter and Mr Ellis and neither of them gave the man a good character. Mrs Moncrief has relieved them several times. I am informed his friends are in a good position and have relieved him several times. The parish authorities have an order to remove the family to Steyning Workhouse. The home is in a most destitute state.
Referred to poor law, Orfeur Cavenagh

24 May 1872
Further information respecting this case: Miss Crisp, 15 Norfolk Terrace, called at the office yesterday and stated she should feel obliged if I would make enquiries about a family she would send to the office which turned out to be this man Soughton. I find since this case was before this society he has not had any regular work. I saw Mrs Sheppard, 1 Clermont Terrace, Preston. She states he has occasionally worked for them.
Entered, RJ [Robert Johnson, secretary]

Letter from Miss Crisp, 15 Norfolk Terrace, Brighton, to the Mendicity Society, undated, Tuesday am
Gentlemen, I have much pleasure in handing you my subscription for the Mendicity Society feeling it will be a great benefit wherever it is adopted.
Remain yours truly S E Crisp
Can you make a grant to Soughtons to help them off to Canada? I think it is a very deserving case.

[259] Canadian passenger lists, 1865-1935, Library and Archives Canada RG-76C.
[260] Archives of Ontario, Toronto, Canada, series MS935; reel 181.

Letter from John Haynes, Town Missionary, 1 New England Road, Brighton, to the Mendicity Society, 21 May 1872
Sir, as it is probable you may hear of a petition I have just written for a family about to emigrate I think it advisable to acquaint you with the facts. The name is Alfred Soughton with a wife and five children. They reside at 17 Providence Place alias Elder Place. He is now a labourer. They have resided in this part of the town about 13 months and during this time have lived decent and respectable lives. In the winter he was ill some weeks. His brothers and sisters are all very respectable persons. They do not ask for ordinary charity as vagrants but to be helped to go to Canada with their family. As such I recommend them. I am yours faithfully, John Haynes, town missionary

Letter from Miss Crisp, 15 Norfolk Terrace, Brighton, to the Mendicity Society, 22 May 1872
Sir, the bearer of this will tell you all particulars of the case. I hope you will find them deserving of the assistance of the benevolent to help them out to Canada and your recommendation will be all powerful to help them and if they are all right I am sure you will feel a pleasure in recommending them to our society and others respond to assist them with kind respects, I remain sir yours very truly, S E Crisp
Their name is Soughton, Providence Place, Brighton

Letter from Mrs Bright, 19 Goldsmid Road, Hove, to the Mendicity Society, 10 June 1872
Mrs Bright begs to place the case of Mrs Soughton once more before the committee of the Mendicity Society. She has now raised money for the passage of herself, husband and family but is still £1 short for the journey to London and other little expenses and if the society can thus aid her Mrs Bright will be very glad and is sure it will be well bestowed. The family must leave tomorrow morning as their ship tickets are taken for sailing on Wednesday morning and they must be on board tomorrow afternoon so any delay would render assistance useless.

73 MATILDA CURTISS, 57, TAILORESS, 9 NELSON PLACE, BRIGHTON

Matilda Curtiss was born in Bexhill in about 1816. In 1851 she was enumerated at 4 Bell Yard, Westminster, with her widowed mother, Frances Curtiss, a 70-year-old annuitant who was born in Warbleton. Ten years later she was living at Canterbury Hall, Northgate Street, Canterbury, with her mother; brother, George Curtiss, a carriage proprietor; and his wife Ann. The 1871 census shows Matilda Curtiss still living with her brother and sister-in-law but now at the Esplanade Post Office, Ryde, Isle of Wight, where George Curtiss was employed as a general carrier.

According to her application form Matilda Curtiss arrived in Brighton in about June 1871 and since leaving Ryde had been living at 8 William Street, Portsmouth. She had been resident at 9 Nelson Place for three months where she paid weekly rent of 1s 6d for a single upstairs room but had fallen six shillings in arrears. Her case was sent to the charity by a Miss North, and Mrs Ashdown of Richmond Street was given as a reference.

In 1881 Matilda Curtiss was living at 18 Gloster Road, Brighton and was still employed as a dressmaker. In 1891 she appeared on the census as a boarder living at 6 Park Crescent Road, Brighton, and she was enumerated for the last time in 1901 when she was 84 and resident at Brighton Workhouse. She died in the September quarter of 1903.

16 February 1872
Statement: Matilda Curtiss wants a little assistance till she gets work.
Report: I have made enquiries respecting the woman and find she is a hard-working woman but cannot get work. Mrs Ashdown gave her a character and says all she wants is work. The home is in a destitute state.
Relieved by payment as a temporary arrangement pending reference to poor law,
Orfeur Cavenagh
NB payment of three shillings to be expended in the purchase of food.

13 February 1875
This woman applied at the office this morning for a little assistance. Lately she has had very little to do. Her home is in a destitute state and she is not known to parish authorities.
Grant of 5s, R P Hooper

18 November 1875
This person applied at the office on Monday for a little temporary assistance. I find that she has very little work and her home is in a destitute state.
WC [William Collingham]
Grant of 5s, R P Hooper

22 November 1875
This person who was very grateful for the grant given her three weeks ago applied at the office on Monday for a little further help. Her house is still in a destitute condition. WC [William Collingham]
Final grant of 5s, AH

Letter from the Reverend C S Chilver, 27 Eaton Place, Brighton, 22 July 1877[261]
The Rev C S Chilver would be glad to have a report on Mrs Curtis, 30 Vine Street. She tells Revd Chilver that she has been relieved by the C O Society and that they think well of her but Rev Chilver would like to know if that is really so. Will you send report to Mrs C Pugh, 64 Upper Lewes Road, as Rev Chilver is leaving home tomorrow

24 July 1877
The Reverend C S Chilver requests a report of this case. Miss Curtiss now resides at 30 Vine Street and still does a little needle work. During the last month the parish have allowed her 1s 6d and a large loaf of bread a week and Mr Borager of 25 Park Crescent has occasionally assisted her. WC [William Collingham]
Report to Mr Chilver, HK

74 CAROLINE SKINNER, 32, NEEDLEWOMAN, 29 EDWARD STREET, BRIGHTON

Caroline Skinner was born in Bexhill in about 1840 and arrived in Brighton, via Lewes, two weeks before her case was forwarded to the Mendicity Society by Miss Thursby of 18 Brunswick Terrace, Hove.[262] *The application form does not contain an entry showing the weekly rent she was paying for her bed at Mrs Seymour's house, 29 Edward Street, but on his visit to her lodgings William Collingham paid the landlady 1s 6d for food and lodgings.*

It proved impossible to find any census entries that could categorically be assigned to this Caroline Skinner: a 36-year-old woman by this name was enumerated in Hastings working as a domestic servant but the ages are not congruent and there is no evidence in any of the other documentation to suggest she was employed as a servant.

As the correspondence and reports suggest, Caroline Skinner made her way back to Hastings where she intended to enter the workhouse. Hastings Workhouse creed registers record 45 admissions for her between 8 July 1877 and 15 February 1899.[263] *Periods in the workhouse varied in length between two nights and almost three months but the majority of stays lasted between three and four weeks.*[264] *Most of the entries show her trade as hawker and she is usually recorded as being Church of England but she is occasionally listed as a Roman Catholic.*

The name Caroline Skinner also appears in the local press. It is not possible to verify whether the woman mentioned in these reports is this Caroline Skinner, as the newspapers

[261] The Reverend Charles Samuel Chilver, curate of the Diocese of Brighton.

[262] Probably Sophia Thursby, born Holmschapel, Lancashire, c1841, daughter of William Thursby, formerly curate of Worsthorne, Lancashire.

[263] Creed registers recorded the inmate's religion but also act as an index to surnames when no other index to admissions survive.

[264] ESRO: HH 20/5-8.

do not record her age, but all of the entries coincide with times that she was not staying at Hastings Workhouse. The Sussex Agricultural Express recorded that a woman named Caroline Skinner pleaded guilty to being drunk and disorderly at New Shoreham on 17th June 1893.[265] *PC Bastable, who proved the case, stated that she was making a great noise and was being followed by a crowd of children. She was given one day's imprisonment. A Caroline Skinner appeared before Hastings magistrates after being found in a drunken and helpless state at West Marina. She asked the constable to take her somewhere and he conveyed her to the police station. Skinner was discharged with a caution.*[266] *One month later Skinner, described as a tramp, appeared before Eastbourne magistrates charged with drunkenness but was discharged after promising to leave the town.*

The year of her death is not known but a woman named Caroline Skinner, aged 62, died in Brighton in the March quarter of 1903 and this seems to be the most likely match.[267]

Letter from Caroline Skinner to Reverend Sir, 12 February 1872

I beg to take the liberty of thus writing to tell you I did not know what to do for the best. I could not get enough to take me up to where I wanted to go into rent amongst my own relations and I came on to Lewes to see if I could get back to my place.[268] I feel sure I could have done if it had not been for parties she had about her which made it unpleasant for her and myself too when I was there. I cannot get into anything and duly I feel so weak and badly I have scarce strength to get about. Will you be so kind as to be a friend to me? You was going to do something for me but owing to the weather I could not get to see you. I should turn you my sincere thanks if you could do a little for me. I want to come back and will go into the Union again. I have quite made up my mind to do that but I cannot walk there. I shall be better off than what I am now. I go about all day long, I scarce have anything in my lips the whole of the day to eat or drink. I am got down weak and low. Would you be so kind as to let me hear from you in a day or two? I do not have sufficient to keep my strength up. I would never trouble you again. Would you be so kind as to address to me the care of Mrs Seymour, 29 Edward Street, Brighton. I do assure to pay for lodgings [and] have had to put some of my own clothes away and I feel the cold so much. If I could but get my warm shawl out again may I entreat of you to be a friend to me? You did promise me something. If I cannot get amongst my own I will come into the Union again. My duty to you. I remain your ever humble servant, Caroline Skinner. I do not know what to do – I have nothing to help myself with I do go hungry all day long

265 Sussex Agricultural Express, 24 June 1893.

266 Sussex Agricultural Express, 21 May 1898.

267 Death of Caroline Skinner registered Q1 1903 Brighton 2b 168.

268 This is probably a reference to Hastings.

Letter to Miss Thursby from the Reverend C L Vaughan, rector of Christ Church, St John Villa, delivered by William Thursby, Ash Wednesday, [14] February 1872[269]
My dear Miss Thursby, I venture to ask you to be so kind as to send the enclosed 5s to the writer of the appeal which I also enclose. She appears to be at Mrs Seymour's, 29 Edward Street, Brighton. I do not like to send straight to that address for the poor thing may have been turned into the street by this time. I was away when her letter came – she is a weak creature in bad health and with a bad temper still I think meaning to do well. I can't help thinking the Union is the best place for her till better weather arrives. I have had a three-week holiday and found all well on my return. I trust your stay at Brighton has been satisfactory and that your father and mother are well. Mrs Vaughan sends her kind love. Very faithfully yours, C L Vaughan

Letter from Miss Thursby, 18 Brunswick Terrace, Hove, 15 February 1872
Miss Thursby presents her compliments to the secretary and hopes he will excuse her again troubling him. She has received the enclosed letters, Mr Vaughan is a clergyman at St Leonards who has requested her to give the 5s in stamps to Caroline Skinner who has applied to him for relief. She thinks it will be more satisfactory to hand the matter over to the Mendicity Society to make proper enquiries into the case. If she is recommended as a deserving person Miss Thursby will be happy to relieve her. The Reverend W Thursby (her father) has subscribed to the Society.
The agent to make early enquiries and if necessary to expend the 5s in such manner as he may deem most expedient submitting his report at next meeting, Orfeur Cavenagh

17 February 1872
Statement: Caroline Skinner would like to go back to Hastings and go in the workhouse.
Report: I paid Mrs Seymour 1s 6d for food and lodgings for this woman till Monday and then took her shawl out of pledge and paid her railway fare to Hastings. Altogether it came to 6s 9d. Miss Thursby paid the extra 1s 9d. Relieved by private person, Orfeur Cavenagh

75 HENRY SHAW, 53, 10 COLLEGE PLACE, BRIGHTON

In February 1872 letters, purportedly from Henry Shaw, were delivered to the Mendicity Society by George Ryder and Charles Gould. When approached by the charity Shaw denied sending them saying that he had never sought relief and refused to provide any further

[269] Charles Lyndhurst Vaughan was the perpetual curate of Christ Church with St John, St Leonards, formerly vicar of St Neot's, Cambridgeshire, 1854-1865.

details. The Brighton Daily News, who published anonymised reports of Mendicity Society applicants, stated that this was a case of mistaken identity.[270] *Henry Shaw was born in Ampthill, Bedfordshire, in about 1819 and was described on the census of 1871 as a retired draper living at 10 College Place with his wife Charlotte, three children and servant.*

The identity of the author of the letters was never established.

Letter from Henry Shaw, 10 College Place, St George's Road, Brighton, 16 February 1872 via Mr Gould, 12 Sussex Square
Sir, I beg to state I am the son of the late Mr David Shaw of this town. I am at present out of employment and my wife an inmate of the hospital suffering with cancer in her breast. I have four children depending on me. My knowing your benevolence has induced me to apply to you for some small assistance in my present distress for which I will be ever grateful. Hoping you will pardon the liberty I have taken. Believe me sir, your most humble servant Henry Shaw

Letter from Henry Shaw, 10 College Place, St George's Road, Brighton, undated, via Mr Ryder, 15 Portland Place
Sir, pardon the liberty I take in applying to you at this late hour. My being out of employment and my wife severely ill I must respectfully ask on behalf of my family some small assistance in my present distress. However small it may be I will be truly grateful. I am sir your most humble servant, Henry Shaw

19 February 1872
Statement: I have not sent to any one for relief and neither do I want any.
Report: I have seen Henry Shaw and he strongly denies having sent a letter to anyone for assistance and says neither does he want any assistance. His wife is not sick. I have seen Henry Shaw and find he is not the man that took the begging letter to Mr Ryder's. Some other person has made use of his name. I searched the tramps' lodging houses but could not find anyone answering the description. I took two men to Mr Ryder's but neither of them was the man. The report of the case to be made to the Chief Constable of police for his information and consideration, Orfeur Cavenagh

76 MARY HOWICK, 40, CHARWOMAN, 16 BRIGDEN STREET, BRIGHTON

Mary Ann Howick (née Godbold) was born in Framlingham, Suffolk, in about 1832 and married Henry Howick at St Nicholas, Brighton, on 6 March 1859 when both were living at 8 Frederick Gardens.[271] *Howick, a carpenter, was born in Easebourne in about 1821 and*

[270] ESRO: DB/B/77/154.
[271] ESRO: PAR 255/1/3/31.

married his first wife, Eliza Hersey or Hearsey, at Easebourne on 29 October 1842. Eliza's death was registered at Midhurst in the June quarter of 1849 but the 1851 census shows Henry Howick still living with other members of the Hersey family at Easbourne.
The couple and their three children were enumerated at 20 Frederick Gardens, Brighton, in 1861. The application form suggests that they moved to their next address, 16 Brigden Street, Brighton, in about 1865 and the 1871 census shows them there living with seven children. The oldest, William, was 15 and employed as a bricklayer's labourer. The second youngest, Kate, was two and was described on the census as 'crippled from birth'.
The Howick family were still living at 16 Brigden Street when their case was sent to the Mendicity Society by Mrs Treacher of 39 Buckingham Place in February 1872. They paid weekly rent of two shillings and were £3 in arrears. Henry Howick had been working for John Howick of 41 Waterloo Street, Hove, but had been out of work for five weeks due to sickness.[272] *His son, William Howick, earned seven shillings per week working as a labourer for Mr Thomas Holloway, builder, of 30 Brigden Street.*

The 1881 census shows Henry and Mary Ann Howick and four of their children sharing the property with five members of the Manning family. By 1891 the household consisted only of Henry, Mary Ann, their daughter, Florence, and a lodger. Mary Ann Howick's death was recorded in the June quarter of 1891 so must have occurred shortly after the taking of the census, which took place on 5th April. The 1901 census shows 16 Brigden Street occupied by Wyndham Howick, his wife Susan, their four children and his father Henry who was 81 and living on his own means. Henry Howick died in Hove in the December quarter of 1907 aged 86.[273]

20 February 1872
Statement: Mary Howick wants a little assistance till her husband gets better.
Report: I have made enquiries respecting this man and find he has been out of work five weeks. He is not a strong man only able to do light work. Mr Howick give him a good character. The wife occasionally gets a day's work. The oldest son's wages come to between 7s and 9s a week. Miss Treacher gave the wife a good character – that lady has relieved them several times. The home is in a passable state.
Referred to the clergyman of the district, Orfeur Cavenagh. I have seen the Reverend Mr Freeman and he will call and see them.[274] He is sorry to say he has known them a long time and has relieved them several times WC [William Collingham]. No further orders, Orfeur Cavenagh

[272] It is not known whether John Howick and Henry Howick were related. John Howick was born in Fernhurst, only a few miles from Easebourne, so there may have been a familial link.

[273] Death of Henry Howick registered Q4 1907 Steyning 2b 179.

[274] Reverend Allan Davidson Freeman of 30 Montpelier Road, curate of Preston with Hove and vice principal of Western College, Brighton.

77 ELIZA PAGE, 30, WASHERWOMAN, 58 CARLTON ROW, BRIGHTON

Eliza Page and her husband Richard lived at 58 Carlton Row with their sons William and Edward aged 10 years and seven weeks old respectively. They had lived at this address for a week when they applied directly to the charity by collecting a ticket from the society's office; they had previously been living at Brighton Workhouse. Richard Page, who is thought to have been baptised at St Nicolas, Brighton, on 31 January 1847, was enumerated at 43 Albion Street in 1851 and 23 Cavendish Place North in 1861 when he was aged 14 and working as a shoe black.[275] *At the time of Eliza Page's approach to the charity Richard Page was employed as a labourer but had been out of work for seven months. The family paid 1s 6d per week rent for one room and were not in arrears.*

20 February 1872
Statement: Eliza Page wants a little assistance till her husband gets work.
Report: I made enquiries respecting this man and find he has only come out of the workhouse a little more than a week since that he has applied to the parish and they have allowed outdoor relief for one week to enable him to get work which he denied having until I told him I had just come from the office: he then admitted it. I have known this man a long time, he never stops anywhere long. He has been convicted for felony. The home is in a destitute state.
Dismissed as undeserving, Orfeur Cavenagh

78 JANE ALCE, 35, WIFE OF A LABOURER, 23 HEREFORD STREET, BRIGHTON

Jane Alce (née Holman) was born in Bath in about 1837 but her application form states that she moved to Brighton in about 1853. In 1862 she married John Alce, a labourer from Lewes who was in born in about 1832.[276]
In 1861 the couple were enumerated at 51 Richmond Buildings and ten years later they were living at 6 Manchester Row. On census returns of 1861, 1871 and 1881 John Alce was described as a general labourer and Jane Alce's occupation is given as charwoman in every instance. At the time of her application to the Mendicity Society the couple lived at 23 Hereford Street with their six children, five of whom attended Dorset Street School. They paid weekly rent of four shillings for the entire house but were £1 in arrears despite John Alce's income of 10 shillings per week which, when he was fully employed, rose to 18 shillings per week.

The case was forwarded to the Mendicity Society by H S Chadwick of Belle Vue, and Miss Gathorne of 24 Upper Rock Gardens was supplied as a reference. The Alce family were enumerated at 90 Spa Street on the census of 1881 and John Alce's death was

[275] ESRO: PAR 255/1/2/14.
[276] John Alce marriage to Jane Holman registered Q2 1862 Brighton 2b 330.

registered in Brighton during the December quarter of 1885. The coroner's inquest into the death of Jane Alce recorded that she was found dead by her son John at 6.45am on 17 August 1907.[277] *The coroner's report described Jane Alce as the widow of John Alce, soap maker, living at 23 Essex Place with her daughter. It recorded that her son John had been at the house the previous evening and, seeing that his mother was feeling unwell, sent for Dr Frederick Relland Baker of 1 Dorset Gardens but he refused to come without an order from the parish. John took his mother a cup of tea the following morning but found she had died during the night. Jane Alce had suffered from chronic bronchitis for years but had not been attended to for four months. The coroner recorded a verdict of death by natural causes and stated that heart failure was the likely reason.*

21 February 1872
Statement: Jane Alce wants a little assistance as the money her husband earns is not enough to keep them.
Report: I have made enquiries respecting this family and find they have been receiving parish relief since last September until about a month ago at the rate of 9s per week. The man is at work now. His wages come to about 16s a week. He has been convicted for felony. The home is in a destitute state.
Dismissed as ineligible, Orfeur Cavenagh

28 April 1877
Mrs Alce, who now resides at 37 Cumberland Place, applied at the office on Thursday for two out-patient letters to the Sussex County Hospital for her daughters Sarah and Mary who are suffering from itch. Mr Witten of the Sloane Street Medical Mission Dispensary who is attending the children states that if the mother carried out his instructions the children would recover in the course of three or four days. WC [William Collingham]
Ineligible, R P Hooper

Application form damaged, c. 1880[278]
Mr Rumbold requests a report of this case. Alce has regular work. His wife goes out charring. Their eldest daughter is married. Jane is in service, the son John jobs about as a porter, Sarah is at home doing nothing. Mary attends Essex Street School, Esther is ill suffering from consumption for which she is attended by Mr E Witten, surgeon. George, aged three, suffers from water on the brain. The family have not troubled the parish since June last. WC [William Collingham]
Report to Mr Rumbold, R P Hooper

277 ESRO: COR 3/2/1907/49.

278 The corner of this application form is missing so the date has been lost but the 1881 census recorded George Alce's age as four which dates this entry to about 1880.

79 JAMES STEVENS, 82, DROVER, 8 SOMERSET STREET, BRIGHTON

James Stevens was born in Brighton in about 1790 and was the oldest of the applicants to the Mendicity Society referred to in this volume. He was enumerated on the 1851 census at 33 Lavender Street employed as a butcher and living with his wife Elizabeth, their daughter, grandson and a seemingly unrelated four-year-old boy called William Goodwin. Goodwin was still living with the family at 4 Paradise Street in 1861 when he was employed as an office boy. 1n 1861 James Stevens was working as a gardener but by 1871 he was described as a widower working as an agricultural labourer lodging at 16 Upper Bedford Street.

At the time of his application to the charity Stevens had been living at 8 Somerset Street for about four months and occupied one room for which he paid weekly rent of two shillings. He was not in arrears with rent payments but had been out of work for two months due to sickness. His case was forwarded to the Mendicity Society by Mrs Edgar of Royal Crescent.

22 February 1872
Statement: James Stevens would be thankful for a little assistance.
Report: I have made enquiries respecting this man and find he used to get his living as a drover for butchers but lately has not been able to do anything. He says he has not got long to live and did not want to trouble the parish authorities. He says when he first fell sick he had a pound or two and has met with a friend or two and so has managed to rub along. Mrs Johnston gave him a good character. The home is in a passable state.
Referred to poor law, Orfeur Cavenagh. NB the result of the response to be reported
This man says he won't trouble the parish. His son in London has sent a trifle and he will try and manage.
Referred to the clergyman of the district, Orfeur Cavenagh

80 WILLIAM MCCARTHY, 60, LABOURER, 79 EGREMONT STREET, BRIGHTON

The McCarthy's case was forwarded to the charity by George Dudley Ryder of 15 Portland Place. William McCarthy was born in Ireland in about 1812 but, according to information given on his application form, had been resident in Brighton since about 1842. McCarthy and his daughter Ellen, or Nelly McCarthy were enumerated on the 1871 census at 79 Egremont Street: they shared the address with a lodger named Jeremiah Crowley and a couple, possibly his son and daughter-in-law, named John and Catherine McCarthy who were 28 and 24 respectively.[279]

By the time of William McCarthy's application to the Mendicity Society in February he was still living with his 18-year-old daughter Ellen at 79 Egremont Street where they paid 2s 6d per week rent for the house. McCarthy had been employed by the town surveyor as a labourer but he had been out of work for seven months. Ellen McCarthy hawked goods for a living and on average earned 2s 6d per week.

William's wife, Johanna, was admitted to the Sussex County Lunatic Asylum on 5 November 1859 in a state of mania but in good physical health.[280] *She had been examined at Brighton Workhouse by George Geere, surgeon, of 21 Broad Street, who stated that she 'had the appearance of an insane person. Has delusions. Thinks she has been trained to be a priest. Does no work, talks incessantly. Has been violent.' Geere went on to state that McCarthy 'Dresses strangely. Washes her clothes in the gutter and hangs them on the lamp post. Has been violent and has threatened to destroy her children.' She remained in the asylum until her death which was recorded on 27 June 1878 at 7.30pm. The cause of death was given as morbus cordis.*[281]

22 February 1872
Statement: William McCarthy wants a little assistance till he gets work. He thinks if Ellen had a licence to hawk they would get their own living.
Report: I made enquiries respecting this man and find he used to work for the parish authorities. His wife is in Haywards Heath asylum. The daughter sells water cress and fish. Canon Rymer gave him a good character. This man denied having relief from the parish but on enquiry I find he is having relief to the value of 2s 6d per week. The home is in a destitute state.
Further enquiry, Orfeur Cavenagh

This man said he did not understand what I meant about relief from the parish and says if his daughter had a licence to sell flowers he thinks they could get their own living
Dismissed, undeserving, R P Hooper

81 JANE PARKER, 39, WIFE OF A LABOURER, 7 BREAD STREET, BRIGHTON

Frederick Parker of 31 Edward Street married Jane Poplar of 84 Nottingham Street at St Nicholas, Brighton, on 23 December 1850.[282] *Both were born in Brighton, Frederick in*

[279] John McCarthy died in the September quarter of 1872 and it is quite probable that his widow, Catherine McCarthy, is the 'widow named McCarthy' referred to in Edward Murray's application to the Charity Organisation Society in September 1877 (see application 105).

[280] ESRO: HC 24/272.

[281] Heart disease.

[282] ESRO: PAR 255/1/3/22.

about 1831 and Jane in about 1833. They were enumerated at 16 Orange Row on the 1851 census but were living at 30 Sun Street with three children in 1861. The 1871 census shows the Parkers living at 15 Upper Gardner Street with seven children and Jane Parker's parents recorded as John Poplett (rather than Poplar), a 70-year-old coffee seller, and his wife Jane Poplett.

Their case was forwarded to the Mendicity Society by the Reverend Robert Poole Hooper, the charity's chairman, when the family found themselves a week's rent in arrears. Frederick and Jane Parker and their six children shared two downstairs rooms for which they paid 2s 6d. Frederick Parker was employed as a labourer on either Church Street or Ship Street and was paid 18 shillings per week.[283] *Two of his daughters were in service but their income was not recorded.*

21 February 1872
Statement: If my husband has done wrong I am sorry for it.
Report: I have made enquiries respecting this man and find he has been working for the parish authorities until about a fortnight ago. Since that he has worked at the new houses at the bottom of Church Street. His wages last week came to about 18 shillings. He is of intemperate habits. Miss Cann, 6 Codrington Place, the District Visitor, visited them on Monday and knows they are not in distress. The home is in a passable state.
Dismissed as undeserving, Orfeur Cavenagh

Letter written by Jane Parker, c1872
Mam, hoping you will pardon the liberty that I take in writing to you but I have been out of work a long time and you know mam I have a large family. Mam I have a job to do to repair a copper but mam I have no bricks or mortar to do it with mam. If you would kindly lend me 2s 6d until tomorrow night I will [be] sure and bring it back again mam. I remain your obedient servant, J Parker, 5 Bread Street

82 WILLIAM LEWRY, 72, LABOURER, 16 PARK CRESCENT ROAD, BRIGHTON

William Lewry was born in Maresfield in about 1800 and married Eliza Parris in Buxted on 17 March 1829.[284] *In 1851 the couple were enumerated at 6 Francis Street, Brighton, where they lived with their three daughters who were born in Maresfield and Buxted between about 1837 and 1846. William was recorded as a labourer and Eliza a laundress. The death of an Eliza Lewry was recorded in Brighton in the June quarter of 1860.*[285]

283 The application form records the last employer as 'Church Street' and the employer's address as 'Ship Street'.
284 ESRO: PAR 286/1/3/1.
285 Death of Eliza Lewry registered Q2 1860 Brighton 2b 122.

Contrary to the information he gave to enumerators in 1851, Lewry stated on his Mendicity Society application form that he moved to Brighton in about 1832. Recently he had been living at 16 Park Crescent Road, where he occupied a single room: previously he had been resident at St Mary Magdalene Street. He paid rent of two shillings per week and was not in arrears.

Lewry was enumerated living with his daughter Emma Jones, her husband and four grandchildren at 41 Cobden Road on the 1881 census. He died in Brighton in the December quarter of 1883.[286]

22 February 1872

Statement: William Lewry would be thankful for a little assistance.

Report: I have made enquiries respecting this man and find he is a respectable man. He used to have a greengrocer's shop in Gloucester Road but lately has been gardening or anything he can get to do. Mr Beal has known this man a long time and says he is a very respectable man. The house is in a passable state and apparently the applicant is not in any want.

Dismissed, ineligible, Orfeur Cavenagh

83 CATHERINE BATTS, 20, WASHER, 30 QUEBEC STREET, BRIGHTON

Catherine Batts had been living in Brighton for only a week when she applied to the Mendicity Society. She was born in Hove and had previously been an inmate of Steyning Workhouse but latterly occupied one upstairs room at 30 Quebec Street for which she paid 2s 6d per week rent. Batts had been working as a washer woman for Mrs Harding of Portslade but had been short of work for three months. Despite this she owed no rent.

Catherine Batts married Henry Richardson, a bricklayer, on 22 November 1879 at Hove, St Andrew.[287] *They were enumerated at 62 Clarendon Road, Hove, on the 1881 census with two children and, ten years later, at 15 Westbourne Street, Hove, now with five children.*

23 February 1872

Statement: Catherine Batts wants a little assistance till Monday when she has got work to go to at Watts Laundry.[288]

Report: I have made enquiries respecting this woman's statement and find it's correct that she has got work to go to on Monday. The home is in a destitute state.

Relieved by grant, 2s 6d, Orfeur Cavenagh

[286] Death of William Lewry registered Q4 1883 Brighton 2b 163.

[287] ESRO: PAR 386/1/3/9.

[288] Goldsmid Road, Hove.

84 MARIA CARTER, 57, NEEDLEWOMAN, 13 MOUNT STREET, BRIGHTON

Maria Carter lived with her three sons at 13 Mount Street: her husband, of whom nothing is known, died at some point before 1861 when the Carter family were enumerated at 187 Eastern Road. Maria Carter was born in Brighton in about 1813 and had been living at Mount Street for 11 years at the time of her application to the Mendicity Society in February 1872. She shared the house with her sons George, a labourer who was short of work but earning 1s 6d a week working for Mr Worsley of West Street; Oliver, a photographer who was not working due to ill health; and James, a clerk at the New Laundry, Lewes Road, who earned ten shillings per week. They paid 3s 6d per week rent for the house and were one week's rent in arrears. George White, the chief constable, forwarded the family's case to the charity after receiving copies of the testimonials shown below.

Maria Carter applied again to the Charity Organisation Society in September 1886 when she was living at 57 Hereford Street.

Testimonials written by James Austen, 6 Egremont Place, Brighton, c. 1872
Madam, the bearer, Maria Carter, is in great distress at the present time having to support her two sons who are out of employment. I's [I am] compelled to appeal to a few benevolent ladies and gentlemen. Should you feel disposed to aid her in her troubles I can answer for the genuineness of this case. Yours obediently, James Austen

Madam, the bearer, Mrs Carter, wishing me to testify as to her character. I can only say I have known her for several years to be a hard-working person and is in great distress at the present time. Yours obediently, James Austen

24 February 1872
Statement: Maria Carter wants a little assistance as one of her sons is out of work and one sick. The other only gets 10s a week.
Report: I have made enquiries respecting this family and find the woman does a little needle work and looks after children for women that go out to work. The oldest son goes out with newspapers once a week for which he gets 18 pence. The next has been sick for some time. The next is a clerk at the New Laundry, his wages is ten shillings per week. The two letters was sent to the police office for investigation and Mr White sent Detective Gibbs to make the enquiry and then sent the letter to me. The house is in a passable state.
Consideration deferred pending the result of Dr Geere's visit, Orfeur Cavenagh

This man has received an order for the workhouse and refused to go saying he is a great deal better and has met with a friend and thinks he shall have work in a few days. Dr Geere says this case is not bad enough for the hospital.[289]
Relieved by grant, Orfeur Cavenagh. NB 2s 6d for the purchase of food for 2nd son

24 September 1886
Mrs Carter applied at the office on Thursday for assistance to tide her over till she can obtain more needle work. She is getting very infirm besides which she is hard of hearing and would doubtless be far better off in the parish infirmary. Her two eldest sons are dead and the youngest lost his situation at the laundry four months ago in consequence of his drinking habits. Since then he has had no regular employment and they are now in a most destitute condition. WC [William Collingham]
Referred to parish, R P Hooper

85 SARAH BERTIE, 63, NEEDLEWOMAN, 28 CARLTON STREET, BRIGHTON

Sarah Bertie's case was forwarded to the Mendicity Society by Dr Geere of 21 Broad Street, Brighton. Bertie stated on the application form that her place of birth was Brighton but that she had only been living in the parish for the last twelve months. She had been at her present address for the duration of that period. Rather confusingly she gave her previous address as 27 Nelson Place which is also in Brighton. She occupied one downstairs room for which she paid two shillings per week rent but, at the time of the application, was 12 shillings in arrears.

Bertie's late husband is not mentioned by name but the form does state that she was widowed about nine years previously and the death of Thomas Bertie was recorded at Brighton in the September quarter of 1864. The marriage of Thomas Bertie and Sarah Ann Upton took place at St Nicholas, Brighton on 6 November 1837.[290]

26 February 1872
Statement: Sarah Bertie if I could get to London I have a sister there and I believe I could get plenty of work.
Report: I have made enquiries respecting this woman and find she has been a widow about nine years. Her husband was a porter at the railway station. She says she has some relations in London and believes she could get plenty of work there. Dr Geere says he thinks the committee would not only be doing good to

[289] This seems to refer to Oliver Carter, Maria Carter's second son who had experienced a period of ill health.
[290] ESRO: PAR 255/1/3/9.

forward this woman to London but be doing good to the town. I am informed she is a little given to drink. The home is in a passable state.
Referred for further enquiry, R P Hooper. In the event of the secretary being satisfied that the sister is willing to receive Sarah Bertie he is authorised to pay her fare (3rd class) to London

18 December 1872
Further information: this person went to Miss Craven, 1 St Peter's Place on Wednesday begging and Miss C, not knowing her, gave her an investigation ticket. Upon enquiry I find that since the case was before the committee in February last, applicant has been in the [work]house for a long time but left three weeks ago and since that she has been lodging at tramps' lodging houses. She has no means of getting a living. WC [William Collingham]
Undeserving, R P Hooper, chairman

86 WILLIAM MEAGER (ALSO GIVEN AS MEAGHER), 62, HAWKER, 3 LAVENDER STREET, BRIGHTON

William Meager seems to have left few firm traces of his life in archival records. He was born in about 1810 at Barming, Kent. A 37-year-old man of this name, also born in Barming, was enumerated on the census of 1851 at Ightham, Kent. He was employed as an agricultural labourer and was married to Elizabeth Meager.

According to the statement on his application form Meager was unmarried (not widowed), moved to Brighton in 1868 and had previously lived at 17 Spa Street, but was not enumerated at that address on the 1871 census. He paid 1s 9d for his single upstairs room.

Meager applied to the charity for a second time in March 1874 after a spell in the workhouse. There is no suggestion in this report that he was in any way ill but a hawker named William Meager aged about 62 and formerly of Brighton Workhouse was admitted to the Sussex County Lunatic Asylum on 27 May 1874.[291] *The asylum's reception papers describe him as a widower whereas the Mendicity Society report records him as single but in all other respects the descriptions seem to match. When examined by the medical orderly David Richards, Meager stated that he had been poisoned by eating peas pudding. He was reported to be always talking, was sleepless and required constant restraint. No next of kin was known and he was considered suicidal but was discharged on 21 October 1875 and was thought to be relieved of his symptoms.*

Meager claims to have married an Ellen Smith at Staplehurst, Kent, but no contemporary record of the marriage could be found. He also refers to a relationship with a woman named either Mary Ann or Emma Smith. A man named William Meagher married a woman named Emma Smith at Brighton in the December quarter of 1888.

[291] ESRO: HC 24/2460.

However, there was no mention of her living with Meager in 1891 when he was enumerated at 14 Manchester Row, lodging with Benjamin Whittington and his family.

26 February 1872
Statement: I have not been able to get five shillings to obtain a new license. I have heard this society has assisted several to get theirs.
Report: I have made enquiries respecting this man and find he is living with some woman as his wife. This man gets his living selling flowers and in the summer on the beach selling fruit. In the summer there is so many complaints of hawkers on the beach the chief constable is obliged to have two special constables there to look after them. This man is one of the worst of them. The home is in a destitute state.
Dismissed, undeserving, R P Hooper

1 February 1873
Miss Butler of Lee House forwarded the annexed letter to the office and requested a report of the case. The above report sent.

Letter from Miss Butler, Lee House [12 Dyke Road], Brighton, 1 February [1873]
Miss Butler presents her compliments to the secretary and begs to know whether the man Meager is a case to be relieved. He lives quite out of Miss Butler's beat but she knows the man by sight and he applies for help.

4 March 1874
This man, who now lodges at the Telegraph beer house, brought in an investigation ticket to the office on Wednesday which was given to him by the Reverend A A Morgan and requested assistance to set him up as a fish hawker to help him over until the fruit season commences.[292] Some time ago he went about the town asking for assistance and gave Mr White, the chief constable's name, as a reference and since then he has been in the workhouse which he left on Tuesday last. He and the woman he once lived with had a quarrel and separated some time ago. WC [William Collingham]
Undeserving, R P Hooper

Letter from the Reverend G F Reyner DD, Staplehurst Rectory, Kent, to Colonel Cuthbert Barlow, Charity Organisation Society, Brighton, 23 January 1885
Dear Sir, I have searched the marriage registers of this parish from 1870 to the present time without finding therein the marriage of William Meagher and Ellen Smith. Believe me, very truly yours George F Reyner

[292] Reverend Aaron Augustus Morgan, vicar of St John's, Carlton Hill.

Report from the Kensington Committee for Organizing Charitable Relief and Mendicity, 27 January 1885
Dear Sir, in November 1876 we were first asked to inquire about this case. The man's age was given as 63 and his wife, Mary Ann, as 64. They said they had a son and two daughters in India. They were living at a common lodging house at Notting Hill and the old man sold bird seed (groundsel) about the streets probably as an excuse for begging. He said he was known to Mr George Hudson farmer at Engleton near Brighton. They had not lived many months at Notting Hill (had previously tramped about the country) and few persons knew them but one or two for whom the wife had done a little work spoke favourably of her. In February 1879, the wife applied here for her rent to be paid. She said her husband had fallen down on the previous Christmas Eve and broken his leg and was then in hospital. She complained of want of food but when advised to go to the workhouse she said she would do without that. So far as we could learn they appeared to carrying on a regular system of house to house begging. The wife this time gave her Christian name as Emma. With reference to your enquiry we have been to 10 Martin Street. The landlady states she has known them some years by their living there from time to time – the last was four months ago. She never heard of the name Smith, always thought the woman's name was Meager. She says they got their living by begging in the streets. They were sober and paid their way. Applicants have frequently been to the relieving officer for medical orders. Yours faithfully, R J Andrews for honorary secretary

21 January 1885
Mrs Tindal Robertson requests a report of this case. Meagher, and the woman Smith with whom he still lives, left Brighton in 1874 and came here from Notting Hill early last spring. According to the man's statement he slipped down in London four years ago and injured his ankle since which time he has walked on crutches and carried his foot in a sling. During the summer he sold cigar lights on the beach. Lately he has sold cabbage nets and no doubt carries his foot in a sling to excite sympathy. Colonel Barlow wrote to the Kensington committee to ascertain what they were doing at Notting Hill and has received a reply to the effect that they appeared to carry on a regular system of house to house begging. The Colonel also wrote to Staplehurst where they say that they were married about eight years ago and has received an answer from the Reverend G F Reyner to the effect that he has searched the marriage registers of the parish from 1870 to the present time but can find no record of the pact. WC [William Collingham]
Report to Mrs Tindal Robertson, F Y Toms, R[oyal] N[avy]

87 ELLEN HILTON, 24, WIFE OF A CHAIR BOTTOMER, 38 THOMAS STREET, BRIGHTON

At the time of Ellen Hilton's application to the Mendicity Society she had been living in Brighton for about a month with her husband Francis and her infant daughter, Rose. They occupied one first floor room for which they paid weekly rent of 3s 6d. The Hiltons owed no rent but Francis Hilton had been sick and unable to work for two days. The family had moved to Brighton from Kingston upon Thames in January 1872.

Francis Hilton was born in Guildford, Surrey, in about 1847; Ellen was recorded on different census returns as being born either in Chelsea, Middlesex, or Reading, Berkshire in about 1848. The 1911 census records that the couple had had 10 children of whom seven were still living at that time, and the children's places of birth on earlier census returns give an insight into their peripatetic life during the 1870s and 1880s. Their son Thomas was born in Brighton in 1873 but subsequent children were born in Godstone, Walton on the Hill and Sunbury on Thames before moving to Portslade in about 1888 when Frank Hilton was born.

The family were enumerated at 20 Crown Road, Portslade, in 1891 when Francis was described as a basket maker. In 1901 Francis was making his living hawking plants and flowers and the family were living at 43 Old Shoreham Road, Portslade. In 1911 Francis was again recorded as a basket maker, now living with Ellen at 83 Trafalgar Road, Portslade. Francis Hilton's death was recorded in the June quarter of 1911.[293]

28 February 1872
Statement: Ellen Hilton wants a little assistance as her husband is sick.
Report: I have made enquiries respecting this man and find he is a chair bottomer. He has been sick two days from a cold. From enquiries made I find a chair bottomer earns from 2s 6d to 3s 6d per day when at work. When I visited the home they were providing a good supper. The home is in a passable state. The time out of work too short to admit of relief being granted. Dismissed as ineligible, Orfeur Cavenagh

88 JOHN BUTLAND, 11, 26 NELSON ROW, BRIGHTON

John Butland's case was forwarded to the Mendicity Society by Christopher Pierpoint, grocer, of 89 Richmond Street, Brighton. The application form does not include a statement from Butland and the charity agent's report seems to be reported speech rather than transcribed from a formal interview and this is perhaps why the information supplied seems to be vague. Despite the paucity of information on John Butland's application it has

[293] Death of Francis Hilton registered Q2 1911 Steyning 2b 175.

been possible to piece together an outline of the family's history as his father, William Butland, applied to the Mendicity Society on 15 May 1872.[294]

John Butland was born in at Upton cum Chalvey, Buckinghamshire in late 1860 or early 1861 and was enumerated, aged four months, with his parents and older sister Louisa in that parish on the census of 1861. William Butland's application form states that the family arrived in Brighton in about November 1871. They lived at 26 Nelson Row from at least March to the end of April 1872 when, according to William Butland's statement, they moved to 26 Chesterfield Street.

William Butland's application to the charity resulted in the family moving to Bath in November 1872.

1 March 1872
Report: this boy has been going about begging for some time saying his father and mother were both ill in bed and that there was seven in [the] family and that they were all starving. His father says he cannot do anything with him and says he was locked up in Reading for the same thing. His father says he has tried to get him sent to some school but cannot succeed. Mr Pierpoint, 89 Richmond Street, will prosecute.
Mr Pierpoint to be requested to prosecute, Orfeur Cavenagh

89 WILLIAM STONE, 81, HAWKER, 24 THOMAS STREET, BRIGHTON

William Stone was born at sea in about 1791. The 1861 census shows the couple at 33 Thomas Street with their sons John born in Dallington in about 1823 and Richard born in Bexhill in about 1835.

On his application for relief Stone stated that he had lived with his wife, Susan, and son, John, at 24 Thomas Street for 16 years. Susan was born in Sevenoaks, Kent, and the form states they had previously lived at Crowbur [probably Crowborough]. They paid weekly rent of 3s 6d for the whole house and were not in arrears with payments. William earned two shillings per week and his son John earned three shillings per week making pegs.

William Stone's death, age 83, was registered at Brighton in the December quarter of 1873.[295]

2 March 1872
Statement: William Stone would be thankful for a little assistance.
Report: I have made enquiries respecting this family and find the man is a hawker and stands in St James' Street at the corner of Broad Street. He says he has stood there for sixteen years. I have no doubt this man gets a good deal given him one time and the other. The wife is not able to work, the son is a

[294] Case number 175.
[295] Death of William Stone registered Q4 1873 Brighton 2b 139.

clothes peg maker. Between them they get a passable living. Mr Toye, the scripture reader, says they are a respectable family and he thinks they do not require relief at present. The home is in a passable state and not in want at present.
Dismissed as ineligible, Orfeur Cavenagh

90 FREDERICK GOLDSMITH, 49, PORTER, 27 GEORGE STREET GARDENS, BRIGHTON

Frederick Goldsmith was enumerated at 8a Sillwood Street, Brighton, on the census of 1851. He was unmarried, living with his brother and employed as a servant. Goldsmith was baptised at St Nicholas, Brighton on 7 January 1824[296] *and married Isabella Morganti (née Lashford) at the same church on 30 March 1863.*[297] *She was born in Brighton in about 1818 and had previously been married to Petric Morganti of Milan. By 1871 Goldsmith was lodging with the Barnard family at 27 George Street Gardens but he was not enumerated with his wife, who was working as a servant at 29 Dorset Gardens. At the time of their application to the Mendicity Society the couple were paying two shillings weekly rent for their second-floor room on which they owed no rent. Their case was forwarded to the charity by Miss Shouldham of 36 Norfolk Road. Isabella earned three shillings a week charring and although Goldsmith had been working for Mr Nunn of the Castle Inn, Castle Street, illness had kept him off work for 12 months. He was admitted to the Sussex County Hospital on 20 September 1871 with an ulcerated leg and was treated there for 24 weeks: he was discharged on 21 February 1872.*[298] *Goldsmith's treatment was recommended by clergyman John Babington of 10 Norfolk Terrace and sureties for his burial were given by his wife, Isabella. The hospital register stated that he had been suffering with this condition for 16 years before his admission but he was considered cured on his discharge.*

Frederick Goldsmith died in the December quarter of 1875 but Isabella Goldsmith was enumerated at 26 Warleigh Road, Brighton, on the census of 1881 where she lived with her daughter from her first marriage Ellen Morganti and earning her living as a nurse.[299] *She died, aged 64, in the December quarter of 1881.*[300]

4 March 1872
Statement: Frederick Goldsmith would be thankful for a little assistance.
Report: I have made enquiries respecting this man and find he has been in the hospital for 22 weeks with abscesses in his legs. He has been out about nine

[296] ESRO: PAR 255/1/2/4.
[297] ESRO: PAR 255/1/3/36.
[298] ESRO: HB 35/3/1871/12277.
[299] Death of Frederick Goldsmith registered Q4 1875 Brighton 2b 124.
[300] Death of Isabella Goldsmith registered Q4 1881 Brighton 2b 144.

days, he is not able to work now. I have seen Mrs Watkins: she gave him a good character and says he worked for them [for] ten years. I have seen Mrs Goldsmith – his brother's widow that keeps the York Arms Inn, Sillwood Street. She has relieved him several times and says he ought to go in the infirmary where I think would be far the best place for him. He has had no regular work for this last 12 months. He applied to the parish authorities but refused to go in the workhouse. The wife occasionally gets a day's work. The home is in a passable state.
Referred to local charity, Orfeur Cavenagh. NB The applicant to apply to the chaplain of the hospital by whom he will be relieved from the Samaritan Fund to be warned with reference to his omission to mention that he had received 3s

91 CHARLOTTE LEIGH, 47, NO OCCUPATION, 22 CROWN STREET, BRIGHTON

Charlotte Forsyth Leigh was born in London on 24 July 1823 and baptised on 2 September 1823 at St Mildred's, Poultry, London.[301] *Her father, Thomas Leigh, married Anna Maria Rowson at Prescot, Lancashire, in September 1812 and subsequently established a solicitor's practice in London.*[302] *Anna Maria Leigh died in Wandsworth, Surrey, in the June quarter of 1843.*[303] *The 1851 census shows Thomas Leigh, who was born in Lymm, Cheshire, living with his daughters Emily and Henrietta at Tulse Hill, Brixton, Surrey. By 1861 he was living at 6 Pembroke Villas, Richmond, with his new wife Martha.*

Charlotte Leigh moved to Brighton in about 1863. At the time of her application to the Mendicity Society she had been living in one room at 22 Crown Street for three weeks. She paid four shillings per week rent and owed nothing but was not in employment. Unusually, her application was dealt with by General Orfeur Cavenagh who usually signed cases off rather than dealing directly with them. This may have been due to Charlotte Leigh's social standing or perhaps her involvement with Lady Elizabeth Abinger, who was a wealthy and probably influential resident of Brighton; when Lady Abinger died on 13 October 1887 her personal estate was valued at £40,682.[304]

It is not known whether Charlotte Leigh ever found the employment she sought but she died at 31 Dean Street, Brighton, on 6 February 1877 leaving personal effects under £300.[305] *Her burial took place at the Parochial Cemetery, Brighton, and was carried out by Attree and Kent at a cost of £16 5s 2d.*[306] *Her father had died aged 83 at 4 Bushey Hill*

[301] Ancestry.com England, select births and christenings 1538-1975.
[302] Lancaster Gazette, 19 September 1812.
[303] Death of Anna Maria Leigh registered Q2 1843 Wandsworth 4 368.
[304] England and Wales National Probate Calendar (index of wills and administrations).
[305] England and Wales National Probate Calendar (index of wills and administrations).
[306] ESRO: ACC 8372/44.

Terrace, Peckham, Surrey, on 22 March 1873, leaving effects of under £400 to his widow Martha.[307]

Letter from Charlotte Leigh, 60 Dyke Road, Brighton, to Lady Abinger, West Cliff House, 142 Kings Road, 29 December [1871]
To Lady Abinger, I trust your ladyship will kindly excuse the very great liberty which I feel I am taking in writing these few lines but, having heard so much of your great kindness, I venture to bring before your notice the very painful position in which I am now placed as my father after having brought me up to every comfort, indeed I may say to luxury, has now refused to support me any longer. My father is 82 years of age [and] has married a second time. He gives no reason but only says he is too poor to allow me any support for the future so that I must now earn my daily bread – though he says he is too poor to support me he is surrounded with every comfort himself and even paying for a house full of warehoused furniture besides the one he now lives in and I have given him no cause of offence. I take the liberty of enclosing one of my papers to your ladyship and should you know of any occupation likely to suit me I should feel most truly grateful. I am in a most painful state of anxiety which must be my excuse for addressing your ladyship and I remain yours respectfully, Charlotte Leigh

Printed handbill produced by Charlotte Leigh, [1871]
A lady (the daughter of a solicitor), now entirely dependent on herself for support is very anxious to meet with some occupation either as a companion to a lady or any other occupation of any kind. Address Y Z, Miss Harman's Library, Sillwood Street, Brighton

Letter from Robert Poole Hooper, 29 Cambridge Road, Hove, to the committee of the Mendicity Society [Camberwell], 31 January 1872
Care of Miss Leigh, referred to Society by Lady Abinger. Gentlemen, I received Miss Leigh's address from Mr Henty yesterday and saw her this morning – also some of the persons whose names she gave me as references. She is the daughter of Thomas Leigh esq, 4 Bushey Hill Terrace, Peckham Road, Camberwell (formerly a solicitor). Her father appears to have allowed his three daughters who left their home on his second marriage, the sum of £100 a year each. This was reduced to £70 in Miss Leigh's case. She is living on a small loan granted her by Messrs Hale, Lloyd and Co Union Bank on the security of her grandfather's will. Her father will not allow her the interest of the few hundreds she will eventually inherit from this source and the capital will soon be dissipated in loans. She has lived in Brighton for many years and has relations who are well

[307] England and Wales National Probate Calendar (index of wills and administrations).

off. I think it a case requiring investigation. I have an impression that there is something yet to be explained and if you will defer coming to a conclusion respecting it till Saturday when I hope to attend the committee I think it will be as well. ~~Case of Mrs Nash: I have spoken to Messrs Jenner about her – they have to vacate… have an opportunity of giving her employment.~~ I am faithfully, R P Hooper

Letter from Charlotte Leigh, 22 Crown Street, Brighton, to the Mendicity Society, 2 March [1872]
Miss Leigh begs to inform the gentleman who called upon her at 17 Upper Market Street some weeks since that she has removed to the above address. Miss Leigh was named to the Society by Lady Abinger – Miss Leigh has been endeavouring in every way to meet with some occupation but cannot do so. Miss Leigh is very greatly in need of it.
Miss Leigh to be requested to wait on the magistrate and state her case on Tuesday morning
Committed the magistrate having no power to interfere

Letter from C J Ribton-Turner, Society for Organising Charitable Relief and Repressing Mendicity, London, to General Orfeur Cavenagh, 2 March 1872
My dear General, I have received the following reply from Camberwell, 'With respect to the case referred to you from Brighton I forwarded it (immediately upon my receiving it) to Mr Fleming in whose parish the gentleman referred to resided – I have seen Mr Fleming this morning and he told me that he had delayed the matter not quite knowing how to deal with it but upon my suggestion he is now going to call himself and will afterwards write to you, Pitt Cobbett'.
Yours truly
C J Ribton Turner

4 March 1872
Statement: I am in great distress – what to do I don't know.
Report: Application made to Camberwell to ascertain whether the father will assist pending the receipt of a reply a grant of 5s authorised. The charity agent waited on Miss Leigh who stated that she was in great distress but she appeared to have the means of obtaining liquor as a glass of porter was on the table Consideration referred, Orfeur Cavenagh. Referred to Poor Law, Orfeur Cavenagh. NB Mr Hooper to be requested kindly to communicate the purport of the decision as well as of her father's statement to Miss Leigh. The result of the enquiry to be communicated to Lady Abinger

Letter from William Thurnall, Camberwell Committee of the Society for Organising Charitable Relief and Repressing Mendicity to R P Hooper, 5 March 1872
Sir, with reference to C Leigh I beg to state that I have called upon her father T Leigh esq of 4 Bushey Hill Terrace, Peckham Road, Camberwell, who is very infirm and he states that his daughter has property in reversion. He allowed her, as long as he able, a sufficient sum to live on but she has no cause to apply for any assistance. He forewarned her years ago that she ought to seek for some employment. As to her statement of his having warehoused furniture he states that that is untrue. He states that he is living in small apartments. Yours obediently, W Thurnall, agent

Letter from C J Ribton-Turner, Society for Organising Charitable Relief and Repressing Mendicity, London, to R P Hooper, 6 March 1872
Dear Sir, I sent you a report in the care of Miss Leigh and am sorry that it was not sent in earlier. Camberwell has only recently joined us and therefore I know very little of the working of the committee. You would be doing an act of kindness if you jogged the memory of any committee who did not give a reply within a reasonable period. I would venture to suggest that you should (if you have not already done so or if the advice does not come too late) ascertain from Miss Leigh her previous address during the last few years (say 3 or 5) and inquire at each of them as to what is known of her and also to ascertain what relations she has alive and where they live with a view to see whether any application to them would be likely to be of use. In great haste, yours faithfully C J Ribton-Turner

Letter from R P Hooper to Mr Henty, 7 March 1872
Dear Sir, I enclose letters received by this morning's post relative to the case of Charlotte Leigh. In haste, yours truly R P Hooper

92A CAROLINE MILES, 27, DRESSMAKER, 23 SCOTLAND STREET, BRIGHTON

Caroline Jane Miles was born in Brighton in about 1845. On the census of 1871 she was enumerated at 30 Over Street living with her sister Clarissa, also a dressmaker; Clarissa's six-year-old daughter Mary; and their widowed mother, E Miles, who was born in Maidstone, Kent in about 1802.

The charity's application form states that when Caroline Miles first applied to the Mendicity Society in March 1872 the family, now without the mother, were previously living at 7 Hanover Terrace but had been renting one room at 23 Scotland Street for about a month. They paid weekly rent of 1s 6d but were 3 shillings in arrears.

The Miles sisters continued to lead a fairly peripatetic lifestyle and according to subsequent letters and applications to the Mendicity Society they also lived at Nelson

Street, St Martin's Place, Meeting House Lane, Hanover Terrace, Oxford Place and Lewes Road. In 1881 they were lodging with the Souther family at 42 Franklin Street.
Miles was a regular author of begging letters and in these lengthy and barely legible missives she regularly claimed a family link to the brewer Henry Hallett. One letter was sent to Hallett suggesting that the claim had substance but the only family member mentioned in Miles' admission to the Sussex County Lunatic Asylum on 11 June 1874 was her sister, Clarisa Miles.[308] *Caroline Miles' reception papers stated that she was living at 41 St Martin's Place and earned a living as a needlewoman. She had been suffering with mania for two weeks and on admission stated to Dr David Richards, the asylum's surgeon, that 'she wishes all persons and doctors and everyone to go to hell. That she deals trade with the devil. Is violent, destroys furniture, tears her clothing, is very abusive and violent in her language and requires constant restraint.' She recovered and and was discharged on 23 December 1874.*

Miles continued to write begging letters until at least 1887; her death was registered in Brighton in the September quarter of 1888.

4 March 1872
Statement: Caroline Miles would like to go to Tunbridge Wells where she believes she could obtain plenty of work.
Report: I have made enquiries respecting this party and find they are regular imposters. This case was before the committee [on] December 30th 1871 when they sent a letter to the Reverend Hooper, 29 Cambridge Road, they were relieved with 2s 6d which I spent on food and by order of the committee I cautioned them that if they were found sending begging letters again they would be taken before the magistrates. They are well known to Reverend Mr Morgan, Mr Hallett, brewer, and several other gentlemen where they are continually sending begging letters. They say if they could get to Tunbridge Wells they could get plenty of work. I have no doubt if they were sent they would be back again in a week or two. The home is in a destitute state. Mr Tamplin was very pleased I called to let him know their character.
Dismissed as undeserving, Orfeur Cavenagh

Letter from Caroline Miles, 7 Hanover Terrace, Brighton, c. 1872
Sir, I beg you will pardon this letter to you for I am very thankful for the assistance you have given us we must have died from exhaustions if we had not had it but nothing could be falser than the statement that I earn a living by begging letters. I always work for what I have but at holiday times we never have any work and our clothes now is not good enough to work at shops. I have been obliged to part with the best of it to save myself from dying of starvation when I am ill for the parochial office will never help us even for one week

308 ESRO: HC 24/2474.

though my father paid rates for many years and we have no relations but the Halletts in Brighton and he never helps unless he is made ashamed of it by others writing to him but I thought if you would be so kind as to help me get to Tunbridge Wells I might get something from my relations there some clothes which we need so much. I trust you will pardon my asking for I should be very thankful if you will be so kind as to pay my fare there. It is not much but I have no means of getting it. The fare is 2s 8d. I am sir your obedient servant Caroline Miles

Letter from Caroline Miles, 9 Oxford Place, Brighton, c. 1872
Sir, I beg you will pardon these few lines to you for I am in such great distress I have been ill for a long time and medicine does me no good because I cannot get any proper food and my mind is full of anxiety for I cannot pay the rent. When I went to the doctor the other morning he said 'you are very ill indeed have you no relations or friends to help you' but I have none but they're in Tunbridge Wells and I cannot get there and I do feel so weak and ill I am afraid I shall die soon if something is not done for me. If you will help me I shall be very grateful indeed, I hope you will pardon my asking again as you did assist me once but I do feel so ill from it [I] do not know where to turn for help. If you will please once more give something to buy us a little nourishing diet I shall be very, very grateful but I should be very glad if I could get to Tunbridge Wells. I am sir yours respectfully C Miles

Letter from Caroline Miles, 9 Oxford Place, Brighton, to H Hallet, c. 1872
Sir, if you will be so good as to give the pound you promised by the mayor I will never trouble you with another letter. I do feel very ill indeed. I am afraid I shall die if something is not done for me. The trials and troubles I have had to encounter in these last four years since we lost our work seems to have crushed and broken my spirit entirely. I was never strong and cannot bear so much though I have tried to bear up and not despair thanking God until [I] raise up some friend to help me and I know I cannot help myself as I feel so weak and ill and I cannot do anything but trust and hope but it appears now that I never shall push another pin to give me even a few shillings to buy us little nourishing diet so that I might have a few days' rest. I have not strength to walk about for work and I do not like to take from the little my sister earns but if I could get to Tunbridge Wells some of my relations might help me out. I shall be very grateful if you will help me for the last time. If you will give the pound my sister can have ten shillings to pay the rent and help me and I can go with the other ten. I might have a shawl to twill my clothes and keep me warm. There is a train at noon I think and trust you will send it to William Miles I shall be very grateful indeed but if you will not give it like this may [*illegible*] can send me there as you

did before. Everyone says you could as you [*illegible as over-written*]. I am sir, yours respectfully, C Miles

Letter from Caroline Miles, 23 Scotland Street, Brighton, c. 1872
They say they [are] all busy at Hanningtons and we might have work if we had better clothes to earn a few shillings is better than nothing but what we need is work at home as [*illegible*] for us but we shall never get that in Brighton. The lies and falsehood that have been told of us is most abominable. I am sure one ought to have some redress now someone has put in the papers that my sister and I have applied at the Mendicity Society for money to get to Tunbridge Wells and have been refused as undeserving. We have never been near the place we do not even know where it is. H[e?] is a most cruel, shameful [*illegible*] and will prevent us selling any work if you did you ought to be punished for the falsehood. The mayor said you said we spent all our money on drink a bare lie then that was never told. If I was one so spiteful I could not do such a thing as injure [illegible] and in the end it will injure you [*illegible*].

Letter from Caroline Miles, 23 Scotland Street, Brighton to Mr Tamplin, c. 1872
Sir, I beg you will pardon the liberty I am taking in writing to you. I have heard that you are [a] kind and charitable gentleman and I beg to make this appeal on behalf of my sister and myself for we are in very great distress. My father was collected [sic] to the gas company for many years and since his death my sister and I have supported ourselves and our mother till her death by needlework but now machines are used it is difficult to get employment and a severe illness compelled me to part with furniture and all the best of my clothing to keep from starving and now it is gone I am not fit to get a shop to work and we have never known such a winter as this we have been in such extreme distress and today I know not where to turn for help. I cannot get any work and we have no food or fire and I should be very grateful indeed for a little assistance if it is but a buffer. I feel ready to despair for I feel feint and ill with going without food for so long. I trust you will pardon my writing to you [*illegible*] I remember when my father died you was so good as to contribute to a fund to help my mother and thinking of this yesterday I feel emboldened to ask you if you will help me once more. I am in the greatest distress and shall feel very grateful for a little help. I am sir yours faithfully, Caroline Miles

18 April 1873
Since this case was before the committee over 12 months ago, when the decision was pronounced undeserving, these people have been lodging in different parts of the town. A short time ago they were in Nelson Street and were continually applying to Mrs Verrall, the District Visitor, for relief. Until Mr Verrall called at the office and learnt their character. A few days ago they removed to 41 St

Martin's Place and since they have been there the Reverend Mr Salmon and the Reverend Mr Jones have assisted them on three or four occasions but before doing anything more for them they wished to have the case investigated to see what could be done for them and when the eldest sister applied on Thursday morning for assistance Mr Jones gave one of the Society tickets and she sent the little girl to the office with the annexed note. Upon visiting the house I found them in the same destitute state as on former occasions. WC [William Collingham]
To be fully reported to the Reverend Mr Salmon, R P Hooper

Letter from Caroline Miles, 41 St Martin's Place, Brighton, c. 1873
Sir, the clergyman of our district has given me this ticket and says you will help us. We are in very great distress and need it at once. I am sir yours respectfully C Miles. If you will call this morning I shall be very thankful as we [are] in such great need

Letter from Ansell Jones, 157 Lewes Road, Brighton, to the Mendicity Society, 2 March 1874
Dear Sir, can you possibly do anything or can you tell me what to do about the two women by name Miles, living [at] 41 St Martin's Place? They are in dreadful distress, almost starving, no bed, fire or food. We are continually assisting them but we cannot support them entirely and they are continually begging. It is really one of the worst cases I know. They will not go into the [work]house – cannot you send an officer up in the morning and I will go with him to them to see them. I know they are not quite so good as they might be but they must not starve. Trusting you will pardon my troubling you. Believe me, sincerely yours, Ansell Jones

3 March 1874
The Reverend Mr Jones having sent the annexed letter to the office Mr Johnson secretary was directed by the committee to call Mr Jones' attention to the report sent to the Reverend Mr Salmon in April 1873. WC [William Collingham]

17 March 1874
The Reverend Mr Salmon gave me the annexed letter which he received from the two sisters Miles and requested me to show it to the committee so that they might instruct him how to expose them to the public without prosecuting them. WC [William Collingham]

Letter from Caroline Miles to Reverend Salmon, vicar of St Martin's [1874]
Sir, we are in great distress and we are starving. We have not strength to keep up even to pray for work. If you do not help us I hope God will curse you. You

take money to give to the poor there is no one on earth in the distress we are now and why should we not have help. C Miles

Letter from Caroline Miles, 15 St Martins Place, Lewes Road, Brighton, to Mrs Lawns or Lanes, c1875[309]
Madam, I beg you will pardon these few lines to you for I am in great trouble. I have been ill in bed for nearly three weeks with inflammation on my chest. I cannot tell what I have suffered but it has left me so weak I cannot get up and I am afraid I shall never recover if unable to procure more nourishing diet. I am most unfortunate, I have but just recovered from a very dangerous illness. I was persuaded [by] them to go into the workhouse but I would prefer death to going there again. The doctor [*illegible*] and most cruelly to me he never paid the slightest attention to me he generally came [*illegible*] and said to him 'Sir you must be aware you are not doing your duty and I was in a position to pay you much [*illegible*]' he never said a word at the time but when I was getting better he had me before the magistrate and said I had used abusive language to him and said I said I would as [*illegible*] for the deal as him but God is the witness no such word ever passed my lips and he will have to stand before God [*illegible*] for the sin I have been ten months at Haywards Heath though my mind has never been affected in the slightest degree it is years since you have assisted me and I thought you would for one give me a meal or Guardians ticket. I shall be very grateful indeed if you will. I am madam, yours respectfully, Caroline Miles

Letter from Mrs Soames, Tramore Lodge, Park Road East, Brighton, 2 November [1875][310]
Mrs Soames would be greatly obliged if this case could be investigated as to the actual need of help as a case of illness. She has previously assisted the writer but found her character so dubious that she dropped further notice of her.

3 November 1875
Mrs Soames forwarded the annexed letters to the office and requests a report of the case. I find that Caroline was ill a little more than twelve months ago and was removed to the infirmary and was afterwards taken to Haywards Heath asylum where she was detained for six months. She is now in a delicate state of health and is in receipt of parish relief besides which the Reverend Mr Salmon and his friends assist her. The eldest sister has work and their home at 15 St Martin's Place is still in the same destitute state. WC [William Collingham]
Case for Union [workhouse], report to Mr Jones, R P Hooper

309 The letter refers to her spell in Haywards Heath asylum: she was discharged in December 1874.
310 Tramore Lodge, 7 Park Road East, Brighton.

17 October [1876]
The Reverend S R Drummond sent the annexed letter to the office and requests a report of the case.[311] The eldest sister and her daughter went to London three months ago expecting that the father of her child would marry her. Caroline is now anxious to join her sister that they may live together. Since my last report there is a little improvement in the conduct and habits of Miss Miles. There is now nothing the matter with her hand. She still takes in needlework and the Guardians are allowing her 3s 6d a week. WC [William Collingham]
Report forwarded to Rev S Drummond, HAD[312]

17 October 1877
Miss Miles, who now resides at 7 Meeting House Lane, requests the Society to grant her a loan of £1 to enable her to get some clothes. She still takes in needle work. The Guardians allow her 5s a week. Her sister Clarissa and her little girl returned from London three weeks ago and the family are still in a destitute condition. WC [William Collingham]
Ineligible, ADF[313]

27 January 1880
The Earl of Chichester requests a report of this case. The applicant now resides at 14 St Martin's Place and still takes in needle work. The Guardians allow her 4s 6d a week. The relieving officer states that she has been begging during the last 20 years. WC [William Collingham]
Report to Earl of Chichester, R P Hooper

18 November 1881
The mayor forwarded the annexed begging letter to the office on Thursday and requests a report of the case. The writer takes in needlework and is in receipt of 4s a week from the parish.
Report to mayor, R P Hooper

13 February 1883
Mr R H Penney of 79 Queens Road forwarded the annexed begging letter to the office this morning and requests a report of the case. The writer still takes in needle work and the Guardians allow her 4s per week. WC [William Collingham]
To be reported to Mr Penney, [*illegible signature*]

[311] Spencer Rodney Drummond, perpetual curate of St John the Baptist.
[312] Signature possibly that of Heneage Dering esq., whose name appears in the list of council members in the Charity Organisation Society annual report of 1877.
[313] Signature probably that of the Reverend Allan Davidson Freeman of 30 Montpelier Road, curate of Preston with Hove and vice principal of Western College, Brighton.

10 April 1885
Mr G Tatham JP brought the accompanying begging letter to the office on Friday and requests a report of the case. The writer continues to take in needle work and the Guardians still allow her 4s per week. WC [William Collingham]
Report to Mr Tatham, R P Hooper

27 March 1886
The Reverend J J Hannah forwarded the accompanying begging letter to the office on Friday and thinks that it is time the writer received a little kind attention from the Society. She now resides at 12 St Martin's Place. The Guardians still allow her 4s per week and she continues to take in needle work. WC [William Collingham]
Report to Reverend J Hannah, Thomas Holland

12 January 1887
Mrs De Laney of 28 Park Crescent forwarded the annexed begging letter to the office on Wednesday and requests a report of the case. The writer continues to take in needle work and the Guardians still allow her 4s a week. WC [William Collingham]
Report to Mrs De Laney, [Major General] A F Bond

18 February 1887
Mrs H S Gates of 44 Montpelier Road forwarded the annexed unstamped begging letter to the office on Friday and wishes the committee to deal with the case. The writer still takes in needle work and the Guardians continue to allow her 4s per week. She has lived principally by writing begging letters for a great many years and when the case was before the committee five weeks ago I asked the relieving officer to caution her which he did but it has had no effect on her. WC [William Collingham]
Undeserving, report to Mrs Gates, R P Hooper

14 March 1887
Mr H Willett of Arnold House forwarded the annexed begging letter to the office on Monday and requests a report of the case. I have nothing to add to my last report. WC [William Collingham]
Report to Mr Willett [Major General] A F Bond

18 February 1888
Dr H Belcher of 28 Cromwell Road forwarded the accompanying begging letter to the office on Friday and wishes the committee to deal with the case. The writer now resides at 4 St Mary Magdalene Street and is still in receipt of parish

relief.
WC [William Collingham]
Report to Dr Belcher, R P Hooper

Letter from Caroline Miles, 128 Lewes Road, Brighton, no date
Dear Sir, I beg you will be so kind as to read this letter and if you will render me a little assistance I shall be very grateful indeed for I have had the misfortune to hurt my hand. I was scrubbing down the street and scratched my hand on a nail and it has fractured the bone and the pain is so great and much hurts and the doctor says I must not work but wear it in a sling. It is in such a dangerous part of the hand that the doctors are afraid to give it the treatment they like lest it should cause my doctor to the amputation of my hand. My hand was injured by an accident [*illegible*] because if you can this once assist me with a few shillings and the pleasure [of] a little nourishing diet I shall be very thankful. You have a great kind heart I know but I know others have set you against me because you [*illegible*] to be so very kind to me. I shall be at home if you wish to see me and to know that it is time [*illegible*] please be so kind as to send a trifle by [*illegible*] and am great need or I would not ask. I am sir yours respectfully, Caroline Miles

Letter from Caroline Miles living with Mrs Sicklemore 7 Poplar Place, Brighton, no date
Sir, I beg you will excuse these few lines to ask if [I] can have a little help from the society. I thought perhaps you will let us have the loan of a pound. I would be quite sure to pay the instalments regularly every week. We are in such need of clothes my sister's little girl has no boots and none of us can go out on a Sunday even to church. What we can earn will not buy clothes unless we can pay for it in instalments and those men that give credit only let them that are [*illegible*] have it and they want so much interest. I should be very thankful of a little help in this way. I am sure if [*illegible*] once needed help we do now. I am yours respectfully, Caroline Miles

Letter from Caroline Miles, 14 St Martin's Place, Brighton, to the Earl of Chichester, 24 January 1880
To his Lordship the Earl of Chichester, my lord, I beg you will pardon the liberty I take in addressing these few lines to you for I am in such distress I feel I must venture something. My father was collected [sic] to the gas company and clerk at Palmers and Green for a great many years and since my father's death I have supported myself by dressmaking. I used to be able to earn sufficient to keep myself but now I cannot for everything is done by machine and I have not one and have tried several times to save the money but [*illegible*] time I have had a serious illness and always have bad health and am now so very badly off for I have had no work for a fortnight it is so very slack at this time of the year. The winter is something terrible to get things to act but if I had a machine I could

hem mill in busy times and save for winter if I could get some influential gentleman or lady to fund a subscription I could get one. I have heard that your lordship is so kind to the poor thus I venture to hope you will assist me. I shall indeed be grateful if you will. I am my lord, your lordship, most obedient, humble servant, Caroline Miles

Letter from the Earl of Chichester, Stanmer House, 26 January 1880
Dear Sir, I shall be much obliged by a report upon the enclosed. If the case should prove deserving I should like to know whether the applicant has been for any length of time a resident in Brighton and thus eligible for the Peischell Charity, Chichester.[314]

Letter from Caroline Miles, 33 Whichelo Place, Islingword Road, Brighton to the mayor of Brighton [William Hallett][315], 17 November 1881
Sir, I beg you will take some notice of this request for I am in such distress words have not power how bad it is. I have had so much illness and it has brought me so low it is impossible to get up again without assistance. If you will not give it me [*illegible*] and ought not to be ashamed to take it if you are not ashamed to give it so when you have given me nothing for so many years, not much since you were last elected mayor the other pound you promised through Mr McQueen we have never had and for years back you [*illegible*] in a letter to me you [*illegible*] would be of more permanent service to me [*illegible*] after saying that I might have had a little help in illness or when unable to obtain work if I had a little help I should not have got down in this way but you have taken no notice of my respectful appeal to you for a little help [*illegible*] this claim on you I am [*illegible*] the only one I have on my father's side it is cruel indeed to let me be starving while give to others for them to appear good. Can you send it me by two o'clock when I am in, Caroline Jane Miles

Letter from Robert Horne Penney, 79 Queens Road, Brighton, 13 February 1883
I enclose you a letter from Caroline Miles whom I do not know anything about. Will you be kind enough to give to me all the information you can respecting her. Yours sincerely, Robert H Penney

Letter from Caroline Miles, 29 Franklin Street, Franklin Road, Brighton, to Robert Penney, [February 1883]
Sir, I feel I am taking a great liberty in writing to you but I trust you will excuse it for necessity makes us do what we should otherwise shrink from. I am in great

314 Subscriptions to Charles Peischell's Charity were split between the direct relief of the poor and funding of Brighton dispensary and infirmary. The Earl of Chichester was a trustee.
315 William Henry Hallett was elected mayor of Brighton in 1866, 1867 and 1881.

need and hearing others speak of you as a good and generous hearted gentleman I feel emboldened to make this request on you but your being in a superior position makes a difficulty I do wish to borrow a little money and I have no security but I would give a large interest for the apparent [*illegible*] though God knows I would not deceive anyone that [*illegible*] and if you would lend me a pound I should be very thankful. I am in such poverty and cannot get up again without some such assistance. We, my sister and I, have been so long without work so bad has work been this year and to keep from starvation almost I have had to keep pawning my clothes. I feel the degradation so much I can never go out on a Sunday and I wanted the [*illegible*] to get it back I would not mind giving 5s interest for the loan of a pound. It is no fault of mine I am in this position it is not idleness or drink [*illegible*] and have very little – it is work being so bad and having bad health but I feel I can explain better in speaking to you than in writing and if you will not mind calling on me or allow me to call on you. I know you by sight having seen you at the Booths meeting. I should be so thankful, so grateful for a little in this way and I will be quite satisfied if you will trust me you could lend it me I could pay instalments as there is a difference in my position. I am sir yours respectfully, C J Miles

Letter from Caroline Miles to Robert Penney
Sir, I am quite aware I am making a strange request expecting a stranger to trust me but there are times in life when we feel we must continue trusting to God to guide us. His I feel I am. I am sir, your obedient servant, Caroline Miles

Letter from Caroline Miles, 12 St Martin's Place, Brighton, to G Tatham, magistrate, Old Steine, 10 April 1885
Sir, I beg you will pardon these few lines to ask if you will assist me a little if I may have a loan from the poor board. I am brought down so low I never can get up again to get a livelihood without such assistance. I have been nearly starved this winter having in pledge every article of clothing to save me though I have a relative rich. I am related to Mr Hallett the brewer and once he wrote in this way to me said he wished he could be of more permanent service to me but instead of being of service he has been the ruin of me. I should be thankful for a little help to get back clothes. The lady Mrs Tatham would I think know me again as I used to bring and get mantles and jackets from Mr Riddlestress's. I work for him for many years. I am sir, your obedient servant, Caroline Miles

Letter from the Reverend J J Hannah, Brighton, 10 April 1885
My dear sir, the enclosed is the third letter which I have received from the same writer. I know nothing about her but as she seemed to make out a very pitiful case I sent the second letter of which by the way she omitted to pay the postage to Mr Salmon in whose parish she lives with a view to helping her if I got a

satisfactory report. I enclose you the postcard which I received in reply. It strikes me that it is time she received a little kind attention from the C O S.[316] Your obedient servant, J J Hannah

Postcard sent to the Reverend J J Hannah, from RSS, 23 March 1886
The best thing you can do with Caroline Miles is to give her in charge as an ardent imposter. She makes her livelihood by writing begging letters – she ought to be shown up. She is quite incorrigible. Yours, RSS

Letter from Caroline Miles to the Reverend J J Hannah, 26 March 1886
Sir, I beg you will pardon my [*illegible*] letter [*illegible*] is sufficient to be the successful. We, my sister and I, trust you will do something for us. I may not have liked [*illegible*] I have been to France I might to New Zealand [*illegible*] and chocolate nothing is to be [*illegible*] when one is in distress so great and overwhelming prevented from ever getting work again for [*illegible*] is a little help even as a loan [*illegible*] my letter it would be a [*illegible*] in my part [*illegible*] sinking for want of nourishment to spare resulting [*illegible*] my feet and must have bought me a little milk [*illegible*] I must not do it but rather trust that it will for sure be taken in and read without it as by [*illegible*] as I have no means to pay for a stamp in my extremity I may hope that help will come from some corner I must beg ask again leaving it to you to decide [*illegible*] where [*or when*] it is [*illegible*] I am most respectfully, Caroline Jane Miles
Dr Hannah [*illegible*], I feel so [*illegible*] the procedures I am [*illegible*] when completed [*illegible*]

Letter from Mrs C De Laney, 28 Park Crescent to Colonel Barlow, Charity Organisation Society, 11 January 1887
Dear Sir, being frequently troubled with such assurances as the enclosed from Caroline Miles, 12 St Martin's Place, Lewes Road I am induced to ask if she is known to the C O Society as a deserving object of charity. I have relieved her but a few times in consequence of being informed that she has for the last twenty years traded in begging letters – otherwise I should give her a little assistance occasionally. I hope I am not wrong in thus addressing you on the matters – if so pray kindly pardon the same. I am sir, yours faithfully, Mrs C De Laney

Letter from Mrs H S Gates, 44 Montpelier Road, Brighton, 17 February 1887
Mrs H S Gates writes with her compliments and begs to forward the enclosed letter. It seems a fitting case for relief. Mrs Gates has very many applications from the poor. They do not understand she gives her <u>thoughts</u> and her <u>pen</u> to

[316] Charity Organisation Society.

them as a general body but she cannot undertake to relieve their necessities individually.

Letter from Caroline Miles, 12 St Martins Place, to Mrs Gates, 14 Montpelier Road [16 February 1887]

To Mrs Codling Gates, madam, I beg you will pardon my addressing these few lines to you for [*illegible*] desire that you take an interest in the poor that I venture to hope that you will take notice of the appeal. I am in such great, such very great need [and] have never found a winter so hard to get through as this. Many a day we have had no fire or even bread to eat. My sister and I can get no work anywhere this year – in three weeks we have not earned half a crown. I am sure I do not know what we shall do. I am too perplexed to sleep and should be grateful - very, very grateful for a little help to tide one over a week or two at Easter there will be a chance of more work [*illegible*] praying that God will [*illegible*] assist me with a little money to get food and fire we have been very nearly starved this year. We can do very [*illegible*] little girls' frocks or little boys [*illegible*]

Madam, I do hope you will pardon sending my letter [*illegible*]. I am indeed sorry to do but do trust you are [*illegible*] I am afraid to spend my last penny but do hope you will not be offended. I am madam, yours respectfully, Caroline Jane Miles

Letter to Mr Colt or Mr Catt from Caroline Miles, 12 St Martins Place [c. 1887]

Sir, I beg you will pardon the liberty I take to address these few lines to you for I have heard it said that you are good and charitable to the poor so I venture to make this appeal to you [*illegible*] you will help me a little. I am in great need: my sister and I earn a livelihood as dressmakers, needlework [*illegible*] this last winter has been beyond all expression terrible for as we have not been able to get any work we have been very nearly starved. I do not know what to do. We have [*illegible*] with clothes to save us [*illegible*] we are bought so low. I should be grateful, very grateful for a little assistance to help us through one more week when there may be some chance of getting more work. I am sure something ought to be done for us for though we are in such great need we are related to those well to do. I and my sister are related to one Alderman Hallett [*illegible*] my grandfather and [*illegible*] Hallett were brothers both at [*illegible*] Street, Tunbridge Wells [*illegible*] for a little assistance is not made I trust Mr Hallett, Mr Alderman Hallett [*illegible*] how very bad off we are so near, so very near starvation. I feel so ill for want of more nourishing diet I shall be very grateful to any gentleman that will take up our cause [and] speak to Mr Hallett and get him to do something for us but in the meanwhile I should be very thankful for a little help if only a trifle, if only a shilling. I cannot afford the penny for a stamp but do not like to send [*illegible*] though two pence is nothing to you but a penny is a matter of life and death to me so great is my need. Hoping, praying, trusting that I may find someone to befriend. I am yours faithfully, Caroline Jane Miles

Letter to Mr W H Hallett, 141 Madeira Parade [c. 1887]
Whatever we shall do I cannot think. We can get no work and must starve if no one will help us. Surely the money Mr Hallett gives to other poor ought to be given to us [*illegible*]. I shall be grateful if you can do anything for us but not through the church or [*illegible*] security – we are not beggars but live by much honour [*illegible*]

Letter from Caroline Miles, 4 St Mary Magdalene Street, Brighton, to Dr Belcher, Steine Street [undated]
To Dr Belcher, sir I beg you will excuse a few words [*illegible*] to acknowledge and thank you for the card you sent me. I ought to have done so before but I have so much trouble lately it has been the very worst winter I have known. In regard to work I can get none though try my utmost for it. Nearly a month I have been without any work and I cannot live on the trifles the Guardians allow me when I cannot get work I have to pledge clothes and it makes one so depressed for fear I may get down this low as some have done and [*illegible*] in consequence but I do trust god in his providence will send work or assistance [*illegible*] I thought while unable to get proper diet it might do me more harm than good and I had better to act but the worst if it is the cards are [*illegible*] but perhaps you will [*illegible*] for one on my portions [*illegible*] I thought the doctor [*illegible*] would get me one bottle of it [*illegible*] are so marvellous but he did not answer my letter. I shall keep the card and ask you to give me little [*illegible*] the month and I can get back to buy food too. I am yours, Caroline Jane Miles

92B ELIZABETH FLOATE, 39, CHARWOMAN, 11 MODEL LODGING HOUSE, CHURCH STREET, BRIGHTON

The Floate family had been living at the Model Lodging House for eight years at the time of their application to the Mendicity Society and before that had been resident at 62 Pimlico. Elizabeth Dean was born in Brighton and married Henry Floate at St Nicholas, Brighton, on 12 November 1858.[317] *At the time of the application the family consisted of Henry Floate, a 43-year-old drover born in Steyning, Elizabeth and their three daughters.*[318] *The 1871 census recorded Elizabeth's mother, Hannah Dean, also living at the address. Dean was a 63-year-old widow who was employed as a bather but she was not shown on the charity's application form.*

[317] ESRO: PAR 255/1/3/31.

[318] The census of 1871 recorded Henry Floate's place of birth as Steyning: the registration district of Steyning includes Hove which is probably Floate's true place of birth.

Henry Floate was earning seven shillings per week and Elizabeth five shillings per week. They were paying four shillings per week for four rooms and were 25 shillings in arrears. Mr Miles of Bond Street, presumably Henry Floate's employer, was given as a reference.[319]

5 March 1872
Statement: Elizabeth Floate wants a little assistance as her [daughter] Elizabeth is sick with a sore throat.
Report: I made enquiries respecting this case and find all three children has been sick. The three youngest is got alright, the oldest one is better but wants a little nourishment. The man is a drover. Mr Miles, Bond Street, gave him a good character and says he is a very steady trustworthy man. The wife goes out to work but since the children has been sick she has not been able to leave home but a very little. The home is in a passable state. I have known them a long time and believe them to be very industrious people.
~~Referred to poor law~~
Relieved by grant (2 shillings), Orfeur Cavenagh. NB the woman to be instructed to wait on the relieving officer in every future similar case

93 ANNA BOOTY, 38, CHARWOMAN, 18 MARINE VIEW, BRIGHTON

Anna Collins was born in Swanage, Dorset, in about 1834. She married Henry Booty, fishmonger, in Watford, Hertfordshire, in the March quarter of 1855 and in 1861 was enumerated at 158 High Street, Watford, living with Henry, their three children, a servant and a lodger.[320] *According to the charity's application form the family arrived in Brighton in about 1865 and by 1871 Anna Booty, now widowed, and her three children were living at 18 Marine View, where they had been living for five years: prior to that they had been resident at 7 Rock Street. Booty had been short of work for the last four months and her case was forwarded to the Mendicity Society by her former employer Laura Soames of Tramore Lodge, Park Road East. Booty lived with her daughters Anna and Matilda and her 14-year-old son, Henry, who had been employed as a labourer by Mr Bostell of Black Lion Street but had been short of work for three weeks.*

The family paid three shillings per week rent for the whole house but were 15 shillings in arrears at the time of the application. Laura Soames suggested that money should be found to take Anna Booty to Lincolnshire or Yorkshire where work could be found for the family but Alsager Hay Hill, the renowned social reformer, firmly stated that this would not be an advisable course of action.

6 March 1872
Statement: Anna Booty wants a little assistance till she gets work.

[319] H Miles, butcher, 20 Bond Street, Brighton.
[320] Anna Collins marriage to Henry Booty registered Q1 1855 Watford 3a 249.

Report: I made enquiries respecting this case and find this woman is well known to the Reverend Mr Morgan and the Reverend Mr Snowden Smith and Miss Soames. All of them have relieved her several times. Mr Toye has known this woman a long time and says he cannot recommend her for relief. The oldest girl is paralysed, the son has been out of work three weeks. This woman goes out cooking and charring but has had no work lately. The home is in a passable state. Miss Soames says she heard there was plenty of work for women down in Lincolnshire. The woman states that she has applied to the relieving officer who offered her an order for the workhouse.
Dismissed as ineligible, Orfeur Cavenagh. NB the woman to be instructed to wait upon per the relieving officer her case being one for the consideration of the Guardians.

31 August 1872
On recommendation by Miss Soames to assist Mrs Booty and her children to migrate to some industrial centre where workers are in demand.
Having made fresh enquiries respecting this person I find she was cook to Mrs Robarts, 4 Lewes Crescent, for seven weeks during which time she conducted herself to the entire satisfaction of her mistress. Miss Soames and the Reverend S Smith likewise give her a good character. Mrs Robarts is out of town but the person in charge of the house says that Mrs Booty is a very industrious and trustworthy woman. WC [William Collingham]
Case with particulars to be communicated to Mr Alsager Hill, R P Hooper, chairman

Letter from Miss Laura Soames, Tramore Lodge to R Johnson, Mendicity Society, 16 September 1872
Sir, I am much obliged for your information about Mrs Booty. I have told her I let you know whether she can find any girls between 13 and 18 to assist her. If however she cannot find any I think perhaps we might raise money for her travelling expenses if she is sure of finding employment when she gets to the work. Please let me know where it is that labour is wanted and what it would cost to send her and her three children there. I am yours truly, Laura Soames

Letter from Alsager Hay Hill, Saracen's Head, Bristol, to R Johnson, Mendicity Society, 4 September 1872
Dear Sir, your letter with particulars of [the] Booty family has reached me here. I am afraid if only two members of the family are available for work that a northern employer might be reluctant to advance expenses of removal and I find charwomen rather opposed to the regularity of factory work. If the woman could obtain two or three respec[table] and able girls to accompany her, ages

between 13 and 18, she might do well. I will however enter on my books and see what can be done. Faithfully yours, Alsager Hay Hill

Letter from Alsager Hay Hill to R Johnson, Mendicity Society, 20 September 1872
Dear Sir, your note addressed to me in London in the matter of the Booty family has been forwarded to me here. I cannot advise any benevolent lady to send Mrs B and her children on spec to Leeds as I think it very uncertain whether they would obtain immediate employment. The expenses of removal are of course a mere question of calculation from the railway guide which I have not to hand here but I advise very great caution in the matter of removal under any circumstance. Your article on street beggars has not reached me therefore I cannot comment on it. Faithfully yours, A H Hill

Letter from Laura Soames, Blackheath, Surrey, 26 September 1872
Sir, I am sorry to hear that the arrangement I proposed for Mrs Booty is not approved of for I am afraid I cannot take the responsibility of recommending young girls to go under her care, Laura Soames

94 ANN NICHOLLS, 29, CHARWOMAN, 44 CUMBERLAND PLACE, BRIGHTON

Ann, or Hannah, Nicholls had a troubled relationship with the Mendicity Society, and later the Charity Organisation Society, that stretched from March 1872 to her death in December 1906. She made multiple requests for relief and over 40 letters of enquiry were sent to the charity by members of the public keen to know more about her before offering relief. Nicholls used a number of aliases which appear to have confused the public and committee members alike. She is one of the few applicants that we have a physical description of: references to her diminutive stature were made on separate occasions by Charity Organisation Society staff in June 1892 and May 1905.

Ann Nicholls, née Fowler, was born in Norwich in 1843 but stated on the application form that she had been living in Brighton since about 1850.[321] *In 1871 she was enumerated at 33 Derby Place with her husband William, an agricultural labourer born in Brighton, and their two children the eldest of whom, Matilda, was born in Croydon in about 1866. By the time of their first approach to the Mendicity Society in March 1872 the family were resident at 44 Cumberland Place where they paid four shillings rent per week for the whole house. They were eight shillings in arrears and William Nicholls, who had previously been working for Mr Marshall of Ditchling Road, had been short of work for a month.*[322]

In May 1877 a number of letters were written to the Charity Organisation Society regarding the family. It appears that Nicholls had approached a Mrs Austen of 8 Palmeira Square and in turn Mrs Austen had asked the C O S whether they viewed her as a worthy

[321] Ann Fowler birth registered Q1 1843 Blofield (Norfolk) 13 27.
[322] John Marshall, builder, Stanford Villas, Ditchling Road.

cause for assistance. The charity decided that due to the Nicholls' intemperate habits she should not receive any relief but a letter written by George Herbert in June 1877 paints Mrs Nicholls in a different light. He stated that she was not the notorious Mrs Nicholls that was well known to magistrates but a hard-working, sober woman that had been deserted by her husband 15 years previously. Poverty had induced her to move in with William Nicholls some years before but the couple never married. Herbert stated that the couple were looking to the church to improve their lot and had had their four children baptised at All Souls the day before.[323] *He also stated that Hannah and William Nicholls wanted to marry but could not do so due to insufficient funds to buy the ring but 'God answered my prayers and sent means for them to get married and money for the ring'. The marriage of a William Nicholls and Hannah Fowler was recorded at Brighton in the June quarter of 1877, suggesting that there was some veracity in George Herbert's statement.*[324]

The family had moved to 42 Egremont Street by the time of their application for relief in December 1878 but they were enumerated at 30 Egremont Street on the census of 1881 and stayed there until at least December 1884.

Hannah Nicholls regularly used aliases in order to fool individuals and the authorities into relieving her on multiple occasions without detection. The first obvious instance of this occurred in February 1883 when she used the name Eldridge but she also used the surnames Mitchell, Whitting, Stringer, Harley and Hill: the last of these was the name of the man she lived with after leaving her husband in about January 1885.

William Collingham's report for the Mendicity Society states that Nicholls was sentenced to 14 days' hard labour for begging In December 1891, but no record of this could be found in local press. In February 1894 she appeared in court as a plaintiff following an assault by Elizabeth Webb in Carlton Hill.[325] *Webb appears to have struck Nicholls and knocked her down but Nicholls was accused of writing malicious letters to Webb's mother, which caused a rift between the two women. Magistrates heard 'a good deal of contradictory evidence' but gave Nicholls a five shillings fine plus costs or seven days' hard labour.*

Hannah Nicholls and Elizabeth Webb's lives continued to be intertwined over the course of the next decade. They were enumerated together at 4 Oxford Place in 1901, when both women earned a living as field workers on a farm. In December 1902 Webb was again assaulted by Nicholls and another woman named Jane Prevett.[326] *She stated that she had lived with the defendants for some years but had recently left and gone to live in Oxford Street. Nicholls came to Webb's house and struck her in the face blacking her eye; Prevett called later and struck her in the mouth. Nicholls claimed that she was responding to an insult whereas Prevett claimed she was acting in self-defence. The case against Prevett*

[323] Matilda, William, Hannah and Rose Nicholls were baptised at All Souls, Brighton, on 20 June 1877 (ESRO: PAR 257/1/2/3).

[324] This appears to have taken place at a non-conformist church as no record of their marriage could be found in Brighton parish records.

[325] Brighton Gazette, 22 February 1894.

[326] Brighton Gazette, 6 December 1902.

was dismissed but Nicholls was found guilty and was bound over in the sum of £5 to keep the peace and paid the costs.

Relations between the two women did not improve and one month later Nicholls was summoned for breaking a window at 4 Oxford Place, the home of Elizabeth Webb,[327] *doing damage to the amount of 6s 6d.*[328] *Webb told the magistrate that between six and seven on Saturday evening Nicholls came to her house and threw a loaf of bread through the window. Nicholls explained that they had been out drinking together and they were 'as bad as one another, 'we really were sir' said the defendant; 'for I threw one loaf and she threw two loaves.' The comment caused laughter in court and the case was dismissed with Nicholls bidding the magistrate 'Good morning sir, very much obliged to you'.*

The last enquiry about Hannah Nicholls was made in March 1906 when she was living at 44 Hereford Street, and the response from the charity gave a concise summary of her activities over the previous 20 years or so. Her death from pneumonia was recorded at 2.45pm on 10 December 1906 by the charity agent George Collingham on a postcard addressed to his father and colleague William Collingham. She was buried at Bear Road cemetery on 14 December 1906 aged 67.[329]

6 March 1872
Statement: Ann Nicholls wants a little assistance till her husband gets work.
Report: I made enquiries respecting this case and find the man has been out of work a month and got work yesterday. His wages when in full work is about 18s per week. The wife occasionally gets a day's work. The home is in a passable state. Mr Marshall gave the man a good character. Mr Toye the scripture reader says they do not require relief at present.
Dismissed as ineligible, Orfeur Cavenagh

22 March 1876
Mrs Fife of Redfern House, College Road, is anxious to assist this family to Queensland but before doing so she was recommended by the Reverend A T Waugh to apply to the society for a report of the case.[330] Nicholls now resides at 19 Egremont Street and is doing a little labouring work. Three years ago the wife had a hawker's licence and for a long time they lived entirely by imposing on a lady in Sussex Square. Both the man and his wife are given to drink and in my opinion it is very doubtful whether they would leave Brighton if their request was granted.

[327] There is an inconsistency in the newspaper reports as 4 Oxford Place is given as the home of both Ann Nicholls and Elizabeth Webb, despite Webb allegedly moving out in November or December 1902.

[328] Brighton Gazette, 10 January 1903.

[329] ESRO: BH/L/3/1/11 - Woodvale Cemetery burial plot ZLX 50.

[330] Reverend Arthur Thornhill Waugh, incumbent of St Mary's, Brighton.

WC [William Collingham]
Undeserving, report to Mrs Fife, JD[331]

Letter from Ann Nicholls, 22 Essex Place, Bedford Street, Brighton, [to Mrs Austen, 8 Palmeira Square, Hove, May 1877]
Madam, I am sorry for troubling you with this letter but as the shopkeeper has sent me in his bill for the money that I owe him and a note with it asking for the money as he is pressed for payment of his own bills. As you have been very kind to us during our illness I hope you will not be offended at the liberty I have taken by writing to you. If you will be so kind as to help me out of the present difficulty I shall be sincerely thankful for your kindness. I have been weak and poorly since I was at your house. My husband has only been able to work [for] four days – he was forced to leave it off, his arms are so bad he can't get any strength in them. I am troubled to get out far from home or I would not have bothered with this letter from yours humbly, Mrs Nicholls

Letter from A Henstridge, 8 Palmeira Square, Hove, to Mr Sharp, 33 Buckingham Road, Brighton, [May 1877]
Dear Sir, the enclosed are the letters respecting the woman you called about last evening. Miss Austen returned her the bill this morning but would do nothing further for her until she had heard from you. Yours truly, A Henstridge

11 May 1877
Mrs Nicholls applied to Mrs Austen of 8 Palmeira Square for assistance to enable her to pay a grocer's account but before relieving the family Mrs Austen requests a report of the case. The husband who has lately been ill is now able to work. His wife was confined two weeks ago. They have four children at home. Both Nicholls and his wife were drunk and quarrelling in the street a few days ago.
WC [William Collingham]
Undeserving, to be reported to Mrs Austen, R P Hooper

Letter from George Herbert, 34 Upper St James Street, [to Mrs W D Savage, Ellerslie House, Freshfield Road, Brighton], 21 June 1877[332]
Dear Madam, I respectfully beg to state the few following facts in respect of Mrs Nicholls and the vicissitudes of her life. She unfortunately got married to a very bad man 18 years ago. He was both a lazy and a drunkard [sic] and sadly abused her. He left her and went away with another woman 15 years ago and she has not seen or heard of him since. Poverty induced [her] to go with William

331 Signature possibly that of John Deverell whose name appears in the list of Charity Organisation Society council members in the annual report of 1877.

332 Mrs Savage was probably the wife of William Dawson Savage, chemist, who ran his business from 109 St James's Street.

Nicholls and she did not marry him as she had no one to take it in hands (and I may say afraid of the law as there is a love for the rich but not for the poor). I have fully investigated the case and find her to be a sober and industrious woman. There is another woman, the name of Nicholls, that has been in gaol several times and most likely the magistrate has taken this party for the other as this woman never was in gaol nor got drunk. William Nicholls has done nothing the last four months and now he is able to work (although not strong) and willing he cannot get it (I enclose you the marriage licence) added with her difficulties is four small children. They were all christened yesterday at All Souls' church and I feel as said by having them married and the children and baptised I hope and trust and God's help it will be the means of them leading a different life. Since I was recommended to them by the visiting lady (Miss Jefferson) they have attended a place of worship twice, sometimes three times, a week and I think they are very wishful to follow Him and if it is possible to get them out of that neighbourhood for [the] sake of the poor children as the language coming out of the public house opposite is dreadful for children to hear and if it is our bounden duty to point them to our saviour and to raise up them that fall – he came for the wicked. She is backward in her soul. When I spoke to you you was very busy and you told me to call the next week and God answered my prayers and sent means for them to get married and money for the ring and I thought that I would call upon you after they was married. I would be very happy if you would kindly grant an interview. I will wait upon you on Saturday morning for the favour of your reply. I am madam, yours faithfully,
George Herbert
PS Mrs Nicholls bids me to return you many sincere thanks for what you have kindly done for her and destitute children

Letter from [Mrs Savage], Ellerslie House, [Freshfield Road, Brighton], 23 June 1877
Some time ago Mrs Savage visited and relieved the persons mentioned in the accompanying letter but subsequently, having heard a very unfavourable report of them, ceased to do. Now that another application is made Mrs S would like to ascertain through the Charity Organisation Society if they are deserving of any relief?

25 June 1877
Mr W D Savage, Ellerslie House, Park Road East, requests a report of this case. Nicholls is now at work for W Botting, builder, the wife does a little charring. Herbert the writer of the letter sent to Mrs Savage is an old sailor from Cornwall, now a seller of ferns. According to his statement he was once a hard drinker but now a total abstainer. He professes to be very religious and no doubt receives a great deal of charity. WC [William Collingham]
To be reported to Mrs Savage, R P Hooper

24 December 1878
Mr S Gurney, 48 Sussex Square, brought to the office on Monday a ticket for the Maternal Society to be given to Mrs Nicholls and requested a report of the case.[333] The family now reside at 42 Egremont Street. Nicholls has had no work since the frost set in. His wife is near her confinement. Their home is in a destitute condition. WC [William Collingham]
To be reported to Mrs Gurney

18 November 1880
Miss Tugwell, 7 Clifton Terrace requests a report of this case. Nicholls now resides at 30 Egremont Street and is in full work. WC [William Collingham]
To be reported to Mrs Tugwell, Hayter Johnson

27 January 1882
Mrs Ellis, 2 Chichester Place, requests a report of this case. Nicholls is not at work in the Queens Park. His wife is a low drunken woman and quite unworthy of charity. WC [William Collingham]
Report to Mrs Ellis, R P Hooper

Letter from Heneage W Dering, 39 Brunswick Place, Hove, 25 March [1882]
My dear Colonel, will you get Collingham to make enquiries about a Mrs Nicholls who lives at 30 Egremont Street. She has been begging here lately, says her husband is a labourer and that she has a child ill with whooping cough. Sincerely yours, Heneage W Dering

27 March 1882
Mr H Dering requests a report of this case.[334] Nicholls is in full work and his wife is out begging nearly every day with a woman named Darling. WC [William Collingham]
Undeserving. Report to Mr Dering, R P Hooper

7 February 1883
Mrs Nicholls, knowing that her case was unfavourably reported to Miss Tugwell by the society in November 1880, kept away from the lady for two years and early in November last she called to Miss T again. She then gave the name of Eldridge saying that she resided at 14 Bedford Buildings and applied for assistance to tide her over till her son, who had had a sunstroke on board the

333 The Maternal Society for Assisting Poor Married Women was established in 1813 to provide poor married women with bed linen, clothing and nourishment for the period of their confinement, The Fearless and the Fabulous: a journey through Brighton and Hove's women's history, Louise Peskett.

334 Heneage Dering's name appears in the list of council members in the Charity Organisation Society annual report of 1877.

Britannia at North Shields, could get his wages which were due to him, namely £20. Believing the woman's statement Miss Tugwell advanced her money from time to time but in December last she doubted the genuineness of the story and requested the society to enquire into the case. At that time the woman could not be found but I have since ascertained that it is Mrs Nicholls. Miss Tugwell is an aged lady and whenever she has been out for a walk Mrs Nicholls has waylaid her and frightened her and has obtained altogether £18. Instead of her son being ill with sunstroke he is undergoing a sentence of five years penal servitude. WC [William Collingham]
Report to Miss Tugwell with recommendation to prosecute which she declined

15 February 1884
Mrs Phillips of 8 Clifton Terrace called at the office on Wednesday [and] stated that she had been assisting a woman named Nicholls of 20 Grosvenor Street who represented that her husband was in London and now wanted to help to enable her to join him but before relieving her again Mrs P requests a report of the case. Mrs Nicholls still resides in Egremont Street her husband is not away from home and she is constantly out begging with the woman Darling. WC [William Collingham]
Report to Mrs Phillips, recommended for prosecution and declined

Letter from Heneage W Dering, 39 Brunswick Place, Hove, 12 December 1884
My dear Colonel, please to enquire through Collingham into the case of one Mrs Nicholls who states that she lives at 30 Egremont Street. Her husband, a labourer, [is] out of work and five children she begged of my wife this morning in the street and on Mrs Dering recommending her to apply to the C O S answered that she did not can [sic] to do that as she fancied that they had some objection to her! I have been a prisoner for a few days, a touch of bronchitis, or would not have bothered you with a letter. Sincerely yours, Heneage W Dering

12 December 1884
Mr H Dering requests another report of this case. The family still live at 30 Egremont Street. The husband is seldom out of employment and his wife is a thorough imposter. WC [William Collingham]
Report to Mr Dering, R P Hooper

Postcard sent by Mrs Tindal Robertson, 9 Belgrave Terrace, 3 March 1885
Will Colonel Barlow kindly report to Mrs Robertson on the case of Mrs White, 20 Manchester Row

5 March 1885
Mrs Tindal Robertson forwarded the annexed postcard to the office on Tuesday

asking the society to investigate the case of Mrs White of 20 Manchester Row but on calling in Manchester Row I found that no one named White lived there and on Wednesday morning I ascertained that Mrs Nicholls is the woman who begged of Mrs Robertson in the name of White. She left her husband three months ago and now resides at 36 Derby Place. She has an institution card in her possession and pads herself to represent that she is near her confinement to excite sympathy. WC [William Collingham]
Report to Mrs Robertson, R P Hooper

Letter from O Shelley, 83 Edward Street, Brighton, c. 1885[335]
Dear Sir, I forwarded your bill as I am press[ed] for money. I hope you will try and settle it. I am sorry for your wife and your long illness. Yours faithfully, O Shelley

Letter from Mrs Henry, 17 Belgrave Place, Brighton, 16 April [1886]
For enquiry: Mrs Mitchell, 23 Grosvenor Street, has a ticket from Mrs Roxby for the Lying in Institution.[336] Husband out of work but expects to get some soon. Sent by Mrs Henry

19 April 1886
This person begged of Mrs Henry 17 Belgrave Place on Saturday last produced an institution card and gave the name of Mitchell but before assisting her the lady wishes for a report of the case. She is now cohabiting with a stableman named Hill and still lives principally by begging. WC [William Collingham]
To be reported to F Y Toms R[oyal] N[avy]

Letter from Miss Garnett, Furze Hill Lodge, Hove, 28 September 1886
Dear Sir, Mrs Whitting, 23 Grosvenor Street, Brighton, has applied to me for help. She says she has a baby one month old and several other children and a husband not in regular work. Is she deserving of help? I would also be glad if you could tell me something of a Mrs Martin, Cavendish Street, a flower woman. She did <u>not</u> beg from me so I should not like her to know I questioned the truth of what she told me. I was anxious to buy flowers from a good flower woman and asked her name <u>liking</u> her appearance. I hope she is deserving, yours truly, C D Garnett

30 September 1886
Mrs Nicholls begged of Miss Garnett of Furze Hill Lodge on Monday and gave the name of Whitting but before assisting her Miss G wishes for a report of the

335 O H Shelly, grocer.
336 The Lying in Institution was situated at 76 West Street.

case. She still cohabits with the man Hill by whom she has a baby six weeks old and continues to live principally by imposing on charitable persons. WC [William Collingham]
Reports to Mrs Nicholls [sic], R P Hooper

Letter from Mrs Gay, 5 Percival Terrace, Brighton, 22 December [1886]
Mrs Gay will be much obliged if the Charity Organisation Society would enquire into the case of Mrs Nicholls or Mitchell, the <u>former</u> I think – 23 Grosvenor Street. She has just brought the enclosed [*enclosure does not survive*] at the same time begging for flannel. I thought something seemed wrong so am sending the card to you. <u>Please return it</u> if it is right

23 December 1886
Mrs Nicholls begged of Mrs Gay of 5 Percival Terrace on Wednesday for 6d to pay the deposit money on blanket ticket but before relieving her the lady wishes for a report of the case. WC [William Collingham]
Report to Mrs Gay, R P Hooper

Letter from Mrs Barclay, Exton House, Second Avenue, Hove, 8 February [1887]
Mrs Barclay will be much obliged to the Charity Organisation if they will tell her if Mrs Frederick Hill, 23 Grosvenor Street is deserving of help. She has applied personally to Mrs Barclay. She says her husband is [a] cab driver out of work and that they are starving

9 February 1887
Mrs Nicholls begged of Mrs Barclay of Exton House, Second Avenue, on Tuesday and gave the name of Hill but before assisting her Mrs B wishes for a report of the case. She still cohabits with the man Hill and lives entirely by begging. WC [William Collingham]
Report to Mrs Barclay, [Major General] A F Bond

2 April 1887
Mrs Crichton of 18 Adelaide Crescent requests a report of this case. Mrs Nicholls continues to cohabit with the man Hill and still lives entirely by begging. WC [William Collingham]
Report to Mrs Crichton, [*signature illegible*]

Postcard to Colonel Barlow, Charity Organisation Society, from Mrs Gay, 5 Percival Terrace, 23 November 1887
Kindly investigate the case of Mrs Mitchell, 16 Chesterfield Street as let me know the result as soon as possible. Mrs M applied here yesterday with a baby in arms. Mrs Gay

23 November 1887
Mrs Nicholls now of 18 Chesterfield Street [sic] begged of Miss Gay, 5 Percival Terrace, on Wednesday and gave the name of Mitchell but before assisting her the lady wishes for a report of the case. She still cohabits with the man Hill and continues to live by begging. WC [William Collingham]
Report to Miss Nicholls [sic], R P Hooper

24 January 1888
Miss Garnett of Furze Hill Lodge requests another report of this case. Mrs Nicholls still resides at 18 Chesterfield Street and continues to live by begging, JHK
Undeserving and report sent to Miss Garnett

20 August 1888
Mrs Nicholls called at 12 Queen Square last Saturday afternoon and asked to see the lady of the house. On being told she was out she asked if any of the family were in, stating that she had been sent by the lame sister at St Mary's House for assistance to pay the deposit on an institution card. Consequently the servant took her to her mistress Mrs Farringdon at 5 North Street Quadrant where she produced the card and asked for 11d to pay the deposit saying that her daughter, Mrs Stringer of 22 Cannon Street, had been in strong labour all day: therefore Mrs Farringdon gave her 11d and some tea and sugar. There is no one named Stringer living at 22 Cannon Street. Mrs Nicholls has been using institution cards for begging purposes for some time past and should the committee consider the case a fit one for prosecution Mrs Farringdon is willing to give evidence against her. WC [William Collingham]
Referred to the honorary solicitor for prosecution, [Major General] A F Bond

Letter to Colonel Barlow from Griffith and Eggar, solicitors, 47 Old Steine, Brighton, 22 August 1888
Dear Sir, re: Mrs Nicholls, we return the papers in this case which Mr Collingham handed to us yesterday. We think there is scarcely sufficient evidence at present to warrant a prosecution under the Vagrant Act but if Mr Collingham can find that Mrs Nicholls obtained other sums of money than the 1s from Mrs Farringdon on a fraudulent pretence the case is one in which we should be strongly disposed to prosecute. Mrs Nicholls might now be prosecuted for obtaining the 1s by false pretences but we think the case would be one for the sessions. Under the Vagrant Act we want to show that she was going about obtaining charitable contributions and at present there is only evidence of her having obtained contributions from Mrs Farringdon. Yours faithfully, Griffith and Eggar

23 August 1888
The honorary solicitors have considered this case and do not think that there is sufficient evidence at present to warrant a conviction under the Vagrant Act. WC [William Collingham]

4 April 1889
Mrs Nicholls applied to Miss Beaumont of 45 Regency Square a week ago for £2 to enable her daughter-in-law to be admitted into the Lying in Institution as she was very near her confinement. She gave the name of Stringer and her address 20 Artillery Street both of which were false and she has no daughter-in-law but as she produced an institution card the lady gave her altogether £1 4s 6d.
Report to Miss Beaumont, Thomas W Holland

9 April 1889
Mr G D Turnbull wishes a report as to where Mrs Nicholls obtained the institution card from, who filled it in for her and who signed it. She obtained the card from Chipperfield and Butlers in the Western Road and it was filled in and signed by Mr J A Barnes, shop-walker [sic]. WC [William Collingham]
Report to Mr Turnbull, [*signature illegible*]

2 December 1891
On Tuesday morning the Hove police called here to ask if I could give them any information respecting a woman named Stringer whom they wanted for obtaining money by false pretences. Knowing that Mrs Nicholls sometimes gives that name I took the officer to her house. She at once admitted that she was the person wanted and on Wednesday she was sentenced to 14 days' hard labour.
To be recorded, R P Hooper

16 June 1892
On Tuesday last Mr H Johnston called at the office and stated that on two occasions a short woman had begged of him for 6d to pay the registration fee on a dispensary letter filled up in the name of Ellen White, servant, of 12 Cannon Street, but on calling at that address I found that no such person resided there, consequently I afterwards saw Mrs Nicholls at 45 William Street when she admitted that she was the woman who begged of Mr Johnston but he does not wish to give evidence against her. WC [William Collingham]
To be recorded, R P Hooper

Letter from Mrs Dewe, 28 Buckingham Place, Brighton, 21 July 1892
Mrs Dewe will feel greatly obliged for information regards Mrs Nicholls, 18 Derby Place, Edward Street. The woman is frequently coming to the house to ask help for one purpose or another. She says she now requires money to enable her

to get her daughter's clothes out of pawn so that she just may go into a situation at Grafton House, Grafton Street, on Monday next. Mrs Nicholls says her husband is a labourer out of work and they have eight children – the youngest of whom is very delicate. Mrs Dewe would feel very grateful if the woman's story could be investigated [and] wishes to know if the man as well the woman are sober people and also respectable, Mrs D's servants tell her Mrs Nicholls smelled very strong of liquor the day when she called last week. The clothes were pawned to procure nourishment for the girl when she was suffering from [a] bad throat a few months' since.
[*on reverse of letter*] Ellen White – servant, 12 Cannon Street

21 July 1892
Mrs Nicholls now of 18 Derby Place has been in the habit of calling on Mrs Dymoke of 13 Chichester Terrace for some time past asking for letters to the medical charities. Flannel and other articles which have been given her but before assisting her again the lady wishes for a report of the case. WC [William Collingham]
Report to Mrs Dymoke, R P Hooper

22 July 1892
Mrs Dewe of 28 Buckingham Place has written to say that Mrs Nicholls is frequently calling at her house to ask help for one purpose or another and she has relieved her on several occasions but before doing so again she wishes for a report on the case. WC [William Collingham]
Report [to] Mrs Dewe, R P Hooper

10 August 1892
Mrs W Money of 21 Cambridge Road requests a report of this case. It appears that Mrs Nicholls has long been in the habit of calling at the house begging and is often abusive to the servants. WC [William Collingham]
Report [to] Mrs Money, R P Hooper

Postcard sent to Colonel Barlow, 59 Preston Road, Brighton, from Mrs L Jennings, Victoria House, 51 Old Steine, Brighton, 28 October 1892
Will you enquire about Mrs Nicholls, 18? Derby Street – says that she wants help to get a daughter into a situation. Kind regards to Mrs Barlow and yourself.
Yours truly, L Jennings
Saw our friends at 89 Montpelier yesterday[337]

[337] Ann Nicholls was in fact living at Derby Place. The mutual friends referred to at 89 Montpelier Road may have been W H Warton and family living at Redland House.

29 October 1892
Mrs Nicholls applied to Mrs Jennings of 51 Old Steine on Friday for assistance to get some clothes out of pawn for her daughter to enable her to go to a situation in London but before complying with her request she wishes for a report of the case. WC [William Collingham]
Report [to] Mrs Jennings, R P Hooper

6 February 1893
Mr G D Turnbull of 100 Lansdowne Place requests a report of this case. Mrs Nicholls now resides at 13 Derby Place. The previous reports will show that she is a notorious beggar and for several years she has lived entirely by imposing on charitable persons. WC [William Collingham]
Report to Mrs Turnbull, EMM

Letter from Mary Ann Skirrow, 3 Codrington Place, Brighton, 4 March 1893
Sir, I shall be obliged by your informing me if you know anything of Mrs Mitchell, 13 Derby Place. She comes to me for money to get clothes out of pawn. She also comes for hospital letters and is troublesome. I know nothing about her. She generally brings a poor sickly looking girl with her. Believe me, yours faithfully, Mary Ann Skirrow (Miss S -), Saturday

6 March 1893
Mrs Skirrow of 3 Codrington Place requests a report of this case. It appears that Mrs Nicholls has recently called there on several occasions begging in the name of Mitchell for one purpose or another and the previous reports will show that she is utterly unworthy of encouragement. WC [William Collingham]
Report to Miss Skirrow, JF, R P Hooper

Letter from Mrs G H Hammond, 8 Third Avenue, 20 May [1893]
Sir, I shall be much obliged if you can tell me if Mrs Nicholls, 13 Derby Place, is deserving of help. Yours truly, Mrs G H Hammond

23 May 1893
Mrs Hammond of 8 Third Avenue requests a report of this case. Mrs Nicholls has lately gone about asking for dispensary letters for her daughter who is in good health and obtains the letters simply as an excuse to beg 6d to pay for the registration fee. WC [William Collingham]
Report to Mrs Hammond, Thomas W Holland

Letter from Frank Loyd, 55 Wilbury Road, Hove, 8 November 1894[338]
Mrs Nicholls, 12 Cumberland Place, Brighton has a son (F Nicholls) age 9 years. He suffers from fits she tells me and is 'in general ill health'. She seeks relief for this child either as an in-patient or out-patient. She does not live with her husband, who is a labourer, she does not know where he is – has not seen him for years. Mrs Nicholls only came to me as a stranger this afternoon. I have therefore had no opportunity of making enquiries about her. Frank Loyd

Letter from C E Boothby, The Royal Alexandra Hospital for Sick Children, Dyke Road, Brighton, 9 November 1894
Dear Sir, may I trouble you to inform Colonel Loyd of 55 Wilbury Road, Hove, a member of the committee of this hospital, whether the case mentioned by him in enclosed letter is a deserving one? Yours faithfully, C E Boothby

10 November 1894
Mr C E Boothby, Royal Alexandra Hospital, wishes the committee to forward a report of this case to Colonel Loyd, 55 Wilbury Road. Mrs Nicholls returned from hop picking a fortnight ago since which time she has resided at 12 Cumberland Place and lived by begging. Her son Frederick, aged nine, is said to be in bad health but he has attended Circus Street school 10 times this week and the previous reports will show that she has been known to the society since March 1872 as a thorough impostor. WC [William Collingham]
Report to Colonel Loyd

22 March 1895
Mrs Nicholls has called on Mrs Friend of Stoneleigh, Preston Road, begging on several occasions lately and has generally been assisted but before relieving her again the lady requests a report of the case. WC [William Collingham]
Report to Mrs French, C P Boger

Letter from A M Waterhouse, 3 Lewes Crescent, Brighton, 19 November [1885]
Dear Sir, I am opening you a lot of trouble but I have been so deceived and this must be my apology. A woman came this morning for assistance to get a pedlar's licence, her name is Hannah Nicholls, 4 Oxford Place, Brighton. Will you kindly let me know if she is deserving of assistance and oblige. Yours truly, A M Waterhouse

20 November 1895
Mrs Nicholls has applied to Mrs Waterhouse, 3 Lewes Crescent, for assistance to set her up as a pedlar but before complying with her request she wishes for a

[338] Lieutenant-Colonel Frank K Loyd.

report of the case. During the past summer she has gone flint picking in the neighbourhood of Falmer and the previous reports will show she that has been known to the society as a thorough imposter since March 1872. WC [William Collingham]
Report to Mrs Waterhouse, C P Boger

16 January 1897
Mrs Crichton, 20 Vernon Terrace, requests another report of this case. On seeing Mrs Nicholls last evening she informed me that her daughters are living in London, therefore they are not in need of medical relief from the Lying-in Institution here but the previous reports will show that the mother has long been in the habit of obtaining lying-in cards for begging purposes. WC [William Collingham]
Report to Mrs Crichton, C P Boger

9 February 1898
Mr J H Sharp of 21 Palmeira Square requests a report of this case. Mrs Nicholls and her companions have long been in the habit of applying to him for letters to the medical charities in Brighton more especially for cards for the lying-in institution and the previous reports will show that they have been used for begging purposes. WC [William Collingham]
Report to Sharp, [*signature illegible*]

18 December 1899
Miss J E Bell, 48 Marine Parade, requests a report of this case. Mrs Nicholls is not known at 5 Spa Street, the address she gave, and is still living in Oxford Place. During the summer she does a little work in the fields, in the winter she goes out seeking charity with a woman named Webb and the previous reports show that she has been known to the society as a troublesome beggar since 6 March 1872. WC [William Collingham]
Reported verbally on Saturday, [*signature illegible*]

27 January 1900
Mrs Napper, Warnham House, Ship Street, requires a report of this case as Mrs Nicholls has recently applied for help for her grandchildren whose mother had just died in Haywards Heath asylum and the receiving officer was just about to arrange for their admission into the Union [workhouse]. Mrs Nicholls has not lost a daughter as represented neither has she any grandchildren left on her hands and the previous reports show that she is a thorough impostor. WC [William Collingham]
Report to Mrs Napper, F de GM [Miss F de G Merrifield]
30 Jan, reported CW

13 May 1905
Letter from Mr Figgis in which he says 'a poor woman name of Harley has just come to see me in the vestry'. I fear she drinks and gave her nothing. She says that she and her daughter, whose husband has deserted her, are to be turned out of 18 William Street. I dare say that the scene is well known to your visitor (see Histed 10341).[339] Mr Figgis was asked for a description of the woman.

Letter from John Benjamin Figgis, Emmanuel Church vestry to Miss H Woodhead honorary secretary of the Charity Organisation Society, 14 May 1905[340]
Dear Miss Woodhead, excuse a line written here – while the matter is before me I say that what Mrs Harley, 12 Henry Street, told me was that she was summoned for rent which she could not pay because her daughter (who lived with her) had been deserted by her husband. She is not above the middle size nor very stout. She had had (as her breath told) something to drink. I identify her as a woman who used to beg of me (say) ten or fifteen years ago: not lately. The case of the Ballams is very disappointing. Yours truly, J B Figgis

Letter from H Woodhead, honorary secretary of the Charity Organisation Society to the Reverend J B Figgis, 28 Compton Avenue, Brighton, 22 May 1905
Dear Mr Figgis, re: Ann Nicholls aged 63, 12 Henry Street. In your first letter respecting a woman giving the name of Harley you said that she stated that she was living at 18 William Street and so we failed to trace her. Mrs Nicholls who is living at 12 Henry Street has been known to us unfavourably to us [sic] since 1872 and she is evidently the woman who applied to you. We have been asked 40 times for information respecting her by ladies and gentlemen to whom she has applied for charity. She often gives a false name and address. She has given the name of Eldridge, White, Mitchell, Whitting, Hill, Stringer etc. The excuses which she gives also are various. Both she and her husband William Nicholls used to drink and at times when he was in full work she used to live by begging. Her moral character is very unsatisfactory. She left her husband in 1884 and has lived with various people since. She might have been prosecuted many times for fraud except for the difficulty to get people to come forward and give evidence. However, on one occasion she was sentenced to 14 days' hard labour for fraudulent begging. On another occasion she got £18 out of a lady by presenting that she had a sailor son who had been discharged from the navy owing to sunstroke and £20 of his pay was owing to him. This story was quite untrue. Another time the excuse for asking for charity was that her husband was in London and she wanted to join him. He was in Brighton all the time. Another

339 This is presumably a reference to a Mr or Mrs Histed, applicant 10341, whose papers do not survive.
340 Figgis is usually associated the Countess of Huntington's church on North Street but *Figgis of Brighton* by J Westbury-Jones states he was appointed minister at the Emmanuel Church, Norfolk Terrace, Brighton, in 1897.

time she pretended that she had lost a daughter. In 1889 she got £1 4s 6d from a lady on the plea that she had a daughter ill and wanted to get £2 to enable her to go to a hospital. Hospital letters and dispensary letters seem to have been a great source of income to her as several people have assisted her when she produced a properly signed letter. We feel sure that if she calls at your house again you will give her no further assistance. Yours truly, H Woodhead, Honorary Secretary

Letter from Kathleen Beves, St Margarets, Dyke Road, Brighton, 14 March 1906
Dear Madam, I am sorry to trouble you again but can you give me any information about Mrs Nicholls of 44 Hereford Street? I think I remember her begging a good deal some years ago, she assures me my mother was very good to her. I cannot be quite sure of her but I think she is a fraud and feel sure my best way is to ask you for information. Yours truly, Kathleen Beves

17 March 1906
Miss K Beves, St Margarets, Dyke Road, requests a report of this case. Mrs Nicholls now resides at 44 Hereford Street and continues to live almost entirely by begging. WC [William Collingham]

Letter to Miss K Beves, 17 Dyke Road, Brighton, from F Wilkinson, 17 March 1906
Dear Madam, re: Ann Nicholls aged 63, 12 Henry Street. You are quite right in thinking this woman is a fraud. She has been known to us most unfavourably to us since 1872. We have been asked 41 times for information respecting her by ladies and gentlemen to whom she has applied for charity. She often gives a false name and address and has called herself Eldridge, White, Mitchell, Whitting, Hill, Stringer etc. Her moral character is very unsatisfactory. She left her husband in 1884 and has lived with various people since. She might many times have been prosecuted for fraud except for the difficulty to get people to come forward and give evidence, she was however, on one occasion she was sentenced to 14 days' hard labour for fraudulent begging. One quite untrue story which she told a lady thereby getting £18 out of her, was that she had a sailor son who had been discharged from the navy owing to a sun-stroke and that £20 of his pay was still owing to him. Another time the excuse given for begging was that the husband was in London and she wanted to join him: he was in Brighton all the time. Another time she pretended that she had lost a daughter. Hospital letters and dispensary letters seem to have been a great source of income to her; several people assisted her when she produced a properly signed letter. Yours faithfully, F Wilkinson

Postcard to William Collingham from George Collingham, 10 December 1906
Dear Pa, Hannah Nicholls died today, Monday afternoon, 2.45pm. Pneumonia. George

11 December 1906
Postcard from the relieving officer to say that Mrs Nicholls died yesterday of pneumonia at 2.45pm. WC [William Collingham]

95 MARY GOBLE, 22, WIFE OF A LABOURER, 5 GROSVENOR STREET, BRIGHTON

Mary Goble (née Jeffery) was born in Brighton in 1850 and married James Goble at St Nicholas, Brighton, on 20 August 1871.[341] *The couple were living at 5 Grosvenor Place in one room with their five-week-old baby. Their case was forwarded to the Mendicity Society by the wife of the Reverend John Hannah, Vicar of Brighton, who had been approached by Mary Goble requesting the price of a marriage fee: Goble was heavily pregnant and feared dying in a state of sin during childbirth. Mrs Hannah was subsequently approached by Goble a number of times with inconsistent stories which prompted her enquiry to the Mendicity Society.*

The charity's report states that Mary's husband, James Goble, who was born in Brighton in 1852, had been convicted of felony two or three times before March 1872.[342] *He was the son of James and Jemima Goble and local press is peppered with references to his misdemeanours between 1858 and 1867. However, James junior was not the only member of the family to find notoriety in the pages of the local press. His father, James senior, was convicted for assaulting his wife Jemima in August 1861.*[343] *The newspaper account of the trial, which carries the headline 'A Brute of a Husband,' records how James Goble, who was described as 'a man of a most forbidding countenance', assaulted Jemima Goble ten days after she had given birth.*[344] *Jemima Goble had recently discovered that her husband had been cohabiting with a woman in Rock Street and, suspecting him to be at the house, went there and smashed windows at the property. James Goble came out swore at her, struck her giving her a black eye and dragged her into the house but a policeman was quickly at the scene to prevent further harm from being done. The justice, Mr Bigge, sentenced Goble to three months' imprisonment with hard labour and only showed leniency because a longer sentence would have left Mrs Goble with nine children to support singlehandedly. Considerable applause was heard in court at the sentence.*

James Goble junior's transgressions were lesser in nature than his father's but seemingly occurred with more frequency. In November 1858 two 'urchins' James Goble and Edward Colwell were charged with wilfully damaging a wall on the London Road. Goble was fined five shillings, or, in default of payment, to go to prison for ten days. Colwell was discharged.[345] *Goble, now 12, appeared in the magistrates' court on 14 June 1865 on the*

[341] ESRO: PAR 255/1/3/46.
[342] Birth of James Goble registered Q2 1852 Brighton 2b 204.
[343] Brighton Gazette, 22 August 1861.
[344] A later report in the *Brighton Gazette* described James Goble as a 'morose looking man'.
[345] Brighton Gazette, 25 November 1858.

same day as his 11-year-old brother John. Both boys had been charged with stealing boots left on the beach by bathers. James Goble was discharged due to lack of evidence but John was committed to prison with seven days hard labour and ten strokes of a birch rod.[346] *On 20 July 1865 James Goble appeared before the magistrates' court for stealing a flannel shirt from John Fitzgerald's shop on Richmond Street. It was noted during the hearing that nearly all the family had been brought before the Justice and James was the fourth member of the family to appear in court during the last year.*[347] *In November 1865 James, described as 'a very old offender', was charged with stealing a pair of clogs from Matthew McCarthy's shop in North Laine. He was found guilty and committed to prison for two months with hard labour.*[348] *Two years later when Goble would have been about 14 he was charged with throwing a boulder at a seven-year-old boy to whom he lost a game of pitch and toss. The incident, which took place on Richmond Street, resulted in the younger boy sustaining a severe head injury. Goble was sentenced to two weeks imprisonment with hard labour.*[349]

James Goble junior deserted his wife in about August 1872 and emigrated to New Zealand. Nothing more is known of him. By February 1883 Mary Goble was living with a brickmaker named George Green at 23 Tichborne Street. The date of her death is not known but there are no obvious matches to women named Mary Goble who died in Brighton between 1883 and 1940. However, an 82-year-old woman named Mary Jeffery died in Brighton in 1933, suggesting she may have reverted to her maiden name after James Goble emigrated.[350]

Letter from Mrs Hannah, the Vicarage, Brighton, [March 1872]

Mrs Hannah will be much obliged if the following case may be enquired into. Mary Jeffery came to her back in July from Mrs Vicars apparently far advanced in pregnancy asking to have the marriage fees remitted as she was very much afraid of dying during her confinement in a state of sin. Her request was granted and she was married by banns at the parish church on the 20th August 1871 to James Goble. She came begging several times after that and was always relieved and in October during Mrs Hannah's absence from home, wrote to say she had been confined of a stillborn female child, that she had been very ill and of course again asking for relief. During and before this time she gave three different addresses all of which proved to be false as the vicar and one of the curates vainly tried to find her. Again and again she came asking [for] relief, her husband was ill, etc, etc, until at last she was told they were both young had no child, and they must work or go to the workhouse. About a fortnight ago she had the amazing folly to come with a fine male child that she was suckling of

[346] Brighton Guardian, 21 June 1865.
[347] Brighton Gazette, 27 July 1865.
[348] Brighton Gazette, 9 November 1865.
[349] Brighton Gazette, 6 June 1867.
[350] Death of Mary Jeffery registered Q4 1933 Brighton 2b 348.

above a month old which she declared was her own <u>second</u> child and says she is now living at 5 Grosvenor Street near Edward Street. Mrs Hannah wants enquiries to be made in the neighbourhood about her and particularly whether she has ever been confined at all? And if so at which of the times she asserts: October or January? And whether her child was born dead or alive.

6 March 1872
Statement: I told an untruth and I am sorry for it.
Report: I made enquiries respecting this case. The statement was false about the stillborn child. She was confined five weeks ago of a son. She says she thought Mr Hannah would not marry them if she did not say she was expecting to be confined. The man has been convicted two or three times for felony, he is in full work at present. The home is in a passable state.
Dismissed as undeserving, Orfeur Cavenagh. NB the purport of the report to be communicated to Mr Hannah

21 January 1874
Mrs Goble applied at the office on Wednesday for assistance and on enquiry I find that her husband deserted her and emigrated to New Zealand 12 months ago last August. After that applicant supported herself and child by washing up till three months ago when she went into the workhouse but she only remained there a month before she came out again and since she has been out of the house she has done a little more washing but she is now suffering from a poisoned finger and appears to be in a very low, weak state no doubt brought on through want of nourishing food. WC [William Collingham]
Referred to parish authorities, R P Hooper

Note from Dr Willoughby Furner, 6 February 1883
I recommend James Goble for the consideration of the Charity Organisation Society. He requires good food. Willoughby Furner, Sussex County Hospital[351]

6 February 1883
The son John, now of 23 Tichbourne Street, who is suffering from an abscess on his arm, was sent by Dr Furner and applied at the office on Monday for assistance to enable him to get nourishing food. His mother goes out washing three days a week and lives with a brickmaker named George Green. WC [William Collingham]
Grant of 2s 6d per week for two weeks.
Agent to arrange, R P Hooper

[351] For a biography of Dr Willoughby Furner see ESRO: LIB/503507/373.

19 February 1883
The son John applied at the office on Monday for some further relief. Although his arm is not much better he has greatly improved in his appearance since my last report. WC [William Collingham]
2s 6d a week for two further weeks, Thomas W Holland

13 March 1883
The son John applied at the office on Monday for some further assistance. His arm is still bad but he improves very much in his appearance. WC [William Collingham]
2s 6d a week for two weeks, Thomas W Holland

96 MARY MANNEL, 70, NEEDLEWOMAN, 34 CROWN STREET, BRIGHTON

Mary or Mary Ann Mannel was enumerated on the 1861 census at 10 Farm Road, Hove. She was employed as a tailoress but, despite being listed as married, was living in shared accommodation with no other family members. She was born in Dawlish, Devon, in about 1802 and, according to her application form, moved to Brighton in about 1855.

By 1871 she was widowed, living at 12 Dean Street, Brighton, with her widowed daughter, Sarah Castle, and her two-year-old granddaughter Ellen Castle. Both women earned their living by tailoring but in about September 1871 they appear to have parted company: at the time of her application for relief in March 1872, Mary stated that she had been living at 34 Crown Street for six months. Mary Mannel occupied one upstairs room at this address, for which she paid rent of three shillings per week. She was not in arrears, but sickness had kept her out of work for a month. Mannel's case was forwarded to the Mendicity Society by Robert Hooper, the charity's vice chairman.

8 March 1872
Statement: Mary Mannel wants a little assistance till she gets work.
Report: I made enquiries respecting this woman and find she has been a widow five years. She lives with her daughter and one child who is also a widow. They support themselves by needle work. Mr Hooper gave her a good character and thinks she ought to receive parish relief. I find she is not known at the parochial office. The home is in a passable state. I believe this to be a deserving case.
Referred to parochial authorities, R P Hooper. NB allowed by parish 2s 6d per week [Orfeur Cavenagh]

97 HANNAH DANES, 49, NURSE, 12 ST NICHOLAS ROAD, BRIGHTON

Hannah Danes was born in Newington, Surrey, in about 1823. Her application form states that she moved to Brighton in about 1869 and that she had been living at her present address for 10 weeks; previously she had been resident at 7 Windsor Street and 11 Boss Gardens. In 1871 a 49-year-old woman named Danes (no first name was given) was enumerated at 13 Lansdowne Place, where she was employed by Thomas Richings, a retired solicitor, as a lady's maid.

By the time of her first application Hannah Danes was already widowed, earning a living as a nurse and occupying one first floor room at 12 St Nicholas Road. She shared the house with Louisa Mills, who applied to the Mendicity Society on the same day.[352] *Danes paid weekly rent of 2s 6d and was 15 shillings in arrears. She had been working for Miss Wardell of 13 New Steine, but sickness had kept her off work for 10 weeks.*
Danes's name was forwarded to the charity in December 1874 by the Reverend R E H Raines when she was living in a single, first-floor room at 80 North Road.[353] *She paid weekly rent of three shillings and was £1 14s in arrears.*

In 1881 Hannah Danes was enumerated at 154 Lewes Road, where she lodged, still working as a nurse.

8 March 1872
Statement: Hannah Danes wants a little assistance till she gets work.
Report: I made enquiries respecting this woman and find she has been getting her living by nursing but has had nothing to do for this last ten weeks. She and the woman Mills live together. She has pawned nearly all her clothes to live on and is now in a very destitute state. Mrs Lee, 42 Borough Street, gave her a good character. Mrs Hannah at the vicarage has relieved her on two occasions. I told this woman if she could not get nursing to do she should try and get something else.
Dismissed as ineligible, Orfeur Cavenagh

18 December 1872
Further information: applicant came again to the office saying that she had had nothing to do for some time and was in a destitute state. She left some letters in proof of her respectability. She has been kept in part by her landlady for some time and is getting into debt. WC [William Collingham]
Ineligible, R P Hooper

14 December 1874
This person brought the annexed letter to the office on Monday and at the same time applied for assistance. In answer to my questions she stated that she had had no regular employment as a nurse for the last five months but that she had earned a little by needlework. She owes three months' rent. The committee

352 Louisa Mills' application is number 98 in the series.
353 The Reverend Richard Edward Hodgson Raines was a curate at the time of Danes's application but he was vicar of St John Carlton Hill between 1875 and 1879.

dismissed her case as ineligible on two previous occasions on the grounds that being a strong woman provided she could not succeed as a nurse she should go charring, house cleaning or washing. WC [William Collingham]
Ineligible, to be reported to Mr Raines, R P Hooper

Letter from R E H Raines, 6 Park Crescent Terrace, Brighton, 14 December 1894
I have much pleasure in recommending Nurse Danes as an object for relief from the funds of the Charity Organisation Society. I believe her to be thoroughly honest and respectable and that she is now in straitened circumstances entirely owing to her having been unfortunate in procuring employment. Faithfully yours, R E H Raines

30 November 1875
This person applied at the office on Monday for £1 12s to enable her to get her boxes which are detained by her late landlord for a quarter's rent. She has nothing to do and is lodging with a poor widow at 27 Crown Street to whom she owes nearly £4. WC [William Collingham]
Ineligible, R P Hooper

98 LOUISA MILLS, 53, NURSE, 12 ST NICHOLAS ROAD, BRIGHTON

Louisa Mills was born in The Strand, London, in about 1819. At the time of her application to the Mendicity Society she lived at 12 St Nicholas Road: the same property as Hannah Danes, who applied to the charity on the same day.[354] *Mills had been living at that address for five months but had been resident in Brighton for about 18 years. She paid weekly rent of one shilling for her first-floor room but was six shillings in arrears. Mills had been working as a nurse for Mrs Coppard of 42 Temple Street and when in full employment earned 12 shillings per week. However, she had been short of work for two months.*

8 March 1872
Statement: Louisa Mills wants a little assistance till she gets work.
Report: I made enquiries respecting this woman and find she has been getting her living nursing but has had nothing to do this last two months. She is a dressmaker by trade. She lives with the woman Danes. Mrs Hannah has relieved her on two occasions.[355] She has pawned nearly all her clothes and is now in a very destitute state. Mrs Coppard gave her a good character. I told her if she could not get nursing to do she should go at her trade dressmaking again.
Dismissed as ineligible, Orfeur Cavenagh

[354] Hannah Danes's application for relief is number 97 in the series.
[355] Probably the wife of the Reverend John Hannah, Vicar of Brighton.

99 CHARLOTTE COLBRAN, 68, NURSE, 13 MARLBOROUGH STREET, BRIGHTON

Charlotte Colbran's case was forwarded to the Mendicity Society by Mrs H Dering of 16 Upper Brunswick Place. A 57-year-old woman named Charlotte B Colbran was enumerated on the census of 1861 living at 6 Chesham Place with her husband John Baker Colbran, a retired farmer from Herstmonceux.

Charlotte Colbran was born in Brighton and had been living at 13 Marlborough Street since the beginning of February 1872. She paid rent of 2s 6d per week and was up to date with payments despite having been out of work for six months due to the death of her employer Mrs Lloyd of West Street, where she had earned six shillings per week. At the time of her application she was a widow. The date of her husband's death is unclear, but a man named John Colbran died in Brighton in the March quarter of 1863.[356]

The application form states that a relative also named Colbran, living in St James Street had relieved her previously. This was probably James Baker Colbran, a builder, who lived at 4 St Mary's Place, just off St James Street. He was born in Herstmonceux in about 1809 and was probably the brother of her late husband.

8 March 1872
Statement: Charlotte Colbran wants a little assistance till she gets work.
Report: I made enquiries respecting this woman and find she has been a widow [for] eight years. She gets her living nursing. She has been three months in the hospital with a bad leg and left five weeks ago.[357] She applied 12 months ago to the parish authorities but refused to go in the workhouse. Mrs Mansbridge gave her a good character.[358] The clergyman of West Street Chapel has relieved this woman on two or three occasions. Mr Colbran has relieved her several times but cannot continue to do so. He gave me half a crown to give to her this afternoon. The home is in a passable state.
Relieved by grant, Orfeur Cavenagh. NB 2 shillings to be allotted this week and 4 shillings – the 2 shillings to give her a chance of obtaining work previous to applying to the relieving officer

Letter from Miss E Turner, 67 Dyke Road, 4 July 1884[359]
Sir, I was accosted a day or two since by a clean, tidy looking woman who told me she was that day 84 years of age and had not a morsel of bread to eat. She said she was a widow in receipt of 3s 6d a week from the parish 2s 6d of which

[356] Death of John Colbran registered Q1 1863 Brighton 2b 119.
[357] Charlotte Colbran was admitted to the Royal Sussex County Hospital on 1 November 1871. She was recommended for treatment by Somers Clarke and security for her burial was provided by Stephen Peters. No details of her medical condition or date of discharge were given [ESRO: HB 35/3/1871/123415].
[358] Mrs Mansbridge lived at 12 North Gardens.
[359] 67 Dyke Road was the address of Miss Draper's home for invalid gentlewomen.

went for her rent. Her name is Mrs Colbran, 31 Zion Place. As I am somewhat of an invalid and my stay here is drawing to a close I think I cannot do better than bring the case to your notice begging you to enquire into it. Should you find the woman's statement correct may I ask you to let me know if it is the power of your society to relieve her? It seems sad to come to her age and be without necessary food. I am sir, yours truly, Miss E Turner

5 July 1884
Miss E Turner of 67 Dyke Road forwarded the annexed letter to the office this morning and wishes to know whether this is a case that the society can assist. Mrs Colbran receives weekly 3s 6d from the parish, 1s from West Street Chapel and 1s from a lady, besides which she gets a little help from St Nicholas district and also temporary assistance from friends so that she ought to be in fairly comfortable circumstances and not in need of relief. WC [William Collingham]
Report to be sent to Miss E Turner [*signature obscured*]

100 ELIZABETH WRIGHT, 28, WASHERWOMAN, 3 JERSEY STREET, BRIGHTON

Elizabeth Wright was born in Brighton in about 1844 and, according to the Mendicity Society application form, had been living at 3 Jersey Street with her husband William and their three daughters since about 1870. Previously the family lived at 19 Newhaven Street where they were enumerated in 1871 lodging with William Taylor and his family. Taylor was a coachmaker and on the census William Wright's profession was given as coach builder's labourer.

By the time of the family's application to the Mendicity Society in March 1872, William Wright was working for John Marshall at the drainage works where, when in full-time occupation, he could expect to take home 16 shillings a week. Elizabeth Wright usually earned 3s 6d a week from washing, so in normal circumstances they would have had a large enough combined income to cover the weekly rent of three shillings for their two rooms. William Wright had been short of work for three weeks and had run up arrears of 12 shillings.

11 March 1872
Statement: Elizabeth Wright wants a little assistance till her husband gets work.
Report: I made enquiries respecting this case and find the man has been out of work three weeks – the drainage works is completed. He applied to the parish authorities but refused to go in the workhouse. The wife occasionally gets a day's work. The home is in a destitute state. They don't bear a very good character in the neighbourhood and they say they are bad principle [sic].
Relieved by grant, Orfeur Cavenagh

2s 6d to be referred to the agent to expend in the purchase of articles of food provided the man is undeserving to obtain work [sic]

101 JANE PATCHING, 64, WASHERWOMAN, 19 PROVIDENCE PLACE, BRIGHTON

Jane Patching (née Cobby) was born in Brighton and married Henry Patching, who was three years her senior, at St Nicholas, Brighton, on 5 November 1826.[360] *The couple were enumerated on the 1841 census at King Street with their children Henry, Susannah and Jane. Ten years later they were resident at 5 Sun Street where they lived with their children Jane, Elizabeth and William and Jane's widowed mother Susannah Cobby. By 1861 the family, now without Susannah Cobby, were living at 69 Albion Hill Street where, according to their Mendicity Society application form, they stayed until about 1868.*[361]

At the time of their approach to the charity in March 1872, Henry Patching was employed as a labourer for Mr Jackson of London Road but due to lack of work was bringing in only five shillings a week when he could usually expect to earn 15 shillings per week. Jane Patching was employed as a washerwoman but was earning two shillings per week rather than the usual three shillings. They paid two shillings per week for the entire house at 19 Providence Place but were 24 shillings in arrears. Thomas Buchan, a dairyman of 25 Providence Place, for whom Henry Patching had recently been working, provided a reference.

The couple were still living at 19 Providence Place in 1881 when they shared the property with their 18-year-old grandson Richard Patching, who was employed as a porter. Richard Patching died in April 1884 whilst working for Messrs Cochrane, wholesale grocers of Brighton.[362] *The Coroner's inquest stated that he had deposited goods in a lift and replaced a bar which ran across the lift designed to prevent anyone from falling down the shaft. However, a colleague found him with his head between the bar and the top of the lift as it was trying to ascend. The accident broke Richard Patching's neck and a verdict of Accidental Death was returned: he was buried at Bear Road cemetery on 30 April 1884.*[363]

Henry Patching died in Brighton aged 80 and was buried at Bear Road cemetery on 3 September 1886.[364] *Two 80-year-old women named Jane Patching died in the March quarter of 1890: although the dates do not tally precisely it is conceivable that one of these may be the correct person.*

360 ESRO: PAR 255/1/3/5.

361 The death of Susannah Cecilia Cobby was registered in the December quarter of 1854.

362 Buckingham Express, 3 May 1884.

363 ESRO: BH/L/3/1/7 - Woodvale Cemetery burial plot ZGW 41.

364 ESRO: BH/L/3/1/7 - Woodvale Cemetery burial plot ZAF 14.

11 March 1872
Statement: Jane Patching wants a little assistance till her husband gets in full work.
Report: I made inquiries respecting this case and find the man is working for Mr Jackson, London Road. He started work there last week, the wife occasionally gets a day's work. They have applied to the parish authorities but refused to go in the workhouse. The home is in a passable state. They are not wanting relief at present. Mr Buchan gave them a good character. Mr Jackson states that he is not a very hard-working man, that he is inclined to be idle and he prefers giving him [?truck].[365]
Dismissed as ineligible, Orfeur Cavenagh

7 November 1872
Further information respecting this case. Since this case was before the committee in March last applicant has not had any regular employment. He has jobbed about for Mrs Kemp, 43 Norfolk Square, who gave him one of the society's tickets thinking it a deserving case for a little relief. The wife is not able to work. They have applied to the Guardians three weeks running when they gave an order for the [work]house which they refused. The home is in a destitute state.
Ineligible, recommended to go into the workhouse, G D R, chairman[366]

102 JOSEPH BIRNBAUM (ALSO GIVEN AS BERNBAUM AND BERNBAM), 50, MUSICIAN, 43 CAVENDISH STREET, BRIGHTON

Joseph Birnbaum was born in Hungary in about 1822. The marriage of a Joseph Birnbaum to Louisa Jane Board was registered in Exeter, Devon, in the March quarter of 1852, and on the census of 1861 he and his wife were enumerated at 26 Cumberland Place, Brighton.[367] *They shared the house with their three children who were aged between one and six and born in Exeter or Torquay, Devon, and a visiting Hungarian man named Joseph Rudorf. These dates suggest that the couple arrived in Brighton during the 1860s, but the couple's application form stated that they had been resident in Brighton since 1854 and had been living at their present address for 10 months; prior to that they had lodged at 53 Cavendish Street.*

At the time of the application, the Birnbaum's eldest daughter, also Louisa, was working as an ironer at the New Laundry on Lewes Road where she earned three shillings per week. Joseph Birnbaum earned nine shillings per week but although their combined income would usually have covered the weekly rent of 4s 9d, they were 20 shillings in arears with

365 The payment of wages otherwise than in money.
366 Thought to be George Dudley Ryder.
367 Joseph Birnbaum marriage to Louisa Jane Board registered Q1 1852 Exeter 5b 183.

repayments. Birnbaum gave John Cordy Burrows, former Mayor of Brighton, of 62 Old Steine as a reference but no further mention of Burrows was made.

Later reports by the Charity Organisation Society state that the Birnbaums left Brighton at some point after March 1872 but returned in about 1877. By the time of their second application in June 1879 the family were living at 1 Ivory Buildings.

Letter from the Duchess of Grafton, 32 Adelaide Crescent, [7 March 1872]
The Duchess of Grafton presents her compliments to Mr Godden and begs to enquire if he knows anything of a man of the name Bernbaum, a Hungarian who begs about the streets, or his wife. Bernbaum told the duchess that his wife attended St Mary's Church and was known to Mr Godden. He professed to be unable to get employment here or to persuade his wife, who is an Englishwoman, to accompany him to Hungary but says he is half famished. The duchess begs to apologise for the use of pencil owing to bad health

Letter from W W Godden, [44] Devonshire Place, 8 March [1872][368]
Dear Mr Beal, I submit to the committee a letter for their consideration. I have informed the duchess that although <u>little</u> is known of Bernbaum at St Mary's yet nothing is known <u>against</u> him. I find also that my friend and colleague Mrs Coore has become surety for him for a loan but expects to 'smart for it'.[369] Yours faithfully, W W Godden

Letter from Louisa Bernbaum, 43 Cavendish Street, Brighton, [7 March 1872]
Sir, in consequence of the kindness of Mr Reynolds in explaining to you this little affair which has unfortunately happened to my husband – a thing which I promise shall never happen again. I am extremely thankful for your great kindness and will promise by all means nothing of the kind shall never happen again sir. Very thankful for your kindness toward me and my family. I remain your humble servant, Louisa Bernbaum

11 March 1872
Statement: all my best friends are dead. My trade is very bad.
Report: I made enquiries respecting this case and find the man is a musician. He plays and sings about the streets and no doubt gets a good living. He says all his best friends are dead. He admitted sending letters to Mrs Cohen and to James Ashling esq and to several other parties in the town. This man has been in the habit of sending begging letters for years. He has been relieved by the District Visitors over and over again. About two years ago they collected a sum of money to get him some furniture. A few weeks ago he had a loan of £5 to get

[368] The Reverend William Worcester Godden, vicar of St Mary's Chapel, 1869-1873.
[369] The Reverend Alfred Thomas Coore MA, 2 College Road, Brighton.

him some more furniture. The house is in a destitute and filthy state. I believe him to be [a] regular imposter.
Further inquiry, Orfeur Cavenagh
This man I believe has left the town since I have been making enquiries about him, dismissed as ineligible, Orfeur Cavenagh. NB the result of the inquiry to be communicated to the Reverend Mr Godden for the information of the Duchess of Grafton

12 June 1879
Mr Battye Cuming, 34 Brunswick Terrace has been in the habit of assisting this man but before doing so again he requests a report of the case. Birnbaum returned to Brighton about two years ago and still goes about with a guitar. His wife takes in needlework. They have only their youngest son dependent on them. The family appear to get a good living. WC [William Collingham]
Report to Mr Battye Cuming, R P Hooper

103 MARTHA HEWITT, 35, WIFE OF A SHOEMAKER, 13 RIDING SCHOOL LANE, BRIGHTON

Martha Hewitt was born in about 1837: she gave her place of birth as Kingston on the Mendicity Society application form but Westbourne, West Sussex, was given as her birthplace on the census of 1871. The 1871 census shows her husband, Henry Hewitt, was born in Portsmouth in about 1841 and their children were born in Portsmouth, Westbourne and Henfield.

The ages of the children and information supplied to the charity suggest the family moved from Henfield to Brighton in 1868 or 1869. They had been living at 13 Riding School Lane for two years, where they paid weekly rent of 4s 6d for the whole house and were 49 shillings in arrears. Their case was forwarded to the Mendicity Society by Mr Jones, the town missionary.[370] *Henry Hewitt had been working for James Whittaker of 16-17 Meeting House Lane, where he usually expected to earn 15 shillings per week but had been out of work for two weeks due to illness.*

13 March 1872
Statement: Martha Hewitt wants a little assistance till her husband gets better.
Report: I made inquiries respecting this case and find the man is a shoe maker: he has been sick two weeks. A few weeks ago he was sick for six weeks. There is no doubt this man is consumptive. He bears a good character at Mr Whittaker's.

[370] John James Jones of 67 Cobden Road started working as a missionary at Brighton in 1869. In 1873 he helped form the Brighton Band of Hope Union and in 1904 he established a weekly service for vagrants at the casual ward of Brighton Workhouse. The *Brighton Gazette* of 3 July 1909 gave a summary of his achievements and recorded the fortieth anniversary of his time in the role.

Mr Meeres, the clergyman of that district has relieved him and says he believes this to be a very deserving case.[371] The wife is not a strong woman. They receive parish relief at the rate of 9s per week. The home is in a destitute state. Mr Smith the relieving officer says the best thing they can do is go in the workhouse.
Dismissed as ineligible, Orfeur Cavenagh

104 JOHN READING, 43, HAWKER, 5 EGREMONT STREET, BRIGHTON

The Reading family's case was originally forwarded to the Mendicity Society by Mrs Fox of 1 Chesham Place in March 1872. The marriage of a John Reading to a Sarah Wooldridge was registered in Brighton in the June quarter of 1860.[372] John, a match seller, Sarah and their children Anne, Charles, Sarah and Martha, aged between 8 years and two months old, had shared one room at 5 Egremont Street for the previous two years.[373] They paid weekly rent of 1s 6d but were 5s 6d in arrears. John Reading brought home four shillings per week and Sarah Reading usually earned 6d per week from charring but had been unable to work since giving birth in January 1872.

Their case was forwarded to the charity again in December 1873: this time by Miss Johnson of West Street House. The family were living in one room on the first floor of 39 Thomas Street. They paid three shillings per week rent and were up to date with payments. The Readings had moved to 22 Hereford Street by the time of their next application in June 1874 when Mr Bennett of the School Board Office recommended them to the society.

John, Sarah and their youngest daughter, Sarah, aged 11, were enumerated at 55 Sloane Street on the census of 1881. The census records John as being blind, which tallies with the reports made by William Collingham, the Mendicity Society's agent. The next contact with the Charity Organisation Society was made after their case was forwarded by Miss Emmett of 12 Eaton Place in March 1884 when the Readings were resident at 43 Essex Street. By this time John and Sarah's son, Charles Reading, had emigrated to Canada but no record of the precise date can be found.

The 1891 census shows John Reading, now described as being subject to fits; Sarah; their daughter Sarah and granddaughter, Daisy Anne Reading living at 43 Egremont Street.

14 March 1872
Statement: John Reading wants a little assistance – he does not want to go in the workhouse.
Report: I made enquiries respecting this case and find the man hawks matches. This man suffers from weak eyes. His wife occasionally gets a little charring but since her last confinement she has not been able to work. The home is in a

[371] Henry William Meeres, curate of Brighton.
[372] John Reading marriage to Sarah Wooldridge registered Q2 1860 Brighton 2b 326.
[373] John Reading gave his age as 43 when the census was taken in April 1871 and to the Mendicity Society in March 1872 but stated he was 57 in 1881 and 67 in 1891.

destitute state. The Reverend Snowden Smith has relieved them on several occasions. He says the best thing they can do is go in the workhouse – he gave me a shilling to give to the wife. They are well known to the parish authorities: they received parish relief during the wife's confinement and now have an order for the workhouse. The man says the reason he went up to Mrs Fox was he heard the lady was very good to the poor.
Referred to Poor Law, Orfeur Cavenagh

16 December 1873
A short time after this case was before the committee in March 1872 the whole family went into the workhouse where they remained until about four months ago. Since then they have lived in a small furnished room in Thomas Street. The man who is very near-sighted continues to sell matches, the wife does a little charring. Neither of the children have attended any school since they came out of the workhouse. Their home is in a destitute state. The Guardians still consider this a fit case for the workhouse and on two recent occasions they gave them an order for the [work]house. Miss Johnson knows nothing of the family but seeing the children running about the streets in a destitute condition she sent them a loaf of bread and an investigation ticket in the hope that something might be done for the children. WC [William Collingham]
Referred to parish and to be reported to Miss Johnson, R P Hooper

10 June 1874
The man Reading applied at the office on Tuesday for three pairs of boots for his children to enable them to attend school. Since my last report he has lost his youngest child. His general circumstances are much the same but lately I have often seen him return home at night the worse for drink. His wife is looking after a furnished house in Percival Terrace. The Guardians adhere to their previous decision and on Tuesday last again offered him an order for the [work]house. WC [William Collingham]
Referred to parish, R P Hooper

Letter from Ada Bright, 19 Goldsmid Road, Brighton, 26 October 1875
Dear Mr Johnson, a woman of the name of Reading living in 22 Hereford Street has been to me today concerning placing a boy of hers in the Brighton Boys' Home and we are anxious to know if her statement is correct. She says she is too delicate to work herself and her husband is nearly blind and also unable to work [and] that she has three children to support. Will you let us know if it is an urgent case and one desirable to be taken into the Destitute Boys' Home? Yours truly,
Ada Bright

26 October 1875
Mrs Bright requests a report of this case. I find that the husband now sells shrimps. The school board have remitted the children's school fees for the last 12 months. The home is in a destitute state. WC [William Collingham]
Case to be reported to Miss Bright and recommended to assist the boy into the boys' home, R P Hooper

Letter from Miss Emmett , 12 Eaton Place, Brighton, 24 March [1884]
Sir, the wife of the bearer is a most respectable woman and has supported her husband for some time by charring who is unable to work himself [sic]. Mrs Reading has worked for some years at Miss King's, 10 Eaton Place, and very often for myself. I have never found a more trustworthy woman. She is now ill and does not know how the rent is to [be] paid. If you could do anything for her I should feel obliged. Yours truly, J R Emmett

28 March 1884
Mrs Reading was sent by Miss Emmett of 12 Eaton Place and applied at the office on Thursday for some temporary assistance. Her husband still sells matches and a fortnight ago the Guardians granted him a pair of boots. Applicant has lately been poorly, suffering from rheumatism, but will be able to work next week. Her son Charles is in Canada. The daughter, Sarah, is at service in London, the eldest is dead and the parents appear very poor. WC [William Collingham]
Grant of 2s 6d, Thomas W Holland

105 MARGARET MURRAY, 29, HAWKER, 84 SPA STREET, BRIGHTON

Edward Murray and his wife Margaret stated on the Mendicity Society's application form that though they were both born in Ireland they had been resident in Brighton since about 1848. The marriage of Edward Murray to Margaret Harrington took place at St Nicholas, Brighton, on 27 August 1863 when Edward was living at 67 Egremont Street and Margaret at 68 Egremont Street.[374] *Margaret Harrington's name had appeared in the local press in June 1861 when she, along with her parents, was apprehended for causing a disturbance on Edward Street due to her late return home one evening.*[375] *The Chief Officer said he did not know 'what had come to the Irish lately but for the last few days they had kept the top part of Edward Street in a perpetual disturbance with their weddings and wakes'. Harrington admitted to being drunk and was discharged with a caution.*

Her husband, Edward Murray, had a long and troubled relationship with the local police force which lasted throughout the 1860s. In February 1862 Murray, then 17, was charged

[374] ESRO: PAR 255/1/3/37.
[375] Brighton Guardian, 19 June 1861.

with begging on Kings Road and was sentenced to seven days' hard labour.[376] *On 29 August 1862 he was charged, along with James Sullivan, with being drunk and annoying persons at the upper part of Edward Street.*[377] *The men were hawkers of fish and both were dressed as mariners. They were apprehended by PC Terry but Murray refused to go peacefully stating that he would 'split Terry's brains out'. Sullivan stated that they were going hopping on Monday which produced some mirth in court. They were fined five shillings and costs or in default a week's imprisonment.*

In October 1863 Edward Murray and William Macarthy were brought before the court: Macarthy for causing wilful damage to the house of Samuel Clark at 43 Derby Place and Murray for assaulting Clark by pulling his whiskers.[378] *Murray was fined one shilling plus costs, Macarthy five shillings plus costs for kicking in a door panel.*

There appears to be no mention of Murray in the local press between October 1863 and November 1866 but his court appearances became steadily more serious in nature from this point onwards. On 19 November 1866 Murray was summoned for leaving his wife chargeable to the parish. The assistant overseer, Mr Thorncroft, stated that Murray's wife had been left in 'a most destitute and pitiable condition'. [379] *The hearing was also covered in the Gazette which quoted Thorncroft as saying, 'the parish was troubled with many ... men like the defendant who spent all their earnings on drink and left their wives for the parish to keep.'*[380] *The piece also quoted the District Visitor, William Barber, who stated that a month previously he had visited Mrs Murray at 62 Hereford Street where he found her in a destitute condition, 'he found no food or fire in the room and the woman was suffering from pregnancy, fever and venereal disease... her husband could support her if he liked... but went sotting about the town from one public house to another.' Mrs Murray was reluctant to say too much against her husband for fear of the repercussions but a neighbour spoke up for her and supplied a list of the pubs that Murray frequented. The Bench considered it a gross case and committed him to prison for three weeks with hard labour.*

In December 1866 Murray, along with James Terry, was charged with stealing a Witney coat worth 22s 6d from the shop of Oliver Watson, 79 North Road: Terry was sentenced to 12 months' hard labour; Murray was found not guilty as witnesses could not be absolutely certain of his identity.[381]

When Murray appeared before magistrates again in March 1867, charged with assaulting his wife, he was described as a 'violent-looking man'.[382] *Margaret Murray, of 62 Hereford Street, stated that on hearing that her husband had been out drinking with a party she went to look for him and returned between five and six pm to find him sitting at*

[376] Brighton Gazette, 27 February 1862.
[377] Brighton Guardian, 3 September 1862.
[378] Brighton Guardian, 14 October 1863.
[379] Brighton Guardian, 21 November 1866.
[380] Brighton Gazette, 22 November 1866.
[381] Brighton Guardian, 2 January 1867.
[382] Brighton Guardian, 13 March 1867.

1: General Sir Orfeur Cavenagh

2: The Reverend John Benjamin Figgis

3: Marriage Wallis

4: Richard Patching

5: The Reverend Robert Ingham Salmon

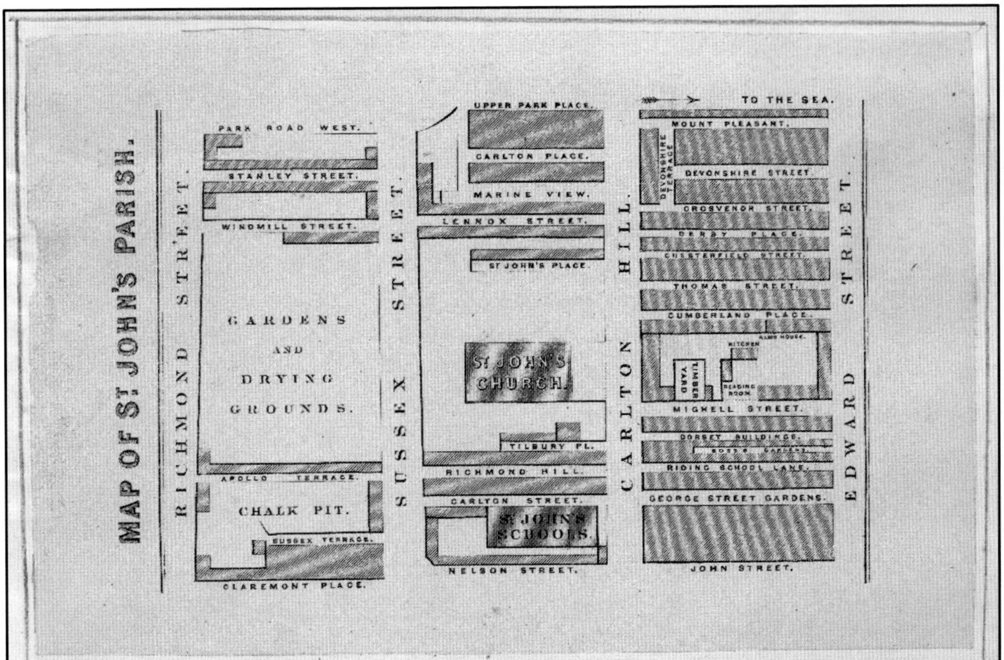

6: The Reverend Canon Henry Rymer

7: Daniel Hack

8: Plan of St John's parish

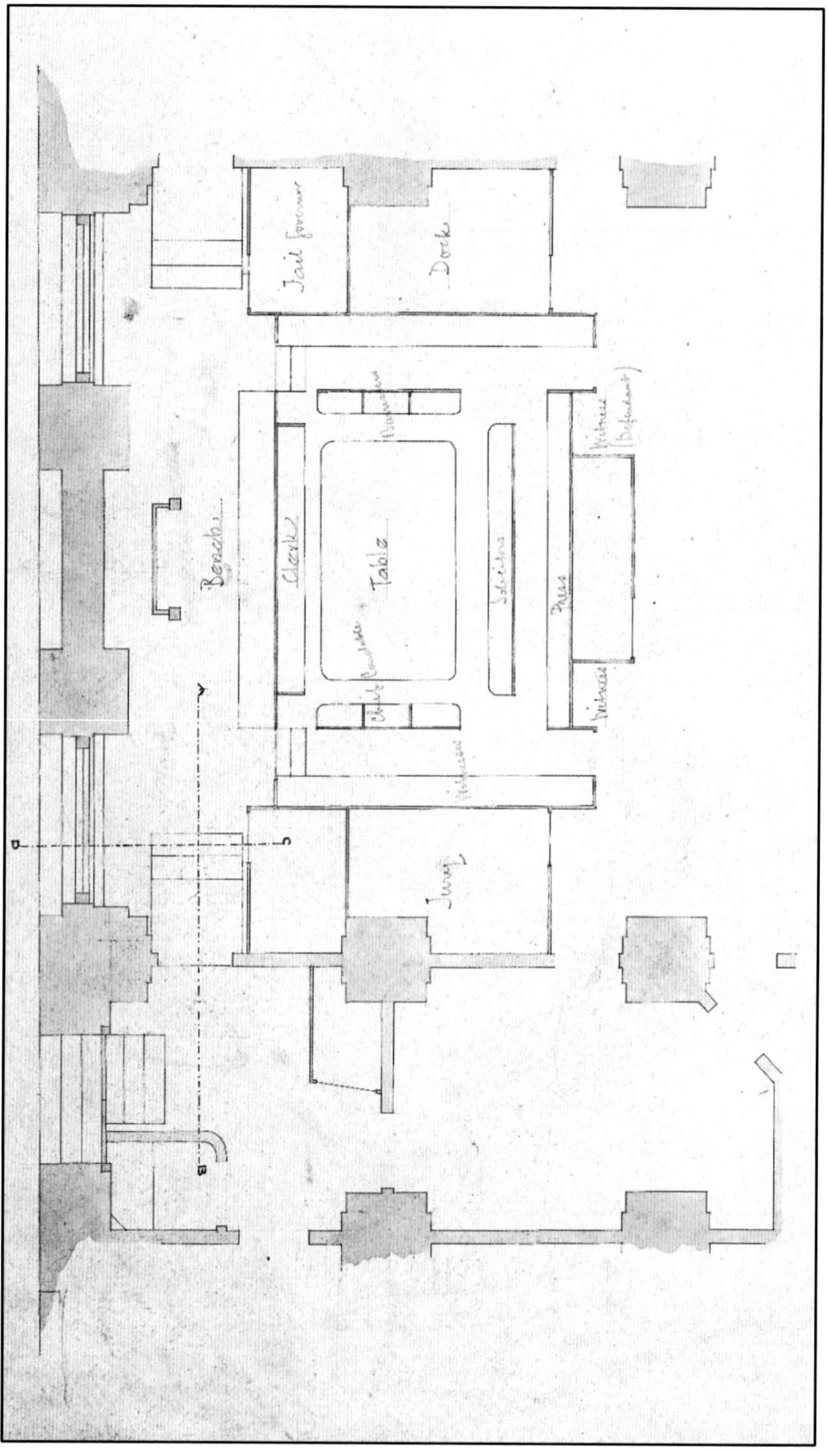

9: Plan showing the layout of Brighton Magistrates' Court

BLOCK OF DWELLINGS FOR FIFTEEN FAMILIES TO BE ERECTED IN CHURCH STREET, BRIGHTON.

10: Print of the Model Lodging House

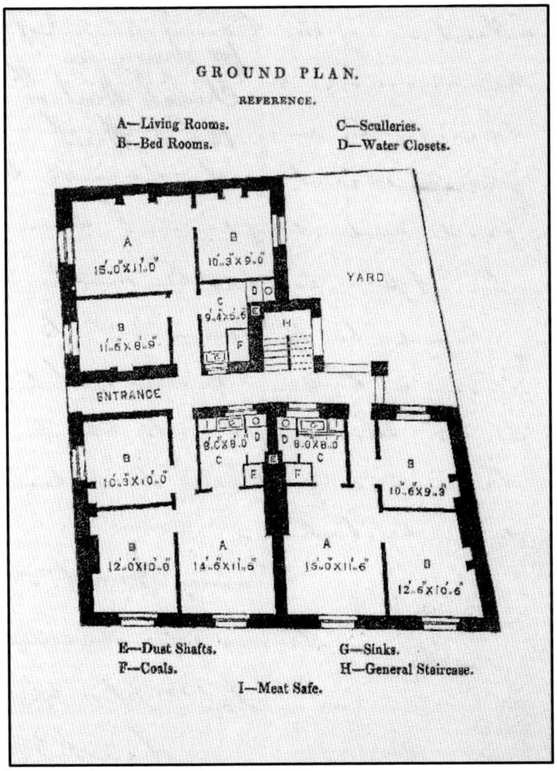

11: Floor plan of the Model Lodging House

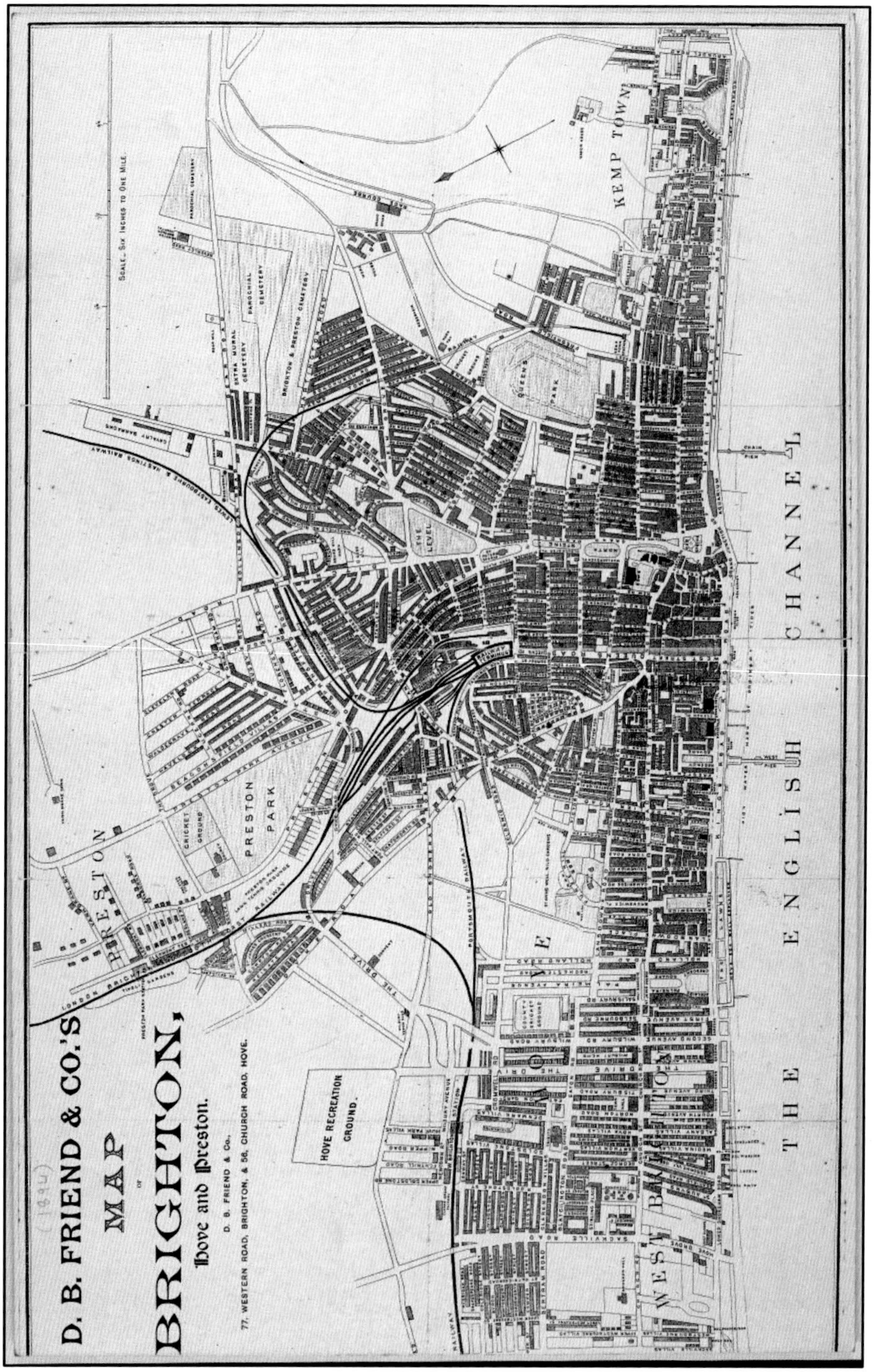

12: *D. B. Friend's Map of Brighton, showing location of applicants' addresses*

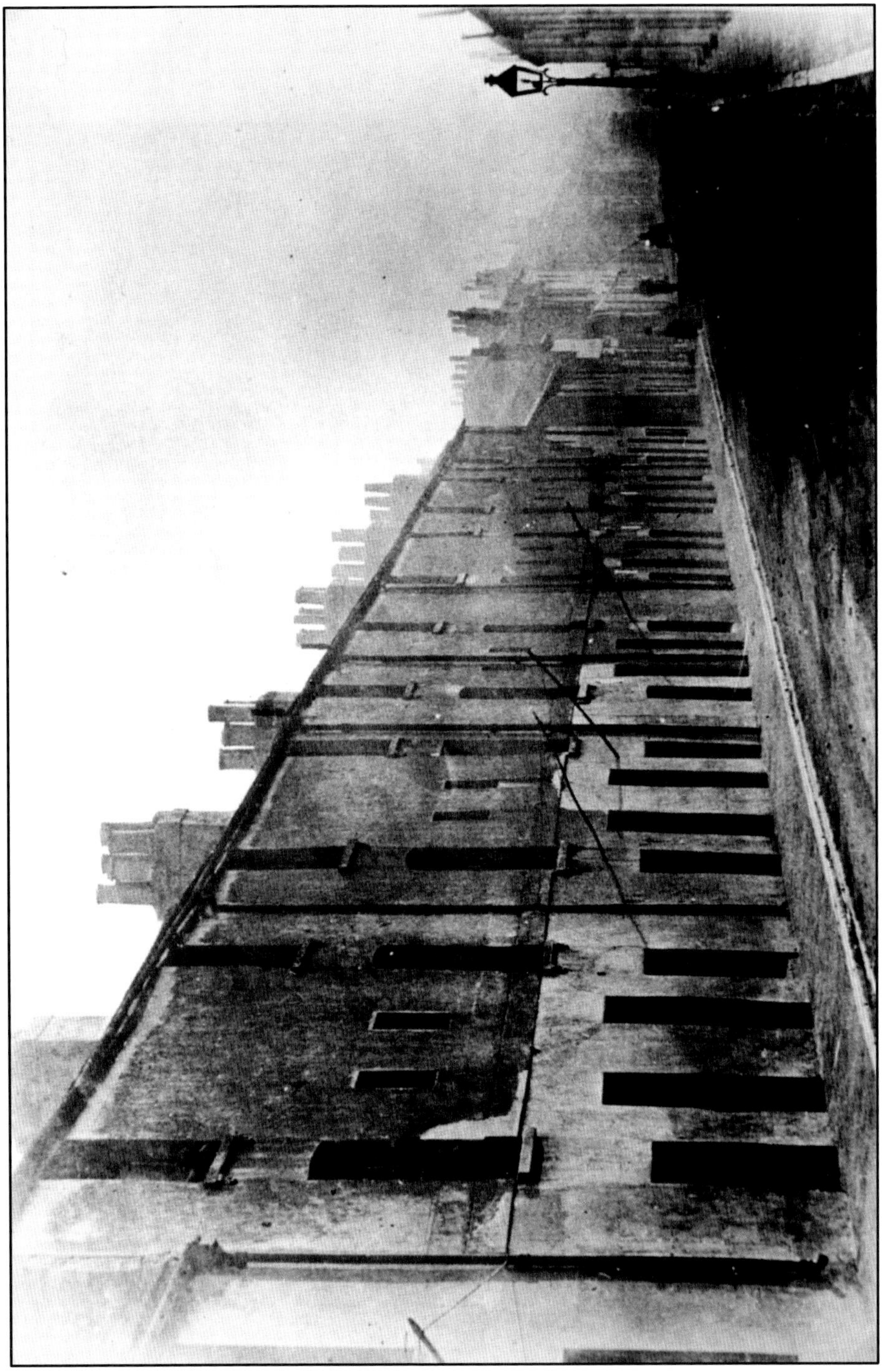

13: Slums in Hereford Street

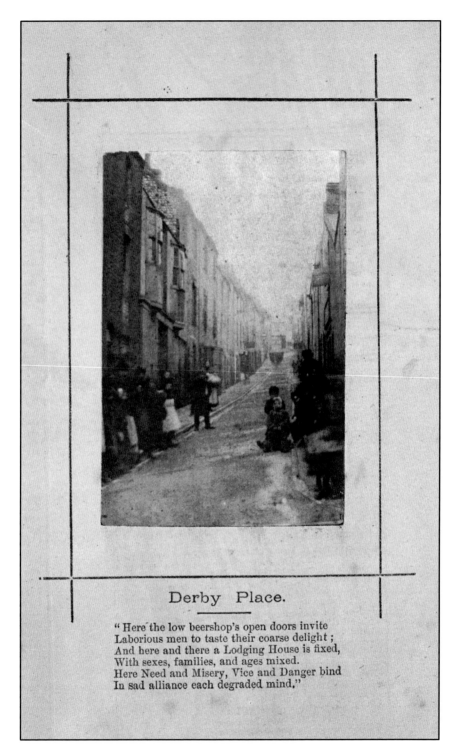

Derby Place.

"Here the low beershop's open doors invite
Laborious men to taste their coarse delight;
And here and there a Lodging House is fixed,
With sexes, families, and ages mixed.
Here Need and Misery, Vice and Danger bind
In sad alliance each degraded mind."

14: Derby Place

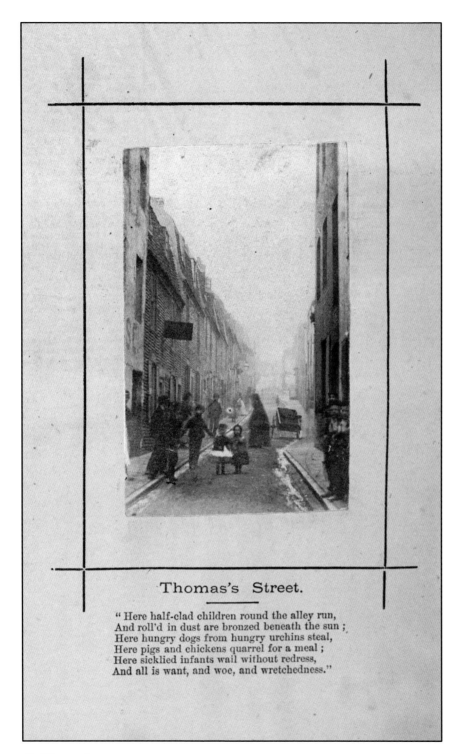

Thomas's Street.

" Here half-clad children round the alley run,
And roll'd in dust are bronzed beneath the sun ;
Here hungry dogs from hungry urchins steal,
Here pigs and chickens quarrel for a meal ;
Here sicklied infants wail without redress,
And all is want, and woe, and wretchedness."

15: Thomas Street

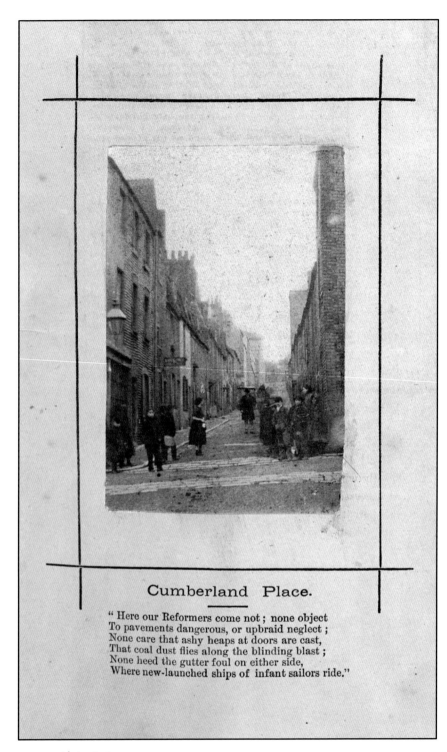

Cumberland Place.

" Here our Reformers come not ; none object
To pavements dangerous, or upbraid neglect ;
None care that ashy heaps at doors are cast,
That coal dust flies along the blinding blast ;
None heed the gutter foul on either side,
Where new-launched ships of infant sailors ride."

16: Cumberland Place

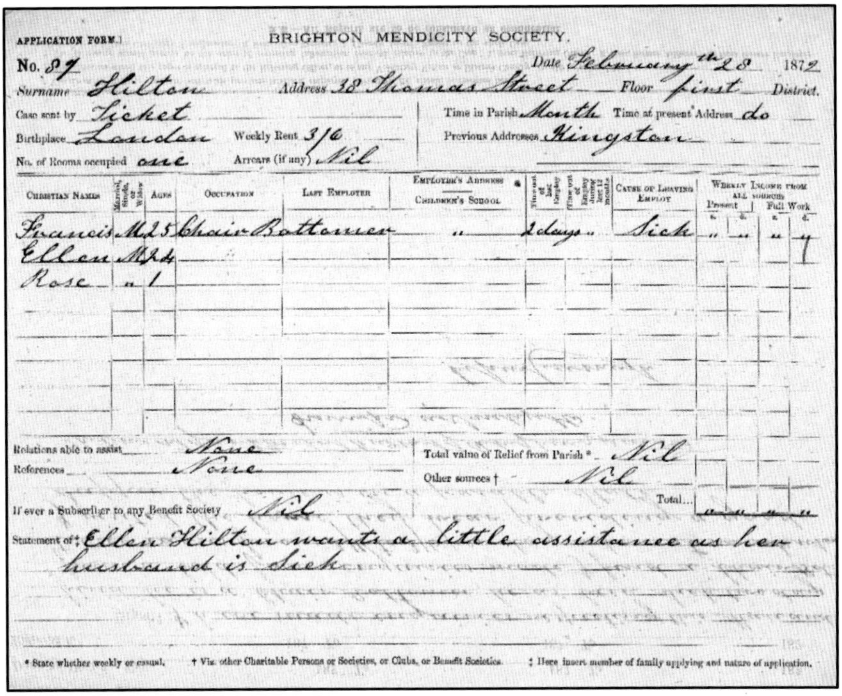

APPLICATION FORM.] BRIGHTON MENDICITY SOCIETY.

No. 87 Date February 28th 1872

Surname Hilton Address 38 Thomas Street Floor first District.

Case sent by Ticket Time in Parish Month Time at present Address do

Birthplace London Weekly Rent 3/6 Previous Addresses Kingston

No. of Rooms occupied one Arrears (if any) Nil

Christian Names	Married, Single, or Widow	Ages	Occupation	Last Employer	Employer's Address & Children's School	Time out of last Employ	Time out of Employ during last 12 months	Cause of Leaving Employ	Weekly Income from all sources: Present s.	d.	Full Work s.	d.
Francis	M	25	Chair Bottomer		"	2 days	"	Sick	"	"	"	7
Ellen	M	24										
Rose	"	1										

Relations able to assist None

References None

Total value of Relief from Parish * Nil

Other sources † Nil

Total

If ever a Subscriber to any Benefit Society Nil

Statement of ‡ Ellen Hilton wants a little assistance as her husband is Sick

* State whether weekly or casual. † Viz. other Charitable Persons or Societies, or Clubs, or Benefit Societies. ‡ Here insert member of family applying and nature of application.

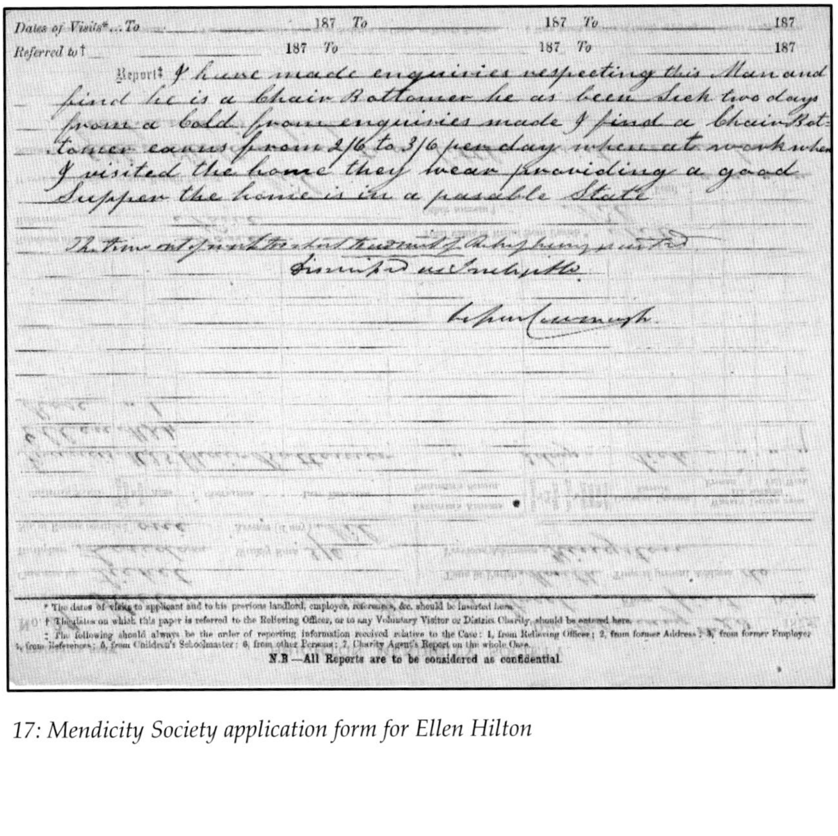

Dates of Visits* ... To 187 To 187 To 187

Referred to † 187 To 187 To 187

Report ‡ I have made enquiries respecting this Man and find he is a Chair Bottomer he as been Sick two days from a Cold from enquiries made I find a Chair Bottomer earns from 2/6 to 3/6 per day when at work when I visited the home they wear providing a good Supper the home is in a pasable State

[illegible]

[illegible]

[illegible]

* The dates of visits to applicant and to his previous landlord, employer, references, &c. should be inserted here.

† The dates on which this paper is referred to the Relieving Officer, or to any Voluntary Visitor or District Charity, should be entered here.

‡ The following should always be the order of reporting information received relative to the Case: 1, from Relieving Officer; 2, from former Address; 3, from former Employer; 4, from References; 5, from Children's Schoolmaster; 6, from other Persons; 7, Charity Agent's Report on the whole Case.

N.B.—All Reports are to be considered as confidential.

17: Mendicity Society application form for Ellen Hilton

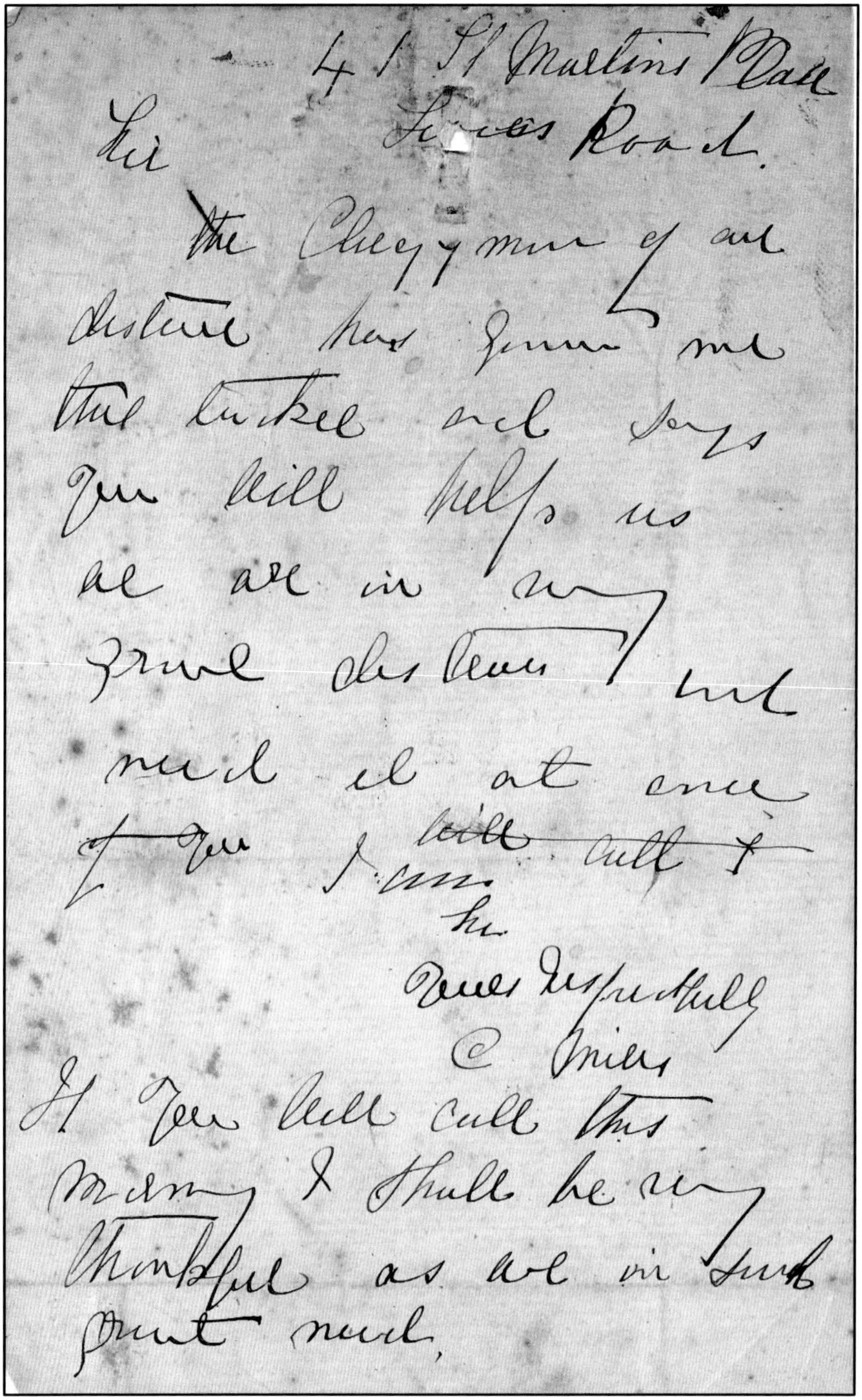
41 St Martins Place
Lewes Road.

Sir

the Clergyman of our district has given me this ticket and says you will help us as we are in very great distress and need it at once ~~if you will call~~ I am Sir

Yours respectfully
C Miles

If you will call this morning I shall be very thankful as we are in such great need.

18: Begging letter written by Caroline Miles

home.[383] *She asked where he had been and he replied that 'she need not care'. Some potatoes were in the room which they were going to have for supper and Margaret struck Edward Murray with the pot that held them. Edward Murray's mother and sister appeared and ordered Margaret Murray to go for Mr Savage or to the hospital to find someone to attend to his wound.*[384] *Margaret Murray stated that her mother-in-law said he ought to get up and strike her in return. Edward Murray was about to leave the room when his mother stopped him: he turned around and struck his wife rendering her insensible. Margaret Murray remembered nothing further of the evening but she produced 'half a hat full of her hair – a portion of which was about a yard long'. Margaret was again reluctant to see her husband punished but asked for him to be bound over to keep the peace. The Bench considered it to be a public scandal and Murray was sentenced to two months' prison with hard labour.*

Murray was charged with being drunk and disorderly in February 1868 when he was walking along Western Road striking or insulting nearly everyone he met.[385] *He was fined five shillings plus costs and was again charged with being drunk and disorderly at West Street on 15 March 1869 after being apprehended by PC William Collingham: he had been ejected from the Grand Concert Hall where he had been stealing other people's drinks and was fined five shillings.*[386, 387]

The Murray family's case was forwarded to the Mendicity Society by George Dudley Ryder. On the 1871 census they were enumerated at 32 Little St James Street with their three children Daniel, Margaret and Ellen, who were aged six, four and two respectively: all were born in Brighton.

At the time of the first application to the charity in March 1872, Edward Murray, who was 26, was working as a labourer and expected to earn 18 shillings per week when in full employment. Margaret Murray, who was 29, hawked fish and was earning 12 shillings per week. They paid two shillings per week rent for two rooms at 84 Spa Street where they had been living since about June 1871 and now had a fourth child named John.

The first application was made the day after the burial of their daughter Ellen, and a note was made on the Murray's record sheet in December 1872 recording the decease of another child, almost certainly John, whose death was registered in the March quarter of 1872. The charity stated that both children died from attacks of bronchitis. Margaret Murray's death was registered in the December quarter of 1874 and the death of a nine-year-old girl named Margaret Murray was registered in the December quarter of 1875, though no mention of this is made in the charity's records.

By the time of his next application to the Charity Organisation Society in September 1877, Edward Murray was living at 75 Spa Street but seems to have spent time living

383 Brighton Gazette, 14 March 1867.

384 William Dawson Savage, JP and chemist.

385 Brighton Guardian, 12 February 1868.

386 William Collingham was later employed as the Mendicity Society's agent and was responsible for transcribing most of the depositions referred to in this volume.

387 Brighton Guardian, 17 March 1869.

with his son Daniel and his mother at 16 Egremont Street, together with a widow named McCarthy. The charity officer did not state the latter's first name but it may well have been Catherine McCarthy, who was also born in Ireland and who, in 1871, was living at 79 Egremont Street with her husband John McCarthy and William McCarthy (who applied to the Mendicity Society for relief on 22 February 1872).[388] *John McCarthy, a hawker of fish, died in the September quarter of 1872. It is unclear whether this McCarthy family were related to Edward Murray's associate William Macarthy with whom he ran into trouble in October 1863.*

A 31-year-old man named Edward Murray was buried at Bear Road cemetery, Brighton, on 3 April 1878.[389]

14 March 1872
Statement: my husband is gone to work today. If he keeps sober he can get a good living.
Report: I made enquiries respecting this case and find the man is living with his wife again. He is gone to work today. He is of intemperate habits: he lives with his wife a month or two and then lives with his mother for a month or two. They buried a child yesterday. The wife sells fish, the home is in a destitute state. If the man and his wife was to keep sober they could be as well off as any working people in Brighton. They are known at the parochial office having received parish relief.
Dismissed as ineligible, Orfeur Cavenagh

7 December 1872
Further information respecting this case: upon inquiry I find that a fortnight after this case was before the committee the applicant lost another child. Both the children died of bronchitis. Their home is in a passable state.

18 September 1877
This man applied at the office this morning for an out-patient's letter to the Sussex County Hospital. He has recently returned from hop picking in consequence of a violent cold. He lost his wife two years ago and now he sometimes lives with his mother and son and sometimes with a widow named McCarthy.
Granted, CAB[390]

18 December 1877
This man, who resides with his mother at 16 Egremont Street, requests a little

[388] ESRO: AMS 6930/6/80.

[389] ESRO: BH/L/3/1/5 - Woodvale Cemetery burial plot ZKK 110.

[390] Probably Colonel C A Baines who is listed in annual reports of the period as a member of the council of the Charity Organisation Society.

assistance to tide him over till his friend can get him into Brompton Hospital. He is now ill and has recently left the Sussex County Hospital. WC [William Collingham]
Grant 5s and refer to parish, H W Kirby

106 FANNY LEWIS, 30, WIFE OF A HAWKER, 11 DERBY PLACE, BRIGHTON

Fanny Lewis was born in Pimlico, London, and had been living in Woolwich and Margate, Kent, before she and her 34-year-old husband Thomas and two young daughters arrived in Brighton in February 1872. At the time of their first application to the Mendicity Society they had been living in one second-floor room at 11 Derby Place for three weeks. Their case was forwarded to the charity by the Reverend Aaron Morgan, vicar of St John's, Carlton Hill. They paid 3s 6d per week in rent and were not in arrears. Thomas Lewis would usually expect to bring home about 18 shillings per week but was earning only seven shillings per week at the time of the application.

Thomas Lewis, a hawker, had received some kind of financial help from a Mr Cobb of Margate. However, the banker Anthony Cobb who wrote to the Mendicity Society could not confirm this, as the Mr Cobb in question had recently died and appeared to have kept no record of this transaction.

The family were enumerated at 36 Derby Place on the census of 1881. It is conceivable that their neighbours, William and Elizabeth Webb at 35 Derby Place may have been related to their friends Charles and Florence Webb, who wrote to the Lewis family in 1889, encouraging them to emigrate to Winnipeg. where they were living.

The Lewises did not contact the Charity Organisation Society again until 1889 when they were living at 27 Derby Place and trying to raise funds to emigrate to Canada. Ellen Nye Chart, the renowned manager of the Theatre Royal, Brighton, took an interest in their case and, although the charity's documents do not record the outcome of their efforts, Thomas and Fanny Lewis with their children George, Minnie and Charles left London for Quebec, sailing steerage class aboard the Grecian, on 17 April 1890.[391] *The census of Canada for 1901 records the family in Winnipeg and the 1906 census of Manitoba records the family living at 372 Aberdeen Avenue, Winnipeg.*[392]

14 March 1872
Statement: Fanny Lewis wants a little assistance to get a hawker's licence.
Report: I made enquiries respecting this case and find the reason this family came to Brighton was on account of their daughter who is an invalid suffering from abscesses in her leg. This man hawks wire work. He has plenty of wire and says if he had a licence he could get a good living. The girl is a great deal better

[391] Canadian passenger lists, 1865-1935, Library and Archives Canada RG-76C.
[392] Census of Canada, 1901, and Census of Northwest Provinces, 1906, RG31-C-1.

already – she is an out-patient at the hospital. Mr Shears has wrote to Mr Cobb, Margate, respecting this case.
Relieved by grant, Orfeur Cavenagh. NB the agent to procure a licence at the cost of 5s provided he is satisfied that the man has the materials to enable him to gain a livelihood

Letter from Anthony B Cobb, Margate Bank, to D F Shears, Brighton Mendicity Society, 15 March 1872
Sir, in reply to your enquiry respecting Thomas Lewis we think that he must have been assisted (if at all) by Mr Cobb who is recently deceased as we do not know the name nor can we obtain any information from the police. It is quite possible that Mr Cobb did help the man without our knowing anything about it therefore we should be sorry to prevent him from obtaining assistance from our ignorance in the matter. Doubtless you will be able to judge how far the story is a true one. Yours truly, Anthony B Cobb

Letter from Charles and Florence Webb, 17 Prairie Street, Winnipeg, Manitoba, Canada, 30 April 1889
Dear Fannie, we received the paper and note quite safe today and were glad to hear you are all quite well as I am glad to say we are at present. Flo has had the whooping cough but it is better now. Dear Fannie we feel sure you would do better out here – better than you are doing at home. Why, you yourself could get lots of work – that is if you went out and they give a dollar or 4s 2d a day and often as much food as you can bring home and you are not worked so many hours as you are at home because I know what it is to go out to work for I went when we was at Littlehampton. Here you work so many hours a day and if over you get over pay. I used to do several single men's washing and it paid very well but I gave it up when Edith was born and I have no need to take it up again. I hope you will come, Charlie says you will get a job directly. We should like him to get on in the coach yard because there the work is light. There is one thing – you will have a place to come to when you get here if you come. Come at once or as soon as you can for the work is plentiful from May to July but there is always plenty of work here. Trusting to see you soon, we remain with love all round, Charles and Florence Webb
PS this is a copy of a letter we have just got, please send the copies back

Letter from Thomas and Fanny Lewis, 27 Derby Place, Brighton, 21 May 1889
Dear Madam, me and wife and four children are about leaving Brighton to Canada. We want to leave by the ship that sails from London on June 14th but we have not got all the money. We have been in Brighton 18 years. I make air balls – you may have seen my wife outside the pier for years but everything being so dull, and our family growing up we think by going there we shall better the

condition of our family. We have got £20 towards £38. Dear madam if you would assist us we should be very thankful and remain your very obedient servants, Thomas and Fanny Lewis

Letter from Ellen Nye Chart, Theatre Royal, New Road, Brighton, 25 May 1889
Dear Sir, will you kindly have enquiries made re the enclosed letter and report to me. Yours faithfully [Ellen] Nye Chart

28 May 1889
Mrs Nye Chart of the Theatre Royal requests a report of this case. Lewis and his wife have supported themselves and their four children for several years by selling air-balls and are now anxious to emigrate to Winnipeg in Canada at a cost of £38 towards which the Emigration Society have granted them £10 10s and the wife has collected £9 10s thus leaving £18 to be raised. The family are recommended as quiet, sober people and are considered worthy of any help that can be rendered them. WC [William Collingham]
Report to Mrs Nye Chart, Thomas W Holland

8 June 1889
Mrs Lewis was sent by Mr Bird, Town Missionary, and applied at the office this morning for a donation towards raising the balance now required, namely £16 15s.[393] WC [William Collingham]
Ineligible, E G

26 July 1889
Mrs Lewis applied at the office on Thursday for a donation towards raising the balance now required, namely £12 10s. WC [William Collingham]
Ineligible, R P Hooper

11 April 1890
Mrs Lewis applied at the office on Thursday for a donation towards purchasing the outfit to enable the family to emigrate to Winnipeg. They have succeeded in raising the passage m[oney] and are anxious to start on Thursday next.[394] WC [William Collingham]
Ineligible, R P Hooper

[393] George Bird is listed in *Pike's Directory* of 1891 as Town Missionary living at 71 Southover Street.
[394] Page damaged.

107 MARGARET HARRINGTON, 64, WASHERWOMAN, 3 ESSEX PLACE, BRIGHTON

Margaret Harrington was born in Ireland in about 1808. When she approached the Mendicity Society in March 1872 she had been living in Brighton for 20 years and had been living in a first-floor room at 3 Essex Place for the previous six years. She was a widow and had been short of work for two weeks. When in full work Margaret Harrington could earn about ten shillings per week, but had fallen three shillings in arrears on her weekly rent of 1s 6d.

A 67-year-old woman named Margaret Harrington was enumerated in Brighton Workhouse in 1881. She was born in County Cork and is described as a farmer's widow. The death of a 77-year-old woman named Margaret Harrington was registered in Brighton in the March quarter of 1891.[395] *It is unclear whether she is related to Margaret Murray (née Harrington), the wife of Edward Murray, who applied to the charity on the previous day.*[396]

15 March 1872
Statement: Margaret Harrington would be thankful for a little assistance. My son who is a soldier occasionally assists me.
Report: I have made inquiries respecting this woman and find she lives with a married daughter. She used to go washing but lately she has not had but a very little to do. Her son who is a soldier occasionally assists her. She applied to the parish authorities but refused to go in the [work]house. The home is in a passable state. Mr Rymer the priest gave her a good character.[397]
Relieved by grant, Orfeur Cavenagh. NB the agent authorised, as a purely temporary measure, to expend 2s 6d in the purchase of food. No further relief will be given.

108 ORPHA MOPPETT, 43, WASHERWOMAN, 31 HEREFORD STREET, BRIGHTON

Orpha Moppett (née Hutson) was baptised in Rodmell on 8 June 1834.[398] *Her husband Edward Moppett, a dairyman, was baptised in Ovingdean on 24 September 1826.*[399] *They*

[395] Death of Margaret Harrington registered Q1 1891 Brighton 2b 201.
[396] Applicant 105 (ESRO: AMS 6930/6/105).
[397] The Reverend Canon Rymer, Catholic Chapel House, Bristol Road.
[398] The entry in the baptism register (ESRO: PAR 464/1/2/1) refers to her as Orphee Hudson. However, despite the discrepancy in the spelling of the surname this does appear to be the correct entry as her parents are given as John and Lucy Hudson. Her father is also referred to in the entry for her marriage.
[399] This does not tally with the age of 43 that was reported to the Mendicity Society. However, no other entry for an Edward Moppett could be found in the Ovingdean baptism register for this period. His

were married at St Nicholas, Brighton, on 9 February 1857 when both were living at 14 Millfield Cottages.[400] *In 1861 they were enumerated at 10 Sloane Street where they lived with their two young children, Orpha Moppett's parents, John and Lucy Hutson, and another couple named Thomas and Ann Hutson and their infant son.*

The 1871 census shows Edward Moppett described as an agricultural labourer and Orpha Moppett as a laundress. The couple were living at 31 Hereford Street with their five children and John and Lucy Hutson, who were then aged 81 and 80 respectively.

The Moppett's case was forwarded to the Mendicity Society by Mrs Kennedy of 6 Marine Terrace in March 1872 when the family, now without Orpha Moppett's parents, were still living at 31 Hereford Street. They paid four shillings weekly rent for the whole house but were 12 shillings in arrears. Edward had been labouring for a Mr Miles of Kemp Town, but he had been sick for the previous three weeks and Orpha for the previous two: when in full work he could expect to bring home 15 shillings per week and she could earn 3s 9d. They had recently received eight shillings outdoor relief from the Guardians. The children attended schools at Warwick Street and Spa Street.

The census of 1881 shows the family living at 42 Essex Street with four daughters. Orpha Moppett applied to the Charity Organisation Society in February 1897 when she was living at 9 Park Place. The report on the family stated that Edward Moppett had died in April 1885 but this appears to have been a mistake: no death was registered in 1885 but the death of an Edward Moppett was registered in Brighton in the June quarter of 1886.[401] *Orpha Moppett's death was registered in the June quarter of 1911 when she was 77 years old.*[402]

15 March 1872

Statement: Orpha Moppett wants a little assistance till her husband gets better.

Report: I have made inquiries respecting this case and find the man has been sick three weeks. I have known him a long time and believe him to be a very industrious man. He bears a good character at Mr Miles' where he has been at work. The wife occasionally does a little washing. The elder daughter could go to service if she had a place to go. Miss Gathern, 24 Upper Rock Gardens, the District Visitor has relieved them several times. They receive parish relief, the home is in a passable state.

Relieved by grant (5s), Orfeur Cavenagh

Postcard from Mrs Gay, 5 Percival Terrace, Brighton, 2 January 1888

Mrs Gay will be glad to have a report of Mrs Moppett, 2 Sloane Street, formerly

father is referred to as John Moppett in both the baptism register and the St Nicholas marriage register (ESRO: PAR 436/1/2/1).

400 ESRO: PAR 255/1/3/29.

401 Death of Edward Moppett registered Q2 1886 Brighton 2b 127.

402 Death of Orpha Moppett registered Q2 1911 Brighton 2b 121.

of Mount Pleasant and if deserving please send her up on Thursday for flannel and an order. The man Townsend, Cromwell Street, has not called for the shirts.

3 January 1888
Mrs Gay of 5 Percival Terrace requests a report of this case. Mrs Moppett, who resides at 2 Sloane Street, lost her husband in April 1885 and has since gone out nursing but she suffers from rheumatism and cannot earn much. Her children are off her hands, the Guardians allow her 2s 6d per week and she continues to bear a decent character. WC [William Collingham]
Report to Mrs Gay, CWBH

17 February 1897
Mrs Moppett applied at the office this morning for an out-patients letter to the Sussex Eye Hospital. She continues to go out nursing and has a cataract forming on her left eye. The Guardians are allowing her 3s per week and she is recommended as a quiet, sober woman. WC [William Collingham]
Granted, Thomas W Holland

109 FRANCES HEMSLEY, 55, CHARWOMAN, 7 IVORY PLACE, BRIGHTON

Frances Hemsley and her son Henry, a 20-year-old railway fireman, were enumerated at 40 Bread Street on the 1871 census. The property was home to two other families and in total 12 people lived at the address. When Frances Hemsley approached the Mendicity Society in March 1872 she had been living at 7 Ivory Place for two weeks. She estimated that her usual earnings would amount to ten shillings per week but due to sickness over the previous three months she was 1s 3d, or week's one rent, in arrears for her first-floor room.

Frances Hemsley stated that she was born in Brighton and her death, aged 59, was registered in the town during the March quarter of 1877.[403]

15 March 1872
Statement: Frances Hemsley wants a little assistance till she gets work.
Report: I made inquiries respecting this woman and find she was in the workhouse about six weeks and left two weeks ago. She gets her living washing and charring or anything she can get to do. Miss Beal gave her a good character. Mr Meeres the clergyman of that district has relieved her on one or two occasions. She is well known to the parish authorities and can have an order for the [work]house. The home is in a passable state.
Referred to Poor Law, Orfeur Cavenagh

[403] Death of Frances Hemsley registered Q1 1877 Brighton 2b 128.

110 AMELIA RIGG, 32, NO OCCUPATION RECORDED, 72 ISLINGWORD ROAD, BRIGHTON

Amelia Rigg (née Grigg) was baptised at St James, Westminster, on 25 December 1839.[404] *The Grigg family were enumerated on the census of 1841 in Regent Square, London, and Amelia's father, William Grigg, was described as a stationer. In 1851 Amelia Grigg was enumerated at a private boarding school in Ealing and by 1861 she was living with her brother William Grigg, a banker's clerk, at 22 Park Road West, Stoke Newington, London. Amelia Grigg married George James Rigg, a clerk at the Union Bank of London, at St Mary's, Stoke Newington on 6 October 1863: their witnesses were William Grigg senior, William Grigg junior and Ellen Doddemeade.*[405] *The couple had three children, Alice, Arthur and George, who were born between about 1864 and 1868. George Rigg senior died intestate on 16 November 1869 leaving effects of under £600. The couple had been living at 4 Bournemouth Road, Peckham Rye, but by the time the letters of administration were granted to Amelia Rigg in March 1870 she was living at Thanet Cottage, Belvedere, Kent.*[406] *The couple enumerated at this address in 1871 were Amelia Rigg's father, William Grigg, and his second wife Amelia (née Doddemeade) who married at St Mary's, Stoke Newington, on 26 May 1860.*[407]

In June 1870 Amelia Rigg approached the Provident Clerks' Benevolent Fund in the hope that she would receive enough votes to entitle her to one of their widow's pensions of £20 per annum. She received 21 votes but failed to garner enough support for an annuity.[408]

Amelia Rigg's contact with the Brighton Mendicity Society in March 1872 was prompted by a letter from John Robertson of Norfolk Road who had been approached by Rigg. She was renting two rooms at 72 Islingword Road at a cost of 4s 3d per week and was not in arrears. Rigg had lived there with her two younger children Arthur, 6, and George, 4, since about March 1871: her daughter, Alice, was living at the Wanstead Infant Orphan Asylum and she was hoping to ensure a place there for Arthur.

Rigg gave her previous addresses as 1 Carlton Place and 53 Old Steine and it is this last address that appears in her letters to the officers of the charity. Following the death of her husband in 1869 she made her way to Brighton, via Belvedere, to set up a lodging house in partnership with the wife of a man named Walter Royle. The partnership proved financially disastrous for her and it was dissolved in April 1871.[409] *The breakdown of the partnership coincided with Rigg contracting smallpox, the treatment of which took a further toll on her finances.*[410]

[404] *England, Births and Christenings, 1538-1975*. Salt Lake City, Utah: FamilySearch, 2013.
[405] London Metropolitan Archives: p94/mry/015.
[406] England and Wales National Probate Calendar (index of wills and administrations).
[407] London Metropolitan Archives: p94/mry/015.
[408] London Evening Standard, 10 June 1870.
[409] Morning Post, 8 April 1871.
[410] No admission record could be found for her at the Royal Sussex County Hospital in 1871.

It is unknown whether Amelia Rigg did manage to secure a place for her son Arthur at the Wanstead Infant Orphan Asylum. Her death was registered at Dartford in the September quarter of 1876 suggesting that she made her way back to Thanet Cottage, Belvedere, to stay with her father and step-mother.[411] *William Grigg senior died aged 85 at Thanet Cottage on 11 January 1885 leaving a personal estate of £7,411 16s 7d to his widow and son William who was living at 28 Riggindale Road, Streatham.*[412] *He was buried at St John the Baptist, Erith, on 17 January 1885.*[413] *William's widow, Amelia Grigg died at Thanet Cottage, Bedonwell, Belvedere, on 5 May 1915 leaving effects of £4551 16 2d.*[414] *She was buried at St John the Baptist, Erith, on 10 May 1915.*[415]

Amelia Rigg's daughter Alice was enumerated at 13 St John's Villas, Islington, in 1881 where she lived with Sarah Kays, a 73-year-old annuitant. Alice Rigg married Robert William Mead, a doctor of medicine, at All Saints, Belvedere on 3 June 1890, suggesting that she eventually found refuge with her grandfather after the death of her mother.[416] *The younger son, George, described as a silk merchant on his marriage certificate, married Amy Elizabeth Grigg of 28 Riggindale Road, Streatham, on 28 December 1893 at St Leonard's, Streatham.*[417] *Amy Grigg was the daughter of George's uncle, William Grigg, and his first cousin.*

Letter to William Henty, Brighton Mendicity Society, from John Robertson, 12 Norfolk Road, Brighton, 14 March 1872
Dear Sir, a woman dressed like a widow sent up to me by my servant the enclosed card today about two o'clock. I went down stairs to her and saw that she had a little boy with her. The case seems to merit attention. She says her name is Rigg and that she lives at number 72 Islingword Road. Yours sincerely, John Robertson

16 March 1872
Statement: Amelia Rigg wants to get her son Arthur in the Infant Orphan Asylum, Wanstead, and then take a situation as governess and put George out to nurse.
Report: this woman states her husband was clerk at the Union Bank for 16 years and died from consumption. They had a little money then and since that [sic] she and another woman took a lodging house at 53 Old Steine. After she had been there three months she fell sick with the smallpox. She has not been doing anything since. What she wants is to get the oldest son in the Infant Orphan

[411] Death of Amelia Rigg registered Q3 1876 Dartford 2a 220.
[412] England and Wales National Probate Calendar (index of wills and administrations).
[413] Bexley Local Studies and Archive Centre: PA137/1/E/3.
[414] England and Wales National Probate Calendar (index of wills and administrations).
[415] Bexley Local Studies and Archive Centre: PA137/1/E/7.
[416] Bexley Local Studies and Archive Centre: PA137C/1/D/1.
[417] London Metropolitan Archives: p95/len/075.

Asylum, Wanstead, and then take a situation as governess. She could put the youngest out to nurse. She states she is well known in London to Mr Lawrence, 154 Fenchurch Street, London, who is assisting her to help get her son in the Infant Orphan Asylum, Wanstead. The home is in a passable state. The woman states she has been a widow two years and that she was not aware she was doing wrong by taking the card about to get money to buy votes with.
Further enquiry from Mr Lawrence and the superintendent of the asylum
References satisfactory. Referred to private sources, R P Hooper

Letter to William Henty from Amelia Rigg, 72 Islingword Road, Brighton, [March 1872]
Sir, having read an appeal to the public some few weeks since that you so kindly inserted in the Brighton Observer on my behalf may I ask whether or not you received any response. My boy is elected into the Wanstead Asylum but not without a loan from a friend which as you can readily believe I am very anxious to receive as soon as possible. Therefore, if you have collected a trifle however small it will be most thankfully received by yours, respectfully, Amelia Rigg

Letter to the chairman of Brighton Mendicity Society, from Amelia Rigg, 72 Islingword Street, Brighton, [March 1872]
Sir, as your society has very kindly taken interest in my case the thought has occurred to me that perhaps you might wish to be in possession of further particulars relating to it. I came to Brighton to enter into partnership in a lodging house at 53 Old Steine, my partner Mrs Royle agreeing to find experience and I capital. However, I soon saw she knew no more of the management of a lodging house than I did myself. I placed £200 of my late husband's life policy in the business. I had not been in it more than six weeks when I unfortunately was taken ill with malignant smallpox for some weeks being on the verge of the grave, my doctor telling my friends he never in all the years he had practised had seen such a terrible case. The expenses of this of course very considerably reduced the residue of my policy. Not agreeing my partner gave me three months' notice to dissolve partnership which time expired. During my illness they lived as extravagantly as it was possible to live, consequently a few weeks since I received a notice of the meeting of the creditors of Walter Royle (my partner's husband). I have every reason to believe my money was appropriated to other than its legitimate purpose whether or not I am not at all likely to get 6d in the pound from the bankrupt. My money is now gone with the exception of a trifle. I have no means whatever of procuring votes for my boy and I must get 600 more in order to ensure his admission. If I can only accomplish this I intend D V establishing myself in a school or taking a situation for the support of self

and little one.[418] If you will help me on my uphill journey through life I shall be very, very thankful. Trusting I have not trespassed too much on your valuable time I am sir yours truly, Amelia Rigg

Draft letter to Alfred Hays esq, 43 Wellington Road, St Johns Wood, London [and] W Grigg esq, Beadonwell, Belvedere, Kent written by an officer of the Brighton Mendicity Society regarding Amelia Rigg, [March 1872]
The case of Mrs Rigg a widow who states that she wishes to get her child Arthur into the Wanstead Orphan Asylum has been brought to the notice of the Brighton Mendicity Society as the case appears to be deserving of assistance. The society will be glad to know how she can be helped – your name being mentioned as one of the gentlemen who are willing to receive proxies. They hope you will kindly afford the necessary information

Letter to D F Shears, Brighton Mendicity Society from Henry W Green, Infant Orphan Asylum, Wanstead, 2 April 1872
Sir, I fear that I cannot give you a definitive reply without learning more particulars than your letter discloses. All the votes issued by this and kindred asylum are bought but this is so obvious that you must intend something more by the question you have put. If the votes are fraudulently bought – which your letter doesn't say – there is no chance of a child gaining admission by them if the fraud is known by us. If you will favour me with some distinct information I shall feel obliged. Yours obediently, Henry W Green

Letter from George Bush, Hockwell Cottage, Chobham Road, Stratford, 3 April 1872
Sir, is the Mendicity Society at Brighton established under an Act of Parliament? If so will you kindly give me the title of it or how otherwise? Yours obediently George Bush

Letter to D F Shears, Brighton Mendicity Society, from W E Lawrence, 154 Fenchurch Street, 6 April 1872
Sir, I have known Mrs Amelia Rigg for very many years and can vouch for the truth of her statements as contained in your note. Her husband, who died about two and half years ago, was for many years a clerk at my bankers: the Union Bank of London and she is now trying to get another child into the Infant Orphan Asylum, a task in which I and many others are aiding her. In addition to her trouble she has lately suffered from smallpox which has much disfigured her and given her an additional claim to our sympathy. I trust your society will consider this a sufficient guarantee that her case is genuine. I remain sir, yours very truly, W E Lawrence

[418] D V is an abbreviation for Deo Volente or God willing.

111 HARRIETT NAPPER, 47, WASHERWOMAN, 10 SCOTLAND STREET, BRIGHTON

Harriett Napper was born in Petworth in about 1825. According to her application form to the Mendicity Society she had been living in Brighton since 1870. In 1871 she was enumerated at 50 Scotland Street where she and her four-year-old daughter Emma lodged with the family of William and Ellen Reeves, who were born in Billingshurst and Petworth respectively. Emma Napper was born in Portsmouth and Harriett was a widow.

By the time of Harriett Napper's approach to the charity in March 1872 she was living with her daughter Emma in one room at 16 Scotland Street. She had been sick for five months and therefore unable to earn her usual income of 7s 6d per week washing clothes. Weekly rent came to one shilling and she was 17 shillings in arrears.

By the time of the application made on 14 January 1878, Napper was living at 3 Southampton Street. The report of January 1881 records that her daughter was 'off her hands' but Emma Napper was enumerated with her mother at 53 St Mary Magdalene Street on the census of 1881. The death of a 73-year-old woman named Harriett Napper was registered in Brighton in the September quarter of 1893.[419]

16 March 1872
Statement: Harriett Napper wants a little assistance till she gets work.
Report: I made enquiries respecting this case and find this woman was in the hospital nearly three months and left when the fire was. She used to get her living washing but lately she has not been able to do hard work only a little charring or needlework. Mr Greaves the scripture reader gave her a good character. He has relieved her on several occasions. She applied to the parish authorities but refused to go in the workhouse. The home is in a passable state.
Referred to parish authorities, R P Hooper

2 March 1874
Further information: this woman, who now lives at 6 Hollingdean Road, applied at the office on Monday for assistance to enable her to purchase a pair of boots. On enquiry I find that applicant works at Tutt Laundry, Lewes Road, and earns on an average about 7s 6d a week. The daughter goes to the new school in Bear Hill. WC [William Collingham]
Grant of 5s for a pair of boots, R P Hooper

14 January 1878
Mrs Napper applied at the office on Saturday for assistance to enable her to purchase a pair of sheets. She now works for Mrs Cole, laundress, 10 Hampden Road, and earns about 7s 6d a week. Mrs Cole gave her a good character. Her

[419] Death of Harriett Napper registered Q3 1893 Brighton 2b 167.

home is in a destitute state. WC [William Collingham]
Referred to clergyman of the district and to report again, T Hayter Johnston

16 January 1878
The Reverend A T Waugh, in whose district applicant resides, has promised to see her case. WC [William Collingham]
To be recorded, T Hayter Johnston

18 February 1878
Mrs Napper, who obtained a rug a month ago applied at the office today for assistance to enable her to purchase a pair of boots. WC [William Collingham]
Ineligible, R P Hooper

10 August 1878
Mrs Napper, who now resides at 43 St Mary Magdalene Street, applied at the office this morning for an out-patient's letter to the Sussex County Hospital.[420] Applicant is suffering from an internal complaint and, the case being urgent, the secretary granted the letter. WC [William Collingham]
Approved, R P Hooper

28 January 1881
This person, now of 53 St Mary Magdalene Street, applied at the office on Friday for assistance to enable her to purchase boots. Lately she has been earning 6s 3d per week. Her daughter is off her hands. WC [William Collingham]
Ineligible, R P Hooper

3 March 1893
Mrs Napper applied at the office on Friday for some temporary relief for her daughter. She went into a situation with Mrs Amber of Marlborough House, Burgess Hill, last Friday but returned on Tuesday suffering from a cold and as she expects to be able to go back to her situation next Wednesday there seems very little need for the application to have been made. George Collingham
Not requiring relief, R P Hooper

112 JOSEPH ROSSI, 75, HAWKER, 36 CUMBERLAND PLACE, BRIGHTON

When Joseph Rossi applied to the Mendicity Society in March 1872 he had been living in Brighton for six weeks: two weeks at 36 Cumberland Place and the earlier period at 7

[420] No record could be found for Harriett Napper's admission to the Royal Sussex County Hospital in August 1878 (ESRO: HB 35/4).

Chesterfield Street. He had come to Brighton from Guildford, Surrey, but was born in Italy in about 1797.

Rossi's case was forwarded to the Mendicity Society by the Reverend Aaron Augustus Morgan, vicar of St John's, Carlton Hill when he owed one week's rent of 2s 6d. He usually expected to make 15 shillings per week when in full work but illness had prevented him from earning for three weeks.

18 March 1872
Statement: Joseph Rossi wants a hawker's licence to hawk fancy flowers. He has been sick three weeks and his licence expired on the fifth of March.
Report: I made enquiries respecting this man and find he is living with a married son who is also a hawker of fancy flowers. He is not known to the Reverend Mr Morgan nor to Mr Toye the scripture reader. The man bears a good character but I do not consider this a case for the society.
Ineligible, R P Hooper, chairman

113 JAMES ETHERIDGE, 33, WATERMAN, 21 ESSEX STREET, BRIGHTON

James Etheridge was born in Brighton in 1841[421] *and married Charlotte Easen at St Nicholas, Brighton, on 28 November 1870.*[422] *The entry in the marriage register records Etheridge's address as the Park Brewery and his occupation as waterman; Easen was living at 60 Crescent Cottages, Upper Bedford Street. In 1871 the couple and their one-year old daughter Charlotte were enumerated at 6 Dorset Street. Two other families shared the same house and in total 12 people lived at the address.*

On 30 June 1871 James Etheridge appeared at the magistrates' court charged with acting as a waterman without a licence.[423] *The town clerk stated that charges would not have been pressed if Etheridge had not been carrying passengers. He had taken out 11 people in his boat the Happy Jack when he was licensed to take only six. Etheridge stated that as the party comprised many children he thought he would be allowed to take extra numbers. The magistrate, Mr Bigge, felt that the large number of children meant that loss of life was more likely so fined Etheridge 20 shillings plus costs as it was his first offence.*

James Etheridge was admitted to the Sussex County Hospital on 27 September 1871 having suffered with pleurisy for seven weeks.[424] *Etheridge was recommended to the hospital by W B Smith, relieving officer for the parish, and sureties for the cost of his burial were given by the Reverend William Worcester Godden, vicar of St Mary's Chapel.*[425] *Etheridge absconded after three weeks.*

[421] Birth of James Etheridge registered Q2 1841 Brighton 7 235.
[422] ESRO: PAR 255/1/3/45.
[423] Brighton Guardian, 5 July 1871.
[424] ESRO: HB 35/3/1871/12297.
[425] Each subscriber to the Royal Sussex County Hospital could forward a certain number of names commensurate with the sum they gave to the hospital annually. On admission each patient was

By the time of his application to the Mendicity Society in March 1872 Etheridge and his wife had been living at 21 Essex Street for seven weeks and before that had been resident at 17 Hereford Street. They paid two shillings per week rent but were five shillings in arrears with payments. In a usual week the couple had a joint income of 15 shillings but due to Charlotte Etheridge's pregnancy, and with James Etheridge being short of work, their joint earnings were only two shillings per week.

Just prior to the application to the Mendicity Society, James Etheridge had spent five weeks at the Sussex County Hospital.[426] *William Collingham, the charity's agent, recorded that Etheridge had asthma but the admission register states that he was admitted on 7 February suffering from secondary syphilis and had been living with the condition for seven years. James Etheridge was treated by Dr Edward Latham Ormerod and his case notes state that on admittance Etheridge appeared 'pale and cachectic looking'.*[427] *Ormerod went on to give some background on Etheridge's case: he described him as a labourer from Brighton who had had syphilis nine years ago but had developed a sore throat which had troubled him intermittently for the last seven years. The whole of Etheridge's soft palate was 'swelled and flabby looking especially on the left side where there is an ulcerated fissure more than an inch long.' Etheridge appeared to make steady progress until 20 February when he had bouts of vomiting which continued for three days, but he recovered sufficiently to be discharged as an out-patient on 5 March. Ormerod also observed that Etheridge's left pupil was much smaller than the right due to a blow he had received 16 years previously.*

Charlotte Etheridge appeared at the magistrates' court on 8 January 1875 when she was the defendant in a case brought against her by Ann Sampson.[428] *Etheridge was accused of assault and battery by Sampson, who stated that they were neighbours both living in Little St James Street. Sampson claimed that Etheridge had abused her and challenged her to a fight. When Sampson refused to resort to fists Etheridge allegedly entered her house and struck her in the face two or three times. Etheridge replied that she did not touch Sampson until Sampson had kicked her and denied entering her neighbour's house. The Brighton Guardian reported that 'the volubility of the women in the court room was considerable and there was evident ill feeling between them. Defendant acknowledged 'slapping the chops' of complainant, but said it was after she had been kicked and taunted to do so'. Etheridge who, like Sampson, appeared in court holding a small child, was fined one shilling and costs or, in default, seven days' hard labour.*

James Etheridge drowned on 21 April 1878 when he was baiting for whelks near the Chain Pier. The inquest recorded that at about 11am a small boat named the Happy Jack was being rowed under the pier by Etheridge and Edward Paskins when a large wave

required to name a person that would guarantee the payment of funeral expenses should they not survive.

[426] ESRO: HB 35/3/1872-535.

[427] ESRO: HB 62/15.

[428] Brighton Guardian, 13 January 1875.

flooded and capsized the craft throwing the men into the water.[429] *A life-buoy was thrown and caught by Paskins who could not swim. Etheridge swam to the second station of the pier but when the boat righted itself he returned to it and Paskins, but following a heavy swell was struck by the boat's sail after which he appeared to sink. His body was found later that afternoon where it had washed ashore near the aquarium. The Borough Coroner, A F Gell, returned a verdict of 'found drowned' but reported that Mr F Merrifield, who had seen the accident, wished to start a fund for the benefit of Charlotte Etheridge. Gell concurred and offered a sovereign towards the fund; an additional thirty-one shilling was raised by the members of the jury.*

19 March 1872
Statement: James Etheridge wants a little assistance. He expects his wife to be confined in a week or two.
Report: I made enquiries respecting this case and find the man is a waterman. He did work for the town authorities a short time and then was in the hospital two weeks suffering from asthma and left two weeks ago. The wife did go charring. She is not able to work now. They are not known to the Reverend Snowden Smith nor to Mr Hart the District Visitor. The home is in a passable state. They applied to the parish authorities but refused to go in the [work]house. The relieving officer states they can have relief during the wife's confinement.
Relieved by grant of 2s and six soup tickets, R P Hooper, chairman

Letter from the Reverend A T Waugh, 8 Charlotte Street, Brighton, 16 May 1878[430]
Dear Sir, it has been intimated to me through Captain Kirby that the Charity Organisation Society might be able to assist in placing a child of Etheridge (the fisherman drowned on Easter Day) at Egremont Place Industrial School. It appears likely that a sum of £100 will be available from a subscription made for the sufferers and of this the gentleman to whom the distribution is entrusted would pay £25 in five annual sums towards the maintenance of the oldest girl, eight years of age. A lady has offered an annual donation of £1 thus £4 a year has to be raised. Can your committee aid? Yours faithfully, A T Waugh

18 May 1878
Captain Kirby mentioned this case to the committee a week ago. On Thursday the Reverend A T Waugh forwarded a letter to the office requesting the society to assist him in placing Mrs Etheridge's oldest daughter in the Brighton and Hove Girls Industrial Home, Egremont Place, for five years. The husband was drowned near the Chain Pier on Easter Sunday. At the inquest a subscription

429 Brighton Guardian, 24 April 1878.
430 Arthur Thornhill Waugh, incumbent of St Mary's, Brighton.

was started for the relief of the widow and her three children and also for Etheridge's companion who lost his boat. Mrs Etheridge who is a sober, respectable person now receives 10s a week from the funds thus raised. Out of the £100 already subscribed it is intended to pay £25 towards the girl's schooling. A lady has promised £1 a year for five years and four more annual subscriptions of a like sum are wanted to complete the arrangement. WC [William Collingham]
Case to be advertised and grant of £1, R P Hooper, chairman

114 JOHN COOPER, 52, LABOURER, BAKERS BOTTOM, BRIGHTON

On the census of 1871 John Cooper was enumerated at Middle Road, Preston, where he lodged with the Goodsell family. He was described as a labourer and he was employed doing similar work when he applied to the Mendicity Society in March 1872. Cooper was born in Nether Wallop, Hampshire, in about 1820 and, according to his Mendicity Society application form, arrived in Brighton in March 1871.[431] *He was unmarried and had been living at an unspecified property in Bakers Bottom for two weeks, where he paid two shillings per week rent and was two shillings in arrears.*[432]

Cooper had been labouring for Mr Brook of Preston but had been out work for seven weeks due to sickness; when in full employment he could expect to bring home 11 shillings per week.[433] *Mr Brook acted as his referee.*

20 March 1872
Statement: John Cooper would be thankful for a little assistance for a week or two when he thinks he shall be able to work.
Report: I made enquiries respecting this man and find he did work for Mr Brook at Preston. He has been sick for seven weeks. He thinks he shall be able to work in a week or two. The house is in a passable state. Mr Brook gave him a good character. I believe this to be a deserving case.
Relieved with a grant of 2s and case reported to Mr Brook the master for further enquiries, R P Hooper, chairman

I have seen Mr Brook again. He states he is very pleased this society has relieved this man. He believed him to be a very deserving man. He did not give me anything for him.
Relieved from private sources and grant of 2s on Tuesday next, 23 March 1872, R P Hooper, chairman

431 The census records Cooper's place of birth as Lower Wallop.

432 Bakers Bottom was at this time a rural settlement which was in the vicinity of what is now Sutherland Road, Bute Street and the Craven Vale estate.

433 Possibly Joseph Brook junior, brewer of Preston.

115 SARAH BENNETT, 63, COOK, 3 OVER STREET, BRIGHTON

Sarah Bennett was forwarded to the Mendicity Society by Mrs Kennedy of 6 Marine Terrace. Bennett was born in Hailsham in about 1809 but according to her application form had been living in Brighton since 1852. She was a widow but nothing is known of her late husband.

Sarah Bennett had been living at 22 Kensington Place but had moved to 3 Over Street in about January 1872. She paid 1s 9d per week rent for her room and was not in arrears. Her previous employer, Miss Phipps of 37 Brunswick Terrace, had paid Bennett 10s 6d per week but had left Brighton three months' previously since which time she had been out of work.

20 March 1872
Statement: Sarah Bennett would be thankful for a little assistance.
Report: This woman states she fell down stairs last Tuesday week, she is now ill in bed. She says Miss Phipps has left the town. Mrs Kennedy states she was in her services a short time about three years ago and was discharged through her intemperate habits. She has applied to the parish and will be relieved today. The house is in a destitute state.
Ineligible, R P Hooper, chairman

116 CATHERINE BRICKLEY, 23, HAWKER, 37 CUMBERLAND PLACE, BRIGHTON

Catherine Brickley (née Carey) was born in Brighton in about 1849 and married James Brickley at St John the Baptist Catholic Church, Brighton, on 7 May 1868.[434] *James Brickley was born in Ireland in about 1841 but was enumerated at 30 Egremont Street, Brighton, on the 1851 census where he lived with his parents and two younger brothers. The ages and birth places of the younger children suggest that the family came to Brighton between about 1843 and about 1850. In 1861 James Brickley was employed as a labourer and living with his parents and younger siblings at 58 Egremont Street. In February 1867 the Brighton Gazette reported a fracas in Egremont Street involving two brothers named Brickley.*[435] *A woman named Catherine Colman saw the brothers fighting and shouted to one of the men to let his brother go. A man named William Kirby pushed Colman over telling her not to interfere. On 23 March 1867 a man named James Brickley was admitted to the Sussex County Hospital but was formally discharged on 3 May after leaving the hospital and failing to return due to intoxication.*[436]

When Catherine Brickley applied to the Mendicity Society in March 1872 the couple and their three-month-old daughter Margaret were living at 37 Cumberland Place, where

[434] ESRO: CAT 18/1/3/2.
[435] Brighton Gazette, 28 February 1867.
[436] ESRO: HB 35/10.

they had been for three months. They paid weekly rent of four shillings for the whole house and were a week's rent in arrears. Both James and Catherine Brickley earned their living hawking goods and expected to bring home 29 shillings per week when in full employment but had recently taken only 12 shillings per week.

Catherine Brickley appeared at the Magistrates' Court in July 1873 charged with assaulting Catherine Coleman of Spa Street.[437] *Coleman stated that when she opened her door on Saturday night Brickley threw a brick at her and struck her heavily on the knee. The report of the hearing in the Brighton Guardian described Brickley as 'a violent woman' and recorded that she was committed to hard labour for a month. It seems reasonable to assume that the Catherine Colman pushed over by William Kirby in February 1867 and the Catherine Coleman assaulted by Catherine Brickley in 1873 are one and the same. Catherine Coleman's name also appears in case 116 when she was involved in an altercation with a woman named Mary Brickley in June 1863. The relationship between Mary and Catherine Brickley is not known.*

James Brickley applied to the charity again in May 1876 in the hope of obtaining an in-patient's letter for the Sussex County Hospital. He had been admitted to the hospital on 16 March 1876 with an urgent case of albuminuria.[438] *His surgeon W Ainslie Hollis stated in his case notes that Brickley's present illness manifested itself with a slight swelling of both feet and his stomach. He had had a similar attack five years previously: after six weeks of out-patient care he was greatly relieved but not cured.*[439] *Six years previously Brickley had rheumatic fever which lasted for five or six weeks and included a period of 14 days when he was unable to move any of his limbs. Having recovered from that illness Brickley got drunk and slept outdoors one night but got very wet in the rain causing him to catch a severe cold. Seven weeks later he noticed a slight swelling of his feet but rather than visit a doctor he took advice from neighbours and the swelling decreased so he took no further measures. Hollis went on to describe James Brickley as 'a man of average height, inclined to be stout, muscles fairly developed, of intemperate habits … rather inclined to be constipated'. Brickley was discharged from the hospital on 1 April 1876 relieved, but not cured, of his symptoms. The death of a James Brickley was registered in Brighton in the September quarter of 1876.*

No further applications were made to the Mendicity Society by Catherine Brickley but her name appeared in the local press in April 1877.[440] *She was described by the Brighton Guardian as being a fish hawker who had been convicted of drunkenness several times before. She was sent to prison for 14 days with hard labour for being drunk and disorderly and using obscene language at a beerhouse near Market Place on Monday 2 April.*

[437] Brighton Guardian, 9 July 1873.

[438] Albuminuria is a condition where protein is present in the urine causing swelling in the ankles, hands, belly or face, ESRO: HB 35/3.

[439] ESRO: HB 62/33.

[440] Brighton Guardian, 4 April 1877.

Catherine Brickley went before the Brighton Bench again in May 1878 when she was charged with being drunk and fighting with Elizabeth Poole on Surrey Street.[441] *The Eastbourne Gazette recorded that this was Poole's fourteenth appearance and Brickley's seventh appearance in the Police Court. They were fined ten shillings and costs or serve one month in prison. Brickley declared that she had no money and prison would kill her.*

On 11 September 1879 Catherine Brickley was admitted to the Sussex County Lunatic Asylum at Haywards Heath suffering from chronic mania.[442] *However, the reception document recorded that she had been transferred from Littlemore Asylum, Oxford, where she was admitted on 25 June 1879.*

Edward Pearl, the surgeon who assessed Catherine Brickley at Littlemore, stated, 'she says that the almighty has put it into her heart that she is to be shot or eaten up alive. She also says that last night her child was, for a long time, outside her cell calling to her.' Pearl reported that Superintendent Hayes of the borough police said that 'last night she climbed to the top of her cell, put her legs through the bars over the top of the door, exposed her bosom and called upon him to come and shoot her'.[443] *Local press reported that Brickley had been charged at Windsor with being drunk in public streets but in answer to the charge Brickley stated that she was ready to die and then made incoherent remarks during the hearing.* [444] *The landlord of the Bachelor's Arms, Mr Smith, stated that Brickley had entered his pub, already drunk, at about 8.15pm on Friday night. She drank a customer's glass of ale and would not leave. Once in custody Superintendent Hayes established that Catherine Brickley visited the area every year to pick peas for Mr Allen at Old Windsor. The magistrates remanded her for a week and, convinced of her insanity, arranged for her transfer to Littlemore Asylum.*[445]

Brickley was discharged from the Sussex County Lunatic Asylum on 1 November 1879 and was considered recovered, but she was readmitted on 8 March 1880 suffering with acute recurrent mania which the reception document stated she had experienced for a year.[446] *Between being discharged in November 1879 and readmitted in March 1880 Brickley stated that she had been an inmate at Brighton Workhouse. The supposed cause of Brickley's mania was alcohol and she was considered a danger to others: the workhouse surgeon, David Richards, stated that Brickley 'says that she is quite dead, is very violent and dangerous to herself and others – breaks windows and furniture, bites, refuses food – is sleepless and requires constant restraint.' She was discharged from the Sussex County Lunatic Asylum, not improved, on 12 August 1889 and readmitted on 28 July 1891 when she was described as 'incoherent but uses filthy language – is quarrelsome and very*

441 Eastbourne Gazette, 1 May 1878.

442 ESRO: HC 24/3669.

443 Superintendent Hayes probably worked for the Borough of Windsor police.

444 Windsor and Eton Express, 28 June 1879.

445 Reports of a woman named Catherine Brickley who was apprehended in a drunken state appear in newspapers published at Reading on 4 October 1873, 15 April 1876 and 16 March 1878 but there is no way of knowing whether this is the same person. The proximity to Windsor makes it noteworthy.

446 ESRO: HC 24/3751.

indecent'.[447] *The case book which records Catherine Brickley's next 12 years as a patient described her variously as, 'quite demented, does nothing and takes little interest in her surroundings', 'incoherent and rambling in speech', 'quite lost; at times dirty and spiteful', 'dirty in habits and hoards rubbish.'*[448] *The case book records that Catherine Brickley died, aged 63, of fatty degeneration of the heart and pulmonary congestion at 2.40pm on 5 June 1913. She was interred at the asylum's burial ground on 9 June 1913.*[449]

Anonymous letter sent to Brighton Mendicity Society, 16 March 1872
Catherine Brickley, 36 or 37 Cumberland Place, Edward Street, St James Street
A lady who has been applied to for relief from a person giving the above address which she has no reason to believe is one of much distress desires to draw the attention of the Mendicity Society to make enquiries being herself a visitor and unable to render any further assistance to the case.

20 March 1872
Statement: I never begged in my life.
Report: I have known this family for this last eight years. The man hawks fish and the woman flowers. They are both very industrious and both very much given to drink. The home is in a passable state.
Undeserving, R P Hooper, chairman

3 May 1876
This man who resides at 59 Egremont Street is suffering from rheumatism and dropsy. What he now wants is an in-patient's letter to the Sussex County Hospital. He was an in-patient for nearly three weeks and left of his own accord about three weeks ago. Mr Langdale, house surgeon, states that this is more of a case for the infirmary than the hospital. WC [William Collingham]
Referred to parish, R P Hooper

117 THOMAS MITCHELL, 30, CLERK, 75 SHRUBLAND ROAD, HACKNEY, LONDON

Thomas Mitchell's case was raised with the Brighton Mendicity Society as a result of a circular he sent to the charity in March 1872. This missive does not survive but he had clearly sent it to a number of other similar societies in the hope that he might raise enough money to start a business in Hastings: a move designed to alleviate the consumption he had been suffering with for 18 months.

[447] ESRO: HC 24/6398.
[448] ESRO: HC 55/25.
[449] ESRO: HC 27/1.

Mitchell was enumerated at 75 Shrubland Road, Hackney, on the 1871 census, where he lived with his wife Ellen and their four children. He was born in Shoreditch in about 1842 and was employed as clerk for the publishers Longman from 1863 but had been unable to work due to his illness. Aside from his full-time work Thomas Mitchell was also the author of two books: 'The Stepping-Stone to Architecture', published in 1869,[450] *'A Rudimentary Manual of Architecture: being a history and explanation of the principal styles of European architecture, ancient, mediæval, and renaissance, with their chief variations described and illustrated,' published in 1870.*[451]

Mitchell's referee was the Reverend John Ross of Haggerston, east London. No further enquiry was made by officers of the Brighton Mendicity Society.

Letter from the Hackney Committee of the Charity Organisation Society and for Improving the Condition of the Poor, 19 March 1872
Sir, with respect to the enclosed document I have to say that others have been received here for enquiry and I give briefly the same report as to others. Mr Mitchell has been for nine years correspondence clerk at Messrs Longmans and is now in an advanced stage of consumption. To provide for his family he issued – by advice – this circular with the object of raising capital to start a business at Hastings were he hopes to regain some measure of restored health. £300 is required towards which £200 has been gathered and is now in the bank in the name of Reverend J Ross – St Mary's, Haggerston. This gentleman speaks most highly of applicant having known him for some years. Mr Mitchell has written a book on architecture, published by Longmans, which was not very profitable. The case is most deserving of sympathy and help and is recommended by many other gentlemen one of whom, Major Whyte-Melville has promised £50 and Messrs Longmans a like sum. These amounts are included in the £200 in the bank and promised. I am sir yours very obediently, [*signature unclear*]

118 MARIAN FLOWERS, AGE NOT GIVEN, OCCUPATION NOT GIVEN, 30 SOUTHAMPTON STREET, READING, BERKSHIRE

Little is known about Marian Flowers. Her case was forwarded to the Mendicity Society by Mr C Hartmann of 13 Cavendish Place, Brighton. Flowers's link to Brighton is not known.

20 March 1872
Mr Hartmann, 13 Cavendish Place, had a begging letter sent to him by Marian S

450 T Mitchell, *The stepping-stone to architecture* (London, 1869).

451 T Mitchell, *A Rudimentary Manual of Architecture: being a history and explanation of the principal styles of European architecture, ancient, mediæval, and renaissance, with their chief variations described and illustrated* (London, 1870).

Flowers, number 20 Southampton Street, Reading, and a few weeks ago a friend of his received one similar. He then went to the Chief Constable respecting it: he referred him to this society. Mr Shears wrote to the superintendent of police, Reading, and this is the answer. I have since seen Mr Hartmann and shown him the answer. He does not wish to take any further steps in the case.
Answer referred to Mr Hartmann, R P Hooper, chairman

Letter from James Purchase, Chief Superintendent of Reading Police, 21 March 1872
Sir, in answer to your letter with reference to Marian S Flowers I beg to inform you that she resides at number 20 Upper Southampton Street (formerly Hill Cottage) and from inquiries made I am informed that there is nothing the matter with her and is in very comfortable circumstances there being no necessity for making such an application. I am sir your obedient servant, James Purchase, Chief Superintendent

119 ELLEN SMITH, AGE NOT GIVEN, OCCUPATION NOT GIVEN, 3 QUEENS ROAD, HORNSEY, LONDON

Little is known of Ellen Smith: there is no obvious record of her residency in Brighton and street directories carry no entries for a greengrocer's shop at 10 King Street run by anyone named Smith, which corroborates William Collingham's findings.

Letter from W J Paton and P Irving, honorary secretaries of the Islington Committee for Organising Charitable Relief and Repressing Mendicity, 4a Park Street, Islington, London, 21 March 1872
Sir, Ellen Smith widow at present of 2 Queens Road, Hornsey Road, London north, has applied here for assistance. She states that she left Brighton in May last and has since followed the occupation of a hawker having no fixed residence until now. She further states that her late husband was a greengrocer in business at 10 King Street and at his death which occurred three years ago she was compelled to part with the business to pay his debts and expenses of his funeral. In the interval between the death of her husband and the date of her leaving Brighton she resided for various periods at 24 Elm Grove, 24 Over Street and other places and she refers for character to Mrs Train of 24 Elm Grove. We shall feel greatly obliged if you will institute enquiries at the foregoing address and favor us with a report at your earliest convenience. Yours obediently, W J Paton and P Irving

22 March 1872
Report: I made enquiries respecting this case and find the whole of this woman's statement is false. Number 10 King Street is a second-hand shop and has been for years. At number nine about three years ago a party that went by the name

of Tuppen had a greengrocer's shop there and the man deserted his wife and no one knows what has become of her. At 24 Over Street the name is not known. At 24 Elm Grove no one by the name of Train lives there. I made enquiries at several other places and no one knows the name.

120 WILLIAM NORTH, ABOUT 35, LABOURER, 22 EASTERN ROAD, BRIGHTON

The circumstances of William North's early years are difficult to ascertain: during the course of his long life he gave many inconsistent estimates of his age. A boy named William North was baptised at St Nicholas, Brighton, on 23 July 1837 to James and Ann North of Edwin Place and this seems the most likely candidate for the man recorded in these papers.[452] *The family were enumerated at the same address in 1841 and 1851, but by 1861 William North was living at a lodging house at 20 Derby Place.*

When he first applied to the Mendicity Society in March 1872 he had been discharged from the Sussex County Hospital two weeks previously and since then had been living at 22 Eastern Road. He expected to make 18 shillings a week when in full employment as a labourer but had recently only been making 10 shillings a week working for Joseph Boniface, a beer retailer, of Essex Street. North had been in and out of hospital since the 1860s and was applying for money to tide him over until being admitted to the workhouse infirmary. Due to his hospital visits and transgressions much is known of his life during the 1860s.

On 17 September 1863 William North, now describing himself as 26, was charged with the assault of Julia Johnstone of Wellington Place, Brighton. The Brighton Guardian referred to him as 'a rough looking fellow' and Julia Johnstone went on to describe how she and her sister were walking on Race Hill near the rifle ranges on the previous day when North came up behind her very suddenly, put his arm around her neck and threw her to the floor, tumbling over her.[453] *Johnstone's sister, Louisa, was walking a short distance ahead and on hearing her sister scream alerted Laurence Walker, who was riding in the vicinity. Walker followed North until he crossed under the railings of the race course: he could not follow on horseback but asked another passer-by, George Johnson, to follow North and keep him in view. North picked up some large stones and said he would throw them at anyone who attempted to touch him but he was eventually apprehended by PC Billingshurst of the East Sussex Constabulary, who was stationed at Falmer and happened to be near the Race Hill in the parish of Ovingdean. North claimed that he caught his foot in Johnstone's dress and fell upon her as a result of the accident but his version of events was not believed and he was given six months' imprisonment with hard labour.*

[452] ESRO: PAR 255/1/2/10.
[453] Brighton Guardian, 23 September 1863.

The following August William North was charged with being drunk and indecently exposing himself on the steps of the Presbyterian chapel, Church Street.[454] *PC Rudd stated that at about 12.45pm on Saturday his attention was called to North and a female accomplice, who were behaving indecently. When Rudd arrived both parties ran away but William North was caught heading towards North Lane.*[455] *North denied lewd behaviour but confessed to the act following the deposition of Ann Betteridge who lived close to the chapel and saw the incident. North stated that 'he was drunk and he was very sorry'. The Chief Constable referred to North's previous appearance before the Bench and the JP, Mr Bigge, fined North 40 shillings and costs or 14 days' imprisonment, adding that he was sorry he could not make the sentence harsher.*

In June 1865 William North was charged with sleeping in one of the borders near the North Lodge of the Royal Pavilion, but was discharged with no fine.[456] *North claimed that he had been drunk and did not remember how he came to be there. The Bench considered that North may have thought he was scaling the wall of the workhouse where he had previously been an inmate.*

North appeared before the Bench again on 7 August 1865 charged with stealing onions from the garden of PC Slater on Sussex Hill.[457] *He was found guilty and committed to the House of Correction for 14 days with hard labour.*

At some point between August 1865 and April 1866 William North was admitted to Brighton Workhouse, and on 26 April 1866 he appeared before magistrates again, this time charged with selling a pair of boots that he had stolen from the institution.[458] *Edward Sattin, master of the workhouse, stated that North had sold the boots to a woman in the Lanes for three shillings, that he was now 'in a state of disease and had several times misconducted himself'. The Bench committed him to hard labour for a month. In August 1867 a man named William North was struck in the face at Brighton Workhouse by another inmate, Ezekiel Burton, when the two men were oakum picking.*[459] *Burton was fined 2s 6d.*

The 'state of disease' that Edward Sattin referred to in his deposition became apparent when North was admitted to the Sussex County Hospital on 17 February 1869 with spinal meningitis.[460] *His surgeon, Dr Henry Moon, described William North as a 38 year-old labourer who served six years in the navy where he picked up syphilis. He had suffered with acute rheumatism six years previously and was considered to be moderately temperate. In January 1869, after getting wet, his knee and ankle joints became tender and swollen confining him to bed for three weeks. Dr Moon goes on to list in great detail the symptoms and treatment of North's disease. By 23 June he is described as having 'no*

[454] Brighton Guardian, 3 August 1864.
[455] North Lane is probably a reference to North Road rather than the area of North Laine.
[456] Brighton Gazette, 22 June 1865.
[457] Brighton Gazette, 10 August 1865.
[458] Brighton Guardian, 2 May 1866.
[459] Brighton Guardian, 31 July 1867.
[460] ESRO: HB 62/22.

sensation now beneath the knees' but was removed to the workhouse on 28 June. North was readmitted on 20 January 1870 with tingling sensations in his feet and discharged on 16 March 'to visit a sister – jerking in the limbs have disappeared and he walks more firmly'.

In January 1871 a 41-year-old man named William North was charged with obtaining relief under false pretenses.[461] *He had visited a woman by the name of Hunt who lived at Bedford Square, stating that he had recently fallen from a scaffold. Mrs Hunt gave North five shillings and an order upon her butcher for a shoulder of mutton. He was found guilty and committed to hard labour for a month.*

William North was enumerated on the 1871 census aged 37 living with his parents at Essex Cottages and made his first application to the Mendicity Society in March 1872. He was re-admitted to the Sussex County Hospital on 24 April 1872 with a condition that was described as feigned epilepsy, but it is conceivable that this symptom was a product of his spinal meningitis which made his limbs jerk.[462]

North appeared before the Brighton Bench again in June 1877.[463] *The Brighton Herald described the hearing: 'William North, 47, a cripple, lodging in Cumberland Place, who has been before the Bench on seven previous occasions for indecent conduct and other offences was sentenced to six months' hard labour for disgusting behaviour towards a girl ten years of age. It was stated that [the] prisoner was mobbed by a crowd of children who nearly stoned him to death'.*

In January 1880 North claimed to have spent another 15 months in hospital but no record could be found of him in the admission registers of the Sussex County Hospital.

William North was again convicted of indecent assault on 8 February 1883: 'An Old Beast – William North, 54, a villainous looking cripple was charged on a warrant with indecently assaulting Lydia Jane Biggs, aged 14, of 32 Meeting House Lane.'[464] *Biggs had been walking along Brighton Place carrying a baby when North grabbed her by the arm and used offensive language to her. He tried to drag her behind some carts but, at the appearance of a man coming out of a nearby public house, let her go. North denied being present in the Lanes on the night in question but was sentenced to six months hard labour.*

In February 1885 he spent time in Woolwich, south east London, and an agent of the Woolwich Society for Organising Charitable Relief and Repressing Mendicity contacted the Charity Organisation Society, Brighton, to enquire about North, who had recently been charged with begging and indecently assaulting a girl, for which he was sent to prison for one month.

By 7 December of 1885 William North was being chased by F S Champion, solicitor, of North Gate House, Brighton Pavilion.[465] *The precise reason for F S Champion's enquiry to Champions solicitors of Eastbourne is unknown but it is probable that North owed*

461 Brighton Guardian, 11 January 1871.
462 ESRO: HB 35/3/1872-1918.
463 Brighton Herald, 2 June 1877.
464 Brighton Guardian, 14 February 1883.
465 ESRO: ACC 8859/3/C/94.

money to one of his clients. The letter enquires whether there is any knowledge of 'the address of a man named William North – he is a cripple and was imprisoned at Lewes in 1884 being sent there from Hastings. He is now believed to be at Eastbourne making picture frames and hawking them about. If you enquire at the police station they will probably be able to tell you his whereabouts.' A note on the reverse of the letter states that North was staying at common lodging house but had left about a fortnight since and was thought to have gone to Brighton.

Reports on North's movements made by the charity show that between 1885 and 1900 he also spent time at Sandgate Road, Folkestone, Kent, where he lived with Ann Cresswell and her daughter or granddaughter, Emily. When North and Cresswell returned to Brighton they lived at 39 William Street and Mrs Bradley of 31 William Street and Mr G King, pastor of the Baptist chapel, Mighell Street, provided references for North. The living arrangement between North and Cresswell lasted until at least 1910 but there is no evidence that they were related in any way despite North's claims.

The Charity Organisation Society was contacted about North by the secretary of Mr Adam Mortimer Singer in 1914. Singer was related to the sewing machine manufacturers and was a renowned yachtsman; when he died in June 1929 he left effects of £462,225.[466] *It seems that Singer's late wife had started funding North some years previously but the reason for the connection is not known.*

William North's last contact with the Charity Organisation Society took place in February 1915 and his name does not appear to have been mentioned in press after this date. The death of a 92 year-old man named William North was registered at Brighton in the June quarter of 1922.[467]

22 March 1872
Statement: William North wants a little assistance to help him over till Wednesday when he is going in the infirmary.
Report: I made inquiries respecting this man and find he is not known at the address given. He is well known at the town hall having been three times convicted. The Reverend Mr Cooper has relieved him on several occasions and says he is not at all sorry he is out of his district now. Mr Boniface did not give him a good character. Mr S North, his uncle, relieved him on several occasions but cannot continue to do so.
Dismissed, undeserving, R P Hooper

Letter to Miss Knollys, from H B Jordison, 44 Lavender Street, Brighton, 22 January 1876
In reference to W North I can speak well of him and consider him to be quite deserving of any assistance you may be kind enough to render him as he is a

[466] England and Wales National Probate Calendar (index of wills and administrations).
[467] Death of William North registered Q2 1922 Brighton 2b 244.

sober man and, I believe, [an] industrious man. I have written this note for him as it is a long journey for him to Mr Sattin only being able to use his crutches. If you will accept this as a recommendation I shall feel obliged.
Yours obediently, H B Jordison, a tradesman

24 January 1876
The man North applied to Miss Knollys of 28 York Road for assistance on Friday last but Miss K refused to assist him unless he produced a recommendation from Mr Sattin instead of which he got Mr Jordison, a small grocer of 44 Lavender Street to give him one and on Saturday he took it to Miss K who again refused to relieve him and sent his recommendation to Mr Sattin, master of the workhouse who sent it to the office for investigation. All Mr Jordison knows of North is that he has been in his shop two or three times in the course of the last four months and believing him to be a respectable man he gave him the letter as requested.
WC [William Collingham]
Undeserving, to be reported to Mr Sattin [*signature illegible*]

Letter from Edward Sattin, master of Brighton Workhouse, 24 January 1876
Dear Sir, can you tell me if there is such a person and would you mind asking him if he wrote the enclosed – our experience of the man North is quite the reverse. The lady would not appear to prosecute but her kindness is very often attempted to be abused by persons leaving here. I am sir yours truly, E Sattin, master

Letter from J Bright, 19 Goldsmid Road, Hove, 3 March [1876]
Dear Sir, William North, residing at present at 44 Upper North Street with a person named Wilton, called on me today for an out-patient ticket to the hospital. He says he has been a cripple for years and a patient in the workhouse infirmary for many years [and] that he left because he was improperly treated and wants to get into the hospital. As I rather doubt his statements I should like to know something about him and think it a great pity he should not have the relief from the [work]house if he can get it. I never heard of anyone not being well treated there before.
Yours truly, J Bright

6 March 1876
Mrs Bright forwarded the annexed letter to the office and requests a report of the case. On enquiry I find that instead of his address being 44 Upper North Street he resides with his mother in Essex Place. North is very well known: sometimes he goes into different hospitals, sometimes he gets sent to prison and at other times he is either begging about the town or else he is in the workhouse. His first conviction was in 1863 when he was sentenced to six months imprisonment for

indecently assaulting a child named Johnson. Since then he has been convicted for exposing himself, for stealing onions also twice for stealing boots and once for begging. WC [William Collingham]
Undeserving, to be reported to Mrs Bright, R P Hooper

Letter from William North [to Mr J Long, 50 Marine Parade, January 1880]
Dear Sir, I trust you will forgive the liberty I take in addressing these few lines to you. I have been in hospital 15 months and now am much better. I wish to ask if you would grateful enough [sic] to favour me with the sum of 7s 6d to go home to Southampton. I shall be truly thankful to you promising never to trouble you again and thanking you a thousand times for your kindness. I remain your humble servant, William North

10 January 1880
Mr J Long 50 Marine Parade brought the annexed begging letter to the office on Friday and stated that he had been assisting North during the last few months but before relieving him again he requests a report of the case. The letter represents that North has been in hospital 15 months and that he now wants 7s 6d to take him home to Southampton. He is a native of Brighton and gave Mr Long a false address. Since my last report he has been convicted on two or three occasions. Lately he has been lodging at 2 Thomas Street. On Thursday he and several of his companions left the town and are said to have gone to Lewes. WC [William Collingham]
Undeserving report to Mr Long, recommended to prosecute, R P Hooper – declined

Letter from C H Mannsell, 19 Cannon Place, Brighton, 17 November 1882
Dear Sir, I shall be much obliged if you would investigate the case of William North now staying at 4 Easton Road[468] who has applied to myself and another clergyman for help. He says he has lately left a convalescent home at Blackheath. He has previously applied to us some time since. Faithfully yours, C H Mannsell

[18] November 1882
The Reverend C H Mannsell of 19 Cannon Place requests a report of this case. North, who returned to Brighton a short time ago, still gets his living by begging and is now lodging at 3 Chesterfield Court instead of 4 Easter Road [sic] which address he gave Mr Mannsell. WC [William Collingham]
Report to Reverend Mannsell, R P Hooper

[468] This is probably Eastern Road in Brighton rather than Eaton Road in Hove.

Letter from James Harrington, agent of the Society for Organising Charitable Relief and Repressing Mendicity, 5 Eleanor Road, Woolwich, London, 5 February 1885
Sir, a man who states to be William North, widower, age 62, stated himself to be a tailor. He goes on two crutches, states he lost the use of his limbs by being run over by a waggon about 13 or 14 years ago.[469] He gets his living by begging. He was charged by police near here with begging and indecently assaulting a girl. He was sent to prison for one month and is only out about six weeks. [470] He was sent here for enquiry to be made into his case by a subscriber of whom he begged. Most of his statements at this office I find to be untrue. From further enquiry I have been told he lived at 11 Chesterfield Court, Brighton, and that he had tickets printed with that address on it and wound up with 'chairs caned and pictures framed'. Would you kindly make as much enquiry as you can and get as much of his antecedents as possible. His case is going before committee on Tuesday next. Would be very thankful for as much information as you can get as he is determined to beg about here and likely I may be obliged to give him into custody. An early answer will greatly oblige. Yours respectfully, James Harrington, agent

6 February 1885
The agent of the Woolwich Committee has written to say that North is there begging and requests a full report of his case. So far as I can ascertain he has not been seen in the town since the seventh of February 1883 where he was charged with indecently assaulting a child and sentenced to six months hard labour. WC [William Collingham]
Report to Woolwich Committee, R P Hooper

Letter from W Hodges, 14 Buckingham Place, Brighton, [May 1900]
Dear Miss Heathcote, I have had an inquiry this morning of a man asking for help in Hove. He gave his name as William North, 39 William Street, a picture frame maker just out of the Sussex County Hospital. He is described as a cripple and very dirty. If anything is known of him at the office I would be glad if the visitor who comes to C Rose this afternoon would bring me word. Yours truly, W Hodges

5 May 1900
Statement: I am sorry I left Folkestone and should be very glad if I could be assisted to return as often I do not take 6d a day.

469 Dr Moon's case notes state that North was run over by a gun carriage in 1855, presumably when he was serving with the Royal Navy (HB 62/22 folio 70).

470 No account of this trial could be found in south London press.

Report: the committee will see by the previous reports that North has been a very bad character and since he returned to Brighton in 1897 he has offered small picture frames for sale as an excuse for begging besides which he often begs at private houses. His references now recommend him as a quiet, decent man and the Brighton police have no convictions recorded against him since 7th of February 1883. He is cohabiting with a woman named Cresswell and appears a fit subject for the poor law authorities to deal with. WC [William Collingham]
Report to Mr Hodges as undeserving, Thomas W Holland, 8 May 1900

14 May 1900
Having heard that North had applied to Mrs Hammond, 8 Third Avenue, on several occasions for help I called there this morning to inform the lady as to what the committee knew of him besides which I also gave particulars regarding several other well-known beggars who are in the habit of sending there for assistance and Mrs Hammond was very much obliged for the information given her. WC [William Collingham]
To be recorded, [*signature illegible*], 15 May 1900

21 May 1900
North has been in the habit of begging of the Reverend W N Dampier, 29 St Nicholas Place. Therefore I called this morning to inform Mr Dampier as to what the society knew of the applicant and he was very much obliged for the particulars given him adding that the man is often begging in the neighbourhood. WC [William Collingham]
Report to Chief Constable, [*signature illegible*], 22 May 1900

9 June 1900
Report: North applied at the office on Friday for 10s 6d to enable him and the woman Cresswell to return to Folkestone. He has recently done very badly here and often does not take 4d a day. Their railway fare there however would cost 12s 6d but the previous reports show that he is a fit subject for the Union and the woman is well able to earn her livelihood by her own industry. WC [William Collingham]
Undeserving, HS, 12 June 1900

Letter from W W Sandeman, 1 Denmark Terrace, Brighton, 17 July 1901
Dear Sir, a man named William North, 26 High Street, Edward Street, Brighton – he seems a sober sort of poor man. He says at some period asked the Charity Organisation Society to get him a licence to sell picture frames which he carves himself. I would be pleased to pay for the licence if you could get it for him. I am leaving Brighton tomorrow at 10am for two days. I remain yours truly, W W Sandeman

18 July 1901
North now resides at 24 High Street and continues to cohabit with the woman Cresswell. When I visited this morning he said he wanted 3s for stock and mentioned that his licence does not expire before next April but the police cannot trace his name on their books as a licensed pedlar. WC [William Collingham]
This man was recently detected begging from house to house for some 20 or 30 surgical aid letters although the two he actually required had been given to him. Reported to Captain Sandeman, CWM

Letter from Mrs J G Barclay, Exton House, Second Avenue, West Brighton [Hove], 13 January 1902
Mrs J G Barclay will thank Colonel Dodd to inform her if William North, 4 Bond Street Row, Brighton, is deserving of help. He came to this door a few days ago for money to buy wood to make little frames (a 1s was given to him) – he goes about on crutches.

15 January 1902
Mrs J G Barclay, Exton House, Second Avenue, requests a report of this case. North is now residing at 4 Bond Street Row. The woman Cresswell is still living with him and the previous reports show that he is utterly unworthy of encouragement. WC [William Collingham]
Reported to Mrs Barclay

30 March 1903
Report: General Holland called the attention of the society to the fact that this man takes a little girl about with him apparently of school age. Letter to J Carden, clerk to Brighton School Board, copy appended.
April 2nd – letter from Mr Carden appended in reply to ours of 30th March.
Recorded 30 March 1903

Letter to J Carden from M E Heathcote, honorary secretary, Charity Organisation Society, 30 March 1903
Re: William North, Bond Street Row. Dear Mr Carden, this man, who is a cripple who stands in the street selling picture frames, has a little girl about with him who is apparently of school age. North is a man of the worst possible character and the child is the child of the woman he lives with. Would you kindly let the attendance officer see into the case? Our attention has been called to it by more than one person.
Faithfully yours M E Heathcote, honorary secretary

Letter from J Carden, clerk to the education committee, Brighton Borough Council, 1 April 1903
Dear Miss Heathcote, I have caused enquiries to be made into this case but the officer of the district reports that the child referred to by you will not be five years of age until September next. When the child reaches the proper legal age, if the family remains in Brighton, steps will be taken to enforce attendance at school. I am, yours faithfully, John Carden

Letter from Jeremiah Colman, Wick Hall, Hove, [12 October 1905]
Dear Sir, will you kindly advise me re: William North of 2 Jew Street, Church Street. Is he a respectable man and deserving of charitable assistance? I feel sure he must be known in your office as the cripple who goes about the town on crutches. Yours faithfully, Jeremiah Colman

13 October 1905
Mr J Colman of Wick Hall requests a report of this case. North now resides at 2 Jew Street where he cohabits with the woman Cresswell. The previous reports show that he has been most unfavourably known to the society since 22 March 1872 and he is still considered a fit subject for the Poor Law Authorities to deal with. WC [William Collingham]
Reported to Mr Colman, EGM, 17 October 1905[471]

Letter to Jeremiah Colman, Wick Hall, Hove, 14 October 1905
Dear Sir, William North, 2 Jew Street. The above has been known to this society since March 1872. He has undergone two terms of imprisonment for criminal assault and another for indecency. He usually states that he became a cripple through saving life in a carriage accident but there is no evidence of this and there is abundant evidence that he has begged under false pretences. He has subsisted on charity ever since we first knew him. The child he calls his grandchild is no relation but the child of the woman Cresswell with whom he cohabits. He is utterly unworthy of any assistance whatever. Faithfully yours, M E Heathcote

Letter from Mrs Henry Cooke, 27 Wilbury Road, Hove, 3 January 1906
Mrs Henry Cooke presents her compliments to the Reverend Canon Hoskyns and begs to apologise in troubling him but she is anxious to obtain help for an old man (nearly 87) living at 2 Jew Street which she thinks must be in Canon Hoskyns' parish. William Ford [sic] walks on crutches and has been coming to Mrs H Cooke <u>constantly</u> during the last few weeks and she has helped him with

[471] Probably the signature of the Reverend E G May who was listed as a council member in the annual report of 1908.

money and tea and sugar at Christmas besides buying some frames (which he makes himself) and also lent him some books but it is not in her power to continue giving him money etc constantly. William Ford tells Mrs H Cooke that he lives with a widowed daughter and three small children in three rooms and that he gets no help from 'parish or parson' though he has applied for Bates Charity and that on Christmas Day they had only bread and butter and tea. The son of a former master pays his rent and a lady in Hove gives him 6d a week and coals occasionally. His daughter and daughter-in-law cannot go out to work on account of the children as he is too infirm to attend to them. He does not wish to go into the Union as he has always had an outdoor life and is fond of his little house. He is a clean looking old man as a rule and scarcely strikes Mrs H Cooke as a professional cadger so she hopes the Reverend Canon Hoskyns may be able to have the case seen into and some help given. Mrs H Cooke would be glad to know if anything can be done

2 February 1906
The Reverend E Heath of Saints Mary and Mary Magdalene, Bread Street, gave this letter appended which was addressed to Canon Hoskyns and sent on to him to him to the honorary secretary.[472] He asks the society to report direct to Mrs Henry Cooke.
Letter to Mrs Cooke

Letter to Mrs Henry Cooke, 11 Guildford Road, Brighton, from M E Heathcote, honorary secretary, 2 February 1906
Re: William North (not Ford), 2 Jew Street. Dear Madam, the Reverend E Heath has handed your letter regarding the above which Canon Hoskyns forwarded to him, to us, and requests us to report direct to you. North has been known to us since 1872. It would be difficult to find a greater scoundrel anywhere. He has twice served terms of imprisonment for indecently assaulting little girls, once for exposing himself and several times for theft. He never was married and has neither a widowed daughter nor grandchildren. The woman with whom he cohabits, who is a woman of bad character, has a child: if you have seen three at the house the others must have been procured for the purpose of begging. He has never done any work, but when not in prison, has lived by begging and fraud. It is quite true that he gets nothing from the parish; his character is too notorious. Speaking generally, one may be quite sure that if a man of his age in Brighton is not in receipt of parish relief, there is very good reason for it. He is utterly unworthy of any assistance whatever.
Faithfully yours, M E Heathcote

[472] Reverend Edward Heath of 34 Buckingham Sreet, Brighton.

Letter from Mrs Henry Cooke transcribed on society agent's report sheet, [February 1906]

Mrs H Cooke presents her compliments to Miss H[eathcote] and begs to thank her for her communication about William North who has pained her much.
Copy of card

Letter to Miss Ellen Rutter, 11 Wilbury Gardens, Hove, 1 February 1908

Dear Madam, re: William North. This man has been known unfavourably to us since 1872. It would be difficult to find a greater scoundrel. He has served terms of imprisonment for assaulting little girls indecently, for exposing himself and for theft. He never was married but cohabits with a woman. He has lived by begging and fraud; it is true he has had nothing from the parish but his character is too notorious.
Yours faithfully, T Bowalter Tait, secretary

Letter from Evelyn S Miller, 2 Kings Gardens, Hove, 10 February 1910

Dear Madam, a case has come under my notice in some time which, if not troubling you, I should like your society to inquire into (privately of course). The old man's name is William North and he lives at 60 William Street, Edward Street, Brighton. My husband has given the old man a little money at various times and now he has written to me. I should be very much obliged if you could find out if North's is a deserving case.
Truly yours, Evelyn S Miller

Copy of a letter sent from the Charity Organisation Society to Evelyn Miller transcribed on the reverse of the letter transcribed above, [12 February 1910]

Copy of answer re North: Dear Madam, I am sorry for the delay in answering your enquiry respecting the above. Our case papers had been accidentally put in the wrong place and we did not find them till we had searched several times. We have known the old man William North unfavourably for nearly 40 years and we have been asked for information respecting him a very large number of times. We believe him to be a thoroughly bad man and needless to say we have always agreed that no charitable assistance should be given to him. He is well known to the police and numerous convictions are recorded against him starting back from 1863. He has twice undergone a sentence of six months hard labour for moral offences against children. He has several times been convicted for felony and also was convicted for begging and for another moral offence. He usually gives a false address but being a well-known character we have had no difficulty in ascertaining his correct address. We believe he has never been married but he has been living with a woman named Cresswell.
H[ilda] Woodhead, honorary secretary

Letter from Evelyn S Miller, 2 Kings Gardens, Hove, 14 February 1910
Dear Madam, re: North. Many thanks for your letter – the character you have given of the above is such that he will receive nothing further from us. I frequently wondered about that old man and am much obliged to you for the information. It is certainly a lesson not to give promiscuous charity. Truly yours Evelyn S Miller

Letter from Miss Johnston, Milton Hill, Steventon, Berkshire, 10 December 1914
Dear Sir, for some years Mr A Mortimer Singer has been making a fortnightly allowance of 5s to William North of 60 William Street, Brighton. When sending the allowance I send also a receipt postcard which the man signs and returns to me. These are always written in the illiterate manner of No. 391 enclosed herewith. The last one, however, (No. 409) is evidently not written by William North himself and I should be grateful if you could make enquiries as to whether the man is still living and also as to whether he continues to be a deserving object of charity. Perhaps you could be so kind as reply to me direct, addressing your reply to: Miss Johnston, secretary, Steventon House, Steventon, Berkshire. Yours faithfully M M Johnston, secretary

11 December 1914
Report: letter from Miss Johnston, secretary to A M Singer esq. Called at 60 William Street and saw North. He is an old man well known to this society. He is now in two rooms with a woman and one girl. He said the woman was his daughter and the girl his grandchild. It was the girl who signed the receipt No. 409. North says owing to the wet weather he has been unable to get out with his picture frames lately. He has been receiving this money – 5s each fortnight for about two and a half years. He was under the impression I was from Mr Singer and wished to be remembered to Clara

Letter from Mary Tudor, secretary, Charity Organisation Society, Brighton to Miss Johnston, 14 December 1914
Dear Madam, I regret to tell you that this man has been known most unfavourably to us since 1872. The last enquiry we had about him was in 1910. He has been notorious as a beggar. He has been in prison several times; twice for indecent assaults on little girls, once for another form of indecency and other times for theft. He used to cohabit with a woman who was not his wife and took her little girl about with him when begging. At the present time he is living with a woman and girl whose identity we do not know but who probably are the same people as before. He used to refer to them as his widowed daughter and grandchild. Your last postcard was signed by the girl. When one agent visited, North guessed that he came from Mr Singer and asked to be remembered to Clara – of course we do not know what he means by this but thought it as well

to let you know. We should be interested to know how it was that Mr Singer started his generous help and would venture to suggest that North should be left to return to the workhouse. Yours truly, Mary Tudor, secretary

Letter from Miss Johnston, Milton Hill, Steventon, Berkshire, to Mary Tudor, secretary, Charity Organisation Society, Brighton 29 December 1914
Dear Madam, I am greatly obliged to you by your letter of the 14th inst re William North and much regret that press of Christmas work has prevented my replying before. Mr A Mortimer Singer regrets extremely to hear such a bad report of the man in question. The charity was, however, begun by the late Mrs Singer who, of course, knew nothing of the recipient's character, but pitied his crippled condition and Mr Singer feels that, under the circumstances, and as the man must now be old, he would not like to discontinue the small allowance which ought to be an assistance to him to keep honest. Again thanking you for your kind trouble in the matter, I am, dear Madam, yours faithfully M M Johnston, secretary

Pro forma letter to Mary Tudor, secretary, Charity Organisation Society, Brighton from Mutual Registration of Assistance, Brighton Bureau Offices, 4 Richmond Terrace, 19 February 1915
To Miss Tudor: these families have been reported by the undermentioned agencies in the months noted – North, William, 60 William Street. December 1914 – Bates Charity was received at Christmas (596)

121 JANE SAUNDERS, 39, DRESSMAKER, 21 HIGH STREET, BRIGHTON

Jane Saunders' case was forwarded to the Mendicity Society by Laura Soames of Tramore Lodge, 7 Park Road East, when her husband, George Saunders, was apparently looking for work in London. George Saunders had been working as a porter for Markwells Hotel, Kings Road, Brighton, but had been out of work for three months. When in full employment he could expect to earn 18 shillings per week and Jane Saunders, who was a dressmaker, ten shillings per week but the family had been living on her reduced wage of five shillings per week for three months. The couple rented the whole of 21 High Street, which they shared with their six children and for which they paid five shillings per week rent. Miss Gardener of Dorset Gardens also acted as a referee for the family.

Little else is known about the family: Jane Saunders stated that she was born in Brighton and a couple named George Nicholson Saunders and Jane Figg married in Brighton in the September quarter of 1862 though no record of this event was found in the marriage register of St Nicholas, Brighton, for that period. George Saunders was enumerated on the census of 1881 as a widower working as a waiter and living with four of his children at South Terrace, Hastings.

26 March 1872
Statement: my husband has gone to London to look for work. I should be thankful for a little assistance.
Report: I made enquiries respecting this case and find this woman's statement is false. Instead of her husband being in London he is at work for Mr A Cowley, Pool Valley.[473] He was at work there last week, his wages were a guinea and instead of his being out of employ three months it's only two and when he was in work instead of his wages being only 18s per week it was a guinea. Miss Soames and Miss Gardener, the District Visitor, have relieved them on several occasions. Mr Moppet, the scripture reader, has also relieved them. The home is in a passable state. Mr Markwell says Saunders is a very good man to work [sic]. Dismissed, undeserving. Collingham to report case to Miss Soames and Miss Gardener, R P Hooper, chairman

122 ANN JONES, 37, CHARWOMAN, 37 ST MARY MAGDALENE STREET, BRIGHTON

Ann Jones was born in Fishbourne in about 1835 but, according to her application form, moved to Brighton in about 1852. In 1861 she was enumerated at 4 Albion Street where she lived with her husband, William, a 21-year-old labourer who was born in Brighton. At the time of her first application in March 1872 Ann and William Jones had been living at 37 St Mary Magdalene Street for nine months. They lived with their four children and rented the whole house for which they paid 3s 6d per week rent. The family were 13 shillings in arrears and their case was forwarded to the Mendicity Society by the Reverend Salmon, vicar of St Martin's.

William Jones had been working for Mr North of 17 Newark Place and usually expected to earn about 18 shillings per week when in full employment, but had recently been taking home only around 7s 6d: Ann Jones had been working as a charwoman, for which she would earn three shillings per week, but had not made any money in recent weeks.

In 1881 the family were recorded living at 24 St Peter Street with three children aged between 17 and seven years of age. Ann Jones was still working as a charwoman and her husband was employed as an excavator: he died in a work-related accident in September 1885. The Coroner's inquest, which was held at the Maltster's Arms, Western Road, stated that Jones, who was living at 5 Picton Street, was working as an excavator lowering and cleaning a well at Mr Smither's brewery, North Street.[474] *Jesse Clyde of 28 Albion Hill*

[473] A Cowley, pastry cook and confectioner, 7-8 Pool Valley.
[474] Brighton Gazette, 7 September 1885.

took a sub-contract to lower the well and hired Jones to help him.[475] *The well was over 100 feet deep and Jones descended by attaching a rope to himself rather than using the iron ladder in the well shaft. When he had been lowered about 55 feet down the well shaft the rope bearing Jones' weight snapped and he fell to the pumping stage of the well which was about 20 feet from the bottom suffering a severe scalp wound. He was still alive when help reached him but he died on the way up to the surface and was pronounced dead by Mr Roger, a surgeon who had been summoned. The rope was examined and was deemed to have been in good condition but it snapped because it had been used with a pulley which put more pressure on it rather than the usual system of lowering a man perpendicularly. A verdict of Accidental Death was recorded on Jones, who was described as the oldest well digger in Brighton and a man of great experience.*

Ann Jones also suffered a severe scalp wound in September 1889: the Mendicity Society report stated that she fell from a swing in North Road but it is unclear what this means. She was admitted to the Sussex County Hospital on 23 September and discharged, cured, on 26 October.[476]

27 March 1872
Statement: Ann Jones would be thankful for a little assistance.
Report: I made enquiries respecting this case and find the man is at work for Mr North. He says he is a good man to work [sic] but never stops long at one place. His wages will be about 18s per week. I am informed he and the wife are both given to drink. The home is in a destitute state. The little girl Eliza is a poor sickly looking little thing: the wife states it has never been well since it had the smallpox about 10 months ago. I believe this to be a case for the children's hospital.[477] I have informed the Reverend Salmon the result of my enquiry.
Dismissed, ineligible. The case of the child referred to in report relieved with a dispensary letter, R P Hooper, chairman

2 October 1889
Mr C G Woolley, contractor, of Lewes Road informed me on Tuesday that there were two children in a destitute condition at 21 Arnold Street and he thought it a case that the society might assist. Their father died four years ago, their mother, who is still addicted to drink, fell from a swing in North Road a week ago last Monday and has since been seriously ill in the hospital. Their daughter Kate, aged 15, occasionally sells flowers, her brother Alfred, aged seven, attends school and the neighbours have recently been supporting them. WC [William Collingham]
5s per week for two weeks, R P Hooper

[475] Brighton Guardian, 9 September 1885.
[476] ESRO: HB 35/5, 23 September 1889.
[477] No record of Eliza Jones could be found in the admission register of the Royal Sussex County Hospital for this date.

16 October 1889
The daughter applied at the office on Wednesday for some further relief. Dr Paley certifies that her mother is much better and will be able to leave the hospital in the course of a week or ten days. WC [William Collingham]
Grant 5s, Thomas Holland

30 October 1889
Mrs Jones sent to the office on Wednesday for assistance to tide her over until she is able to resume work. She came out of the hospital on Saturday last but will not be fit for work for some time and as she is a low, drinking woman the case now appears a fit one to refer to the parish authorities. WC [William Collingham]
Referred to parish, Thomas W Holland

14 December 1889
The Reverend J H Bishop of 32 York Road, Hove, requests a report of this case. Mrs Jones now resides at 23 Arnold Street, is still unable to work and has an order for the Union in her possession. WC [William Collingham]
Report to Mr Bishop, R P Hooper

123 JAMES COOPER, 41, LABOURER, 22 ABERDEEN ROAD, BRIGHTON

James Cooper was born in Hackney, London, in about 1831. His application form states that he had been living in Brighton since September 1870, and until September 1871 had been living at 1 Melbourne Street. He was enumerated at this address in 1871 where he was described as 39 years of age, unmarried and employed as a wood chopper.
Cooper paid weekly rent of three shillings for his bed on the first floor of 22 Aberdeen Road and he was four weeks' rent in arrears. He stated that when fully employed he expected to earn 11 shillings per week but had been short of work for four weeks.

27 March 1872
Statement: James Cooper would be grateful for a little assistance till he gets work.
Report: I made enquiries respecting this man and find he did work for Mr McKellow, wood merchant, Lewes Road, and left a month ago. Since that he has been up to London to try for work but could not succeed. This man is a cripple having only one leg. He has a licence to hawk but has not got anything to sell. Mr McKellow gave him a good character and says he shall have work for him again in the winter. I believe this to be a deserving case.
Relieved with grant of 2s 6d, R P Hooper, chairman

20 August 1873
Further information: this man who resides at 24 Baker Street has for a long time been working for Mr Holloway, wood merchant of Sussex Place until six weeks ago and since that he has been ill – suffering from an abscess on the top of his head caused by a blow from a piece of wood. At first he was an out-patient at the hospital and after that he was in the infirmary for three weeks which he left on Monday. He is getting better but at present he cannot earn much. He therefore hopes the committee will take a favourable view of his case and grant him a little temporary assistance. On enquiry I find applicant's statement as to the cause of the injury he received is correct. I am told that although generally of good character and attentive to his work he occasionally indulges in the evening.
WC [William Collingham]
Grant of 5s, R P Hooper, chairman

124 ANN GREY, 38, CHARWOMAN, 13 LITTLE ST JAMES STREET, BRIGHTON

The Grey family's case was forwarded to the Mendicity Society by Mrs Bright of 54 Ship Street. They presented references from Canon Rymer of St John the Baptist Catholic church, Bristol Road, and Mrs Sharp of 8 Grafton Street. Ann Grey lived at 13 Little St James Street with her husband Richard and their five children who were aged between 11 and 19 years of age. Ann Grey gave her place of birth as Ireland and stated that she had been living in Brighton for nine years: the last five of those had been spent at their current address; previously they were resident at Pimlico, Brighton, and before that they were living in Norwich.

The Greys paid rent of 2s 1d per week for the entire house and were not in arrears, despite the fact that Richard, a sailmaker, had been short of work for five years due to illness. Ann Grey could expect to make eight shillings per week charring when in full employment but presently was earning only five shillings per week.

The couple were successful in raising funds for their passage to Canada and set sail for Quebec with their three youngest children, Mary, Ann and Richard on the Scotland on 20 May 1872 from London via Plymouth.[478]

27 March 1872
Statement: Ann Grey would be thankful for a little assistance to enable them [to] emigrate to Canada. The two oldest sons are not going; they want to go to sea.
Report: I made enquiries respecting this case and find this is the man that goes about with a music on wheels called the fun of the fair. He states he has two brothers out in Canada and that he could work at his trade, sail making, if he could get there. The wife goes out charring. The two oldest sons are gone to

[478] Canadian passenger lists, 1865-1935, Library and Archives Canada RG-76C.

Portsmouth to join the Navy. The oldest daughter has been in service but left to go with her friends to Canada. They state the sum they want is £18. The home is in a destitute state. Mrs Sharp gave a good character. I have not seen Canon Rymer, when I called he was out.
Deferred for further enquiry, R P Hooper, chairman

30 March 1872
Further information respecting this man: he states he joined the naval brigade in 1853 at Sunderland and went from there to the Baltic and in 1856 he lost the use of his legs at Sebastopol caused by a splinter of a bombshell. The name of the ship he was in was [HMS] Driver. He was then invalided home and discharged with six months' pay - £23.
Referred for further enquiry, R P Hooper

Undated report, c. 1872
This man states it was about five years ago that he worked at Shoreham. It was only a short time and he has forgotten the name. His discharge [papers] from the Navy, he states, he has lost. He states he used to average about 15s a week but lately it was not worth going out for. Canon Rymer gave them a good character and believes them to be a deserving family.
Grant of £1 on condition that the balance of the sum required to enable the family to emigrate is forthcoming. Collingham directed to mention the case to the emigration officer.
R P Hooper, chairman

Printed appeal, c. 1872
Richard Grey and family respectfully appeal to the Christian public under the following circumstances: they are most anxious to emigrate to Canada where he can find constant employment at good wages. He and his family are often reduced to great privations from his being so often out of work. His friends in Canada are all doing so well, they are desirous of joining their relatives in that colony as part of the family (one son and one daughter) have been promised help from the Juvenile Emigration Society, the others have joined the Sussex Emigration Club No 1. Under these circumstances they appeal for kind assistance of the Christian public to help them with a money contribution to enable them with their own savings to raise funds sufficient to defray the expenses of their passages and outfits and give them the chance of leaving England in May when the juveniles take their departure so that the whole family may leave together in the same ship. The family are well known for honesty, sobriety and industry and we believe this appeal is deserving of support: Neil Crispin, 137 Elm Grove; William Tomlinson, 34 Great College Street; E S Sharp, 8 Grafton Street

125 FRANK KENT, 50, FISHERMAN, 24 CAMBRIDGE STREET, BRIGHTON

Frank, or Francis, Kent was baptised at St Nicholas, Brighton, on 11 November 1821.[479] *His parents Francis Kent, a carpenter, and Elizabeth Kent gave their address as Blucher Place in the baptism register. Francis Kent junior was enumerated on the 1841 census as a fishmonger living on Upper North Street with his wife Hannah and daughter Mary Ann. On Saturday 14 September 1844 a man named Francis Kent, along with James Marchant and Thomas Miles, all fishermen, were charged with assault by PC Duval.*[480] *Duval stated that they were following a man along North Street between one and two in the morning and that they had previously assaulted him. All three men were committed to the house of correction for 14 days.*

On the 1851 census Kent was enumerated with his wife Hannah, an ironer, at 2 Regent Court with their three children. By 1861 Kent was recorded as a widower and was living with his eldest daughter, Mary, at 16 Regent Row. The census of 1871 records Francis Kent, now married to Jane Kent, living at 24 Cambridge Street with four children and they were still living at that address when Frank Kent applied to the Mendicity Society in March 1872.

The application form to the Mendicity Society stated that the family had been living at 24 Cambridge Street for three years but were resident at Bread Street before then. Kent usually earned 12 shillings per week, they paid rent of five shillings per week for the whole house but had arrears of £4. He paid into a net insurance scheme. The family's case was forwarded to the society by Marriage Wallis.

The census of 1881 shows that Frank and Jane Kent were still living at 24 Cambridge Street, but by 1891 they had moved to 135 Albion Hill. Frank Kent's death was recorded at Brighton in the September quarter of 1900, aged 78.[481]

29 March 1872
Statement: when he belonged to the Net Insurance Society he could not keep his arrears paid up.
Report: I made enquiries respecting this case and find this man has been going about with a begging petition to enable him to get some new nets. He states he collected about £8 and that Mr Mills, solicitor, Bond Street, got up the petition. From enquiry I find it's true he lost nets and things to the value of about £12 two months ago. He states about a fortnight ago a policeman was going to lock him up for going about with the petition. Mr Beal took down his case. He was told to attend the Provident and District Committee but did not do so. About ten years ago he collected £8 in the same way. This man has got a boat of his value £70 [sic].
Dismissed, ineligible, R P Hooper, Chairman

479 ESRO: PAR 255/1/2/3.
480 Brighton Gazette, 19 September 1844.
481 Death of Francis Kent registered Q3 1900 Brighton 2b 119.

126 SAMUEL BURTON PALMER, 73, COAL AGENT, 13 TORONTO TERRACE, BRIGHTON

Samuel Burton Palmer was born in Brighton in about 1800 and married Elizabeth Kennard in Havant, Hampshire, on 23 February December 1826.[482] *Their son, also Samuel Burton Palmer, was baptised at St Nicholas, Brighton, on 11 February 1831*[483] *but died the following year and was buried at St Nicholas on 31 March 1832.*[484] *Palmer established an ironmongery business at 86 St James' Street in 1826, which continued to operate from the same premises until 1851.*

Brighton Commissioners' accounts[485] *show that for the period 30 June to 31 December 1834 Palmer had been paid £124 14s 9d for iron work on the Commissioners' watering account*[486] *and £51 18s 10d for the following six months.*[487] *He billed the Commissioners for maintenance work in January and February 1835*[488] *but lost a contract for the supply of ironwork with Brighton Guardians to Palmer and Green*[489] *in March 1836.*[490] *Regarding this last contract, Mr Ridley of the Guardians expressed his preference for Palmer and Green whereas Mr Stone proposed Samuel Palmer. Another Guardian, Mr Herritt, stated that Palmer and Green had received little work from the parish but had paid a lot in rates whereas Samuel Butler Palmer had carried out a lot of work but had not made commensurate payment of rates. On 20 March 1839 Palmer won a contract to erect cast iron fencing from Kings Road battery to the western boundary of Brighton, for which he was paid £259 3s 2d.*[491]

Palmer appears to have had a strained relationship with his neighbour John Hallyar, butcher, of 84 St James Street. The two men appeared in court on 23 November 1848, Hallyar being accused of cutting the hose of Palmer's water engine with a meat cleaver.[492] *Hallyar admitted to cutting the hose but stated that he had been provoked into this action by Palmer's repeated use of the hose to wash his windows; Hallyar stated that when the wind blew form the west the water splashed over his meat, rendering it unsaleable, and he estimated that he had lost £20 to £30 worth of stock in this manner. Mr Borrer JP was sympathetic to Hallyar but stated that as he had admitted the misdemeanour he had no*

482 Sussex Family History Group marriage index.

483 ESRO: PAR 255/1/2/7.

484 ESRO: PAR 255/1/5/5.

485 Brighton Commissioners were responsible for the regulation of the town and for improvements to streets and facilities. They were established by the Brighton Town Act 1773 and wound up in 1855 following the incorporation of Brighton as a municipal borough in 1854.

486 Brighton Gazette, 23 April 1835.

487 Brighton Gazette, 24 September 1835.

488 ESRO: AMS 6432/2/18.

489 Palmer and Green, ironmongers of North Street, was owned by William Palmer and Thomas Green. Samuel Butler Palmer's brother was named William but it is not known whether the sibling and owner of the firm were one and the same.

490 Brighton Gazette: 24 March 1836.

491 ESRO: DB/B 66/33.

492 Brighton Gazette, 30 November 1848.

option but to fine him 12 shillings plus costs of 11 shillings. Hallyar stated that neighbours would almost certainly help him pay the fine such was their frustration with Palmer for the same reasons. A week later Joseph Welfare, an employee of Palmer's, appeared in court accused of turning the hose on Hallyar and soaking him.[493] *Welfare claimed that he was defending himself but he was found guilty of assault and fined ten shillings plus costs.*

In March 1849 Samuel Burton Palmer appeared in court again when he attempted to recover £18 from S A Mantell, innkeeper of the Dolphin, Lewes.[494] *Palmer had quoted for removing old equipment, laying new gas pipes and installing lamps. Mantell had agreed to the price but had not paid on completion of the work; the judge ordered that Mantell should repay in full.*

On 10 July 1849 Palmer was chosen to be the creditors' assignee in the bankruptcy case of William Tomsey Creech, owner of the Golden Cross Inn, Pavilion Street, Brighton.[495] *It is unclear why Palmer was chosen to carry out this role (he may have been a creditor) but, for whatever reason, he was clearly considered to be reliable enough to execute his responsibility properly.*

In 1851 Samuel Palmer, his wife, Elizabeth, their two daughters aged 17 and 10 and a servant named Susannah Sherwood were enumerated at 86 St James Street where Palmer ran his ironmonger's shop employing seven people. However, business had clearly not been good because on 12 May 1851 Palmer signed an indenture assigning all his estate and effects to Samuel Haines, accountant, and Edward Totty, merchant, for the mutual benefit of his creditors.[496]

Samuel Burton Palmer appeared at the county court, Hove Town Hall, with his son William on 11 November 1856.[497] *Exactly what happened is unknown but William Palmer was summoned to show why he should not find sureties to keep the peace, but the summons was withdrawn, presumably at his father's behest.*

The bad feeling between father and son apparently continued and William Palmer appeared before magistrates again on 6 June 1860, charged with being drunk and committing wilful damage to his father's property.[498] *The press report described William Palmer as an 'undutiful son... a dissipated looking young man of about 25 years of age'. Samuel Palmer, who was described as deeply affected by the sad position of his son, deposed, 'I live in Wyndham Street. The prisoner is my son. The charge against him is that yesterday morning he came to my house and kicked up a disturbance there. It was about eight or nine o'clock in the morning. He was very tipsy at the time.' After questioning by Mr Bigge, JP, Palmer went on to state that William was employed as an agent in the book trade and that he had threatened his father's life over and over again which prompted Palmer senior to fetch a policeman, who helped eject his son. William returned and tried*

[493] Brighton Gazette, 7 December 1848.
[494] Brighton Gazette, 1 March 1849.
[495] ESRO: AMS 6610/9/3.
[496] Brighton Gazette, 5 June 1851.
[497] Brighton Gazette, 20 November 1856.
[498] Brighton Guardian, 13 June 1860.

to break open the door and then smashed the window. The newspaper report states that at this point William interrupted the hearing to state, 'Oh! I was tapping at the window to make the old boy hear when the glass broke.' Mr Bigge dismissed the comment and Samuel Palmer went on to describe how he barricaded himself in a room and sent for a policeman whilst his son threatened him and his wife. Palmer requested that his son be spared a custodial sentence and instead be sent away from Brighton where his behaviour had become reprehensible. William Palmer was asked if he wished to make a statement; he apologised and stated that he would be willing to leave town as his job would be at risk if his employers discovered his misdemeanours. Palmer was fined five shillings and costs for being drunk, 1s 6d for damaging the window and bound over to keep the peace for 12 months or one month's imprisonment with hard labour.

Four months after the incident involving his son, Palmer's daughter, Charlotte, died aged 20 at the family home at 13 Wyndham Street.[499]

Samuel Burton Palmer, now described as a coal agent, and his wife Elizabeth were enumerated at 13 Wyndham Street on the 1861 census where they lived with their daughter Elizabeth. In July 1862 Palmer applied for the job of porter at the North Gate, Brighton Pavilion, but it was given to Richard Martin.[500]

Palmer, now trading from 13 Cranbourne Street, was required to surrender himself to Ewen Evershed, registrar of the county court on 13 June 1868 and was adjudged bankrupt on 24 June.[501] *Evershed was the official assignee and Anthony Runnacles, of 21a Ship Street, acted as solicitor.*

On the census of 1871 Palmer, his wife and daughter Elizabeth were enumerated at 6 Toronto Terrace but had moved to 13 Toronto Terrace by the time of his first contact with the Mendicity Society in March 1872. Palmer, now 73 years of age, stated on his application form that he had paid into many charitable institutions over a number of years and as a result felt that he was deserving of relief. He had been employed as an agent by Mr Beves, coal merchant of Dyke Road, where he earned three shillings per week and he was given nine shillings per week by the parish. He was paying rent of six shillings per week but had arrears of £7. Mr Relf of Reigate Road and the Reverend Thomas Cooke of Lennox Road supplied references but the Mendicity Society were aware of begging letters that Palmer had sent to the Reverend Hannah and Laurence Peel esq in the months before his application.

In his begging letters Palmer refers to a bad accident sustained by his wife. William Collingham's report states that this occurred in September 1870; Elizabeth Palmer died of bronchitis in February 1873. At this stage Palmer, now 74, was receiving 7s 2d of parish benefit. In about 1874 he started to supplement his income by petitioning local people to support him in efforts to access a pension fund that he claimed to have set up with the Iron, Hardware and Metal Trades Pension Society. Palmer kept a book in which he recorded the

[499] Brighton Gazette, 11 October 1860.
[500] Brighton Gazette, 17 July 1862.
[501] London Gazette, 30 June 1868.

names of people who supported him and the sums of money they donated. He stated in his collections book that he was 'endeavouring to obtain the pension allowed from the Iron, Hardware and Metal Trades Pension Society, London. To do this 3000 votes have to be applied to [sic] and the stamps, envelopes and cards etc will cost £30.' Curiously he pasted a printed statement regarding the society into the front of his collection book, which appears to have been put there to lend weight to his application, but the appeal was written and printed by his brother, William Palmer who, according to the contact at the pension society, was a bona fide member of the scheme. The pension society's clerk confirmed that Samuel Burton Palmer was not a member and that no such sum of money had to be raised.

By the time of Palmer's fourth application to the Charity Organisation Society on 15 March 1875 he had moved to 5 Franklin Street but ten days after this application he had been charged with begging by the Charity Organisation Society.[502] *Mr Lamb, who represented the COS, stated that Palmer had been asking for money under the representation that he needed £30 to enable him to access funds at the Iron, Hardware and Metal Trades Pension Society. The society's agent, William Collingham, was called and he deposed that on Wednesday evening he saw Palmer in New Road and followed him to the Seven Stars beer house on Ship Street. On coming out of the pub, Palmer proceeded to East Street and then North Street, calling at various houses on the way. In North Street he obtained 2s 6d and then returned to the Seven Stars, where Collingham found him with a bun and spiced ale. Collingham asked to see the collecting book, which Palmer denied knowledge of, but Collingham found it in Palmer's hat. The society decided not to press charges but the magistrate warned that if Palmer persisted in begging he would be sent to prison.*

Palmer applied to the Charity Organisation Society again in May 1877, by which time he was living with his daughter Elizabeth at 90 Upper Lewes Road, and he continued to live with her until his death in the June quarter of 1878.[503] *Elizabeth Palmer was enumerated as a lodger at 67 Lewes Road, Brighton, on the 1881 census. She was enumerated at 3 St Martin's Place, Brighton, on the census of 1891.*

Letter from Samuel Palmer, 13 Toronto Terrace, to Sir Laurence Peel, [32 Sussex Square], 10 January 1872

Sir, I hope you will pardon the liberty I take in writing to you. I beg to state my poor wife has had a dreadful accident. She was coming down stairs (more than a year ago W H)[504] without a light, missed her step and fell from the top of the stairs to the bottom, she broke her right arm at the wrist joint, it was quite smashed, and greatly injured her left arm also at the wrist joint. It is considered to be a very bad case at her time of life. She is in the 75th year of her age, she is now helpless, she has lost the use of her right hand and can only use the thumb

[502] Brighton Herald, 27 March 1875.

[503] Death of Samuel Burton Palmer registered Q2 1878 Brighton 2b 132.

[504] This aside was made by the Mendicity Society member that was reviewing the case.

and forefinger of her left hand. My daughter has hitherto supported herself by her needlework which she has had to give up to nurse her mother who requires constant attention. She requires much nourishing food in her weak state, I am sorry to say it is out of my power to get her sufficient. If sir you will be so kind as to give us a little assistance in our present trouble and distress we shall be greatly obliged to you and ever remember your kindness with gratitude. I am sir your obedient servant S B Palmer
PS I beg to say I was formerly an ironmonger in Brighton but through misfortunes and losses in trade I gave up my business. Since then we have been in very reduced circumstances
The parish allows 9s 2d per week. The daughter (a dressmaker) is wholly engaged in attending to the mother. Enquire of Reid -- successors to Palmer and Green – if they know what his friends do for Palmer

Letter from Sir Laurence Peel, Frogmore Cottage, Windsor, 13 January 1872
Mr Beal, I do not understand the changes which have, of late, taken place at the district society but being away from home I return to trouble you with the enclosed note and ask you to referee the case for me. If you find it deserving of attention I do not think I ever knew the writer though I have known others of the same name in Brighton who were engaged in the iron trade. Yours truly, Laurence Peel

Undated note, c. 1872
Mrs Cohen would feel much obliged by Mr Beal sending her a report of the enclosed case to 32 Park Lane, West London

Letter from Samuel Palmer, 13 Toronto Terrace, to the Mendicity Society, 28 March 1872
Sir, I hope you will pardon the liberty I take in writing to you. I beg to state my poor wife has had a dreadful accident. She was coming downstairs without a light, missed her step and fell from the top of the stairs to the bottom, she broke her right arm at the wrist joint, it was quite smashed, and greatly injured her left arm also at the wrist joint. It is considered to be a very bad case at her time of life. She is in the 75th year, she is now helpless, she has lost the use of her right hand her left hand is very little better. My daughter has hitherto supported herself by her needlework which she has had to give up to nurse her mother who requires constant attention. She requires much nourishing food in her weak state, I am sorry to say it is out of my power to get her sufficient. If sir, you will be so kind as to give us a little assistance in our present trouble and distress we shall be greatly obliged to you and ever remember your kindness with gratitude. I am sir your obedient servant S B Palmer

PS I beg to say I was formerly an ironmonger in Brighton but through misfortunes and losses in trade I gave up my business. Since then I have been in very reduced circumstances. I beg to say I have letters of recommendation by me
Referred to agent for full enquiry

28 March 1872
Statement: I have paid into all the charitable institutions in Brighton and I do not see why I should not have something out.
Report: I made enquiries respecting this case and find this man had an ironmongers shop in St James Street from 1826 to 1851. He then failed in business and then some time after that he had some money left him. He then opened a shop in Cranbourne Street and after about two years failed again. I am informed when he was in business he used to drink freely. He also had a son of very intemperate habits and was a great trouble to him. Since that he has earned a few shillings doing a little writing. He now collects a few orders for Mr Beves, coal merchant. He receives parish relief at the rate of 9s per week. The Reverend Mr Cook has relieved him on several occasions. He states it was in September 1870 when his wife met with her accident. I have no doubt this man gets relief from several gentleman in the town that knew him when he was in business and that he has been on the habit of sending begging letters a long time. He sent one to Dr Hannah in 1871 and one to Laurence Peel esq 10 January 1872.
Dismissed, underserving. Collingham to communicate with parish authorities and report further, R P Hooper, chairman

Identical letters from Samuel Palmer, 13 Toronto Terrace, to female recipients unknown except Miss Beckwith of 4 Denmark Terrace who received her letter on 22 April; 9, 15 and 22 April 1872
Madam, I hope you will pardon the liberty I take in writing to you. I beg to state my poor wife has had a dreadful accident. She was coming down stairs without a light, missed her step and fell from the top of the stairs to the bottom, she broke her right arm at the wrist joint, it was quite smashed, and greatly injured her left arm also at the wrist joint. It is considered to be a very bad case at her time of life. She is in the 75th year, she is now helpless, she has lost the use of her right hand her left hand is very little better. My daughter has hitherto supported herself by her needlework which she has had to give up to nurse her mother who requires constant attention. She requires much nourishing food in her weak state, I am sorry to say it is out of my power to get her sufficient. If madam you will be so kind as to give us a little assistance in our present trouble and distress we shall be greatly obliged to you and ever remember your kindness with gratitude. I am madam your obedient servant S B Palmer
PS I beg to say I was formerly an ironmonger in Brighton but through misfortunes and losses in trade I gave up my business. Since then I have been in

very reduced circumstances. I have a letter of recommendation from a reverend gentleman by me

Letter from W Howick, Relief Office, Parochial Offices, Church Street, Brighton, 21 May 1872
Sir, I beg to return the letters written by S Palmer and to inform you that I told him to appear before the Board this day which he did and stated that he had not written a letter of that description since he was there about three or four weeks ago. I am sir your obedient servant, W Howick, Relieving Officer

Letter from Samuel Palmer, 13 Toronto Terrace, to an unknown male recipient, possibly Sir Laurence Peel, 12 April 1873
Sir, I hope you will pardon the liberty I take in writing to you. Some time since you sir, very kindly and handsomely, help[ed] me in [sic] behalf of my very poor wife who had the misfortune to break her arm. I am very sorry to inform you sir of our sad bereavement in the loss of my poor dear wife who died of bronchitis. She was taken alarming ill in the middle of the night on the Tuesday and died nine days after. Her suffering was very great. The doctor saw her at 7 o'clock the evening she died; he said he thought there would be no change for the worst during the night but we had better watch her which my daughter intended to do as she had done every night during the week being her mother's only nurse and she so very ill she could not venture to take scarcely any rest. We are quite overwhelmed with grief at her loss – we hoped she would get better but each day she got rapidly worse. Will you sir have the kindness to pardon the liberty I take in asking you to give me a little assistance in my present trouble as I am sorry to say the various necessary expenses attending the funeral etc are more than I am at present prepared to meet. Your kindly helping me we shall much appreciate and ever remember with gratitude myself and daughter write sir in presenting our duty to you. I am sir your obedient servant, S B Palmer
Wife died in February, Charles Sawyer

21 April 1873
Report: Mrs Hankey brought the annexed letter to the office on Monday afternoon which she received from the man Palmer whom she stated she had assisted on two or three occasions but before doing so again she thought it best to make some enquiries to see whether he was known to this society. I informed Mrs Hankey that Palmer was well known to the society as a begging letter writer for which he had been cautioned by the society and also by the parish authorities. Upon enquiry I find his wife died at the end of February. He receives 2s cash, 2s meat, 2s groceries and 1s 2d bread from the parish: weekly total 7s 2d. Upon asking him the reason why he had commenced sending begging letters again he stated that since he had been cautioned he had not written to any

strangers only to one or two of his old friends. Since my report to the committee over 12 months ago on the 14th of May the case was reported to the Guardians and several of his letters was sent over for their inspection. He was then cautioned by them that if he did not discontinue sending begging letters his outdoor relief would be taken off. WC [William Collingham]
To be reported [to the] Guardians and Mrs Hankey, R P Hooper

Notebook embossed 'S B Palmer, ironmonger, 86 St James Street, Brighton' but written when Palmer was resident at 13 Toronto Terrace, c1874
Printed petition for the Iron, Hardware and Metal Trades Pension Society
The votes and interest of the subscribers and members of the above institution are earnestly solicited on behalf of William Palmer, 40 Tidy Street, Brighton, aged 65 years, who was for 40 years partner in the late firm of Palmer and Green of Brighton but from reverses in business and heavy personal affliction which has latterly assumed the form of chronic rheumatism he is [sic] become quite helpless and incapable of performing the duties of life. This case is strongly recommended by R W Kennard MP, Messrs Kennard and Co, 67 Upper Thames Street, London; W Udall, Birmingham; W F Dixon, Sheffield; S Hawkins, Dyke Road, Brighton; Every and Newman, 27 Station Street, Brighton; J Crowther, 67 Upper Thames Street, London; D Hulett, 55 High Holborn, London; Messrs R and W Wilson, Wardour Street, London; George Spearing, 28 Clifton Terrace, Brighton; Messrs C and J Reed, 26 North Street, Brighton; Mr Packham, 68 Western Road, Brighton; R Green, 66 Grand Parade, Brighton and Frederick Allen, North Road, Brighton

Subsequent manuscript entries, 1874-1875
13 Toronto Terrace, Albion Hill: S B Palmer, ironmonger, is endeavouring to obtain the pension allowed from the Iron, Hardware and Metal Trades Pension Society, London. To do this 3000 votes have to be applied to [sic] and the stamps, envelopes and cards etc will cost £30. S B Palmer earnestly solicits the kind aid of the generous public to aid him in his views. The names of the subscribers are over[leaf].
11 November 1874: E Gates, Chesham House, 5s; Miss Chapman, Belmont, 10s; J Evershed, 5s; Miss Jefferson, 5s
13 November: Jacob Boys, 5s; E Evershed, 5s; Cordy Burrows, 5s; William Morgan, 10s
21 November: Vallance and Catt, 10s
23 November: Hanningtons, 10s
27 November: [*name illegible*] 5s and S J 2s 6d
1 December: E N Hall, 10s
7 December: Daniel Hack
10 December: William Stevens, 5s

15 December: J Havelock, 5s
18 December: Major Hallett, 5s; Henry J Gillwood, 5s; Miss Clarke, 2s 6d; J L Chilver, 2s 6d; Edwin Booth, 5s
8 January 1875: Thomas Lulham and Sons, 5s and H L senior, 2s 6d
20 January: RP, 2s 6d
22 January: R Needham, 2s 6d
23 January: A J Mills, 2s 6d; J Furner, 2s 6d; R Bacon, 2s 6d; J Dallimore, 5s; L Saunders, 2s 4d; George Duncombe, 2s 6d
2 February: Miss Robertson, 10s
4 February: Thomas King, 5s; [*name illegible*], 2s; Henry Jones, 2s 6d; Mr Peart, 2s 6d; John Moate, 2s 6d; George Callard, 2s 6d; J W Staples, 2s 6d; G W Smith, 2s 6d; J Rose, 2s 6d
20 February: W Saunders, 2s 6d; Edward Graves, 2s 6d; J F S, 2s 6d; S N Soper, 2s 6d; E L, 2s 6d; J C, 2s 6d; Mr White, 2s 6d; Dr Ruge, 7 Park Crescent, 2s 6d; H R, 2s; M D, 2s 6d; D S, 2s 6d
8 March; W Banfield, 5s; John Beal, 2s 6d; C Wren, 2s 6d; C Vaughan, 2s 6d; Robert Hamilton, 2s 6d; John M Newnham, 2s; G W P, 2s 6d; J L, 2s 6d; L L, 2s; Robert Crowhurst, 5s; [*name illegible*], 2s 6d;
Parker and Smith, 2s 6d

Testimonial at rear of notebook
Sir, understanding you are about to apply for assistance from the Iron, Hardware and Metal Trades Pension Society. Having known you as a reputable tradesman for upwards of forty years I can bear testimony to you having held for many years a good position as a furnishing ironmonger, but of late been very unfortunate and in much distress. I hope therefore you will be successful in your application. I remain sir, yours respectfully, Richard M Webb

20 March 1874
Report: Mr Smith forwarded the annexed letters to the office and requests a report of the case. I have no fresh information respecting Palmer. His circumstances are about the same. WC [William Collingham]
To be fully reported to Mr Smith, R P Hooper. NB letter returned to Mr Smith at his request, RJ secretary

8 March 1875
This man who now resides at 5 Franklin Street called on Captain Cuthbert for assistance a few evenings ago. Captain C[uthbert] refused to relieve him and called at the office that I might enquire into the case. I find that there is an Iron, Hardware and Metal Trades Pension Society at 5 New Bridge Street, Blackfriars, and Palmer is collecting money to enable his daughter to write for votes to enable him to obtain a pension. He is not now in receipt of parish relief both he

and his daughter are supported by friends.
WC [William Collingham]
Secretary to write to Iron, Hardware etc Pension Society on subject, R P Hooper

Letter from Benjamin Burford Rawlings of the Iron, Hardware and Metal Trades Pensions Society, 5 New Bridge Road, Blackfriars, London, 10 March 1875
Sir, in reply to your enquiry I beg to inform you that no person named S B Palmer has been admitted a candidate for a pension of this society. A Mr William Palmer of your town is already a pensioner and has been so since December 1868 so that your question can scarcely refer to him but if you have further information I shall be obliged by another communication and will gladly assist you in discovering the truth. I am yours truly B Burford Rawlings, secretary

Letter from R Johnson, Charity Organisation Society to the Iron, Hardware and Metal Trades Pensions Society, 5 New Bridge Road, Blackfriars, London, 11 March 1875
Re: S B Palmer – Sir, this man who was formerly and for many years an ironmonger in this town is brother of William Palmer, now a pensioner on your society. On looking at the notice on the cover of your reports I see that candidate must have procured a certain printed form and filled it up with the particulars required and that they must also be recommended by two subscribers. As S B Palmer is going about collecting money for the expense of his canvass you will oblige the committee by informing me whether he has obtained, filled up and returned an application form with the recommendations as required by the notice referred to. The number of impositions practiced by applicants for charity under various pretences will, I think, be sufficient excuse for thus troubling you a second time. The question I would briefly put is this: has Palmer a right to go about collecting money under the circumstances named before he is a candidate by complying with the conditions of the society?
Yours truly, R Johnson

Letter from Benjamin Burford Rawlings of the Iron, Hardware and Metal Trades Pensions Society, 5 New Bridge Road, Blackfriars, London, 12 March 1875
Sir, in reply to your questions, I beg to inform you that S B Palmer has not sent in an application to be admitted a candidate for a pension: so far as I am aware he has not been supplied with a form for the purpose. He is therefore out of order in describing himself as a candidate and in soliciting contributions toward the expense of his canvass. Yours faithfully, B Burford Rawlings

13 March 1875
Case to be submitted to the honourable solicitor for opinion, R P Hooper

15 March 1875
Report: Mr Brandreth, honorary solicitor, advises that Palmer should be cautioned, told to give up his collecting book and then if he continues to collect money to prosecute him for begging. WC [William Collingham]
Agent to carry out advice of Mr Brandreth, R P Hooper

25 March 1875
On Wednesday evening I saw Palmer go into the Seven Stars public house, Ship Street, and I afterwards saw him begging at several shops in North Street and the neighbourhood, returning to the Seven Stars again where he regaled himself with spiced ale and a bun for which he paid with a half crown that he had just received from Messrs Parker and Smith of North Street. I then took him into custody and this morning he was brought up before the Bench. Mr Lamb conducting the case in the absence of Mr Brandreth, honorary solicitor, informed the Bench that the society did not wish to press for a conviction but merely to stop the prisoner from begging. The magistrates discharged him with a caution. WC [William Collingham]
To be recorded, R P Hooper

Letter from Robert Poole Hooper, Charity Organisation Society to M Brandreth, honorary solicitor, Charity Organisation Society, 64 Middle Street, Brighton, 25 March 1875
Dear Sir, re Palmer, Collingham took the man Palmer, whose case you are acquainted with, into custody last night and he is to be brought before the magistrates at 11 this morning. He is an inveterate beggar and we have lots of productions in the way of begging letters. He has been cautioned by us several times but I do not think it advisable to press for his conviction. There is much sympathy felt for him in some quarters as an old Brighton tradesman and if we could, through you, get him dismissed with a strongish reprimand from the Bench I think would be better for the society. I came here early (9.30) thinking I might catch you here though I told Collingham to appoint 10.30 but being in the neighbourhood thought it well to come for the chance of seeing you. However, I have said all I could have done in an interview. Yours faithfully, R P Hooper

Letter from W Wooldridge, to Mr Johnson, secretary of the Charity Organisation Society, Brighton, 10 May 1877
Sir, the enclosed has been left at my house. Speaking from memory I should say that I do not know the person mentioned in the letter. I should be sorry to be uncharitable and would willingly help the applicant if it be right to do so. Yours obediently, W Wooldridge, Withdean

11 May 1877
Report: Mr Wooldridge of Laine House, Withdean, requests a report of this case. Palmer is now very infirm and confined to his house. His daughter resides with and attends to him. The parish allow them 5s a week. A friend pays their rent and they receive a little help from charitable persons. Since Palmer was before the Bench in March 1875 he has begged very little. WC [William Collingham]
A condensed report of case to be sent to Mr Wooldridge, R P Hooper

Letter from William C Tamplin, Phoenix Brewery, Brighton, 11 October 1877
I enclose a letter brought to me yesterday and for the present have partially relieved the case but should be glad to know if the statement in the letter is correct and whether it is a deserving case. Yours faithfully, William C Tamplin

12 October 1877
Mr W C Tamplin, brewer, has forwarded one of Miss Palmer's begging letters to the office and requests a report of the case. I find that Palmer and his daughter are in the same condition as they were in May. I have therefore nothing to add to my last report. WC [William Collingham]
Above report to be forwarded

Letter to W Wooldridge esq, Laine House, Withdean, from Miss E Palmer, 90 Upper Lewes Road, Brighton, 30 April 1879
Sir, I hope you will please have the great kindness to pardon the liberty I take in writing to you. I am sorry to say my dear father is quite ill, he has been very ill indeed for more than a year. His long illness has rendered him very weak indeed. He is suffering from exhaustion of the system, he requires more nourishing food than we can procure. May I ask the great kindness of you sir to give my father some assistance. Whatever, sir, you will have the goodness to give him he would be glad and thankful to receive and ever remember your great kindness sir in helping him now he is ill and in adversity. My father is in his 79th year, we desire to present our duty to you sir hoping you are quite well. With our grateful thanks for your former great kindness and sympathy to my father previous to my mother's death. I am sir, your obedient servant, E Palmer

Letter to W Wooldridge esq, Laine House, Withdean, from Miss E Palmer, 90 Upper Lewes Road, Brighton, 29 September 1879
Sir, I hope you will please have the great kindness to pardon the liberty I take in writing to you. I am sorry to say my dear father is quite ill, he has been very ill indeed for more than a year. His long illness has rendered him very weak indeed. He is suffering from exhaustion of the system. This is the fifth illness my father has had since my dear mother's death. My father requires more nourishing food than we can procure. May I ask the great kindness of you sir to

give my father some assistance. Whatever, sir, you will have the goodness to give him he would be glad and thankful to receive and ever remember with gratitude your kindly helping him now he is ill as it would enable me to procure him better diet which he so much requires to strengthen him. Your kind compassion and sympathy sir we should ever appreciate and gratefully remember. We desire to present our duty to you sir, hoping you are quite well. With our grateful thanks for your former goodness to my father. I am sir, your obedient servant, E Palmer

127 JOHN CLARKE OF LONDON

It has been impossible to find any further information on John Clarke from the information supplied by the East End Division of the Charity Organization [sic] Society. Nobody by the name of Dawkins is listed living in North Road in the street directories of the day. It is probable that Clarke was an assumed name.

Letter from A E Lindsay-Kaye, Charity Organization Society, East End Division, 139 Belgravia Street, Stepney, 26 March 1872
Sir, a person named John Clarke, labourer, states he has resided at 10 Chichester Street, Brighton for 3 years and has worked for Mr Dawkins near North Road, Brighton. Would you kindly give me any particulars you may have should he be known to you, yours faithfully A E Lindsay-Kaye pro hon[orary] Sec[retary]
Referred to agent for enquiry, R P Hooper, chairman Mar 28 [18]72

28 March 1872
Report: I made enquiries respecting this case and find the [name] of Dawkins is not known in North Road and at No 10 Chichester Street I saw Mrs Saunders the landlady of the house. She states no one by the name of Clark [sic] has lived there within this last nine years.
Reply to be sent by Hon Sec, R P Hooper, chairman Mar 30 [18]72

128 GEORGE BASSETT, 43, FISHERMAN, 29 DORSET STREET, BRIGHTON

George Bassett was born in Brighton in about 1829 and married Jane Ann Barnard in Brighton during the summer of 1858.[505] *In 1861 George Bassett, a fisherman, and Jane Bassett, a laundress, were enumerated at 9 Orange Row, where they lived with their two young daughters. The neighbouring family was named Barnard and there may have been a familial link between Philip Barnard the 39-year-old fisherman and 33-year old Jane Bassett (née Barnard).*

[505] George Bassett marriage to Jane Ann Barnard registered Q3 1858 Brighton 2b 263.

Jane Bassett's death was registered at Brighton in the June quarter of 1870.[506] *By 1871 George had moved to 5 Dorset Street, where he lodged with his youngest daughter in the house of another fisherman, Thomas Harman. This was next door to James Etheridge, who applied to the Mendicity Society on 19 March 1872 and who was drowned on Easter day 1878 [see case 113].*

When he applied to the Mendicity Society in March 1872, George Bassett had recently moved from 8 Shuters Gardens to 29 Dorset Street. His two daughters attended Dorset Street school and Bassett rented one room at the house, where he paid weekly rent of 1s 6d. He was 14 shillings in arrears and although he expected to make seven shillings a week when in full employment he had recently only been making four shillings per week. His case had been forwarded to the charity by Reverend C Young, who ran a gentlemen's boarding school at 35 Sussex Square.

By 1881 George Bassett was lodging at 45 William Street. His death was registered at Brighton in the March quarter of 1908.[507]

30 March 1872
Statement: the reason I went to the Reverend Mr Young was that he has relieved me several times before.
Report: I made enquires respecting this man's statement and find it's false. He is not known to the Reverend Mr Young nor neither did he give him the ticket. This man gets his living shrimping and I have no doubt gets a great deal more than what he says he does. The home is in a destitute state. He is well known to the parish authorities having received parish relief on several occasions until this winter when they gave an order for the [work]house.
Dismissed, undeserving and ordered to be cautioned by agent, R P Hooper, chairman

11 March 1874
Further information: this man brought an investigation ticket to the office on Wednesday which was given him by Mr Duddell's servant and requested assistance to enable him to pay off his arrears of rent. On enquiry I find he has earned very little lately and he has in his possession and order for the [work]house. WC [William Collingham]
Ineligible, GDR [George Dudley Ryder], chairman

[506] Death of Jane Bassett registered Q2 1870 Brighton 2b 123.
[507] Death of George Bassett registered Q1 1908 Brighton 2b 148.

129 CAROLINE TESTER, 48, IRONER, REGAN'S LODGING HOUSE, BRIGHTON

Little is known of Caroline Tester's early life; her application to the Mendicity Society states that she was born in Brighton in about 1824 but no certain record of her baptism could be found and she does not appear to have been enumerated on any census returns.[508]

Despite the lack of information from official sources, Caroline Tester's life was regularly scrutinized by the local press, which recorded her numerous appearances at the magistrates' court. Her first known appearance was on 1 June 1864, when she was charged five shillings for being drunk and causing a disturbance.[509] *The Brighton Guardian described her as a 'decently dressed woman' and went on to quote PC Kenward, who apprehended Tester 'sitting in a chair helplessly drunk in front of 4 Norfolk Place'. She was brought in to the police station on a truck in a 'beastly state of intoxication.' Tester stated that it was 'true she took a glass of beer and it overcame her'; she was very sorry.*

On 30 August 1864 Caroline Tester appeared before the Bench for being drunk and disorderly in Carlton Street at 1.30am the previous morning.[510] *PC Pollard stated that he found Tester sitting on a doorstep singing and could not get her to be quiet. She could not walk so was taken to the town hall in a wheelbarrow. She again apologised for her actions and stated that if she was drunk at least she was not quarrelsome. She was fined five shillings.*

A similar charge was put against Tester on 20 September 1864, after she was found drunk and incapable at Bartholomews.[511] *The Brighton Gazette recorded that she attempted to cry in court and stated that she was not drunk but was suffering a fit which was brought on by drinking only small quantities of beer. Mr Thorncroft, assistant overseer, who was sitting in the court, stated that Tester got drunk by begging off charitable persons, and the magistrate Mr Scott fined her five shillings and costs or, in default, seven days' imprisonment with hard labour.*

Tester's distressed state appeared to worsen, and she appeared in court on Tuesday 4 April 1865 when she was charged with attempting to commit suicide.[512] *PC Luxford stated that he found Tester on the beach below the western entrance to the Chain Pier the previous evening at about 10.30pm. Her clothes were wet and a number of people had gathered around her. Amongst the onlookers was a Henry Neve who described seeing Tester going into the water before he followed her into the sea with others to rescue her. PC Luxford took her to the town hall and placed her in a cell where she attempted to strangle herself. This report states that Tester had been in prison twice before and had made a similar attempt on her life some time ago; the Brighton Gazette additionally stated that Tester was*

[508] A Caroline Tester was baptised at Dorset Gardens Wesleyan church on 18 October 1821 (Mormon IGI) and a Caroline Elizabeth Tester was baptised at St Nicholas, Brighton, on 30 June 1822, daughter of George Tester, butcher (PAR 255/1/2/3).

[509] Brighton Guardian, 8 June 1864.

[510] Brighton Guardian, 31 August 1864.

[511] Brighton Gazette, 22 September 1864.

[512] Brighton Guardian, 5 April 1865.

'an exceedingly tall woman'.[513] *She was remanded until the following Monday when she expressed sorrow for her conduct the previous week.*[514] *The Brighton Guardian reported that Tester's conduct in prison was good and she was discharged with an admonition from the Bench.*

Caroline Tester's next appearance at the magistrates' court was on 12 April 1865, two days after she was discharged from gaol for attempting suicide. She appeared in court with bloodied hands and was charged with being drunk and disorderly on Church Street, where she broke a square of glass at the house of Mr Thorncroft, the assistant overseer: Tester was aggrieved because Thorncroft would not give her an order for the workhouse.[515] *She was committed to one month's hard labour.*

Tester again attempted to commit suicide by drowning herself on 11 July 1865. She appeared before the Bench on 12 July when James Woolley, a carter, stated that at about eight o'clock the previous evening he saw Tester go from the bottom of Middle Street gap towards the sea.[516] *She took off her bonnet and shawl and ran in and lay down. A policeman assisted Woolley in bringing her back to the shore and from there to the town hall. She was bound over in her own recognizances and ordered to find two sureties to keep the peace for two months. James Woolley was presented with five shillings for his actions.*

On Monday 25 September 1865 Caroline Tester made another appearance before the bench, this time charged with being drunk and causing a disturbance at Old Steine on Sunday night. The Brighton Gazette referred to her as 'a tall woman' and recorded that she was fined five shillings.[517] *The Brighton Guardian added that PC Reed had enormous difficulty conveying her from the Old Steine to the Town Hall.*[518]

Tester's next known appearance at the magistrates' court was on Tuesday 27 February 1866, when she was charged with being drunk and willfully breaking a window at the parochial offices.[519] *Mr Thorncroft, assistant overseer, stated that she had then created a disturbance outside his house on Church Street at about midnight. She was fined 6d with five shillings damages, with 14 days' hard labour in default.*

On 12 August 1867 Tester was charged by PC Fry with being drunk and disorderly on Kings Road, and was sentenced to seven days' hard labour.[520] *She was convicted of the same offence after being apprehended by on St James's Street on 17 October 1867.*[521]

Tester appeared at the magistrates' court again on 10 November 1871, charged with being drunk and disorderly the previous evening.[522] *PC Mann stated that he found Caroline Tester drunk, shouting and quarrelling; she lay down and had to be carried to the*

[513] Brighton Gazette, 6 April 1865.
[514] Brighton Guardian, 12 April 1865.
[515] Brighton Guardian, 19 April 1865.
[516] Brighton Guardian, 19 July 1865.
[517] Brighton Gazette, 28 September 1865.
[518] Brighton Guardian, 27 September 1865.
[519] Brighton Guardian, 28 February 1866.
[520] Brighton Gazette, 15 August 1.
[521] Brighton Gazette, 24 October 1867.
[522] Brighton Guardian, 15 November 1871.

police station. By this point she was such a familiar face in the court room that the officials made a joke of the occurrence: Mr Bigge, the magistrate, asked Mr White, chief constable, if the prisoner had appeared before. White responded, to some laughter, that this was the 19th time. Mr W R Smith added that Tester had only been out of the workhouse for a week, and it transpired that she had only recently undergone a severe operation.[523] *The magistrates took this information into account and let her off with a fine of five shillings, stating that she should not be drinking at all given that she was ill. They stated that they would not be so lenient if she appeared before the Bench again.*

When Caroline Tester applied to the Mendicity Society on 30 March 1872 she was living at Regan's Lodging House and had been there for three months.[524] *She stated that she had been living in Brighton for five years but, as her long list of court appearances attested, this was false information. Tester supplied Hugh Saunders of 142 North Street (the Blacksmith's Arms) as a reference and stated that she was paying 2s 4d a week in rent and was one week in arrears, despite earning 15 shillings per week as an ironer.*[525]

Caroline Tester was admitted to the Sussex County Lunatic Asylum from Brighton Workhouse infirmary on 27 July 1872 suffering with melancholia and in a precarious physical state due to breast cancer.[526] *David Richards, surgeon, examined Tester on her admittance to the asylum and found her suicidal and a danger to others. Richards made the following statement following the examination, 'says that she has a scorpion in her insides, that she has been robbed of her great wealth and that she will kill Jesus. Is sleepless, refuses food is violent to others and requires constant restraint.' Tester was considered recovered by the committee of visitors and discharged on 4 September 1872. However, two days later she was charged with being drunk and disorderly on Junction Parade. The Brighton Guardian reported that she had been making a noise and when spoken to laid upon the ground and became helpless.*[527] *PC Geall proved the charge but Tester accused him of telling a 'tissue of falsehoods' and the magistrate, Mr Bigge, stated that 'there seemed only two places where it seemed possible for her to live – namely the lunatic asylum or the gaol.' Tester retorted that she had only been singing Rule Britannia and that she had been ill and was having to undergo an operation but was not believed, this being her 24th court appearance. She was fined 10 shillings plus costs and left the court making a 'deplorable noise'.*

523 This was probably an operation for breast cancer, which Tester was reported to be suffering from when she was admitted to Sussex County Lunatic Asylum in July 1872. However, no record of her treatment could be found in the admission registers of the Royal Sussex County Hospital.

524 The 1871 census shows the lodging house run by Thomas Regan situated at 41-42 Derby Place.

525 In May 1872 a woman named Caroline Deighton (applicant 187) applied to the Mendicity Society. Charity officials felt that this may have been an alias used by Caroline Tester and the evidence does suggest this to be the case.

526 ESRO: HC 24/2088.

527 Brighton Guardian, 11 September 1872.

Caroline Tester's death was recorded at Brighton in the December quarter of 1874 aged 50.[528]

30 March 1872
Statement: Caroline Tester would be thankful for a little assistance.
Report: I made enquiries respecting this case and find Miss Saunders does not know this woman. Mr Toye the scripture reader says it would do more harm than good to relieve this woman. She is well known to the parish authorities. I have known her this last seven years: she is one of the worst women in Brighton. She has been convicted nineteen times through her intemperate habits and the last I saw of her was on Sunday afternoon about three o'clock. Two policemen were wheeling her to the town hall drunk on a barrow.
Dismissed, undeserving, R P Hooper

130 MARY PURSER, 36, HAWKER, 47 CHESTERFIELD STREET, BRIGHTON

Mary Purser, her husband Joseph and their three children arrived in Brighton only one week before she applied to the Mendicity Society. Purser was born in Ireland but had previously been living in Croydon. She expected to earn three shillings per week when in full employment but had been out of work for three weeks. Joseph Purser also earned his living as a hawker and was earning five shillings per week. The family paid 3s 6d for a single room at 47 Chesterfield Street.

2 April 1872
Statement: Mary Purser would be thankful for a little assistance. Since her daughter Mary has been out of the Croydon infirmary she has not been able to go out hawking.
Report: I made enquiries respecting this case and find this man hawks walking sticks, the wife hawks oranges. She states that since her daughter Mary came out of the Croydon infirmary she has not been able to go hawking and the reason they came to Brighton was to get the daughter an out-patient of the eye infirmary. The wife states about six months' ago when the child was at play another child scratched its eye with its finger nail and poisoned it. The girl then went into the Croydon infirmary for some time and afterwards was an out-patient but finding the child did not get better they came to Brighton and the Reverend Mr Morgan gave them a letter for the eye infirmary and a shilling grocery ticket. The home is in a destitute state.
Referred for further enquiry, R P Hooper, chairman

[528] Death of Caroline Tester registered Q4 1874 Brighton 2b 132.

I have seen Dr Penfold at the eye infirmary. He states the child would be better at home with its friends than it would be in the infirmary. Referred to Mr Morgan for advice and assistance to amount of 5s.
R P Hooper, chairman

Further information respecting this case. I have seen Mrs Purser, she stated out of the 5s given to the Reverend Mr Fincher she has only received relief at the rate of 4s: 2s meat, 2s in grocery. The Reverend Mr Fincher states she has altogether had relief to the amount of a pound of more.[529] The child is now attended by Dr Moon and is progressing favourably.[530]
Woman's statement discredited, R P Hooper, entered RJ [Robert Johnson, secretary]

25 June 1872
Further information respecting this case. Mr Plumer, 162 North Street, states Purser's licence having run out they are now in a destitute state and if the committee will give 2s 6d he will [give] 2s 6d.[531] WC [William Collingham]
June 25, case differed, R P Hooper, chairman

131 RICHARD POCKNEY (ALSO GIVEN AS POCKNEE), 74, NO OCCUPATION, 9 NELSON STREET, BRIGHTON

Richard Pockney was the son of John and Jane Pockney[532] *of Portslade, and was baptised at St Nicolas, Portslade, on 18 August 1797.*[533] *His application to the Mendicity Society states that he had been resident in Brighton since about 1817. A man named Richard Pockney was charged with being disorderly in Edward Street on Sunday 30 August 1846.*[534] *A policeman stated that he found Pockney knocking at the Thurlow Arms at two o'clock in the morning. When he refused to go home the policeman pulled him into the road then followed him to Park Street. Pockney verbally abused the policeman all the way and was taken into custody. On their way to the town hall the policeman grabbed Pockney by the collar but he drew a penknife to free himself, nearly cutting the policeman in the process. He later claimed that he did this to prevent being choked. Richard Pockney stated that he was a carpenter and was celebrating the anniversary of his joining a society along with a fellow member. He was discharged with an admonition.*

529 John Moore Fincher, curate, St John the Evangelist, Carlton Hill.
530 Dr William Moon was a teacher and creator of Moon type a reading alphabet for the blind, which was a precursor to Braille.
531 A S Plumer, wine and spirit merchant.
532 Jane Pockney's death was recorded in the diary of Henry Hudson, bailiff, on 9 February 1837 (ESRO: 6942/2).
533 ESRO: PAR 449/1/1/2.
534 Brighton Gazette, 3 September 1846.

Pockney was enumerated on the 1861 census at 39 Newhaven Street where he lived with his wife Elizabeth, who was from Mellis, Suffolk, and was 12 years his junior. Elizabeth Pockney's death was registered at Brighton in the spring of 1865 using the alternative spelling of Pocknee.[535]
Ten years later Richard Pockney was enumerated at 9 Nelson Street, employed as a labourer and living with his nephew, Henry Pockney, a 53-year-old labourer, his wife Susan and their family. The Mendicity Society application form showed that he had been living there for three years and was paying his nephew no rent. Richard Pockney received 2s 6d from the parish authorities per week and gave Mr Bray of Dinapore Street as a reference. His death was recorded at Brighton in the December quarter of 1879 also using the alternative spelling of Pocknee.[536]

2 April 1872
Statement: Richard Pockney would be thankful for a little assistance.
Report: I made enquiries respecting this case and find this man lives with his nephew rent free and receives 2s 6d per week from the parish authorities. Mr Oliver, 39 Ashton Street, the District Visitor, gave him a good character. The nephew works for Mr Durtnall, carrier, North Street, his wages is 18s per week.[537] Mr Dray, dairyman, Dinapore Street, gave him a good character.
Ordered to be communicated to Mr Oliver and the clergy of the district and reported again at next meeting, R P Hooper, chairman

I have seen the Reverend Mr Mears the clergyman of that district.[538] He says there is no District Visitor to that district; that district is about to change hands. He says his district is a very poor one, it extends from Grand Parade taking the south side of Sussex Street to Nelson Street and Dorset Buildings and the north side of Edward Street. He thinks he cannot assist in this case.
Dismissed, ineligible, R P Hooper, chairman

132 MARY RIVERS, 58, BONNET MAKER, 13 JUBILEE STREET, BRIGHTON

Mary Rivers was born in Sheerness, Kent, in about 1814. Her application form stated that she moved to Brighton in about 1842 and had been living at 13 Jubilee Street for four years; prior to that she had been living on Cheltenham Place. She was enumerated on the 1861 census as Mary Ann Rivers, living at 13 Cheltenham Place with her husband Frederick, a 53-year-old dyer from Middlesex.[539] *Mary Rivers was described as a straw-*

[535] Death of Elizabeth Pocknee registered Q2 1865 Brighton 2b 132.
[536] Death of Richard Pocknee registered Q4 1879 Brighton 2b 151.
[537] Durtnall and Son, railway and general carriers, warehousemen etc were listed in *Page's Directory of 1872* at 149 North Street.
[538] Probably Henry William Meeres, curate of Brighton.
[539] Mary Ann Mills marriage to Frederick Rivers registered Q1 1851 Brighton 7 345.

bonnet maker. Frederick Rivers's death was recorded at Brighton in the June quarter of 1861.[540]

The census of 1871 records Mary Rivers employed as a dyer and living at 13 Jubilee Street with her son Charles Rivers, a bookseller, and Grace Mills, her niece, who was employed as a mantle maker.

When Mary Rivers applied to the Mendicity Society in April 1872 she was paying weekly rent of 6s 6d for the whole house. No mention of her niece is made but she was still living with her son Charles, who had been working as a clerk for a Mr Bishop of Maidstone, Kent, but had been short of work for three months. He could usually expect to earn 20 shillings per week when in full employment and Mary Rivers stated that she could usually earn 15 shillings as a bonnet maker, but she had only been bringing in 3s 6d per week and had rent arrears of £2.

Rivers stated that a family member named Anna Mills of Southampton may be able to help her and she supplied Mrs Beal of 108 Church Street as a reference.[541] *Her death was registered at Brighton in the September quarter of 1878.*[542]

5 April 1872
Statement: Mary Rivers would be thankful for a little assistance till her son gets work.
Report: I made enquiries respecting this case and find this woman gets her living making hats and bonnets. She is not able to do but a very little now. She is an out-patient at the infirmary. The son appears to be a very respectable young man. Mr Beal has known her a long time and says she is a respectable woman and that she has had several loans and always paid them up but cannot get security now. Mrs Blencowe, 29 Clifton Terrace, the District Visitor, has relieved her on one or two occasions. The home is in a passable state. I believe this is to be a case for the parish authorities where I find she is not known.
Relieved with grant of 5s
R P Hooper, chairman

133 ELLEN BISHOP, 26, WIFE OF A LABOURER, 42 ELDER STREET, BRIGHTON

Ellen Bishop contacted the Mendicity Society having been given a ticket by Mrs Kemp of 88 London Road. She was born in Chailey in about 1846 but had been living in Brighton with her husband Frederick Bishop, a labourer from Lamberhurst, Kent, since 1867: the

540 Death of Frederick Rivers registered Q2 1861 Brighton 2b 120.

541 F Beal is listed in *Page's Directory of 1872* as the resident agent of the Brighton Provident and District Society Benevolent Loan Fund, the Sick Relief Fund and the Mendicity Society, all of which operated from premises at 108 Church Street.

542 Death of Mary Rivers registered Q3 1878 Brighton 2b 122.

year of their wedding.[543] *They had been living at 42 Elder Street with their children for three months and were previously living at 55 Elder Street. They paid weekly rent of 2s 6d for one bedroom and were not in arrears. Frederick Bishop had been working at the drainage works for Mr Marshall of Islingword Road, where he usually expected to earn 18 shillings per week, but he had been short of work for six weeks and at the time of the application was earning nothing.*

In the 1881 census the family were enumerated at 45 Whichelo Place. Frederick Bishop described himself as a locomotive engine driver but despite the apparent upturn in their fortunes they were sharing a house with another large family.

5 April 1872
Statement: Ellen Bishop would be thankful for a little assistance till her husband gets work. She thinks he will have work next week at the brick field, Portslade.
Report: I made enquiries respecting this case and find this man did work for Mr Marshall at the drainage works and left about six weeks ago when the works was completed. Mr Marshall states he had so many men to work for him it's impossible to recollect anything as to character. I am informed he is of intemperate habits. The wife states he has not received relief from anyone and if she had not pawned a quilt yesterday they must of starved. When I asked her to show me the ticket she brought one pawned the day before. She refused to let me see her room. Upon enquiry I find they have only three children instead of four. I do not believe they pay 2s 6d per week rent for one room in Elder Street. Mrs Kemp does not know them: the woman went there for relief and Mrs Kemp gave her the ticket. The Reverend Mr Coombe, 42 Clifton Road, relieved them and gave them a shilling yesterday which the wife denied.[544]
Dismissed, undeserving, R P Hooper, chairman

134 WILLIAM STAPLEHURST, 65, LABOURER, 28 COBDEN ROAD, BRIGHTON

William Staplehurst was born in Framfield in about 1807 and married Lucy Louisa Leeves at Heathfield on 23 April 1843.[545] *The couple were enumerated at Carters Passage, Lewes, in 1851, where they lived with their daughters Sally, Emily and Mary, who were born in Fletching and Lewes.*

According to the Mendicity Society's application form, the Staplehurst family arrived in Brighton in about 1854 and they were enumerated at 10 Cobden Road on the census of 1871, where they lived with their daughters Mary, Caroline and Ann, who were born in Lewes and Brighton. Staplehurst's case was forwarded to the Mendicity Society by the

543 Marriage of Ellen Parker to Frederick Bisshopp registered Q1 1867 Brighton 2b 248.
544 The Reverend Thomas Coombe, vicar of All Saints Church, Brighton.
545 ESRO: PAR 372/1/3/2.

Reverend Figgis, the minister of Countess of Huntingdon's chapel, when the family had been living at 28 Cobden Road for seven months. They paid 5s 6d rent per week and were a week in arears. The application shows William and Lucy Staplehurst living with their daughters Mary, Harriet, Caroline and Laura: all bar Mary, who was a dressmaker, were employed as collar makers working from premises on Bedford Street. William Staplehurst was employed by Benjamin Inkpen, a dairyman, living on Elm Grove. Between the father and his four daughters the family's weekly income was usually expected to be in the region of 27s 6d but had been reduced to 21s 3d.

The charity agent's report mentions that Lucy Staplehurst was suffering from a debilitating psychiatric condition: she was admitted to the Sussex County Lunatic Asylum on 30 June 1874 suffering from mania.[546] *Her admission papers state that she was living at 70 Hanover Street with William, who was still employed as a labourer, and the cause of her illness was thought to be the scarlet fever which she had contracted three years previously. The admission papers described Lucy Staplehurst's symptoms in the following way, 'Says she has to kiss bricks and does so because she thinks it right and in that way had black eyes etc. She says that she is the She Devil and also the Devil's wife. Is always talking, making a noise and requires constant watching.' She died of exhaustion from an abscess on her chest on 21 May 1878.*

In 1881 William Staplehurst was enumerated as a farm labourer living at 51 Park Crescent Road, lodging with George Lee and his family. Ten years later he was earning his living as a gardener and was living at 62 Arnold Street. He died in Brighton in the March quarter of 1897 aged 90.[547]

5 April 1872
Statement: William Staplehurst would be thankful for a little assistance.
Report: I made enquiries respecting this case and find the man works for Mr Inkpen, Elm Grove. He bears a very good character. The wife is not quite right in her mind. The next to the youngest daughter stays at home to look after her. The oldest daughter is learning dress making, she gets her board at present. The two others work at that large shop at [the] corner of Bedford Street collar making. The home is in a comfortable state. The Reverend Mr Figgis, 32 Clifton Road, said he understood the man was out of work.
Dismissed, ineligible, R P Hooper, chairman

135 GERMAN BUXTON, 37, RAILWAY LABOURER, 51 JERSEY STREET, BRIGHTON

German Buxton's Mendicity Society application form stated that he was born in Sandbach, Cheshire, in about 1835 and that he and his wife Hannah, who was born in

546 ESRO: HC 24/2479.
547 Death of William Staplehurst registered Q1 1897 Brighton 2b 174.

Westmoreland, arrived in Brighton in 1864. On 16 June 1864 Buxton joined Brighton police force, but his employment was short-lived.[548] *At 1.40am on 7 August of the same year Buxton was found lying down asleep on the steps of 49 Norfolk Square by Inspector Foord. He was drunk and the inspector brought him to the town hall where the night constable sent him home. Buxton was kept in the probationary class for another eight weeks and severely reprimanded by the watch committee. On 24 September Samuel Mantle of 36 Bread Street came to the town hall at midnight and complained of having been assaulted by PC Buxton at the Queens Head public house, Steine Street. John Beard, of 2 George Street Court, was present and claimed that Buxton challenged him to a fight. Morris Lakey, of 10 Market Street, also witnessed the incident and stated that Buxton's conduct was very poor. The night constable sent PC Luxton to the pub but by the time he arrived Buxton had gone home. He was discharged from the police force on 28 September 1864.*

Buxton's name appeared in the local press in December 1866 when he was summoned for sureties of the peace by John Alford Denton.[549] *Denton claimed that he had employed Buxton during the summer but had discharged him for abusive conduct. On Tuesday 18th December Buxton spat at Denton whilst Buxton was cleaning the windows of a Mr Histed at the Pavilion Buildings. Denton was concerned that unless Buxton was bound over he would commit bodily harm. Buxton was bound over in his own recognizances of £10 to keep the peace for 10 months.*

German and Hannah Buxton and their five-year-old son, William, were enumerated at 51 Jersey Street on the 1871 census. Buxton was described as a railway labourer; by 31 December 1871 he was recorded as a painter at Brighton railway works, badge number 1146, earning three shillings per day.[550]

By the time of their application to the Mendicity Society the Buxtons were five weeks' rent in arrears. They paid 6s 9d for the whole of 51 Jersey Street, where they had been living for two years.[551] *German Buxton expected to earn 18 shillings per week at the railway works but had been suffering with an abscess in his eye for seven months. Hannah Buxton worked as a charwoman, usually earning four shillings per week, but had also been off sick for seven months. The couple's only source of income was the ten shillings per week that Buxton received from the Railway Club he had paid into.*

In 1881 the Buxton family were enumerated at 8 Norfolk Street: German Buxton was employed as a labourer and his 15-year-old son William was employed as a grocer; no occupation is recorded for Hannah Buxton. German Buxton's death was registered in the September quarter of 1888.[552]

6 April 1872

548 ESRO: SPA 3/17/1.

549 Brighton Guardian, 26 December 1866.

550 The National Archives: LBSCR company records, RAIL 414; piece: 763.

551 The form states that they had previously been living at 11 Washington Street.

552 Death of German Buxton registered Q3 1888 Brighton 2b 141.

Statement: German Buxton would be thankful for a little assistance till he gets better. He thinks in a few weeks he shall be able to do a little light work.
Report: I made enquiries respecting this man and find he did work at the railway station but has been sick this last seven months suffering with [an] abscess in his eye. This man thinks he shall be able to work in a few weeks but the matron at the eye infirmary thinks it will be some time before he is able to work. Mr Samson, 33 Hamilton Road, Prestonville, the foreman at the station, gave him a good character and says he believes this to be a very deserving case and that he shall have work for him as soon as he is able to come. Mr Greaves the scripture reader relieved him on one occasion. This man belongs to what is called the shop club. They pay a shilling a month and have out 10 shillings a week for eight weeks in either of the half year. The station men collected a few shillings for him last week. The house is in a passable state. I have known him about eight years. He was in the Brighton police force a short time and was discharged. Since that I believe he has tried hard for a living. He is not known at the parochial office.
Relieved with 5s and referred to parish authorities, R P Hooper, chairman

Letter from J Short, 25 Ann Street, Brighton, 6 April 1872[553]
Dear sir, I recommend the bearer as a real deserving object of charity. German Buxton has been afflicted with inflammation of the eyes [for] seven months and a poisoned and crushed hand three months. The poor man has been ten months and not earned a penny. With wife and one child six years of age depending on him for support he has worked at the Brighton railway works six years and bore an irreproachable character. His club has seen out for the past month and his [sic] now depending on private charity. His wife has not been able to earn anything owing to his severe affliction for some time. His address is 51 Jersey Street. The necessary enquiries will find this a true statement of facts. Assist the man for the present, I shall advise him to apply to the Guardians on Tuesday next. He is a labourer, painter's labourer [sic], he was four years on the Metropolitan Police Force. Yours respectfully, J Short

Letter from Charles Samson, 33 Hamilton Road, 9 April 1872
Sir, I would very respectfully and earnestly recommend Jarman Buxton [sic] to your kind consideration. His great affliction calls forth all our best sympathies and I have ever found him after working under me for six years to be an industrious good man. Your obedient servant, Charles Samson

[553] *Page's Brighton Directory of 1872* describes John Short as the proprietor of a coffee and eating house.

136 ELIZABETH CAMFIELD, 74, HAWKER, WELLINGTON INN, [THOMAS STREET], BRIGHTON[554]

Elizabeth Camfield's case appears to have been forwarded to the Mendicity Society by Mr Joseph Samuel Cole, landlord of the Wellington Arms, Thomas Street, in April 1872.[555] She stated that she was born in London in about 1798 and had been living in Brighton since about 1850: a woman named Elizabeth Sturt married a George Camfield at Brighton in 1850 but the date of his death is not known.[556] Despite claiming that she had been living at the Wellington Inn for two years she was enumerated at 197 Eastern Road on the 1871 census where she lodged with a pork butcher named Goldsmith, his family and four other lodgers.

The application form states that Camfield paid 2s 4d for her bed and was 2s 6d in arrears. She usually expected to make seven shillings per week hawking items but was currently earning six shillings per week. An 83-year-old woman named Eliza Camfield was enumerated at Brighton Workhouse in 1881. The death of an 82-year-old woman named Elizabeth Camfield was registered at Brighton in the June quarter of 1881.[557]

10 April 1872
Statement: Elizabeth Camfield would be grateful for a little assistance.
Report: I made enquiries respecting this case and find this woman gets her living hawking. I have known her some time and believe she tries hard to get a living. Mr Cole gave her a good character. She is not known to Mr Toye the scripture reader. She is known to the relieving officer. She applied there for relief in January when they gave an order for the workhouse. I believe she is not requiring relief at present.
Ineligible, R P Hooper, chairman

137 SYDNEY BERRY, 17, RAILWAY LABOURER, 72 UPPER LEWES ROAD, BRIGHTON

Thomas Berry, wine merchant, his wife Rebecca and their children Frederick and Agnes were enumerated at 10 Black Lion Street on the 1861 census. Berry Brothers wine merchants were listed in Page's Directory of 1870 with premises at 9, 10 and 17 Black Lion Street.[558] The demise of the business is evident in the census return for 1871 when the same address was occupied by George Richardson, an accountant's clerk, and William Chadburn, a wine merchant's porter.

554 Recorded as the Wellington Arms, Thomas Street, in the petty sessions licensing register.
555 ESRO: PTS 2/6/2.
556 Marriage of Elizabeth Sturt to George Camfield registered Q3 1850 Brighton 7 425.
557 Death of Elizabeth Camfield registered Q2 1881 Brighton 2b 133.
558 This company is not thought to be connected to Berry Bros & Rudd, St James's.

When Sydney Berry applied to the Mendicity Society in April 1872 he was 17 years of age and working as a labourer for the London Brighton and South Coast Railway Company. Although he was not enumerated with his family in 1861 or 1871 he stated on his aplication form that his previous address was 10 Black Lion Street. Berry did not state when he moved to 72 Upper Lewes Road, how much he was earning or how much he was paying in rent.
Berry's application for relief was turned down by the Mendicity Society but funds raised by his referee, Mrs Dingwall, also of 10 Black Lion Street, enabled him to fulfill his wish of emigrating to Canada. On 30 April 1872 Sydney Berry and his younger brother Percy sailed from London to Quebec via Plymouth on the SS Scotland.[559] *The SS Scotland carried 250 passengers and amongst the number were the Lidgold family from Brighton. Like Berry, George Lidgold worked for the London Brighton and South Coast Railway Company; Lidgold applied to the Mendicity Society on 12 April for help with his fare to Canada but was turned down [see case 139]. The SS Scotland docked at Quebec on 20 May 1872 but nothing further is known of Berry's life in Canada.*

Letter to William Henty from Mrs M H Dingwall, 10 Black Lion Street, Brighton, 6 April [1872][560]
Dear Sir, I was yesterday advised by Mrs Bright to ask your kind assistance in a case I have had on my hands for seven weeks. It is that of T S Berry, late of 10 Black Lion Street, wine merchant. Five years ago he took to drinking and utterly ruined himself and family. He is now a miserable wreck hopelessly ill. There are five sons three of whom have supported the family. They are paid so little and their work is so unsuited for them that I wish to help them to something better. Mr Penney has kindly given the eldest a place on one of his vessels for a year's voyage and I am trying to send two of the lads out to America. Miss Crisp and Mrs Bright have kindly consented to send one boy free for the other. I must collect six guineas by next Saturday, also the outfit for the three lads and I am beside allowing Mrs Berry a £1 a week while she and Mr Berry are so ill. If you will assist me I shall feel very grateful. Respectfully yours, M H Dingwall

Letter to William Henty from Mrs M H Dingwall, 10 Black Lion Street, Brighton, Monday [probably 8 April 1872]
Mrs Dingwall compliments and thanks Mr Henty for his polite note. Miss Crisp and Mrs Bright thought that as Mrs Dingwall had given Mrs Berry weekly relief during a serious illness of her own and of Mr Berry (drinking seven weeks) and is still obliged to do so it was hoped that Mr Henty would have relieved Mrs Dingwall by giving a weekly allowance from the funds of the Mendicity Society. To collect £5 by Saturday for the passage money of one of the boys and provide

[559] Library and Archives Canada; Ottawa, Ontario, Canada; Series RG 76-C; Roll C-4527.
[560] William Henty was on the board of the Mendicity Society.

clothes for three is harder work than Mrs Dingwall is fit for. The £1 given by Mr Henty is used for purchasing flannel for shirts for the boy who is going to sea and Mrs Dingwall begs to report her thanks to Mrs Henty, not only for the sum, but for the cheerful kindness with which it was giving [sic] which was most encouraging

Letter from William Henty, 12 Medina Villas, Hove, Tuesday [probably 9 April 1872]
Sir, I enclose letter from Mrs Dingwall respecting a family of three sons of a Mrs Berry. Her previous letter mentioned that three children had to be provided for – one was taken in hand by the Emigration Committee, one was going to sea and money was wanted to pay the passage of the third to Canada (£5 now wanting) that letter said nothing about the Mendicity Society. You can make the necessary enquiries for the information of the committee. I have an engagement to meet a gentleman from London on business which keeps me at home. Yours, William Henty

Calling card of Mrs M H Dingwall, 10 Black Lion Street, Brighton, undated
The case is strongly recommended by Cordy Burrows esq. G W Henty will kindly see Mrs D, she will call on Monday at 9am.

Calling card of Mrs M H Dingwall, 10 Black Lion Street, Brighton, undated
I have a subscription opened and recommended by Cordy Burrows esq, amount collected £4 5s.

Letter to the chairman of the Mendicity Society from Mrs M H Dingwall, 10 Black Lion Street, Brighton, 10 April [1872]
I write to ask your kind assistance in starting three boys in a position which it is to be hoped will enable them to help themselves. Two are going out to America, one to sea. The Emigration Society kindly sent the younger boy free but for his outfit. I require overcoat, pair of boots, handkerchiefs, socks, hat and trousers. For the older boy I must pay on Saturday £5 passage money and require outfits, two under flannels, pair of boots, trousers, hat, socks, handkerchiefs and box. For the boy going to sea I must have warm under flannels, one pair trousers, coat, boots, two wrappers, three pairs overalls, box and handkerchiefs. This poor boy has worked so hard at night work to try to keep his mother that his health has failed. It is hoped the voyage will restore him if he has warm clothing. All this is much more than I can manage minded the time being short – I therefore earnestly ask for kind interest. Mrs Dingwall

11 April 1872
Statement: Sydney Berry would like to go to Canada.

Report: I made enquiries respecting this lad and find he did work at the railway station but has left to go to Canada. His father was for a long time in business in Black Lion Street but failed through his intemperate habits. I have seen Mrs Dingwall and gave her the £1 15s which she was very thankful for.
Case dismissed as being now sufficiently relieved,
G D Ryder, vice chairman

Receipt signed by Mrs Dingwall, 12 April [1872]
Received from the agent of the Mendicity Society, the sum of £1 10s, Mrs M H Dingwall

138 ROSE SIMMONDS, 14, DAUGHTER OF A CARPENTER, 28 SOUTHAMPTON STREET, BRIGHTON

Rose Simmonds was the daughter of Edward Simmonds, a carpenter born in Bushey, Hertfordshire, in about 1811, and Mary Ann Simmonds a laundress from Lea Bridge, Essex, who was born in about 1843.[561] *Rose Simmonds was also born in Lea Bridge in about 1859 but according to the Mendicity Society's application form the family moved to Brighton in about 1863.*

Edward and Mary Ann Simmonds were enumerated at 13 Quebec Street on the census of 1871 where they lived with their four children, of whom Rose was the oldest. The application states that they subsequently moved to 81 Islingword Road before going to 28 Southampton Street three weeks before they applied. Their case was forwarded to the Mendicity Society by Mrs Hart of 24 Grand Parade when Edward Simmonds had been sick for two months and Mary Ann Simmonds had been sick for two weeks. Edward Simmonds had been working for a builder named Chatterton and Mary Ann had been employed as a washer woman by Mrs Packet of Albion Hill.[562] *Simmonds could usually expect to earn 20 shillings when in full employment but was only earning 4s 6d and Mary Ann would usually earn five shillings per week but was presently earning nothing. They paid weekly rent of 6s 6d and were 13 shillings in arrears. They gave the names of Mrs Hart, 24 Grand Parade, and Mrs Hannah of Washington Street, the District Visitor, as their references.*

The death of a 64-year-old man named Edward Simmonds was registered at Brighton in the March quarter of 1875.[563]

561 There are two possible matches: the marriage of Edward Simmonds to a Mary Ann Jarret registered Q2 1860 Hastings 2b 43; the otherEdward Simmonds to a Mary Ann Laxton registered Q1 1859 Islington 1b 273.

562 Possibly S Chatterton, builder, of 14 Upper Rock Gardens.

563 Death of Edward Simmonds registered Q1 1875 Brighton 2b 186.

12 April 1872
Statement: Rose Simmonds would be thankful for a little assistance. My mother will be able to go to work next week.
Report: I made enquiries respecting this case and find this man did work for Mr Chatterton in Southampton Street. He has been sick about two months. He is of intemperate habits. The wife will be able to go to work in another week. Mrs Packet the laundress gave her a good character. Mrs Hart has relieved them on one or two occasions. Mrs Hannah, 90 Washington Street, the District Visitor has relieved them on several occasions. The home is in a passable state. They receive parish relief at the rate of 9s per week.
Grant of 5s in kind through the agent, G D Ryder, vice chairman

139 GEORGE LIDGOLD, 35, RAILWAY LABOURER, 9 STANLEY STREET, BRIGHTON

Cornelius George Lidgold was the son of Sarah and Cornelius Lidgold, a gardener, and was baptised at St Mary, Barnes, Surrey, on 2 June 1833.[564] *He married Mary Cox at Walworth, Surrey, on 16 June 1852 and was described as a milkman on the marriage certificate.*[565] *In 1861 Lidgold was enumerated at Baker Street, Lambeth, with his father who was employed as a carter. George Lidgold, as he appears to have been known, stated on his application form that he moved to Brighton in about 1869, initially residing at 18 Southover Street, before moving to 9 Stanley Street in about 1870 where he was enumerated in 1871.*

By December 1871 Lidgold was employed as a labourer at the London Brighton and South Coast Railway Company where he was earning 3s 4d per day.[566] *He was still employed by the railway company in April 1872 when his family's case was forwarded to the Mendicity Society by Mrs Bright of 19 Goldsmid Road. By this time, he was earning 20 shillings per week and paying 4s 9d rent per week on 9 Stanley Street but had rent arrears of 14 shillings. He lived at the property with his wife Mary and their three young children.*

Lidgold's request for help with the fare to Canada was refused but despite this he appears on the passenger list of the SS Scotland with the rest of the family.[567] *The ship sailed from London to Quebec via Plymouth on 30 April 1872 and docked on 20 May 1872. Amongst the other passengers was Sydney Berry, one of George Lidgold's colleagues at the London Brighton and South Coast Railway Company, who applied to the Mendicity Society for funds to help him emigrate the day before Lidgold (see case 137).*

564 London Metropolitan Archives: Church of England Parish Registers, 1754-1906; DW/T/2325.
565 Ancestry.com England, Marriages and Banns, 1754-1921.
566 The National Archives: LBSCR company records, RAIL 414; piece: 763.
567 Library and Archives Canada; Ottawa, Ontario, Canada; Series RG 76-C; Roll C-4527.

The 1881 census of Ontario shows George Lidgold employed as a farmer living at Muskoka with his family.[568] *The entry in the district of Muskoka register of deaths gives a great deal of biographical information: he died of myocardial failure as a result of Bright's disease at Draper, Muskoka, on 25 August 1919 and was buried at Uffington, Draper, Ontario.*[569] *He had suffered with this condition for some years but outlived his wife.*

Letter from S Bright of the Juvenile Emigration Society, undated
Bearer, George Lidgold, is most anxious to emigrate with his family and has funds enough to do so excepting £1. If he can be assisted to this by [the] Mendicity Society it will be a great boon. The Juvenile Emigration Society are assisting him. S Bright on the part of the committee of the J E S.

12 April 1872
Statement: George Lidgold would be thankful for a little assistance to enable him and his wife and family to emigrate to Canada.
Report: I made enquiries respecting this case and find this man is working at the railway. His wages is £1 a week. Mr Robinson the foreman gave him a good character. The home is in a passable state. From enquiries I made in the neighbourhood where they are living I find they bear a good character.
Ineligible, referred to the Sussex Emigration Society, G D Ryder, vice chairman

140 MARY KENNETT, 52, LAUNDRESS, 27 QUEBEC STREET, BRIGHTON

Mary Kennett's maiden name is not known but she was born in East Hoathly in about 1820. In 1851 she was enumerated at a lodging house in West Street, Brighton, with her husband Joseph Kennett, a butcher, born in Eastbourne in the December quarter of 1844. The couple shared the accommodation with their four children who were aged between eight and two years old all of whom were born in Lewes.

In 1861 the Kennett family were enumerated at 25 Scotland Street. The Mendicity Society application form states that they then went to an address in Cobden Road before moving to 27 Quebec Street in about 1867. It was whilst resident at this address that Mary Kennett first approached the Mendicity Society, on 12 April 1872. She was employed as a laundress and her husband as a butcher; the eldest son Henry was employed as a porter by A Dowsett, chemist, of 16 North Street. Between the three breadwinners the family could usually expect to earn 29 shillings per week but recently had had a lower income of 23 shillings per week. They paid rent of four shillings per week but were £2 in arrears. Like a number of other families during this period they were applying for money to fund their

568 1881 Canada Census; Oakley, Ryde and Draper, Muskoka, Ontario; Roll C-13243; Page 9; Family 93.

569 Archives of Ontario; Toronto, Ontario, Canada; Collection MS935; Reel 256.

emigration to Canada but, unlike the Berrys, the Kennetts were unsuccessful [see cases 137 and 139].

Joseph Kennett applied to the charity again in July 1876, when the family were resident at 43 Islingword Road. He gave a false address and claimed that his wife had recently died, but this statement appears to have been easily disproved by the charity's agent, William Collingham. The Kennetts had moved to 6 Pevensey Road by December 1877 and were enumerated at that address in 1881. Mary Kennett's next approach to the Mendicity Society came in October 1882 when she was recently widowed and living at 22 Newmarket Road.

Mary Kennett appears to have been held in high esteem by the charity officials and those who advocated for her. She remained in fairly regular contact with the Charity Organisation Society until February 1900 and died in Brighton aged 84 in the June quarter of 1904.[570]

12 April 1872
Statement: Mary Kennett would be thankful for a little assistance to enable them to emigrate to Canada.
Report: I made enquiries respecting this case and find this man has not had any regular work since he has been in Brighton. He has been jobbing about and helping unload market carts. He is of intemperate habits. The wife is a very respectable woman. She has had to work hard at laundry work to keep the house together. They have had a large family: one daughter is married and living in Quebec, one son in Ireland in the 17th Lancers, one at sea and two in Brighton – one a carver and gilder working in Union Street, the other a porter at the Star and Garter hotel. The home is in a passable state. They state they want to collect £30 and all they have got is £2 15s.
Ineligible, G D Ryder, vice chairman

Letter to Mr Johnson from Marriage Wallis [of Springfield, Withdean], 25 February 1875
Dear Sir, can you enquire for me about Joseph Kennett, 16 Upper Bedford Street? He says his wife is just dead and he asked me for help. Not being prepos[sess]ed by his appearance, I would rather know his character and the facts of the case before doing anything. Yours truly, Marriage Wallis

1 March 1875
This family did not emigrate to Canada, the man still jobs about with carriers and others and on Thursday last he applied to Mr Wallis for assistance to enable him to bury his wife who he said was just dead and gave his address [as] 16 Upper Bedford Street. On enquiry I find instead of his address being 16 Upper

[570] Death of Mary Kennett registered Q2 1904 Brighton 2b 115.

Bedford Street he lives at 58 Islingword Road. His wife keeps a small general shop and instead of her being dead on Saturday evening she was quite well and serving her customers. WC [William Collingham]
To be reported to Mr Marriage Wallis with recommendation to prosecute, R P Hooper, chairman

11 July 1876
Mrs Kennett applied at the office on Monday for the committee to be security for her for a £5 loan to enable her to pay out a man put in possession £4 12s by Corrall and Co. coal merchants. Applicant now keeps a small general shop at 43 Islingword Street and her husband still jobs about with carriers. WC [William Collingham]
Ineligible, R P Hooper

30 September 1877
Mr Donovan requests a report of this case. The family now reside at 49 Viaduct Road. Kennett, who never helps support his home, has been ill in bed nearly a fortnight suffering from erysipelas.[571] The wife takes in a little washing. Her two sons are both in work. The house is in a destitute state. WC [William Collingham]
Undeserving, R P Hooper

20 December 1877
Mrs Kennett, who now resides at 6 Pevensey Road, applied at the office on Wednesday for assistance to tide her over till her husband gets better. He is suffering from a bad leg. Applicant is in delicate health. They have an order for the workhouse in their possession. WC [William Collingham]
Referred to parish, R P Hooper

16 May 1879
Mr H Willett, Arnold House, Montpelier Place, requests a report of this case. Kennett has been ill a month suffering from erysipelas for which he is attended by the dispensary doctor. His wife will apply to the Guardians on Tuesday for outdoor relief. The home is in a destitute state. WC [William Collingham]
Undeserving, report to Mr H Willett, R P Hooper

Letter from J Greaves, 10 Ashton Street, 14 October 1882
J Greaves, scripture reader, has known Mary Kennett (residing at 22 Newmarket Road) for more than twenty years and has ever found her hard working, cleanly

[571] Erysipelas is an acute skin infection usually occurring on the face, arms, fingers, legs or toes.

and in every way deserving of any help which may be given to her. Her husband died about five weeks ago and she is now in great need.

14 October 1882
Mrs Kennett applied at the office this morning for assistance to tide her over till she can obtain some light employment. Her late husband who was a heavy drag on her for many years died five weeks ago. Applicant earns a trifle by nursing children for persons who go out to work. She has a brother, a grocer, in Lewes Road who is very good to her and her sons also assist her. She is known to the parish authorities and was granted an order for the [work]house on Tuesday last. WC [William Collingham]
Ineligible, R P Hooper

Note from Mrs J O Smith, Richmond Villa, c1883[572]
A very sad and deserving case. I have given 6s 6d for blankets to be taken out of pawn – help is truly needed. Mrs J O Smith, Richmond Villa, Saturday

Letter from Mrs J O Smith, Richmond Villa, 24 July [1883]
Mrs Kinnard [sic], 22 Newmarket Road, Lewes [Road] from Mrs J O Smith. Will you kindly see into the above case and give a little assistance. I have from time to time assisted and know it is a deserving case. Mrs J O Smith, Richmond Villa
On reverse: Mrs Smith would not appeal but just now is doing almost as much as she can manage

26 July 1883
The daughter was sent by Mrs J O Smith of Richmond Villa and applied at the office on Wednesday for some temporary relief for her mother. She still resides at 22 Newmarket Road and has lately gone out charring till 10 days ago when she was taken ill with breakings out on her wrists for which she is attended to by the dispensary doctor and will not be able to work for a week or two. She has always been a sober, hardworking woman and seems very poor. WC [William Collingham]
Grant of 5s per week for two weeks, R P Hooper

8 August 1883
The daughter applied at the office on Wednesday for some further relief for her mother. She is getting better and hopes to be able to work in the course of a few days. WC [William Collingham]
Grant of 5s, R P Hooper

[572] John Oliver Smith, Richmond Villa, Richmond Terrace, Brighton, died January 1892 (ESRO: ACC 5702/85/1).

15 November 1884
This person, now of 90 Upper Lewes Road, was sent by Mrs J O Smith

Letter from Mary P Hack, 31 December 1885
Sir, Mrs Kennett, a widow (hard working), has met with an accident – a severe cut in the leg. She is doctoring it herself so that I do not know if she can have anything from the accident [the Jubilee and Accident Fund] but it prevents her going to her regular work. She is deserving of help. She has been known to Mr Greaves, scripture reader, 10 Ashton Street, for nearly 20 years and we have helped her sometimes. Her daughter who has come over from her place for the day brings this note. Yours truly, Mary P Hack

1 January 1886
The daughter was sent by Miss M P Hack and applied at the office on Thursday for relief for her mother from the Jubilee and Accident Fund. She is now taking charge of an unfurnished house and has a slight scratch on her right shin which does not prevent her from working and the Guardians allow her 3s per week. WC [William Collingham]
Ineligible, R P Hooper

9 October 1890
Mrs J O Smith of Richmond Villa requests a report on this case. Mrs Kennett now resides at 70 Upper Lewes Road. Her brother continues to assist her and the Guardians are allowing her 3s per week. WC [William Collingham]
Report to Mrs J O Smith, Thomas Holland

Letter from Mary Kennett, 38 Round Hill Crescent, Brighton, 1 December 1893
Dear Madam, I beg your pardon for taking the liberty in writing to you after your kindness to me in the summer. I have never forgotten it but I, Mrs Kennett that came to you in the summer, were in distress at the time and I bought my insurance book to you and you were kind enough to pay it for me and you also gave me some fruit. I am sorry to tell you that I have been very ill and just getting about a little now but I am still very bad. I am in great distress. I am so sorry to trouble you again I hope you will forgive me I feel now so sinking for the want of nourishment if I were well enough to work I would not trouble no one. Dear madam, I am sure you will remember the person that has wrote this – I lived at Baker Street when I came to you last summer but I have moved since to 38 Round Hill Crescent and have got two rooms here. Your obedient servant, Mary Kennett

2 December 1893
Mrs Napper, Warnham House, Ship Street, requests a report of this case. Mrs

Kennett now resides at 38 Round Hill Crescent and generally earns a trifle by going out charring but during the past 10 days she has been in ill health. Her brother still assists her and the Guardians continue to allow her 3s per week. WC [William Collingham]
Report to Mrs Napper, R P Hooper

Letter from Winifred J Willett, West House [12 Portland Place], Brighton, 19 November [1896]
Dear Sir, will you kindly give this person 5s for her insurance for us if you think desirable. It appears from the book that it is 5s per week and was last paid on September 14th. Yours truly, Winifred J Willett

Letter from Mary Kennett, 101a Albion Hill, Brighton, 19 November 1896
Dear Madam, I have taken the liberty in writing to you hoping you will not be offended with me for daring so. I am writing to know if you would kindly assist me a little in my insurance as I have been in a great many years now and would not like to get out of it now. I may want it soon for I am 78 years of age coming Xmas and I feel very weak and too old for work. I am sorry to trouble you and would not do so only that I cannot work now. Hoping you will not think I have taken a great liberty in writing to you. I have sent my character for you to see. I remain your humble servant, Mary Kennett

20 November 1896
Mrs Kennett, now of 101a Albion Hill, has applied to Mrs G W Willett of West House for assistance to pay off her insurance arrears and the lady is willing for the committee to give her 5s on her account. At present she only owes 3s 4d. The Guardians are allowing her 3s 6d per week and she has always borne a good character. WC [William Collingham]
Mrs Willett granted 5s, [Captain] C P Boger

Letter from Winifred J Willett, West House [12 Portland Place], Brighton, 3 March [1897]
Dear Sir, kindly assist the enclosed case if it is a deserving one irrespective of whether the woman is in receipt of parish relief or not. Yours truly, W J Willett

Letter from Mary Kennett, 101a Albion Hill, Brighton, 3 March 1897
Dear Sir, I humbly beg your pardon for writing to you and hoping you will not think I have taken a great liberty on myself. I am very sorry to have to trouble you but I have got three weeks behind with my rent and, dear sir, if you would kindly assist me a little I should feel so thankful to you indeed. I have been very bad and feel far from well. Now I feel I am too old for work, I was 78 years of age last Christmas. I have sent my rent book and character for you to see.

Hoping dear sir you will not be offended and that it is quite correct what I have written. Your humble and obedient servant, Mary Kennett

5 March 1897
Mrs Kennett has applied to Mrs G W Willett for £1 1s 1d to enable her to pay off three weeks arrears of rent and the lady wishes her to be assisted if the case is a deserving one. The applicant rents a flat at 1s per week and lodgers pay 3s but her room is empty occasionally. According to her statement she earns 1s 6d a week charring. Her brother still does what he can for her and the Guardians continue to allow her 3s 6d a week. She supports a granddaughter aged 22 who should be in service besides which instead of renting a flat she could move into one room and then she would be able to manage without seeking charity. WC [William Collingham]
Ineligible, C W Mellor

12 February 1900
Mrs Napper, Warnham House, Ship Street, requests another report of this case. Mrs Kennett is not ill as represented by her granddaughter. Her brother continues to do what he can for her and the Guardians still allow her outdoor relief. WC [William Collingham]
Report to Mrs Napper, E A J Drury

14 February [1900]
Reported, CD

141 JAMES AVYES, 34, LABOURER, 3 CUMBERLAND PLACE, BRIGHTON

William Collingham, the Mendicity Society's agent, recorded the surname of this applicant as Avyes but there appears to be no one by this name recorded on any census returns or parish records. It is possible that the man's real name was Avis or perhaps Aves; the 1851 census carries an entry for a James Aves who was born in Rodmell in about 1838 living with his uncle William Wright, an eating-house keeper, at 9 Carlton Street.

The application form for this man stated that he was born in Brighton in about 1838 and had previously been living at 2 Derby Place before moving to 3 Cumberland Place in about December 1871. He was paying 1s 9d rent per week for a bed in a shared room, had no arrears and usually expected to earn ten shillings a week when in full employment. The man's case was forwarded to the Mendicity Society by Miss Jackson of 13 Pavilion Parade.

15 April 1872
Statement: I was at work at Falmer on Saturday when I came over sick and had to come home. I should be thankful for a little assistance.

Report: I have known this man a long time – he generally jobs about in the market. He is of intemperate habits. He has been convicted several times for felony. He is not known to Miss Jackson – he applied there for relief and Miss Jackson not knowing him gave him the ticket. I told him the best thing he could do was to apply for an order for the workhouse. Upon enquiry I find he has done so. He is to go before the board this afternoon.
Ineligible

142 ELIZABETH CALLAGHAN [ALSO GIVEN AS CALLAGAN], 45, HAWKER, 23 CAVENDISH STREET, BRIGHTON

When Elizabeth Callaghan (née Graham) applied to the Mendicity Society she was sharing one room at 23 Cavendish Street with her children James and Elizabeth.[573] *She was born in Sheffield, Yorkshire, in about 1827 but had been living in Brighton for two years. The family moved to Cavendish Street in about April 1871 and had previously been living at 7 Chesterfield Street. They paid weekly rent of 3s 6d, owed no rent and Elizabeth earned four shillings per week by hawking goods.*

Her husband Matthew had returned to Barnsley, Yorkshire, with their 17-year-old son Edward to find work. It is not known whether the family raised the necessary funds to return to Yorkshire.

16 April 1872
Statement: Elizabeth Callaghan wants assistance to get to Barnsley in Yorkshire where her husband is at work.
Report: I made enquiries respecting this case and find this woman's husband worked at the drainage works and when the works was completed about seven weeks ago he left the town. The wife states he has now got work at Barnsley. She gets her living hawking. The husband sends her 5s a week to help support the children. With regard to references she states since she has been living in Brighton she has not made friends with anyone. The home is in a destitute state. She states it would cost about 20s to get down to her husband.
Relieved with grant of 2s 6d pending further enquiry, R P Hooper. The answer from Barnsley being satisfactory, ordered that in case her husband sends a Post Office order for the balance of railway fare this society will give £1 towards the fare the tickets being just procured, Thomas Driscoll, chairman

Letter to R P Hooper from Superintendent George Sykes, West Riding Constabulary, Barnsley, 20 April 1872
Re: Callaghan, a labourer, and his son aged 17 years. Sir, in reply to your letter of yesterday's date upon this subject I beg to inform you that both Callaghan and

[573] Marriage of Elizabeth Graham to Matthew Mark Callaghan registered Q4 1845 York 23 773.

his son are still living at number 6 Greenwood's Square in this town. Callaghan is working at the New Oaks pit as a labourer and when working he receives 3s 6d per day. He only worked two days last week and that was the reason he did not send his wife any money. I am sir your obedient servant, George Sykes, Superintendent

Letter to Elizabeth Callaghan from Matthew Callaghan, 6 Greenwood Square, Barnsley, Yorkshire, 14 May 1872
My dear wife, I received your kind and welcome letter this afternoon and was very happy to hear you and the children is well. As this leaves me at present thank God Edward is getting better – he went to work this morning but the[n] had to come home at noon. He is very weak and could not do the work. I was in good hopes to be able to send you some money to bring you down the next week or two but I will do what I can. The weather has been very bad for the last week. I worked only four days last week and half a day yesterday so I cannot save much when I pay 4s a week for our lodgings and provisions is so very dear here but horses is very cheap and coals is only 9s a ton so if you were here and we to have a horse [sic] we soon could get around and you wanted to know where Matthew was – he went to Gibraltar on a sailing exhibition [sic] and I wrote to him and Mary Ann on Sunday week. They have not answered yet – when they do I will let you know so I now conclude with love to all, Elizabeth and James. Write [to] M Callaghan, No 6 Greenwood Square, Barnsley, Yorkshire. I hope to see you soon, goodbye, with love to all

143 ANN SIMMONDS, 42, WASHER, 21 ST MARTIN'S PLACE, BRIGHTON

When Ann Simmonds' case was forwarded to the Mendicity Society by the Reverend Salmon, vicar of St Martin's, Lewes Road, she was renting two rooms at 21 St Martin's Place, which she shared with her 16-year-old daughter, Rose, and her two sons, Frederick and Thomas aged 13 and 10 respectively. They paid three shillings per week rent and had been at the address for seven months: previously they had been living at 3 St Mary Magdalen Street and had been living in Brighton for seven years. She owed no rent and was earning 15 shillings per week working as a laundress for Mrs Tutt of Lewes Road. The household income was boosted by Frederick who earned five shillings per week as an errand boy for Mr Phillips of Western Road.

Ann Simmonds was born in Albourne in about 1830. Her first husband died and her second husband deserted her in about 1868, but it has not been possible to establish the name of either man.

16 April 1872
Statement: Ann Simmonds would be thankful for a little assistance to help get the remainder of her son's clothes to enable him to emigrate to Canada.
Report: this woman states her husband deserted her about four years ago and left her with five children. Two of them are in service in the country and one is at Mr Batchelor's, 18 Lewes Road. Upon enquiry I find her first husband died about five years ago and some time after that she married again. Her next husband, finding he could not live with her, he deserted and is supposed gone to America. Mrs Hardwicke states she discharged her for most disgraceful conduct. I am informed she is very much given to drink. The home is in a passable state. She states the things she wants will cost about 20s.
Ineligible, R P Hooper, chairman

144 HENRY WHITE, 37, HAWKER, 43 CHESTERFIELD STREET, BRIGHTON

Henry White was born in Brighton in about 1835 but had spent some time in Plymouth, Devon, before returning either in about 1865 or at the beginning of April 1872: the information on his application form is ambiguous. His case was forwarded to the Mendicity Society by the Reverend John Moore Fincher, curate of St John's, Carlton Hill, and Mr Toye, the scripture reader, was given as a character reference.

White described himself as a widower but the report does not refer to his late wife and there are a number of marriage records for men in Brighton named Henry White so it has not been possible to identify this woman. Henry White had started a relationship with a woman named Jane Long who is mentioned on his application of 1875. However, White died in about 1881 so the last three documents transcribed below relate to Jane Long.

16 April 1872
Statement: Henry White wants a little assistance to help him get out a licence. He states he has got 2s 6d and wants 2s 6d more.
Report: I have known this man a long time. He makes children's toys and sells [them] and sometimes sings about the streets. He is of weak intellect. I believe he often goes without sufficient food. The Reverend Mr Fincher and Mr Toye the scripture reader say they believe this to be a deserving case.
Grant of 2s 6d to assist in obtaining license. License to be bought by Collingham, R P Hooper, chairman

8 October 1875
Further information: this man who resides at 6 Thomas Street and who was sent by Mr Witten of the Medical Mission Dispensary applied at the office on Friday for assistance to enable him to purchase his child, aged five months, some

nourishing food.[574] Applicant still sells children's toys and lives with a little woman named Jane Long. This woman is deformed and blind of one eye. She has a boy aged 12 said to be the son of her brother-in-law, Albert Muett of Worthing, a widower, also a girl aged six – an illegitimate child by the same man. For some time she went about begging with these children but for the last two years she has lived with applicant and she now has a baby aged five months on whose behalf the application is made. WC [William Collingham]
Referred to parish, A Hamilton

1 January 1878
White applied at the office on Tuesday for 5s to enable him to renew his hawker's licence. He still lives with the woman Long. She lost her first child by White and now has another baby five months, a poor sickly little thing which is attended by the parish doctor. The relieving officers have had a deal of trouble with White, and the Reverend Dinnick, 86 London Road, states that White is constantly begging at various places of worship. WC [William Collingham]
Undeserving, referred to parish, R P Hooper

26 January 1878
White, who was sent recommended by Mr Jones, town missionary, applied at the office this morning for assistance to enable him to get the baby nourishing food. WC [William Collingham]
Undeserving, R P Hooper, chairman

Letter from Emilin Townsend, [4 Hanover Terrace], [26 January 1902]
Dear Sir, can you give me any information about a poor old woman who sits in the gardens near the queen's statue? Her name is Mrs White. She is a cripple and has only one eye and no means of subsistence except the charity of passers by yet she is refused relief by the parish authorities because she has a son of 19 who is expected to keep her. If her tale is true I should like to help her hence my application to you. I am yours sincerely Emilin Townsend, stamps for reply enclosed

27 January 1902
The previous reports show that this little woman who is feeble minded, a cripple and blind of the left eye is known to the society as Jane Long and has had several children by different men here and in Worthing. The man White died about 21 years ago and since then she has got her living by sitting on the seats in the neighbourhood of the Pavilion to excite sympathy. Her son, who is also feeble

[574] Edward Witten, 18 College Road, Brighton.

minded, is employed by Mr Ludby out of charity.[575] They have made no application to the parish for many years and in my opinion the mother would be far better off in the Union. WC [William Collingham]
Report to Miss Townsend, reported accordingly, copy appended

Letter to Emilin Townsend, 4 Hanover Terrace, 31 January 1902
Re: White [*illegible*], Dear Madam, this little woman who has been unfavorably known to our society since 1872 was never married but has had several illegitimate children by different fathers. She is slightly deficient as is also her son of 19 but as he earns 8s a week and their rent is only 4s she has no occasion to sit in the Pavilion Gardens to excite compassion as she has done now for some years past. They have not made any application to the parish for a very long time. Both would do well to go into the [work]house. Faithfully yours, M E Heathcote, Honorary Secretary

145 JOHN HILL, 26, LABOURER, 10 SHUTERS GARDENS, BRIGHTON

John Hill was born in Horsham in about 1846 and, according to his Mendicity Society application form, came to Brighton in August 1871: first living at 4 Frederick Cottages and a month later moving to 10 Shuters Gardens. His case was forwarded to the charity by Mr Duddell of Queens Park and he received references from the vicar of Brighton, the Reverend John Hannah, and Mr Chisholm of 41 Caledonian Road. Hill was not earning at the time of his application but was not paying any rent for his bed in a shared room at Shuters Gardens (sometimes given as Chuters Gardens) which was situated off West Street.

18 April 1872
Statement: John Hill would be thankful for a little assistance to enable him to emigrate to Canada.
Report: I made enquiries respecting this man's statement and find it's correct. I have seen his discharge, it stated, 'Not fit for further service' and on the bottom it stated his conduct has been good, it was dated 19th of July 1870. Mr Wagner states he does not know him personally, but he has known the family for years. Mr Chisholm states he has known him from a child. He knew him when he attended West Street School. He believes this to be a very deserving case.

[575] Robert Ludby, described on the 1901 census as a general dealer of 35 Jersey Street, Brighton.

146 THOMAS SULLIVAN, 52, HAWKER, 38 THOMAS STREET, BRIGHTON

Thomas Sullivan was born in Ireland in about 1820 and, according to his Mendicity Society application form, moved to Brighton in 1866. On the 1871 census he was enumerated at 17 Egremont Street, Brighton, where he lived with his wife Mary and his six-year-old son John. The census entry recorded Sullivan's occupation as miner and stated that he was blind from an accident. John Sullivan was born in Heffer Combe [sic, probably Hollacombe], Devon.

Thomas Sullivan's name was forwarded to the Mendicity Society by Mrs Howard of 28 Old Steine, who presumably knew Sullivan from his regular pitch on the south side of the Old Steine from where he sold matches. The family had been living in one room at 38 Thomas Street for a month. They paid two shillings per week rent and were not in arrears. He stated that he usually earned seven shillings per week but recently had only been bringing in five shillings per week.

By May 1876 Sullivan had moved to 18 Cumberland Place and he was resident at 34 Derby Place when he applied on 25 June 1879. At the time of his last application in 1886 he was widowed and living at a tramps' lodging house at 82 Egremont Street. The death of a 67-year-old man named Thomas Sullivan was recorded in Brighton in the December quarter of 1888.[576]

19 April 1872
Statement: Thomas Sullivan would be thankful for a little assistance. His trade is very bad at present.
Report: This is the blind man that stands on the south side of the Old Steine with cigar lights. He states his trade has very much fallen off lately and that often he does not get 6d a day. From enquiries made I find he bears a good character. The wife is ill – she is an out-patient at the hospital. The home is in a destitute state. Mrs Howard has relieved them on one or two occasions and believes this to be a very deserving case. Mr Toye the scripture reader has relieved them on two or three occasions. They applied to the parish authorities in January last but refused to go in the [work]house.
Ineligible, having been offered residence in the workhouse by the parochial authorities, R P Hooper

Letter from Mrs Kennedy, 6 Marine Terrace, 24 February 1873
Mrs Kennedy will be glad if the Mendicity Society will inquire into the case of Thomas Sullivan, a blind man, at 38 Thomas Street and if necessary she will contribute a trifle to the relief of family.

26 February 1873
Further information: Mrs Kennedy, 6 Marine Terrace, sent the annexed letter to

[576] Death of Thomas Sullivan registered Q4 1888 Brighton 2b 139.

the office asking for information respecting this case and upon enquiry I find the man still stands on the Old Steine with cigar lights. The wife sometimes sells oranges but for several weeks she has been unable to buy any. The home is in a destitute state. They are not in receipt of parish relief. The Reverend Mr Morgan occasionally helps them. WC [William Collingham]
Report to Mrs Kennedy, G D Ryder, chairman

19 May 1876
This man applied at the office on Thursday for assistance to enable him to pay off his arrears of rent, namely 6d, also for assistance to get his wife some nuts and oranges. The husband still sells cigar lights on the Old Steine and his wife, who has been ill, is now able to go out if she could get about 5s worth of stock to start with. They receive a little help from charitable persons and nothing is known against them. WC [William Collingham]
Grant of 5s to purchase nuts and oranges, R P Hooper

28 November 1876
The man Sullivan who was sent and recommended by Mr Jones, town missionary, applied at the office for a coat. WC [William Collingham]
Ineligible, R P Hooper

30 April 1877
Mrs Sullivan, who has been ill nearly all the winter, requests the society to give her 5s worth of stock that she may earn a little by selling nuts and oranges. WC [William Collingham]
Referred to parish, R P Hooper

15 November 1878
Sullivan, who now resides at 34 Derby Place, still stands on the Old Steine. His wife is suffering from asthma. Their son earns a trifle by selling roasted chestnuts. WC [William Collingham]
To be reported to Mr Robertson

25 June 1879
Sullivan, who was sent by Dr Millard, applied at the office on Tuesday for some assistance. He still stands on the Old Steine. His wife is in delicate health. Their son sells flowers. WC [William Collingham]
Ineligible, report to Dr Millard, R P Hooper

Letter from Mrs Douglas Fox, 1 Chesham Place, Brighton, 13 September [1883]
Mrs Douglas Fox would be obliged by being informed if Thomas Sullivan, a blind man living at 81 Egremont Street, is a deserving fellow.

14 September 1883
Mrs Douglas Fox requests a report of this case. Sullivan now resides at 82 Egremont Street and still sells cigar lights. He lost his wife in March last and since then his son has not lived with him. He has clothes in pawn for 1s 4d and appears to have a hard struggle to keep out of the workhouse. WC [William Collingham]
Report to Mrs D Fox, Thomas W Holland

Letter from Thomas Sullivan to Viscountess Canterbury, 8 December 1883
Dear Lady, I hope you will forgive me for sending to you but I am so bad off that that I do not know what to do for the weather has been so bad that I can not go on the Steine and my health is so bad through a bad cold. Dear Lady would you kindly send me a trifle. I should be very thankful to you and I [sic] coal ticket for I have no fire in my little room and I find it very cold indeed. I beg to remain your sincere servant, Tom Sullivan

Letter from Thomas Sullivan to Viscountess Canterbury, [June 1884]
Would you ladyship kindly help me. I am a poor blind man and lately lost my wife and through that I have got into arrears with my rent and do not know what to do to pay it. If your ladyship would help me I would be most thankful. I am your humble servant Tom Sullivan

Letter from Viscountess Canterbury, Highland, Prestonville, Brighton, 6 June [1884]
Viscountess Canterbury presents her compliments to Colonel Barlow and will be much obliged if he will kindly inform her if Tom Sullivan who has written and brought the enclosed letters is deserving of charity.

Letter from C A Parker, Grosvenor House, 22 Bread Street, Brighton, [June 1884]
I have known Thomas Sullivan 8 or 9 years and believe it to be a great charity to help him. He is always thankful for what is given to him and never encroaches on anyone's good nature. I believe the poor man to be in a very distressed state at the present time. C A Parker

7 June 1884
Viscountess Canterbury of Highlands, Prestonville, requests a report of this case. Sullivan who is very near-sighted but not blind still stands on the Old Steine appears poor and would be far better off in the parish infirmary.
WC [William Collingham] Report to Lady Canterbury, R P Hooper

Letter from Miss Holland, 11 Vernon Terrace, Brighton, 21 October [1884]
Miss Holland presents her compliments to the secretary of the Charity Organisation Society and would be much obliged for some information

concerning a blind man named Sullivan residing at 81 Egremont Street who has applied to her and whom she will be happy to relieve if a proper subject for charity.

22 October 1884
Miss Holland of 11 Vernon Terrace requests a report of this case. Sullivan still stands on the Old Steine and seems very poor. WC [William Collingham]
Report to Miss Holland, H Dering

12 December 1885
Mrs Winans of 1 Chichester Terrace forwarded the annexed begging letter to the office on Friday and requests a report of the case. Sullivan who now resides at 5 Egremont Street still stands on the Old Steine and a few coals would be well bestowed. WC [William Collingham]
Report to Mrs Winnans, R P Hooper

8 January 1886
Sullivan was sent by Mr Lindsay Cox of 6 Lansdowne Mansions and applied at the office on Thursday for 5s to enable him to pay off two weeks arrears of rent. He still stands on the Old Steine and appears poor. WC [William Collingham]
Ineligible, R P Hooper

23 July 1886
Mrs Tindal Robertson of 9 Belgrave Terrace requests a report of this case. Sullivan now resides in a tramps' lodging house at 82 Egremont Street where he owes 6s for rent and still stands on the Old Steine with cigar lights. WC [William Collingham]
Report to Mrs Tindal Robertson, R P Hooper

147 ELIZABETH WELLS, 66, 22 MEETING HOUSE LANE, BRIGHTON

Elizabeth Wells was born in Brighton in about 1807. The census of 1861 enumerates a 53-year-old woman of this name at 26e Meeting House Lane living with her husband, George Wells, a cooper; four adult offspring; a grandson and a visitor named William Stevens. By 1871 the family had moved to 22 Meeting House Lane.

When she applied to the Mendicity Society in April 1872 Wells was widowed. She had been living at 22 Meeting House Lane for six years, had no income but paid no rent at the property. Mr Casselden, bootmaker, of 7 Church Street and the Reverend Hammond acted as her referees.[577]

[577] Reverend R Hammond was a curate at St Paul's, West Street, Brighton.

19 April 1872
Statement: Elizabeth Wells would be thankful for a little assistance.
Report: I made enquiries respecting this woman and find she lives with a married daughter. She minds the children while the daughter goes out washing. The daughter's husband is a sailor, he allows his wife 10s a week. They have three children. The Reverend Mr Hammond, 23 Russell Square, has relieved her on two or three occasions. Mr Casselden, 7 Church Street, gave her a good character. She is known to the parish authorities having received relief a long time during illness until she got better when they gave her an order for the [work]house which she refused. The home is in a passable state.
Ineligible, R P Hooper

148 EMMA ELLYATT (ALSO GIVEN AS EMMA ELLIOTT), 50, WIFE OF A HANDCHAIR MAN, 69 ALBION STREET, BRIGHTON

Emma Charles Ellyatt (née Mackenzie) was born in London in about 1822 but, according to her Mendicity Society application form, had been living in Brighton for 44 years. She married Thomas Ellyatt a carpenter of 50 Albion Street at St Nicholas, Brighton, on 23 February 1852.[578] *The entry on the marriage register described Emma Mackenzie as a spinster of Terminus Road, Brighton, daughter of a tea dealer. Thomas Ellyatt was baptised at St Nicholas, Brighton, on 7 September 1828 and, on the census of 1841, was enumerated at Albion Street where he lived with his parents, Thomas and Betsy Ellyatt and his five siblings.*[579]

In 1861 the couple were enumerated at 61 Albion Street but by the time of their application for relief in April 1872 they had been living at 69 Albion Street for three years and previously at 68 Albion Street. Their 10-year-old son Charles attended school at Richmond Buildings. They paid weekly rent of 4s 6d for the entire house and were 15 shillings in arrears partly due to a shortage of work: Thomas Ellyatt could usually expect to make 15 shillings per week but was earning only 12 shillings per week presently and his was the only source of income. References were supplied by Mr Greaves of 10 Ashton Street and the Reverend Cook.[580]

Emma Charles Ellyatt's death was recorded in the December quarter of 1876.[581] *In 1881 Thomas Ellyat was enumerated at 59 Albion Street with his son Alexander and a man, probably a brother or cousin, named Henry Ellyatt and his family. All three men earned their living as handchair men. A handchair man called Thomas Elliott, whose age and status matches Thomas Ellyatt, was enumerated boarding at 50 New England Street on the census of 1891.*

578 ESRO: PAR 255/1/3/23.
579 ESRO: PAR 255/1/2/6.
580 Possibly the Reverend Thomas Cooke, perpetual curate of St Peter, Brighton.
581 Death of Emma Ellyatt registered Q4 1876 Brighton 2b 118.

Alexander Ellyatt, described as a bath chairman, was charged with stealing a pair of hair cutting machines from a barber's shop run by G F King of 30 Russell Street in August 1901, but was fined only five shillings in recognition of his otherwise good character.[582]

20 April 1872
Statement: Emma Ellyatt wants 5s to enable her to get a hawker's licence.
Report: I made enquiries respecting this case and find that man sells coffee and cakes the first thing in the morning and in the day goes out with a hand chair. I have known him a long time and believe him to be a respectable man but do not think it a case for this society. The home is in a passable state. The wife states she wants to sell cigar lights and pins and needles and shirt buttons.
Ineligible, John Deverell
Letter from the Reverend Thomas Cooke, 20 April 1872
The Reverend Thomas Cooke recommends Mrs Elliott, 69 Albion Street, as worthy of assistance in her effort to obtain a hawker's licence. Witness my hand this 20th day of April 1872, Thomas Cooke

16 January 1884
Ellyatt, now of 59 Albion Street, applied at the office on Tuesday for relief from the Jubilee and Accident fund. Three weeks ago last Friday evening he stumbled over a door mat which was laying on the pavement in Cheapside and broke his left arm for which he is an out-patient at the hospital. He lost his wife seven years ago. His son is in the army. Applicant is very infirm for his age and appears poor. WC [William Collingham]
Grant of 5s per week for three weeks, R P Hooper

5 February 1884
Ellyatt applied at the office on Tuesday for some further assistance. His arm is getting better but he is not likely to be able to work for another two or three weeks. WC [William Collingham]
Grant of 5s per week for three weeks, R P Hooper

19 February 1887
Ellyatt was sent and recommended by Mr S R Simonds of 43 Park Crescent and applied at the office this morning for assistance till he can earn more money. He still draws a hand-chair but has earned very little lately and appears to be doing his best to keep out of the workhouse. WC [William Collingham]
Ineligible, R P Hooper

582 Brighton Gazette, 17 August 1901.

149 JANE RICHARDS, 22, CHARWOMAN, 81 CARLTON HILL, BRIGHTON

Jane Richards, whose maiden name is not known, was born in Brighton in about 1850: the date of her marriage to George Richards, a tailor from Colyton, Devon is also unknown. The couple were enumerated on the census of 1871 as lodgers at 66 Lewes Road.

When Jane Richards applied to the Mendicity Society in April 1872 her husband, a tailor working at Preston Barracks, had been out of work for six weeks due to sickness. He would usually expect to earn 22 shillings per week but since his illness they had to live on the eight shillings per week Jane Richards earned from charring. By April 1872 the couple had a one-year-old daughter called Alice and they shared one room with her at 81 Carlton Hill. They paid weekly rent of 1s 6d and were not in arrears. The Reverend John Davies Trigge, curate of St Nicholas, Brighton, provided a reference.

20 April 1872
Statement: Jane Richards would be thankful for a little assistance.
Report: I made enquiries respecting this case and find the man did work at the barracks. About six weeks ago he went out of his mind and is now in the workhouse. The wife goes to laundry work or charring. From enquiries made I find she bears a good character. The home is in a passable state. I have not seen the Reverend Mr Trigg[e]. I am informed he is living at Horsham.
Ineligible, John Deverell, chairman

150 MARY MITCHELL, 38, WIFE OF A LABOURER, 90 SPA STREET, BRIGHTON

Mary Davey of 49 King Street married Stephen Mitchell, a labourer of 120 Woburn Place, at St Nicholas, Brighton, on 11 July 1858.[583] *Stephen Mitchell was recorded as a widower. He was born in Woodmancote in about 1824, and in 1851 was enumerated at 8 Nottingham Street, Brighton, with his first wife, Sarah and their young children. The date of Sarah Mitchell's death is unknown: four women called Sarah Mitchell or Sarah Ann Mitchell died in Brighton between 1854 and 1857.*

The 1861 census enumerates Mary Mitchell, who was born in Cuckfield in about 1835, and her husband at 2 Circus Grove where they lived with five children: presumably the offspring of both Sarah Mitchell and Mary Mitchell.

When Mary Mitchell applied to the Mendicity Society in April 1872 the couple had eight children. They had been living at 90 Spa Street for five weeks and were previously resident at 62 John Street. They paid weekly rent of 3s 6d for the entire house and were not in arrears. Stephen Mitchell was employed as a labourer by Mr Stringer at Portslade brick works where he usually earned 18 shillings per week when in full employment but

[583] ESRO: PAR 255/1/3/31.

recently he had been earning only 16 shillings per week. Mr Hart the scripture reader provided a character reference.

22 April 1872
Statement: Mary Mitchell would be thankful if the committee would assist her in getting some clothes to send her two eldest daughters to service in [sic].
Report: I made enquiries respecting this case and find this man works in the brick fields at Portslade. From enquiries made I find he bears a good character. The wife used to make paper bags and the two oldest girls sell them but this year no one under the age of seventeen can have a licence. The wife states she would send them to service if she could get clothes for them to wear. The home is in a passable state. They are known to the parish authorities. Mr Hart the scripture reader has relieved them on several occasions.
Referred for further enquiries to be made, John Deverell, chairman

I have seen the Reverend Mr D Smith. He states if the committee will assist him he will attend to the case.
Relieved with grant of 5s, R P Hooper, chairman

151 CHARLES POWELL, 37, SHOEMAKER, 10 NELSON PLACE, BRIGHTON

On his application form to the Mendicity Society Charles Powell stated that he was born in Portsmouth in about 1835, but he gave Lymington, Hampshire, as his place of birth on the 1871 census. In 1871 he was enumerated at 28 Nelson Row with his wife Charlotte, a dressmaker born in Brighton in 1837, and three children. However, the application form, which was produced only a year after the census, states that Powell was a widower, who lived in two rooms at 10 Nelson Place with a 35-year-old single woman named Charlotte and six children. The report produced by William Collingham, the Mendicity Society's agent, suggest that Powell was telling the truth to the charity and lying about his marital status to the census enumerator. The statement also suggests that Powell was considering marriage to Charlotte but no record of the wedding could be found in Brighton parish registers.

Powell's application form states that they had been resident at Nelson Place for five weeks and had previously rented lodgings at 11 Riding School Lane. The family paid rent of three shillings per week and they were a week in arrears. When in full employment Powell earned 15 shillings per week but had recently been earning only nine shillings per week.

Letter from Margaret E Johnstone, 25 Bloomsbury Place, Brighton, 18 April 1872
Sir, I shall be obliged if you will make enquiry as to the circumstances of a shoemaker of the name of Powell who with his wife and four (?) children lodges

in an upper room at No 10 Nelson Place, district of St Peter's. I wish to know if they are worthy objects of charity. I am told they have had illness and been nearly starved through the winter and up to the present time. Mr Douglas Fox referred me to you for correct information as to this case.[584] I am yours faithfully, Margaret E Johnstone

22 April 1872
Statement: Charles Powell would be thankful for a little assistance to help him get a few small tools.
Report: I made enquiries respecting this case and find this man was ill a long time in the winter and during that time he received parish relief but having a large family he was obliged to sell several of his things to the Reverend Mr Meeres who thinks this is not a case for this society. Mrs Johnstone states the reason she wanted enquiries made was a friend of hers had relieved them on several occasions. He states the tools he wants would cost about 7s 6d.
Undeserving but the society strongly recommends the man to marry the woman he is living with and as he expresses himself willing to be married the case is referred to the Reverend Mr Meeres. John Deverell, chairman

152 MARY MAW, 57, WIFE OF A RAILWAY COMPANY ENGINE DRIVER, 27 BOSTON STREET, BRIGHTON

Mary Maw was born in Brocklesby, Lincolnshire, in about 1816 and, according to her application to the Mendicity Society, arrived in Brighton in about 1856.[585] *Her husband George Maw was born in Whitburn, Durham, in about 1816 and was employed as a locomotive engine driver. They appear to have moved south via Stockton-on-Tees, where their son Thomas was born in about 1843, and Derbyshire, where their fourteen-year-old daughter was born. In 1861 the Maws were enumerated at 3 Peel Place, Brighton, and they remained at that address until a week before their application to the Mendicity Society in April 1872.*

George and Mary Maw's case was forwarded to the Mendicity Society by Mrs Cox of 15 London Road. The couple had been living in one room at 27 Boston Street for a week for which they paid two shillings per week rent; they were given 8s 9d every week by the parish and were up to date with rent payments. George Maw still described himself as an engine driver but, due to an unspecified illness, had been unable to work for eight years.

[584] Douglas Fox (1796-1885) was born in Derby and came to Brighton in 1858. He was a philanthropist involved with the Royal Sussex County Hospital, blind asylum, eye hospital and town mission (Brighton Gazette, 7 October 1885).

[585] Mary Maw gave her place of birth as Brocklesby on the 1871 census but stated Brockhurst as her place of birth on the application form. There are several small hamlets with this name at various location throughout the country.

George Maw was enumerated at Brighton Workhouse on the 1881 census where he was recorded as a lunatic. His death was registered in the March quarter of 1882.[586] *Mary Maw was also resident at Brighton Workhouse in 1881 and her death was registered at Brighton in the September quarter of 1884.*[587]

24 April 1872
Statement: Mary Maw would be thankful for a little assistance as the relief the parish allows is not enough to keep them.
Report: I made enquiries respecting this case and find this man did work for the railway company but he has not been able to work for this last eight years. The wife is not able to earn anything. They receive parish relief at the rate of 8s 9d per week. The home is in a passable state. The Reverend Mr Coombe, 42 Clifton Road, states he has relieved them on one or two occasions.[588] Miss Cox, 15 London Road, has relieved them on seven occasions and believes them to be deserving of a little temporary relief at present on account of them being obliged to have a cab to remove from one house to the other.
Relieved with grant of 3s in consideration of removal and good character from parish authorities. R P Hooper, chairman

153 MRS [FANNY FOSTER] CARY, [52], 173 LEWES ROAD, BRIGHTON

The case of Thomas and Fanny Cary was brought to the attention of the Mendicity Society by the Reverend John Hannah, Vicar of Brighton. Hannah had received one letter and had another letter from the same author forwarded on to him; his suspicions were aroused when the two stories did not tally.

Fanny Foster Cary (née Didham) was the daughter of Richard and Maria Didham; she was baptised in Hambledon, Hampshire, on 19 November 1820.[589] *She married Thomas Cary, who was born in Fernhurst in 1813, at St Margaret's church, Fernhurst, on 28 June 1843.*[590] *Cary's father, the Reverend John Henry Spelman Cary, performed the ceremony. Although they were married in West Sussex the couple appear to have been resident near Kings Lynn; the report published in the Norfolk Chronicle described Fanny Didham as the daughter of R G Didham esq, Royal Navy, of Portsdown [Hampshire]: Thomas Cary's address was given as Eau Brink Hall near Kings Lynn, Norfolk.*[591]

Thomas, Fanny and their three children were enumerated at 33 Parsons Mead, Croydon, on the 1851 census, when they were visiting Fanny Bannister, a widow and law stationer working in London. All three children were recorded as having been born in Kings Lynn.

586 Death of George Maw registered Q1 1882 Brighton 2b 191.
587 Death of Mary Maw registered Q3 1884 Brighton 2b 140.
588 The Reverend Thomas Coombe, vicar of All Saints Church, Brighton.
589 Ancestry.com England, select births and christenings 1538-1975.
590 Ancestry.com England, select marriages 1538-1973.
591 Norfolk Chronicle, 9 July 1843.

They appear to have stayed at Eau Brink Hall until early 1854 when an advertisement for the letting of the property appeared in the Norfolk Chronicle in March of that year.[592] *The house, which was situated about four miles to the south west of Kings Lynn, was described as 'late in the occupation of Thomas Cary esq' and had five bedrooms, a water closet and 'every convenience for a family of respectability' and was available at £30 rent per year.*

In 1861 they were enumerated at 1 Kelso Villas, Folkestone, Kent. Fanny Cary's father, Richard Green Didham, also lived in Folkestone, but he had died the previous year and had been buried at Christ Church, Folkestone, on 19 November 1860.[593] *Didham had a distinguished career as a paymaster and purser in the Royal Navy: he served on HMS Sheldrake when it sank the French frigate Salamander in 1806 and was appointed paymaster to HMS Bellerophon in 1847.*[594] *Despite his respectable career Didham left effects of less than £100.*[595]

In 1871 Thomas and Fanny Cary were enumerated at 173 Lewes Road, where they lived with their daughters Fanny and Mary, who were born in Kings Lynn and Emsworth respectively, suggesting that they moved to Hampshire between leaving Norfolk and arriving at Folkestone. Thomas Cary described himself as an annuitant and it is possible that he received income from the will of his father, the Reverend John Henry Spelman, who died in February 1852, leaving a contested will that appears to have been settled on 1 November 1864.[596] *Fanny Cary's letter of 20 April 1872 to the Reverend John Hannah suggests that they were temporarily poverty stricken because of this or another Chancery case depriving them of income. Her letter of 7 March 1872 requests funds from an unknown recipient, possibly the Marquis of Bute, suggesting that her father lived near his estate at Portsdown, Hampshire.* [597]

When they were approached by the Brighton Mendicity Society, Fanny Cary refused to answer any questions about her circumstances. It is unclear when Fanny and Thomas Cary left Brighton but both were buried in Congresbury, Somerset: Fanny on 9 March 1876, aged 54 and Thomas on 22 December 1877 aged 64.[598]

Letter from F F Cary, 173 Lewes Road, Brighton, 7 March [1872]

Sir, I hope you will take no offence in my asking you for a little assistance for a lady who is in great distress. I don't know whether I can bring to your memory a Mr Didham who lived at Portsdown Cottage many years ago near your estate. This appeal is for one of his daughters – seeing your name in a Brighton newspaper and, knowing your well-known generosity, I wrote this application.

592 Norfolk Chronicle, 4 March 1854.
593 Ancestry.com England, select burials 1538-1991.
594 London Evening Standard, 24 September 1847.
595 England and Wales National Probate Calendar (index of wills and administrations).
596 Norwich Mercury, 13 August 1864.
597 The Marquis of Bute is referred to by D G Dodd, chief clerk of the Mendicity Society London in his letter of 6 May 1872.
598 Somerset Heritage Service: Somerset parish records, 1538-1914: D\P\con/2/1/7.

Any small sum would be most gratefully received. I am sir yours faithfully, F F Cary

Letter [to the Reverend John Hannah] from Fanny Foster Cary, 173 Lewes Road, Brighton, 20 April [1872]
Reverend Sir, I feel I am taking a great liberty in writing to you especially as I can take no claim on you except as a parishioner. I am a lady daughter of a deceased naval officer and from an unfortunate law suit reduced to temporary distress. I am compelled to raise a sum for an especial bill which if not settled we then lose even our home. To avoid this I am compelled to ask for a little assistance. My husband is the son of the late Reverend J Spelman Cary, 57 years incumbent of Fernhurst, Sussex, and whose son-in-law still holds it. My husband is in bad health, I have two daughters and two sons. My father's friend, Lord Egmont of Cowdray has forwarded me a small sum who knew the case, also the Duchess of Norfolk [sic]. If kind strangers will still help me I shall feel very grateful as we are unknown here though we have been resident here for two years. My husband is a regular attender of the Reverend E Cley's.[599] Trusting you will be able to give me a little assistance and hoping you will pardon the liberty I have taken. I am reverend sir, yours faithfully, F F Cary

Note from the Reverend John Hannah, St Nicholas vicarage, 23 April [1872]
Mr Collingham, will you find out what you can about the writer of this latter. Another letter has been just forwarded to me from another quarter in which she rests her appeal on quite a different ground, Hannah

24 April 1872
Statement: I want nothing to do with your society. What I want is £500.
Report: I made enquiries respecting this case and find this man has got about £200 a year coming in and that the wife is expecting a large sum of money that was left for her when her mother died, something like £1,800. I saw the man – there is nothing the matter with him. Dr Hannah states in one letter the wife stated he was ill and wanted nourishment. The Reverend Mr North received a letter from a French gentleman in Sussex Square that they wrote to asking for a few pounds. I am informed they are very much in debt at several different places.
Case to be reported to Dr Hannah. Writer of letter to be warned by our agent, R P Hooper, chairman. Ordered to be cautioned, a record to me by agent,
R P Hooper

[599] This is difficult to read and may be E Cleg or a misspelling of E Clay but no Brighton clergyman of these names could be found in *Crockford's Clerical Directory, 1874*.

Letter to F Beal, Brighton Mendicity Society, from D G Dodd, chief clerk of the Mendicity Society London, 13 Red Lion Square, London, 6 May 1872
Two enclosures please return to me. Confidential re Moore and Cary. Sir, I hope that I shall not be taxing you too heavily in asking your help in the investigation of the two enclosed cases: they appear to be of a class asking for more delicacy than we could expect from the police. Hitherto neither appears to have [been] known to us. As you may suppose the Marquis of Bute's marriage has stirred up a good many people to write to him for charity but it will be advisable not to mention his name in the course of the enquiries. With thanks for your forever efficient help. I am sir yours, obliged and obediently, D G Dodd, chief clerk
Answered 9 May 1872, giving an account of Mr Cary's case No 153. Moore's case answered 12 May

154 ELIZA CLARK, 40, WASHERWOMAN, 32 SOUTHAMPTON STREET, BRIGHTON

Eliza Clark (née Wilkins) was born in Brighton in about 1832. She married George Clarke (whose name was given as both Clark and Clarke in various documents but will be referred to as Clark throughout) at St Nicholas, Brighton, on 26 February 1855.[600] George Clark, a bricklayer, was baptised at St Nicholas, Brighton, on 24 May 1835 and lived at 53 Albion Street with Eliza Wilkins at the time of their wedding.[601] In 1861 the couple were enumerated at 90 Woburn Place, where they lived with their two young sons Edward and George.

In July 1865 a 30-year-old man named George Clark was charged with being drunk and disorderly at the Elm Grove Tavern.[602] He had been drinking with Benjamin Tomsett, who had been taken into custody: when Clark realised that his companion had been taken to the Town Hall he walked to the building and threatened to pull the place down if Tomsett was not released. Clark was fined 5d.

On 27 February 1866 George Clark was charged with creating a disturbance in St James's Street but was considered to be insane and removed to the infirmary of Brighton Workhouse.[603] Clark was held at the workhouse for two days and after examination was committed to the Sussex County Lunatic Asylum where he was admitted on 1 March 1866 in a manic state.[604] Clark's admission papers state that he was living at 60 Cavendish Street with Eliza and had become unwell about five days previously. The cause of his insanity was given as an injury to his head sustained during a fall nine years previously. He stated that he was the 'holy son of the saviour' and that 'Miss Nightingale', presumably

600 ESRO: PAR 255/1/3/27.
601 ESRO: PAR 255/1/2/9.
602 Brighton Guardian, 26 July 1865.
603 Brighton Gazette, 1 March 1866.
604 ESRO: HC 24/1061.

a reference to Florence Nightingale, was his friend. The admission papers went on to state that he was very violent but also 'dances, swears, sings and cries out murder.' On 13 March Clark's place of settlement was adjudicated as Alverstoke, Hampshire, by Brighton magistrates and on 17 March relieving officers issued an order for Clark's removal to Alverstoke from where he was to be transferred to Knowle Asylum, Fareham, Hampshire.

George Clark was next admitted to the Sussex County Lunatic Asylum on 22 December 1868 whilst in a state of recurrent mania.[605] *He was living at 15 Claremont Row and had been unwell for about a week. As with all subsequent instances he was transferred from Brighton Workhouse and the examining medical officer, David Richards, stated that Clark referred to himself as the 'tumbler pigeon and is always singing, jumping, whistling, swearing or making a noise.' He was deemed to be sufficiently recovered to be released on 4 August 1869.*

Clark kept out of the asylum until 31 August 1870 when he and Eliza were living at 7 Nelson Place.[606] *He was violent, talkative and thought that both his father and sons were being treated at the asylum. He was discharged on 27 June 1871. While George Clark was being treated at Sussex County Lunatic Asylum, Eliza Clark, who was working as a washerwoman, and her children were enumerated at 41 Quebec Street where they lived with Sarah Wall.*

Eliza Clark applied to the Mendicity Society on 25 April 1872 when the family were living at 32 Southampton Street. George Clark was working as a labourer for Mr Sattin of 12 North Square and earning 15 shillings per week. Eliza Clark would usually earn five shillings per week as a washerwoman but had been sick and off work for a month. The family occupied three rooms and paid 3s 6d per week rent but were nine shillings in arrears. The Clarks' case was forwarded to the charity by Mrs Hart of 24 Grand Parade.

George Clark was re-admitted to the Sussex County Lunatic Asylum with recurrent mania on 18 February 1873.[607] *His previous place of abode was 32 Toronto Terrace but Eliza Clark was resident at Brighton Workhouse and he was admitted from the workhouse infirmary. When assesed by David Richards, the workhouse surgeon, Clark stated that he was a 'soldier to God Almighty and being so must obey orders.' He stood on his head, was sleepless, was always talking, praying, singing or making a noise. He was discharged on 31 October 1873 but was readmitted on 4 September 1874 presenting similar symptoms.*[608] *The asylum's admission papers contain an undated letter from George Clark, 'Doctor Williams sir I wish to tell that I am quite well. I have got work and I thought that you would not mind paying my wife as I only be gone to work where I am last Monday and it would look bad to leave so soon. I was very thankful of the money for it was a little Godsend. I am your humble G Clark.' During this period of George Clark's treatment Eliza Clark applied to the Charity Organisation Society on 21 December 1874 when she was living at 21 Claremont Row but her appeal was dismissed as undeserving.*

[605] ESRO: HC 24/1531.
[606] ESRO: HC 24/1783.
[607] ESRO: HC 24/2212.
[608] ESRO: HC 24/2536.

George Clark was was discharged on 26 May 1876 but he appeared before the Brighton Police Court on 11 June 1877 charged with being a lunatic not under proper control.[609] *The press report stated that although he was already an excellent bricklayer he had learnt the trade of shoemaker whilst confined in asylums. He was transported to Brighton Workhouse infirmary.*

By the time of George Clark's next admission to the Sussex County Lunatic Asylum on 10 July 1878, Eliza Clark was living back at 32 Southampton Street where she had been resident in April 1872.[610] *Clark's condition appears to have worsened: he was 'always talking incoherently in a most violent and disgusting manner – [he] exposes his person to children, is sleepless and requires constant watching.' Despite the seriousness of his condition he was considered recovered and discharged on 27 December 1878.*

Clark stayed out of the asylum for five years and in 1881 was enumerated at 24 St Mary Magdelene Street where he shared the house with his wife and three sons aged 12, 16 and 22. He was admitted to the asylum for the seventh time on 22 December 1883 in a 'wild and excited state'.[611] *Again, he was described as incoherent and a danger to others and he remained there until 28 June 1884. Shortly after his discharge he broke his wife's arm during a tussle and it was when she was rendered incapacitated as a result of the attack that she next applied, unsuccesfully, to the Charity Organisation Society on 30 June 1884.*[612]

George Clark was admitted to the Sussex County Lunatic Asylum for an eighth and final time on 24 April 1886 displaying his usual symptoms of restlessness, aggresion and incoherence.[613] *He remained under the asylum's care until 3 October 1886 when he returned to his wife, who was living at 2 Whichelo Place.*

The death of a 64-year-old man named George Clark was registered in Brighton in the December quarter of 1897.[614] *In 1901 Eliza Clark was enumerated at 32 Southampton Street which appears to have been the home of her employer Mrs Longley: it was an address she had been returning to since at least April 1872. According to the statement she made in her final application to the charity in 1906, Eliza Clark outlived all but one of her 15 children. Her death, at the age of 77, was recorded at Brighton in the September quarter of 1907.*[615]

25 April 1872
Statement: Eliza Clark would be thankful for a little assistance.

609 Brighton Guardian, 13 June 1877.

610 ESRO: HC 24/3410.

611 ESRO: HC 24/4579.

612 Clark appears not to have been charged with assault as no reference to a hearing in the Police Court could be found in the local press during early July 1884.

613 ESRO: HC 24/5071.

614 Death of George Clark registered Q4 1897 Brighton 2b 151.

615 Death of Eliza Clark registered Q3 1907 Brighton 2b 106.

Report: I made enquiries respecting this case and find this man was out of work some time ago but for some time him and the oldest son has been working for Mr Sattin. Their wages is £1 18s per week. I have known this man a long time, he is of intemperate habits. He has been in Haywards Heath asylum on three different occasions. The home is in a destitute state. They are not known to Mrs Hart. They are well known to the parish authorities. Mr Seleger, 8 Hampden Road, the scripture reader states he has relieved them on two or three occasions.[616]
Dismissed, undeserving

Letter from M Soane, North House, [19 Gloucester Place], Brighton, 21 December [1874]
Mrs Soane will be much obliged if you will attend to this case which appears a deserving one. Her husband is in Haywards Heath asylum. M Soane

21 December 1874
Mrs Clark applied to Mrs Soane of North House on Monday for assistance when Mrs Soane relieved her and gave her a note to bring to the office thinking that if deserving the society would do something for her. Mrs Soane requests a report of the case. On enquiry I find that the husband, who is of very intemperate habits, has been in Haywards Heath asylum for the last four months. The wife, who is also very much given to drink, worked sometime for Mrs Key, laundress of 14 Toronto Terrace. Her wages were 10s a week but she was discharged last week for being insolent. The eldest son who works for Mr Newnham, builder, earns 7s per week. The boy William who works for Mr Holloway, wood merchant, can earn 6s per week when he choses but he often absents himself. The son Thomas is dead. When they please to be industrious the family, consisting of the woman and five children, can support themselves respectably. The Guardians offered the woman an order for the [work]house five weeks ago and a fortnight ago gave two of the children boots. WC [William Collingham]
Undeserving, R P Hooper

30 June 1884
Mrs Clark applied at the office on Saturday for relief from the Jubilee and Accident Fund. Her husband was discharged from Haywards Heath asylum a month ago last Wednesday and three weeks ago last Saturday when they were having a tussle he broke her right arm for which she is an out-patient at the hospital and will not be able to work at the laundry again for several weeks. Her husband has had no employment since he came home. They still bear indifferent

616 William Collingham, the charity's agent, has clearly written the name Seleger but no-one of this name appears in any indexes or contemporary street directories.

characters, have no children dependent on them and seem very poor. WC [William Collingham]
Undeserving, F Y Toms R[oyal] N[avy]

25 January 1906
I visited 40 Laurel Row and saw applicant and her sister and noticed that they were very clean and tidy and had a very comfortable home. The applicant informed me that she had a lot of trouble – her late husband had been in the asylum several times and that she had 15 children all dead but one also that she had six sons in the army now all dead. The previous reports show that she was formerly addicted to drink. I saw Miss Longley, 31 Southampton Street [sic], and she informed me that the applicant was a very respectable old woman who had had a lot of trouble with her family, also that she had worked for the Longleys for over 30 years at laundry work and she thought her very deserving. I also saw the relieving officer who states that the applicant is a respectable woman and that she receives the pay as stated in her application, also that she has received parish pay [for] several years during the winter but takes herself off during the summer months when she assists on the beach with the bathing machines.
William Fox

Letter from H[ilda] Woodhead, honorary secretary of the Howard Charity, 26 January 1906
Re: Clark, w[oman] aged 72 (our number 134). Dear Madam, we do not think this woman is in need of any further help. She lives with a sister who gives her a room rent free and also part of her food. We think that any further help would probably benefit the sister rather than the applicant. Yours truly H Woodhead
Report not requiring relief, NVC.[617] Letter to HC

155 ELLEN MOORE, 17, SERVANT, 10 EDWARD STREET, BRIGHTON

Ellen Moore was born in Wick, near Littlehampton, in about 1855. When her case was sent to the Mendicity Society by the Reverend Aaron Augustus Morgan, vicar of St John's, Carlton Hill, she had been resident in Brighton for only one day, having just arrived from her previous employment at Goring. No details of how much rent she paid are given on the application form. Case notes for Fanny Foster Cary, case 153, contains a letter to F Beal, Brighton Mendicity Society, from D G Dodd, chief clerk of the Mendicity Society London, 13 Red Lion Square, London, 6 May 1872 which carries a passing reference to Ellen Moore.

[617] Signature probably that of Mr N V Combe, who is listed as a vice-chairman of the council in the annual report of 1908.

24 April 1872
Statement: Ellen Moore would be thankful for a little assistance till she can get a situation.
Report: This girl states her mother died when she was quite a child and some time after that her father deserted them and after that she lived with Mrs Carpenter at 6 Albert Terrace, Littlehampton, for 18 months and after that she lived with Mrs Markwick at Goring and the reason she lived there was because she was not old enough. From enquiries made I find she is lodging at 10 Edward Street and that she is expecting a situation at 6 Old Steine – Miss West has wrote for her character and if it's a good one she will be able to get into it in about a week.
Grant of 2s 6d pending further enquiry, R P Hooper, chairman
Miss West states after the character she has received she cannot take her into her service. Referred to clergyman of the district, R P Hooper, chairman

Letter to Miss West, 6 Old Steine, from J Markwick, Goring, 28 April 1872
Madam, in answer to yours respecting Ellen Moore I am much surprised at her referring me to you as she is a very bad girl indeed. Mrs Markwick and family have all tried to make her different. I took her from the East Preston Union (with a bad character) with the idea of giving her a chance of redeeming her last character but it is all of no avail. She is given to telling the most abominable falsehoods and, what is more, fearfull dirty. I would not recommend her to anyone where she would have to appear in any decent society. I intended to have taken her back to the Union again but she left my house early on Tuesday morning before any of the family were about. I remain yours respectfully, J Markwick

Letter to Miss West, 6 Old Steine, from Mrs Carpenter, 10 Albert Terrace, Littlehampton, [April 1872]
Madam, according to your request I write to say that Ellen Moore has left me nearly two years and I know she has lived in several places since. I have not very much to say in her favour but I believe she is honest. I think you had better refer to one of her last situation[s]. I remain yours truly, M Carpenter

Letter to [William] Henty from John Harding, East Preston Union, 7 May 1872
Sir, in reply to your letter I beg to say I know very little of the girl Ellen Moore. Her stay in the workhouse was only 47 days. I believe she lived previous to that with Mrs Carpenter and lately with Mr Markwick of Goring. Mr Markwick called and told me she had left rather suddenly in consequence of him looking out for another servant to take her place. He stated he believed her to be perfectly honest. I should think if she had someone strict over her there is no reason why she should not do in service. I think the poor girl is quite friendless

with the exception of a brother and she is quite young, her age being only 15 [sic]. I am sir, yours respectfully, John Harding

156 MARY BRICKLEY, 60, CHARWOMAN, 3 SUGARS COURT, UPPER BEDFORD STREET, BRIGHTON

Mary Brickley was enumerated at 41 Thomas Street on the census of 1871. She was born in Ireland and stated that she was 38, which does not tally with the 60 years of age she claimed to be when her family's case was sent to the Mendicity Society by George Dudley Ryder, who was vice president of the society, in April 1872. The Brickleys stated on the Mendicity Society's application form that they had been living in Brighton for 25 years but information given on the census return indicates otherwise: their 16-year-old daughter Elizabeth was described as born in Ireland while their 15-year-old son Richard was born in Brighton, suggesting an arrival date of about 1856.

Mary Brickley's husband Richard was also born in Ireland. He stated that he was 38 on the 1871 census and 50-years-old on the Mendicity Society's application form. In June 1863 Richard Brickley appeared before the Brighton Bench as a complainant in a case against Catherine Coleman.[618] *The Brighton Guardian reported that Richard's wife Mary was the real complainant. She and the defendant, both Irish women, lived next door to each other on Eastern Road and a quarrel between them resulted in Coleman breaking windows. She pleaded guilty to breaking two of the panes but the case was examined at great length and the whole family disagreement was raised up for the amusement of the court. After nearly half an hour's discussion the Bench fined the defendant, Catherine Coleman, 6d and ordered her to pay 2s 6d, the value of the windows broken.*[619]

In 1865 Mary Brickley again appeared as a complainant in a case against a neighbour.[620] *Edward Crowley lived next door to the Brickleys on Egremont Street and Mary Brickley claimed that the previous Monday at about 6pm, Edward Crowley had thrown stones into her house through her back door. A boy named William Foley gave evidence and stated that on Tuesday afternoon Crowley, who was about 10 years old, had been throwing stones at him: the stones missed him but entered Brickley's house. The case was dismissed due to the inconsistency in times given.*

The Brickley's case came before the Mendicity Society in April 1872. Richard Brickley was out of work; Mary Brickley was earning three shillings per week charring; Richard Brickley junior had been earning ten shillings per week labouring for Mr Fitzgerald of Richmond Street but had left two weeks earlier, and Elizabeth Brickley had been sorting

[618] In 1873 Catherine Coleman was assaulted by Catherine Brickley. The relationship between Catherine Brickley, who applied to the Mendicity Society on 20 March 1872 (Case number 116), and Mary Brickley is not clear.

[619] Brighton Guardian, 3 June 1863.

[620] Brighton Guardian, 7 June 1865.

rags for Mr Fitzgerald earning nine shillings per week. They paid rent of 2s 2d per week for their house and owed nothing.

When Richard Brickley senior died in June 1873 his age was registered as 54. Mary Brickley died in the September quarter of 1886 but the family's case came before the Charity Organisation Society again in August 1893.[621] *The charity had received information that the couple's daughter Elizabeth Brickley had married a man named Walter Watts, and Richard Brickley junior had spent time in the Sussex County Lunatic Asylum, Haywards Heath.*[622] *He was admitted to the asylum on 26 June 1893 suffering with melancholia and was discharged on 2 February 1894.*[623]

26 April 1872
Statement: Mary Brickley would be thankful for a little assistance.
Report: I made enquiries respecting this case and this man sits about the Marine Parade and no doubt gets a little given him. The wife does a little charring. The daughter works for Mr Fitzgerald, 15 Richmond Street, the son did work there but left on his accord a fortnight ago. The home is in a destitute state. Canon Rymer states he has relieved them on several occasions and believes they are very poor. They are well known to the parish authorities.
Referred to parish authorities, R P Hooper. NB. This case was mentioned before the committee on the 23 January 1873 when a report was sent to Lady Radstock. WC [William Collingham]

Letter from Lady Radstock, 135 Marine Parade, [21 January 1873]
Sir, I should be much obliged if you would be good enough to send me some particulars about a man named Brickley living at 8 Essex Place. Lord Radstock will be glad to give a donation of £1 to the society if you will desire someone to call. Yours truly S C Radstock
Report to be sent to Lady Radstock, R P Hooper

12 March 1874
Mrs Brickley who now lives at 5 Little St James Street, and who was sent by Mrs Odling, 68 Dyke Road, applied at the office on Thursday for assistance. Upon enquiry I find that applicant's husband died last June and since then she has done a little charring and cut up a little cloth for Mr Fitzgerald. Her son now sells roast chestnuts. Mrs Odling who assisted the husband during his illness cannot go on assisting the wife and family. Mr Smith, relieving officer, states that this is not a case where the Guardians would be likely to grant outdoor

[621] Death of Mary Brickley registered Q3 1886 Brighton 2b 133.

[622] Confusingly a man named Walter Watts married a Margaret Brickley at Brighton in the March quarter of 1870. No later marriage to Elizabeth Brickley is obviously recorded.

[623] ESRO: HC 24/6915.

relief. WC [William Collingham]
Referred to parish, R P Hooper, chairman

5 August 1893
Mr W Hackett, relieving officer of Hove, wishes for some particulars respecting this family. The husband died at 5 Little St James Street in June 1873, the widow died at 20 Egremont Street in 1886. The son Richard has had no settled address since then. He has generally wandered about the country gathering ferns and is now in Haywards Heath asylum. The daughter Elizabeth is married to a man named Walter Watts. She is residing at 12 Claremont Row and should any further information be required she would be able to give it. WC [William Collingham]
Report to Mr Hackett, R P Hooper

157 ANN HILLS, 34, WASHERWOMAN, 45 HEREFORD STREET, BRIGHTON

Ann Hills was born in Lingfield, Surrey, in about 1838. At the time of her approach to the Mendicity Society she was living in one room at 45 Hereford Street with her husband Joseph, a 42-year-old labourer. Joseph Hills had been working for a Mr Humphrey of Bedford Street where he would normally earn 16 shillings a week, but due to illness had been off work for a week. Ann Hills usually earned ten shillings a week as a washerwoman but recently had been earning only one shilling per week. Miss Mahon of 8 Dorset Gardens supplied a reference.

26 April 1872
Statement: Ann Hills wants a little assistance till her husband gets better.
Report: I made enquiries respecting this case and find the man did work for Mr Humphrey, Bedford Street. He has been sick this week. He bears anything but a good character, he is of intemperate habits. The wife gets a shilling a week for minding a neighbour's child, she is also given to drink and won't work when she can get it. The home is in a destitute and filthy state. Miss Mahon, the District Visitor, states that she cannot say anything in their favour. They applied to the parish authorities but refused to go in the house.
Ineligible, R P Hooper

158 ELIZA CUMMING (ALSO GIVEN AS CUMMINS), 42, WASHERWOMAN, 9 QUEBEC STREET, BRIGHTON

Eliza Cumming (née Virral), whose name in other documents is usually given as Cummins, was born in Eastbourne in about 1830.[624] *She married William Aldridge, a labourer, at St Mary's, Eastbourne on 24 July 1849.*[625] *William Aldridge died aged 34 and was buried at St Mary's on 29 November 1861.*[626] *Her second marriage, to James Samuel Godden, a widowed labourer living at Meads, Eastbourne, took place at St Mary's on Christmas Day 1862.*[627] *James Godden died three and a half years later, aged 33, and was buried at St Mary's on 10 May 1866.*[628]

When the Cummins's case was forwarded to the Mendicity Society in April 1872 Eliza's husband was given as James Cummins, a labourer from Eastbourne. He was baptised at St Mary's, Eastbourne, on 7 December 1845 and his parents were given as Joseph and Ann Cummins.[629] *The Cummins family were enumerated at 17 York Buildings, Eastbourne, on the 1851 census. No record of a marriage between Eliza Godden and James Cummins could be found in the parish records of St Mary's, Eastbourne, but their names appear as witnesses at the wedding of Henry Cummins, a 21-year-old fisherman, son of Joseph Cummins, and Mary Aldridge, 19, daughter of William Aldridge, deceased, at St Mary's on 8 February 1869.*[630] *This then, is the marriage of James Cummins's brother Joseph to Eliza Godden's daughter.*

When their case was forwarded to the Mendicity Society by Mr Greaves of 10 Ashton Street the Cumminses, who claimed to be married, paid weekly rent of six shillings for their house at 9 Quebec Street, where they had been living for nine months. They had moved to Brighton from Eastbourne in about August 1871.

James Cummins was employed as a labourer by Mr Jennings, a contractor, but had been sick for six months and was earning only 8s 6d per week rather than 20 shillings a week, which was his usual wage when fully employed. Eliza Cummins earned 5s 6d as a washerwoman and her 13-year-old son Samuel earned 7s 6d per week labouring. They also received 8s 6d per week from the parish so had a combined weekly income of 21s 6d.

In 1881 the family were enumerated at 22 Islingword Street: both Joseph and Eliza Cummins were employed in the laundry business and they shared the house with three children and two nephews. The Cummins applied to the Charity Organisation Society for a final time in January 1899. The application forms of this period gave a lot more biographical information than the earlier format and from it we know that they had been living at 16 Islingword Street for seven months. Before that they had been at 83 Whippingham Road for three months; 8a Islingword Street for eight years; 22 Islingword

624 An Eliza Verrall was baptised at St Mary's, Eastbourne, on 10 April 1831 (ESRO: PAR 309/1/2/1).
625 ESRO: PAR 309/1/3/2.
626 ESRO: PAR 309/1/5/2.
627 ESRO: PAR 309/1/3/2.
628 ESRO: PAR 309/1/5/2.
629 ESRO: PAR 309/1/2/2.
630 ESRO: PAR 309/1/3/3.

Street for nine years and 27 Southampton Street for six years. Both James and Eliza Cummins were taking in laundry and usually had a combined income of 40 shillings per week but it had recently been reduced to five shillings a week. They were living with Eliza's son Samuel Aldridge, a 39-year-old labourer whose earnings had dropped to almost nothing; her daughter, Eliza Tutt (née Aldridge), Eliza Cummins's 38-year-old daughter, who was employed by her mother and step-father earning eight shillings per week; John Godden, Eliza's 36-year-old son, who was employed as a missionary and James Cummins, the 29-year-old son of James and Eliza Cummins, who was employed as a labourer at the railway station. The combined household income usually amounted to 53 shillings per week but had dropped to 16 shillings per week. The family paid weekly rent of nine shillings but were 15 shillings in arrears and also had other debts of £3 10s. James Cummins senior is recorded as previously belonging to the Nottingham Unity of Oddfellows between the ages of 18 and 30. Character references were supplied by Mr Townshend Martin of 3 West Hill Road and the Reverend Edmund Phillips of 35 Beaconsfield Villas, vicar of Ann Street Congregational Church.

James Cummins was enumerated at 16 Islingword Street in 1901 aged 58 living with his son James and still working at a laundry. Eliza Cummins had died in the June quarter of 1899[631] and James Cummins died in Brighton in the March quarter of 1904.[632]

27 April 1872

Statement: Eliza Cumming would be thankful if the committee would assist them home to Eastbourne.

Report: I made enquiries respecting this case and find the man did work for Mr Jennings, contractor. He has not been able to work this last six months. He wants to go back to Eastbourne where he states his wife could get plenty of work. I have seen the relieving officer, he states he is about to get them removed home. The wife states if they are removed by the parish authorities they will have to go in the workhouse. This, she states, she does not want to do. Mr Greaves the scripture reader gave them a good character and states he has relieved them on several occasions. The home is in a passable state.

Referred to parish authorities, R P Hooper, chairman

1 October 1875

This family refused to be removed home to Eastbourne in 1872 but stayed here till they were irremovable and then obtained outdoor relief which they received till May last when it was stopped in consequence of their receiving charity from all quarters. On Friday Cummins [sic] who is recommended by Mr Jones, town missionary, applied at the office for assistance to enable him to purchase a secondhand barrow that he may fetch and carry home clothes. Applicant suffers

631 Death of Eliza Cummins registered Q2 1899 Brighton 2b 142.

632 Death of James Cummins registered Q1 1904 Brighton 2b 170.

from heart disease. His wife, who keeps a laundry, employs women and has a wringing machine and mangle in her possession. The man and his wife both state that they are converted; they hold prayer meetings at their house and I have every reason to believe that they receive a great deal of charity.
Ineligible, A H, chairman[633]

4 December 1876
Mrs Cummins applied at the office on Monday for some assistance. Her husband is now ill and unable to work and is attended by the parish doctor. The wife and her daughter still carry on the laundry. The sons Samuel and John are both in work. The Guardians offered the family an order for the house a week ago. WC [William Collingham]
Referred to parish, R P Hooper

Letter from Townshend Martin, 3 West Hill Road, 27 January [1899]
Dear Miss Merrifield, the man Cummings [sic] is well known to me as a very steady, industrious person and one who for a long time suffered from heart disease. My knowledge of him extends over a period of nine years. Money spent in the way spoken of by you will, in my judgement, be wisely placed. I may add that I was not cognizant of his application to your society. The Homewood family in Whichelo Place are again in straitened circumstances and have been helped by me in the form of 2s and two gallons of bread. I am yours faithfully, Townshend Martin

27 January 1899
Statement: about 23 years ago Mrs Hornbuckle bought us a basket and wringing machine and gave us her washing to do. Since then we have maintained ourselves in this way, employing my married [paper damaged] daughter at 2s a day and one other woman at 2s 6d. My wife's son Samuel pays us 10s weekly for [paper damaged] and lodging when he has work. Her other son cannot help us regularly as he has so many poor to care for [paper damaged] and lodging when he has work. My wife has been ill six weeks attended by Dr Scott of the medical club for which we pay each 1d weekly. I have [paper damaged] rheumatic attack since last October and it has been difficult to get the work done, besides the wringer is worn out now and we should get along if we could have the wringer repaired and a new tub.
Report: saw Mr Philips who has known Cummings for seven years as an attendary at services which he conducts and has always had reason to think well of him. Recently, during the man's dangerous illness, he went to see him and

633 The chairman of the Charity Organisation Society in 1875 is not known but the annual report of 1877 records the vice-chairman as the Reverend Alexander Hamilton.

visitors sent by Mr Phillips gave a little money – he thinks 10s in all: that was in the autumn, I understood. Failing to see Mr Martin I sent him a note asking as to character and also as to the likelihood of money being well bestowed on the repair of his wringer etc. Answer annexed. The agent reports that this family have had a great deal of charitable help for many years. They ought to have been able to save. The wringer does want repair as stated and the tub is worn out. The character of the family is good but they have shown no thrift. Perhaps if anything is given it should be as a returnable grant. 18s would suffice.
Ineligible, E A J Drury

159 CHARLES BUTLER, 54, HAWKER, 100 HANOVER TERRACE, BRIGHTON

Charles and Frances Butler were enumerated at 28 Quebec Street, Brighton, on the census of 1871. They shared the house with their 17-year-old son William, who was born in Steyning, a 15-year-old nephew named Henry Day and Francis Cadby a confectioner's assistant who boarded with the family. Charles Butler was born in Brighton in about 1818 and his wife Frances was born in Soberton, Hampshire, in about 1820.

At the time of their approach to the Mendicity Society Charles and Frances Butler were occupying two rooms at 100 Hanover Terrace, where they lived rent free for four months. Charles Butler usually earned nine shillings per week when in full employment but had been ill for seven months and consequently was taking home only 7s 6d per week.

Charles Butler's death was registered in Brighton in the June quarter of 1875.[634] *In 1881 Frances Butler was enumerated lodging at 7 Hanover Street earning her living as a nurse. Her death was recorded in Brighton in the March quarter of 1891.*[635]

29 April 1872
Statement: Charles Butler would be thankful if the committee would assist him to get a little stock.
Report: I made enquiries respecting this case and find this is the man that stands up the Dyke Road with a barrow selling ginger beer and sweets in the summer. He states he has not been able to do anything for this last seven months and during that time the parish allowed him relief at the rate of 7s 6d per week. The wife is not able to do anything. They have a grown up son living with them and a nephew. The son works for Messrs Dutton and Thorowgood, East Street.[636] The home is in a passable state. Mr Thompson, 11 Rose Hill, states he has relieved them on several occasions and believes this to be a very deserving case.
Ineligible, R P Hooper, chairman

634 Death of Charles Butler registered Q2 1875 Brighton 2b 144.
635 Death of Frances Butler registered Q1 1891 Brighton 2b 181.
636 Dutton and Thorowgood, shoe and boot makers, 46-47 East Street, Brighton.

160 MARY MARCHANT, 46, WIFE OF A WATERMAN, 23 BLUCHER PLACE, BRIGHTON

Mary Rosina Marchant (née Redding) was born in Fittleworth in about 1826 and married George Marchant, fisherman, in Brighton in the June quarter of 1860.[637] *Two men named George Marchant applied to the Mendicity Society in the first six months of 1872 but it is not known whether they were directly related.*[638] *George Marchant was baptised at St Nicholas, Brighton, on 7 December 1823.*[639] *In 1861 Mary Marchant, who was then employed as a charwoman, was enumerated at 5 Dorset Street, where she lived with her 11-year-old niece Mary Redding, who was born in Petworth. George Marchant was enumerated at sea as one of the crew of the 'Cheering'.*

In January 1866 a woman named Sarah Harman, 43, was charged with stealing a frock, shirt and other articles, which were the property of George Marchant of 5 Dorset Street.[640] *In November 1865 George and Mary Marchant were made in-patients at the hospital but on their return on 6 December the accused's daughter had been living in the house.*[641] *The prosecutor noticed a gown, a Guernsey jumper, a frock and other articles were missing. Charles Longhurst, a second-hand clothes dealer of Cavendish Street bought the frock from Harman for 1s 6d and the Guernsey for 9d: she stated that they belonged to her husband. PC Reed took Harman, who was known as an old offender, into custody from a lodging house on Derby Place. She pleaded guilty and was committed to three months' hard labour.*

When Mary Marchant approached the Mendicity Society in April 1872 the family had been living at 23 Blucher Place for three years. They paid weekly rent of six shillings and were £3 8s in arrears. George Marchant would usually expect to earn 18 shillings per week when in full employment but had been earning only eight shillings per week recently due to illness. Nothing is known about the six orphan children mentioned in the Mendicity Society agent's report who appeared to be in the care of the Marchants. The couple received a good reference from Mrs Sampson of 26 Upper Russell Street.

29 April 1872

Statement: Mary Marchant would be thankful for a little assistance.

Report: I made enquiries respecting this case and find this man is a waterman. He went to work again last week, before that he was ill a long time. The wife is not able to earn anything on account of having six orphan children whose father fell over the cliff at the bottom of Market Street about two years ago. The two oldest are at work, the other four the parish authorities allow 8s per week. Mrs

[637] Marriage of Mary Rosina Redding to John (sic) Marchant registered Q2 1860 Brighton 2b 325.

[638] The other man named George Marchant was baptised at St Nicholas on 23 September 1821 (PAR 255/1/2/3). He worked as fisherman, married a woman named Mary and applied to the Mendicity Society on 19 January 1872 (case 31).

[639] ESRO: PAR 255/1/2/4.

[640] Brighton Guardian, 24 January 1866.

[641] Admission registers for this period do not survive and neither appears to be mentioned in the series of surgeons' case books (HB 62).

Sampson gave them a good character. The home is in a passable state. I am informed they are both very kind to the children.
Ineligible, R P Hooper, chairman

161 THOMAS SIMON, 25 CUMBERLAND PLACE, BRIGHTON

Thomas Simon's application to the Mendicity Society contained no biographical information other than his address. A man named Thomas Simon was enumerated boarding at 15 Peel Place in 1861. He was 32, born in Bingley, Yorkshire, and was employed as an engine turner. Ten years later he was employed as an engine fitter and living at 33 Blackman Street living with his wife, Sarah. This man seems to have been in steady employment so it seems unlikely that he is the man that made this application.

Letter from Thomas Simon to Henry Herbert, 4 Clarendon Terrace, 26 April 1872
Most honoured sir, I the undersigned humble beg your kind consideration under the following statements. I am a Christian Israelite known to the Reverend Mr Stern, principal of the Jews' Home Mission. I am in want of means in order to carry on a business which certainly would prosper had I a few pounds in hand. Knowing most honoured sir your name is associated with the society for promoting Christianity amongst the Jews I therefore humbly crave for a little assistance for which good act I would feel ever thankfully. With all good blessings I remain most honoured sir your most humble servant, T Simon

29 April 1872
Report: I made enquiries respecting this case and find Mr Herbert, 4 Clarendon Terrace, received this letter on Friday and sent it to the office for investigation. When I called at his lodgings he was out and after that he called on Mr Herbert again who told him his case would be investigated. He said 'thank you sir, good morning' and from enquiries I have made he no doubt left the town. From enquiries I have made no doubt he was a regular begging letter writer. 25 Cumberland Place is a tramps' lodging house.
Case to be entered, R P Hooper, chairman

162 ROBERT SEIFORT, 39, MUSICIAN, 3 LAUREL ROW, BRIGHTON

Robert Seifort, his wife Eva and infant daughter Mary were enumerated at 12 Somerset Street, Bath, on the census of 1861. By 1871 they had moved to Brighton and were recorded at 3 Laurel Row on the census of that year. Robert Seifort was born in Lodzen, Germany, in about 1832, and Eva Seifort was born in Hessen, Germany, in about 1838. It is not known when they arrived in England but their children were born in Bath in 1860, London in 1862 and Brighton in 1864 and 1870.

The Seifort family's case was brought to the attention of the Mendicity Society by Mr M R Brandreth, who became the honorary solicitor of the Charity Organisation Society. Robert Seifort was a musician who played with the town band earning eight shillings per week. The family paid weekly rent of 3s 6d and stated that they had been living in the parish for 10 years though the ages of their children on the 1871 census suggest that this was inaccurate.

The death of a 40-year-old man named Robert Seifert [sic] was recorded in Brighton in the June quarter of 1872.[642]

29 April 1872
Report: I made enquiries respecting this case and find the husband died on Monday morning and there is no doubt the members of the band will bury him. I have known them a long time. The wife is given to drink. The home is in a destitute state.
Ineligible, R P Hooper, chairman. Entered, RJ [Robert Johnson, secretary]

163 CATHERINE HOLLISTER, 45, NO OCCUPATION, 24 YORK ROAD, BRIGHTON

Catherine Hollister was baptised Catherine Foreman Bennett at St Mary, Lambeth, on 6 April 1828.[643] *She married John Hollister, a 28-year-old iron moulder of 8 Faringdon Street, Swindon, Wiltshire, at Swindon parish church on 29 July 1855.*[644] *The entry in the marriage register describes her as a straw bonnett maker of New Swindon, and initially records her name as Catherine Freeman Bennett: an amendment signed by both parties records it correctly as Catherine Foreman Bennett.*

John and Catherine Hollister were enumerated at 8 Faringdon Street, Swindon, on the 1861 census. They shared the address with a couple who were probably Catherine's parents: William Bennett and his wife Ann, who were both 64 and from Trowbridge, Wiltshire. Also living at the address were a servant and John and Catherine Hollister's children Ann, four; Mary, two and James, three months, all of whom were born in New Swindon.

Catherine Hollister's application to the Mendicity Society states that the family arrived at Brighton in 1862 which tallies with the dates of their sons: James was born in Swindon in 1861 and John was born in Brighton in 1864.

The second-eldest daughter, Mary, was admitted to the Sussex County Asylum, Haywards Heath, on 15 October 1867 aged eight, described as an 'idiot and epileptic.'[645] *She was recorded as the daughter of John and Catherine Hollister, of 15 Viaduct Road, and*

[642] Death of Robert Seifert registered Q2 1872 Brighton 2b 103.
[643] London Metropolitan Archive: P85/mry1/356.
[644] Wiltshire and Swindon History Centre: 1357/15.
[645] ESRO: HC 24/1316.

was observed to destroy her clothes, bite the flesh off her fingers and attempted to jump out of a window. She died at the asylum on 2 November 1887 of a condition described as 'decay of epilepsy.'

John Hollister's death was recorded in Brighton in the March quarter of 1868.[646] *In 1871 Catherine Hollister was enumerated at 30 Boston Street, Brighton, with her children James, John, Thomas and Rhoda, and her widowed mother, Ann Bennett.*

In April 1872 The Hollister family's case was sent to the Mendicity Society by Miss Westwood, of 12 London Road. They had been living at 24 York Road for about a year and paid weekly rent of 3s 6d.[647] *Catherine Hollister's occupation is not given, but she was receiving eight shillings per week in parish relief and all of the children attended Belmont Street school.*

On 25 October 1873 the Hollister's eldest daughter Ann, like her younger sister, was admitted to the Sussex County Asylum, Haywards Heath, aged 16.[648] *Her mother was living at 57 New England Street and Ann Hollister's mental state was described as 'an idiot.' When examined by the asylum's medical officer she stated that she would 'send him to hell' and thought that her food was being poisoned and her mother dead. She was considered 'very violent to others, dirty in her habits, is sleepless and requires constant restraint.' She died of epilepsy at the asylum on 26 November 1876.*

Catherine Hollister's death was recorded at Brighton in the December quarter of 1877.[649] *No children with the surname Hollister appeared in the admission register of the workhouse school*[650] *or in the creed register of Warren Farm Industrial School.*[651] *The creed register lists pupils' religions but also acts as an index to the admission registers.*

30 April 1872
Statement: Catherine Hollister would be thankful for a little assistance.
Report: I made enquiries respecting this case and find this woman is having parish relief at the rate of 10s per week and in addition to the four children at home there is one in Haywards Heath asylum and one in the workhouse. This woman's mother is an invalid living with her. She receives relief at the [rate] of 5s 9d per week. Altogether this family cost the parish £1 11s 9d per week. They are not known to Miss Westwood nor to the Reverend Mr Coombe, Clifton Road. The home is in a passable state.
Ineligible, GDR [George Dudley Ryder]. Entered, RJ [Robert Johnson, secretary]

646 Death of John Hollister registered Q1 1868 Brighton 2b 128.

647 There is a slight inconsistency in the dates of the family's residence at these addresses: they were enumerated at 30 Boston Street in 1871 but stated on 30 April 1872 that they had been living at 24 York Road for 16 months and that their previous address had ben 15 Viaduct Terrace.

648 ESRO: HC 24/2352.

649 Death of Catherine Hollister registered Q4 1877 Brighton 2b 142.

650 ESRO: R/S 29/2.

651 ESRO: R/S 35/1.

164 LUCY BRUCE, 48, DRESSMAKER, LONDON

Lucy Bruce was born in Great Whelnetham near Bury St Edmunds, Suffolk in about 1824 and was enumerated on the 1871 census lodging at the house of Daniel Cowley, confectioner, at 1 Powis Road, Brighton. From the information given in the letters transcribed below it is thought that she lived at that address between about November 1870 and December 1871.

In 1881 Bruce was enumerated lodging at 8 Bouverie Street, Paddington, and still working as a dressmaker. In 1901 she was living at 15 Cambridge Street, Paddington.

Letter from H Harrison, clerk to the committee of the Paddington Committee for Organising Charitable Relief and Repressing Mendicity, 3 Leinster Street, Cleveland Square, London, 29 April 1872

Re: Lucy Bruce. Sir, the above person has applied for assistance to this office. She states she resided for 13 months at 1 Powis Road, Brighton and left five months since. Will you kindly cause enquiry to be made as to character etc and report result to me at your earliest convenience. Lucy Bruce is 48 years of age, single and a dressmaker. I am sir, your obedient servant H Harrison

29 April 1872
Report: I made enquiries respecting this case and find this woman's statement is correct. She lodged at 1 Powis Road for 13 months and during that time she supported herself by dress making and about five months ago she left and went to London. From enquiries made I find she bears a good character.

Letter from R Johnson, Brighton Mendicity Society, 2 May 1872
Sir, in reply to your letter of April 29 I have to inform you that Lucy Bruce's statement is perfectly correct and I am happy to add that from inquiries made by our agent she bears a good character. R Johnson

165 THOMAS KEEN, 56, HAWKER, 11 DERBY PLACE, BRIGHTON

Thomas Keen's application to the Mendicity Society stated that he was born in Cambridge in about 1816. He came to Brighton via Gravesend, Kent, where, in September 1864, he sustained an injury that resulted in the loss of his right leg. Local press reported the incident in detail, 'on Saturday afternoon last a shocking accident happened to a man named Thomas Keen, in the employ of Mr W Lake of Chalk, whilst engaged at a threshing machine which was at work in a field near Milton church. The unfortunate man, it seems, was in the act of feeding the machine and having placed in it too much corn at once he endeavoured to force it with his foot, which was laid hold of by the machinery and before the engine could be stopped his leg was most dreadfully mangled. The poor fellow having been saved from his perilous position he was at once removed to the infirmary, when it was found neccesary to amputate the leg above the knee, which operation was performed by Dr Granshaw, and the sufferer is now going on favourably.'[652]

Keen stated that he had been living in Brighton since April 1872 and before that had lived at Hastings. He earned five shillings per week and paid weekly rent of 2s 4d for a bed at 11 Derby Place: a lodging house used, at one time or another, by a number of other applicants to the Mendicity Society.

1 May 1872
Statement: Thomas Keen wants a licence to hawk and a little stock of books to enable him to get his living by hawking instead of begging.
Report: This man states he was at work for a Mr W Lake who lives in Donally Road, Gravesend, about seven years ago with a threshing machine and slipped into the drum and was taken from there to Bath Street Infirmary where his right leg was taken off at the knee joint and since that [sic] he has been tramping the country.
Ineligible, GDR [George Dudley Ryder]

166 JOHN THOMAS, 64, NO OCCUPATION, 31 DERBY PLACE, BRIGHTON

John Thomas was born in Brighton in about 1808. The wedding of a John Thomas to an Elizabeth Martin, also of Brighton, took place at St Nicholas, Brighton, on 26 December 1855: Thomas was recorded as a 42-year-old widower living at 8 Hereford Street and employed as a stonemason.[653] *Elizabeth Martin was 33 and living at 50 Park Street. On the census of 1861 John and Elizabeth Thomas were enumerated at 2 Wyndham Street, Camberwell, Surrey: John was recorded as 58 years of age and was employed as a stonemason, Elizabeth's age was given as 37.*[654]

A 60-year-old man named John Thomas was admitted to the Sussex County Hospital on 20 October 1869.[655] *He was suffering with rheumatism but was relieved of his symptoms by the time of his discharge. In 1871 the couple were enumerated at 27 Derby Place, where John was employed as a stone sawyer; at the time of their application to the Mendicity Society in May 1872 they had been living at 31 Derby Place for a year. They paid weekly rent of 3s 6d but were £1 in debt. John Thomas was not in employment, but Elizabeth Thomas earned seven shillings per week either as a charwoman, as she claimed, or as a prostitute, which was stated by the charity's agent.*

652 Gravesend Reporter, North Kent and South Essex Advertiser, 10 September 1864.
653 ESRO: PAR 255/1/3/28.
654 This means she would have been born in 1823. That date is consistent with the age she gave in the 1871 census but does not tally with the age given to the Mendicity Society agent which would have given her a birth year of about 1816.
655 ESRO: HB 35/3/1869-5501.

2 May 1872
Statement: John Thomas would be thankful for a little assistance; he states he does not want to go into the workhouse.
Report: I made enquiries respecting this case and find this man is a stone mason but he has not been able to work for this last four years. He did receive parish relief for some time till about 12 months ago when they gave an order for the house. He went in for a short time and then left. Since that he has been an out-patient at the hospital suffering with rheumatism. Instead of the wife being a charwoman she is a prostitute. The home is in a passable state. I have not seen Mr Toye: I am informed he is in London.
Undeserving, R P Hooper, chairman

167 SARAH TERRY, 46, WASHERWOMAN, 21 GROSVENOR STREET, BRIGHTON

When Sarah Terry applied to the Mendicity Society she was widowed and living at 21 Grosvenor Street with her 14-year-old daughter, Elizabeth, and her three-year-old son, George, both of whom attended St John's School, Carlton Hill. It has not been possible to ascertain the name of her late husband.

Sarah Terry was born in Lewes in about 1826 and, according to her application, came to Brighton in about 1869. She had been living at Grosvenor Street for 10 months where she rented one room for 1s 9d per week and owed no rent: prior to that she was living at 11 Park Place, Brighton but was not enumerated at that address on the 1871 census. Terry earned ten shillings per week working as a washerwoman for Mrs Mills of Marine View. The scripture reader Mr Toye was supplied as a reference.

4 May 1872
Statement: Sarah Terry would be thankful if the committee would assist her and her two children to Liverpool to enable them to emigrate to America.
Report: I made enquiries respecting this case and find this woman works for Mrs Mills and bears a very good character. Mr Toye, the scripture reader, states he does not know but a very little about her. He believes her to be a respectable woman. The home is in a passable state. She states it will cost about £3 to get to Liverpool. WC [William Collingham]
Case referred to Mr Hack,[656] R P Hooper, chairman

[656] Probably Daniel Hack.

168 CHARLOTTE CECIL, 56, NEEDLEWOMAN, 3 DERBY PLACE, BRIGHTON

It has not been possible to discover much about Charlotte Cecil beyond the information she supplied on the Mendicity Society's application form. She claims to have been born in London in about 1816 and states that she moved to Brighton in about 1858. At the time of her application she had been living at 3 Derby Place for a week and before that had been resident at the workhouse infirmary. Cecil's case was forwarded to the society by the Reverend Aaron Augustus Morgan, vicar of St John's, Carlton Hill. She was widowed, occupied one room for which she paid no rent and would usually be able to earn five shillings per week but had been unable to work for five months due to sickness. A 60-year-old woman named Charlotte Cecil died in Brighton in the March quarter of 1880.[657]

8 May 1872
Statement: Charlotte Cecil would be thankful for a little assistance to help her over till next Tuesday when she will apply to the parish authorities for a little outdoor relief.
Report: I made enquiries respecting this woman and find she is the widow of a sergeant who died in India. Since his death she lived with a man named Parker and kept a hat shop in the lanes. Parker died two years ago and through her intemperate habits she soon failed in business. After that she did a little needle work till five months ago when she fell sick and went into the infirmary and left a week ago. She is staying with her daughter. The daughter is known to the police as a prostitute and living with a man. WC [William Collingham]
Dismissed, undeserving – case to be communicated to Reverend A A Morgan, R P Hooper, chairman

169 MARY ANN MOORE, 66, GOVERNESS, 25 NORFOLK ROAD, BRIGHTON

Mary Ann Moore's case was brought to the attention of the Brighton Mendicity Society by the London Mendicity Society of 13 Red Lion Square (though it is unclear excatly what their interest in the case was). Moore was born in Goodrich, Herefordshire, in about 1808 and stated that she had moved to Brighton in about 1859. Previously she had been living at 4 Hampton Place but in about 1867 she moved to 25 Norfolk Road, where she ran a small school for young ladies. Mary Ann Moore was enumerated at that property in 1871 living with Elizabeth Fellingham, a 48-year-old general servant from Brighton.

Weekly rent on 25 Norfolk Road was 14 shillings and although Moore was not in arrears with payments she was earning only ten shillings per week. However, her niece was staying with her and her contributions brought rent down to about five shillings a week, leaving Moore with about five shillings per week to live on.

[657] Death of Charlotte Cecil registered Q1 1880 2b 152.

Moore supplied the names of Mr E S Clifton, hairdresser, stationer and newsagent of 30 Preston Street and W Heathfield, 19 Lincolns Inn Field, London, as her references. She left 25 Norfolk Road in 1875 and subsequently started a small school at an unknown address. This venture failed but in autumn 1876 she managed to find accomodation at almshouses in Wilmington near Dartford, Kent, known as The Retreat.

The death of a 78-year-old woman named Mary Ann Moore was registered in Dartford in the June quarter of 1881. Another woman with this name died in Dartford aged 80 in the March quarter of 1894.

8 May 1872
Statement: Mary Ann Moore would be thankful if she could get into the Governesses Benevolent Institution at London.
Report: I made enquiries respecting this case and find this woman keeps a small ladies-school. Her niece is staying with her and that brings the rent down to about 5s per week. Mr Moore, chemist, Preston Street, is this woman's nephew.[658] The Reverend Mr Trocke states he knows but a very little about her. She was recommended to him by the late Dr King. Mr Clifton, 30 Preston Street, states she is a very respectable woman. WC [William Collingham]
Case referred to Mr Mr Hooper for enquiry and report, R P Hooper. Enquiries very satisfactory. Result to be communicated to Mendicity Society, Red Lion Square, R P Hooper

Letter to the Earl of Chichester from E Moore, 25 Norfolk Road, Brighton, 20 July 1873
My Lord, may I ask your kind interest on behalf of an aunt: an old lady of 68 years of age, sister to the late Mr Moore, chemist, Preston Street, who is now in much distress. She has worked hard all her life as governess and has been keeping a small school but in consequence of unforeseen circumstances is now in great need of pecuniary aid to enable her to keep her home as at her advanced age she has no means of support if compelled to do so. Knowing you are ever ready to aid the distressed I have laid this case before you and trust you will kindly send her a little aid. I can fully satisfy you as to the truth of all I say, being a stranger I am sure you would find it a most deserving case and all I say unfortunately too true but having lived respectably by her own exertions she feels a delicacy in making her case known although she needs help so much. Trusting you will excuse the liberty I have taken. I am your lordship's obedient servant, E Moore

1 August 1873
The annexed letter was sent to the Earl of Chichester who forwarded it to Dr Hannah for investigation and he being away from home the Reverend J J

[658] Moore and Son, chemists and mineral water manufacturers, 67 Preston Street.

Hannah opened it and, not knowing anything of the person referred to, he sent it to the office and would like to have a report of the case. On enquiry I find Miss Moore is in a delicate state of health. The lady who boarded with her at the time of the last report continues to do so. Applicant's niece, a governess who has assisted her on several occassions is now out of a situation and is therefore unable to help her. WC [William Collingham]
Report to be forwarded to Lord Chichester, R P Hooper, chairman

Letter from the Earl of Chichester to the Charity Organisation Society, 6 August 1873
Case 169, Mary Moore. Sir, I am much obliged by the report upon the above case and shall be further obliged if you will be good enough to hand the poor lady the enclose [sic] cheque requesting her to send me a receipt, Chichester

Letter from E Moore, 5 The Retreat, Wilmington, near Dartford, Kent, to the Earl of Chichester, 28 February 1877
My Lord, I take the liberty to write on behalf of a relative, Miss Moore, a poor lady who until recently resided in Brighton. She has been a governess more than 40 years but not being able any longer to teach or to keep her home together is now down here where she has the use of two rooms rent free. A few years since you kindly sent her some help from a fund at your disposal. If you could help her now I should be most grateful as all provisions, coals etc are so expensive. She suffers much from numbness of the limbs, particularly fingers, so she cannot increase her income by fancy work as some ladies do. Any wearing apparel would be most acceptable. Miss Moore was sister to a chemist of that name in Preston Street but he has been dead some years. Trusting you will please pardon the liberty I have taken in writing. I am my Lord, yours most obediently, E Moore
Mrs Duke 17 Preston Street knows Miss Moore well

Letter from the Earl of Chichester to the Charity Organisation Society, 1 March 1877
Dear Sir, I shall be much obliged by a report upon the enclosed letter respecting Moore. Truly yours, Chichester

2 March 1877
The Earl of Chichester requests a report of this case. Miss Moore left Norfolk Road about two years ago. Afterwards she took lodgings and endeavoured to support herself by keeping a small school but soon failed. Last autumn she went to her present address in Kent which is an almshouse. Mrs Duke, 17 Preston Street, who has known Miss Moore many years strongly recommends the case. WC [William Collingham]
To be favourably reported to Lord Chichester, R P Hooper

170 ELLEN KNIGHT, 24, IRONER, 27 GEORGE STREET GARDENS, BRIGHTON

When Ellen Knight applied to the Mendicity Society she had been working as an ironer at the New Laundry on Lewes Road. She stated that she was born in Maresfield and that she moved to Brighton in 1868, first to 58 Cavendish Street and then, in late April 1872, to 27 George Street Gardens.

At the time of her application to the Mendicity Society Ellen Knight should have been earning 15 shillings per week but had been out of work for three months with sickness. The man she claimed was her husband, Thomas Knight, had been working for Mr W Potts, butcher of 41 Edward Street, earning 18 shillings per week until three months earlier. The couple paid four shillings per week rent for one room and were one week's rent in arrears.

Ellen Knight claimed that she married her husband at St Anne's, Lewes. No marriages involving anyone by the name of Knight were recorded in the parish marriage register between 1865 and 1872 but a marriage between Ellen Evans and Thomas Knight was registered in Brighton in 1869.[659]

9 May 1872
Statement: Ellen Knight would be thankful for a little assistance till her husband gets work.
Report: I made enquiries respecting this case and find this man did work for Mr Potts, butcher, 41 Edward Street, and was discharged for absenting himself from his work when his master was away from home. I have known him a long time. When he is in work he stays drinking about till one o'clock in the morning. I am informed they are not married. I asked the wife to show me the marriage certificate, she refused to do so but declared she was married at St Ann's, Lewes. The home is in a passable state. The man applied to the parish but refused to go in the [work]house. The wife stated he went home and lit his pipe with the order. WC [William Collingham]
Undeserving, R P Hooper

171 JAMES NORRIS, 52, HANDCHAIR MAN, 9 PARK CRESCENT ROAD, BRIGHTON

James Norris was baptised at Godalming, Surrey, on 11 March 1821.[660] *In 1851 Norris, described as a draper, and his wife Charlotte, who was born in Wisborough Green in about 1830, were enumerated at 76 Elder Street, Brighton. Ten years later Norris was still earning his living as a draper and the couple were living at Farncombe, Surrey.*

[659] Marriage of Ellen Evans to Thomas Knight registered Q3 1869 Brighton 2b 345.
[660] London Metropolitan Archive: DW/T/5142.

Charlotte Norris died at some point between the taking of the census in April 1861 and the wedding of James Norris and Amelia Holloway at Oxford in the December quarter of 1864.[661] *James and Amelia Norris were enumerated at 9 Park Crescent Road on the census of 1871. By this time Norris was earning his living as a handchair man and Amelia, who was born in Oxford in about 1841, was employed as a needlewoman. The couple had three children: James William, born in Storrington in about 1867, Harry, born in Hove in about 1868 and Louisa born in Brighton in 1870.*

The Norris family's case was sent to the Mendicity Society by the Reverend Robert Ingham Salmon of St Martin's, Lewes Road. James Norris stated that they had moved to Brighton in 1864 (which does not tally with the dates and places of birth of his children given in the census) and that they had been living at their current address for 18 months and previously at 12 Park Crescent. The family paid weekly rent of three shillings for the house but owed £2: Norris was earning 15 shillings per week but his wife was not employed. Mr Potter of 17 Park Crescent was supplied as a reference.

When James Norris applied to the Charity Organisation Society in April 1874 the family were living at 35 St Paul's Street. They had moved to 19 Bedford Buildings by the time of their next application in February 1881 and James and Amelia Norris along with their six children were enumerated at the same address on the census taken on 3 April 1881.

James Norris's death at the age of 78 was registered at Brighton in the September quarter of 1899.[662]

11 May 1872
Statement: James Norris would be thankful if the committee could assist him in getting his chair repaired.
Report: I made enquiries respecting this case and find what this man's chair wants is new tyres. He states they would cost 6s. The Reverend Mr Salmon states he believes this to be a deserving case: he gave him a pair of boots. The reason they are so destitute at present is they have been summonsed for arrears of rent. Mr Potter states he believes him to be a deserving object for charity, he has employed him on several occasions and relieved him on two or three occasions. From enquiries I made he bears a good character. The home is in a passable state.
Relieved with grant of 6s, R P Hooper, chairman

21 April 1874
This man, who stated that he was sent by the Reverend Mr Salmon, applied at the office on Tuesday for assistance to enable him to purchase a new handchair

661 The death of a woman named Charlotte Norris was registered at Farnham, Surrey, in the March quarter of 1861 but as the census was taken in April 1861 this cannot be the same person unless there was an administrative error.

662 Death of James Norris registered Q3 1899 Brighton 2b 168.

which would cost about £40. In answer to my questions he stated that his present chair was so old and shabby that people would not engage him provided there was another chair on the stand. What he now wants is to sell his old chair for about £8 and to have a petition to collect the remainder. Mr Salmon intended the man to apply to the Provident and District Society but says that if this society can do anything to assist the man he should be very pleased, knowing that he is anxious to support his wife and family. Since the case was before the committee nearly two years ago they have had two children, the eldest aged 18 months is in very delicate health and the other is a baby aged seven weeks. In my opinion his present chair might be put in good repair for about £8 and as he knows some ladies who will assist him a loan for the remainder would enable him to make his old chair answer his purpose and while that was going under repair he could hire another. WC [William Collingham]
To stand over for further information, R P Hooper

25 April 1874
Since this case was last before the committee I have obtained the annexed estimate of the cost of repairing the chair, but on seeing the applicant he said that his friends would not hear of his having the old chair repaired and what he wants is a new one. WC [William Collingham]
Ineligible, R P Hooper, chairman

Estimate for repairing hand chair provided by James Mercer, North Road, 25 April 1874[663]
New leather hood, apron and dash; new blue cloth lining; four new straps and trimming - £10 10s
New iron and vallant [vallance], new brass bead and trimming – 12s
18 new felloes to wheels, new set of tyres, new India rubber ditto; plats and trimming on - £3 15s
New brass to handle screws and trimming – 5s
Cleaning of iron work, painting, picking out and varnishing all over – £2 10s
Total £17 12s

22 February 1881
Norris, now of 19 Bedford Buildings, applied at the office on Monday for £6 10s to enable him to purchase four new wheels for his hand chair. In 1874 he sold his old chair and succeeded in raising £40 pounds for a new one. Since then the wooden wheels have gone out of date and he now wants new wire wheels to

[663] J Mercer, coachmaker and wheelwright, 46 North Road.

give the chair a lighter appearance. He has four children dependant on him and his wife is near her confinement. WC [William Collingham]
Ineligible – applicant referred to the Benevolent Loan Fund, 22 February 1881, G Turnbull

172 NICHOLAS GORMAN, 76, NO OCCUPATION, 37 DERBY PLACE, BRIGHTON

The case of Nicholas Gorman and his wife, Catherine, was forwarded to the Mendicity Society by the Reverend Aaron Augustus Morgan, vicar of St John's, Carlton Hill. Gorman was born in Ireland in about 1794; Catherine Gorman's place of birth and maiden name are not known but she was born in about 1804.

According to the statement made to the Mendicity Society the couple arrived in Brighton in about November 1870; they had spent the four days prior to their application in lodgings at 37 Derby Place and were previously resident in Brighton Workhouse. They occupied one room, for which they paid weekly rent of 3s 6d and were one shilling in arrears.

Catherine Gorman's death was registered in Brighton in the September quarter of 1872.[664]

10 May 1872
Statement: Nicholas Gorman wants a little assistance till his wife gets better.
Report: I made enquiries respecting this case and find this man and his wife was in the workhouse but left on Tuesday last. Since that the wife fell sick and is now ill in bed. I have known the man for some time but never knew him to do any work. They are not known to Mr Toye the scripture reader. The man applied to the Reverend Mr Morgan for relief and he, not knowing him, gave him a ticket to have the case investigated. When I found the wife was ill in bed I went back to Mr Morgan and informed him the result of my enquiry. He stated he would attend to the case. The relieving officer states they can have an order for the [work]house. I believe that to be far the best place for them. WC [William Collingham]
Referred to parish authorities, R P Hooper

173 WILLIAM CARSON, 40, LABOURER, 15 CHESTERFIELD STREET, BRIGHTON

William Carson was born in Glasgow in about 1832 and his wife Jane was born in Dublin in about 1837. The wedding of a William Carson and Jane Higgins was recorded at Elham,

[664] Death of Catherine Gorman registered Q3 1872 Brighton 2b 111.

Kent, in the June quarter of 1867.[665] *The couple were enumerated on the 1871 census at Albion House, Christchurch, Folkestone, Kent, where William was employed by Miss Sankey as a general servant and Jane as a cook.*

At the time of their application to the Mendicity Society in May 1872 they had been living at 15 Chesterfield Street with their two infant sons for a week and had previously been resident at Brighton Workhouse. They paid weekly rent of 3s 6d and were already a week's rent in arrears. William had been out of work for nine months and Jane seven months.

13 May 1872
Statement: William Carson would be thankful for a little assistance till he gets work.
Report: I made enquiries respecting this case and find this man and his wife was in the [work]house and left on Monday last. They were there about five months. Mr Sattin, the governor, states during their stay in the [work]house their conduct was very good. He believes this to be a deserving case for a little temporary relief.
Ineligible, R P Hooper, chairman

174 ESTHER BOTTING, 36, WIFE OF A LABOURER, ST MARTIN'S COTTAGE, BRIGHTON

Esther Lidbitter of Pulborough was 28 years of age when she married Henry Botting, a 45-year-old labourer from Cuckfield, at St Nicholas, Brighton, on 21 May 1865.[666] *The marriage register records they were both living at 51 Southover Street, Brighton, at the time of the wedding. According to the Mendicity Society application form the couple, or just Esther – it is unclear – had been resident in Brighton since 1865 and they had been living at St Martin's Cottage for eight months and previously at 23 Francis Street, Brighton.*

At the time of the application Henry Botting was labouring for Mr Leary of Lewes Road and earning 15 shillings per week. The couple paid weekly rent of five shillings per week for the whole house and were not in arrears. They had a four-year-old son William, and twin girls, Eliza and Emily, who were four months old; Emily had asthma.

The family were enumerated at 16 Bedford Buildings on the cenus of 1881 and at 10 Elder Row in 1891, when Esther Botting's occupation was recorded as a laundry woman.

They applied to the Charity Organisation Society on 19 January 1894 when they were living at 49 Elder Row and again on 11 June 1901 following Henry Botting's death in April 1901. The form, which gave far more information in its later format, showed that between 1894 and 1901 they had lived at 15 Picton Street for nine months, 31 Newmarket

[665] Marriage of William Carson and Jane Higgins registered Q2 1867 Elham 2a 1263.
[666] ESRO: PAR 255/1/3/39.

Road for 16 months and 19 Hastings Road for two or three years. The 1901 application form also shows that their case was forwarded to the charity by Miss P Hack, who was probably the author of the undated letter transcribed below.

The form of 1901 also shows that Esther Botting had, until 10 months previously, been employed to wash for W Douglas of Bonchurch Road, where she earned eight shillings per week; her son William earned 20 shillings per week labouring for the Electric Light Company on Church Street; her daughter Emily was in service for Mr Harvey of Ditchling Road, earning 3s 6d per week; Emily's twin sister Eliza was employed by Mr Hylden of 15 Rugby Road but her wages were not recorded. The family received 2s 6d per week during Henry Botting's illness and paid weekly rent of 3s 6d for two rooms. They were two shillings in debt and had 20 shillings worth of goods held in pawn. References were supplied by W Ashdown, builder, of 24 Ivory Place and Mr Rhodes of 51 Vere Road.

Esther Botting's death was recorded at Brighton in the September quarter of 1910.[667]

14 May 1872
Statement: Esther Botting would be thankful if the committee would give her a dispensary letter for her daughter, Emily.
Report: I made enquiries respecting this case and find this man does work for Mr Leary and bears a good character. From enquiries I made in the neighbourhood I find the wife also bears a good character. I believe this to be a deserving case.
Relieved by dispensary letter, R P Hooper, chairman

19 January 1894
Mrs Botting applied at the office on Friday for assistance to tide her over until her husband is able to resume work. He has been employed by the railway company till three weeks ago when he was taken ill with bronchitis for which he is attended by the dispensary doctor and is still confined to his room. His wife earns 6s 3d a week by going out washing. Their house is in a destitute state and a fortnight ago they were granted an order for the workhouse but their son has just been taken on by the corporation, therefore temporary relief would set them up for the present. WC [William Collingham]
5s, R P Hooper

Fragment of a letter thought to be from Miss P Hack to Colonel Dodd, Charity Organisation Society, Brighton, [June 1901]
Sir, a poor woman, Mrs Botting, of 2 Boston Street is applying for help from the Widows' Society. Her landlady Mrs Stevenson of the same address and Mr Ashdown, 13 street [sic] recommend her but as both are strangers to me, and me of them, only appeals from brief knowledge of her. I shall be very glad if you can

[667] Death of Esther Botting registered Q3 1910 Brighton 2b 115.

get me some more information before I lay the case before the committee on [*remainder of letter missing*]

11 June 1901
Statement: my husband died last April and I have had no relief since then. My health has been so bad to do any work, I think I hurt my back in lifting him. My son gives me 12s-14s a week for rent and board for us both. Eliza is in service at a boarding house and seems unable to help me. Emily sometimes gives me a shilling. I have come to the office to ask for a recommendation for the Widows' Fund. Emily was born with asthma and cannot take a heavy place.

175 WILLIAM BUTLAND (ALSO GIVEN AS BUCKLAND), 36, LABOURER, 26 CHESTERFIELD STREET, BRIGHTON

This man is largely refered to as William Butland in the Mendicity Society's reports but was enumerated as William Buckland on the census of 1861. He was enumerated in Upton-cum-Chalvey, Buckinghamshire, where he lived with his wife Maria (née Blackman) who was born in Hillingdon, Middlesex, in about 1835 and their two children, Louisa and John, both born in Chalvey.[668] *The couple were married in Eton, Buckinghamshire, in the September quarter of 1857.*[669]

When William Butland applied to the charity in May 1872, they had been living in Brighton for seven months: previously at 26 Nelson Row but since April 1872 at 26 Chesterfield Street. Butland had been out of work for three weeks but had previously been employed as a labourer at Aldrington gas works where he earned 21 shillings per week. Maria Butland had been prevented from working for three weeks through sickness but had previously been employed as a washerwoman by Mrs Kennard of Jersey Street, who paid her nine shillings per week. The couple paid weekly rent of 3s 9d for the whole house and were 1s 3d in arrears with rent payments. At the time of the application the Butiands had seven children, five of whom attended St John's School. Mr Savage, chemist, of 65 Edward Street, supplied a reference.

William Butland moved to Bath later in 1872 and the rest of the family were accompanied on their journey to Bath by William Collingham, the charity's agent, in November 1872.

15 May 1872
Statement: William Butland would be thankful for a little assistance till he gets work.
Report: I made enquires respecting this case and find this man did work at the gas works but was discharged three weeks ago when they shortened hands. This

[668] John Butland applied to the Mendicity Society on 1 March 1872 (case 88).
[669] Marriage of William Buckland and Maria Blackman registered Q3 1857 Eton 3a 501.

man is the father of the boy Butland, case 88. I find the wife did work for Mrs Kennard, Jersey Street, but she has not been to work since the fire – that was about a month ago. Mrs Kennard states she waited for her some time but finding she did not come back to work she was obliged to take another woman in her place. Mr Savage, chemist, Edward Street, states since the fire they have had in the way of relief in money and goods the value of £12 or more. Upon the whole Mr Savage thinks he is not deserving of relief from this society. Mr Smith, the relieving officer, states the man applied to him for a doctor a week ago but stated he did not want relief. The home is in a passable state which was not the case before the fire. WC [William Collingham]
Undeserving, GDR [George Dudley Ryder], chairman

21 November 1872
After this case was before the committee in May last the whole of the family went into the country where they remained till after the hop picking season was over. They then came back to Brighton and lodged at a tramps' lodging house, 7 Chesterfield Street. During the time they were there the children were in the habit of going about begging until they were taken to the town hall and discharged with a caution.[670] I saw one of the boys begging and I afterwards cautioned the father and I believe the whole family then went into the workhouse. The wife received this letter from her husband at Bath which she gave to Mr Challen and the case was mentioned before the committee on Thursday the 20th instant who directed the secretary to write to his employer at Bath. Mr Johnson has written there and received the annexed answer. WC [William Collingham]

Letter from George Helps, secretary, Bath Gas Light and Coke Company, Upper Bristol Road, Bath, 22 November 1872
Sir, in reply to your enquiry William Buckland is at present in the employ of this company as a labourer at 16s per week, but it is quite uncertain how long he will continue, perhaps only for a week or two. Yours faithfully George Helps, secretary

Letter from Louisa Rachel Nicolls, 26 St James Square, Bath, 29 November 1872
Gentlemen, seeing in the West Sussex [?Gazette] of yesterday a paragraph respecting the family of a man working in the gas works in Bath I beg to know if it is a true statement. If so, I shall be glad to be told the name of the family that I may make some enquiries. I have been just now with the chairman of the gas works and have promised to get any information for him. I remain, Louisa Rachel Nicolls

[670] Brighton police station was based in the town hall.

29 November 1872
On Wednesday morning Mrs Butland applied at the office for assistance to help her and her family to Bath where she stated her husband had got work and from instructions I received last Saturday from the committee I met them at the railway on Friday morning where I took through tickets to Bath and saw the whole party off by the 6.25am train for which applicant was very thankful. The railway tickets came to £1 19s 3d; fly, 2s 9d; refreshments on the journey 2s 6d, total £2 4s 6d; through the advertisement in the Daily News Mr Johnson, secretary, received 12s; Mr Bigge gave me 6s 6d out of the magistrates' poor box and the society £1 grant with 6s in stamps from the applicant's husband: total £2 4s 6d which paid for the removal. WC [William Collingham]
A grant of £1 will be given to the woman on application to enable her and her children to join her husband at Bath, R P Hooper, chairman

176 FRANCES WENHAM, 40, WIFE OF A CARTER, PYECOMBE

The Wenhams were one of the few families to apply to the Mendicity Society who lived outside the parish of Brighton.

In 1841 a 15-year-old boy named John Wenham was enumerated at Hurstbourne Farm, Westmeston, employed as an agricultural labourer and living with Joseph Mighell, farmer. The 1841 census does not record precise place of birth, but later census returns state that he was born in East Chiltington in about 1827.

The marriage of a Frances Rogers, of 18 Spring Street, aged 27, and a John Wenham, a 31-year-old widower employed as a milkman and living at 11 New Dorset Street, was recorded at St Nicholas, Brighton on 12 May 1860.[671] *The census of 1861 enumerates Wenham, employed as a carter at Hamsey, living with his wife Frances, who was born in Newtimber, and his 10-year-old son John, born in East Chiltington. The son's age suggests that he was the product of John Wenham's previous marriage: the wedding of a John Wenham and a Mary Philpot was registered in Lewes in the December quarter of 1850 and the deaths of several women named Mary Wenham were recorded in East Sussex between 1850 and 1860.*

In 1871 John and Frances Wenham were enumerated at Eastwoods Cottage, Pyecombe. John was employed as an agricultural labourer and they lived with seven children. The oldest, Winifred, was born in Cooksbridge in about 1862 but all the younger children, aged between eight and one, were born in East Chiltington.

The case of the Wenham family was forwarded to the Mendicity Society by F Trille of 126 Queens Road in May 1872. Frances Wenham stated that they had moved to Brighton 14 months previously, shortly after the taking of the 1871 census. John Wenham had been employed as a carter by Mr Blaber of Pyecombe where he earned 15 shillings per week, but

[671] ESRO: PAR 255/1/3/32.

there was no reference to his employer since his arrival in Brighton. The family paid two shillings per week rent and were not in arrears with payments.

Frances Wenham's request for relief was turned down but the family remained in Brighton and were enumerated at 26 St Paul's Street in 1881, by which time John Wenham was employed as a labourer on the railway. Their seven-year-old daughter's place of birth was given as Pyecombe, indicating that their residence in Brighton was not unbroken. They shared the house with, amongst others, James Rogers, a 56-year-old gardener from Nyetimber, who was quite probably Frances Wenham's brother.

The death of Frances Wenham was registered in Brighton in the September quarter of 1887.[672] *John Wenham was enumerated on the 1891 census living at 14 Park Street and employed as a gardener. In 1911 Wenham was enumerated as a patient at the Sussex County Hospital, Brighton, where he was described as 84, and formerly a general labourer employed by the corporation works.*

17 May 1872
Statement: Frances Wenham would be thankful if the committee could assist her to get a pair of new boots and irons for her son Benjamin who is a cripple. She states they will cost about 30s and that Mr Blaber will give part of it.
Report: I have not made any enquiries respecting this case, Pyecombe being out of our district, but as the woman appears to be very respectable, I thought it best to put the case before the committee.
Ineligible, R P Hooper. Entered, RJ [Robert Johnson, secretary]

177 MARIA WASHINGTON, 32, WIFE OF A BRICKLAYER, 26 FREDERICK STREET, BRIGHTON

Maria Goble was baptised at St Nicholas, Brighton, on 12 July 1840.[673] *She married Adam Washington, a labourer of 6 Jubilee Court, at St Nicholas on 18 November 1861: the ceremony was performed by Henry Michell Wagner, Vicar of Brighton.*[674] *Adam was the son of Martha and James Washington, a bricklayer of Bread Street, and he was baptised at St Nicholas on 21 July 1839.*[675]

The Washington family were enumerated in Bread Street in 1841 and were living at 26 Bread Street when the following census was taken in 1851. In 1861 Adam Washington and his father, now a widower, were enumerated at 24 Pimlico but Adam had moved out before his marriage to Maria Goble in November 1861. By 1871 Adam and Maria Washington had three children and were living at 26 Frederick Street.

672 Death of Frances Wenham registered Q3 1887 Brighton 2b 158.
673 ESRO: PAR 255/1/2/12.
674 ESRO: PAR 255/1/3/34.
675 ESRO: PAR 255/1/2/11.

When they applied to the Mendicity Society in May 1872 the couple and their three children were still living at 26 Frederick Street, where they paid five shillings rent per week for the whole house. They were £1 in arrears and neither partner was earning an income.

By 1881 the Washington family had moved to 75 Hanover Terrace. They applied to the charity again in March 1884, by which time they had moved to 20 Belgrave Street, but they were enumerated at 9 Kingsbury Road on the census of 1891. On 14 May 1891, about six weeks after the census was taken, Adam Washington was admitted to the Sussex County Lunatic Asylum at Haywards Heath.[676] *His admission papers stated that he had been suffering from mania for about two months and that 'he is restless – is very reticent and can give no account of his recent doings. Admits that he was found in a pond but does not know how he got there.' Washington stated that his brother had been similarly afflicted and the examining surgeon, Dr Douglas McKissock Ross stated, 'He is melancholy and depressed, takes no interest in things around, when interrogated his one answer is 'I don't know.' He wanders about in an aimless manner.' William Davies, the attendant at Brighton Workhouse, stated that he had observed Washington, who was 51, make three attempts to escape over the wall and that he 'is very restless day and night trying all the doors to get away and he gets little or no sleep.' He was considered to have made a full recovery and was discharged on 3 October 1891.*

Adam Washington's death was registered in Brighton in the June quarter of 1893.[677] *In 1901 Maria Washington was enumerated at 32 Victoria Street, Brighton, where she lived with her daughter Mary, son-in-law and their two young daughters. She died in the December quarter of 1909 aged 69.*[678]

18 May 1872
Statement: Maria Washington wants a little assistance till her husband gets work.
Report: I made enquiries respecting this case and find this man did work for Mr Botting, 21 Ship Street, and was discharged three weeks ago through short of work. When at work his wages was £1 13s per week. Upon enquiry I find he bears a good character. He states he believes he will have work in another week or so. The wife does not do anything. The home is in a passable state. They are not known to the relieving officer, Miss Hesketh, 12 Powis Villas. The District Visitor states she has known them a long time and believes them to be a very respectable family. WC [William Collingham]
Ineligible, R P Hooper, chairman

28 March 1884

676 ESRO: HC 24/6331.
677 Death of Adam Washington registered Q2 1893 Brighton 2b 138.
678 Death of Maria Washington registered Q4 1909 Brighton 2b 135.

Mrs Washington, now of 20 Belgrave Street, was sent by Dr Mackey and applied at the office on Friday for assistance to enable her to get her daughter Mary, aged nine, nourishing food. The child has been poorly for some time suffering from gatherings on her neck for which she is an out-patient at the children's hospital. The husband has had no regular work since last November. His wife earns a trifle by going out charring. They have two children dependant on them, appear very poor and have not troubled the parish since October 1873. WC [William Collingham]
Grant 3s a week for seven weeks, Thomas W Holland

178 CAROLINE TUCKER, 47, WASHER, 11 ST PETER'S STREET, BRIGHTON

Caroline Tucker was born in Laycock, Wiltshire, in about 1825 but, according to her statement to the Mendicity Society's agent, came to Brighton in about 1852. Her husband, William Tucker, was born in Patcham in about 1834. In 1851 he was enumerated at London Road, Preston, where he lived with Thomas Bartlett and his family, earning his living as a bricklayer.[679]

By 1861 the couple were living at 2 Frederick Cottages with two other families amounting to 15 people in total. William Tucker was employed as a labourer on the railways and Caroline Tucker was described as a laundress. They had three children under the age of seven.

On 17 August 1867 a 40-year-old woman named Caroline Tucker appeared in court on a charge of felony holding an infant in her arms. The Brighton Gazette reported, 'It appeared from the evidence of Mrs Cruse, the wife of a music-master, residing at 39 Buckingham Road, that the prisoner had been occasionally employed by her as a charwoman. On the previous Tuesday she was working for her and, on leaving work, she saw her go away with a bundle under her arm. The next morning witness missed a linen sheet from a table in the kitchen. The sheet produced belonged to her but it was not the one she missed from the kitchen. Several other things, including a pair of stockings taken from prisoner's feet, were identified by Mrs Cruse. It further appeard that prisoner had pledged several articles at various pawnbrokers, not in her own name. Mr White, in reply to a question from the Bench stated that the prisoner, who lived in the Model Lodging House at the back of the Clarence Hotel, was in a most destitute condition and had three other children. Prisoner pleaded guilty and was sentenced to 14 days' hard labour.'[680]

In 1871 the family were enumerated at 23 Claremont Row and William Tucker had returned to his earlier employment as a bricklayer.

When the Tuckers' case was forwarded to the Mendicity Society by Daniel Hack in May 1872 the family had been living at 11 St Peter's Street for three months. They paid weekly

[679] This couple appear to be no relation to the couple also named William and Caroline Tucker that applied to the Mendicity Society on 26 January 1872, case 39.
[680] Brighton Gazette, 22 August 1867.

rent of 2s 6d for the whole house and were £1 in arrears. William Tucker was unemployed and Caroline Tucker had been off work for three weeks with sickness but usually expected to earn 15 shillings per week washing for her sister, Mrs Hardie, of 4 West Hill Place. All three children attended St John's School, Carlton Hill.[681]

Caroline Tucker's death was registered at Brighton in the June quarter of 1873 but in 1881 William Tucker was enumerated at 7 Francis Street with his second wife Hannah and his 15-year-old son, Edward.[682]

18 May 1872
Statement: Caroline Tucker wants a little assistance till her husband gets work. She states Mr Bartlett at Ditchling is her husband's father.
Report: I made enquiries respecting this case and find Mrs Hardie, 4 West Hill Place, is this woman's sister. She states they have nearly kept the wife and children for several years but cannot continue to do so. I have known the man a long time: he never has any regular work and when he does do any work the money he gets he spends on drink. The home is in a destitute state. They are not known to Mr Hack. The wife applied to him for relief and they, not knowing her, gave her the ticket. The wife applied to go in the workhouse. WC [William Collingham]
I have since seen the Reverend Mr Morgan, he states Dr Griffiths pays the childrens' school
Ineligible, R P Hooper, chairman. Entered, RJ [Robert Johnson, secretary]

179 LUCY CARD, 51, CHARWOMAN, 22 HOLLAND STREET, BRIGHTON

Lucy Card was born in Dublin in about 1821. Her maiden name and the date of her wedding to James Card is not known for certain but a woman named Lucy Ferguson married a James Bennett Card, a servant of 49 Old Steine, at St Nicholas, Brighton, on 27 January 1848.[683] *James Card was the son of a woman also named Lucy Card and was baptised at Hartfield on 16 September 1821 described as the 'base born son of Lucy Card'.*[684]

The couple and their two infant children, both born in Brighton, were enumerated at 44 Upper Edward Street in 1851: James Card was described as a servant and valet. By 1861 they had five children and were living at 24 Albion Street; James Card's profession was given as handchair man. Ten years later the Card family were enumerated at 22 Claremont Place, an address they shared with the Raynsford family.

681 *Page's Directory of Brighton, 1872*, states that N Hardie, tailor, lived at 3 West Hill Place.
682 Death of Caroline Tucker registered Q2 1873 Brighton 2b 140.
683 ESRO: PAR 255/1/3/19.
684 ESRO: PAR 360/1/2/1.

According to the Mendicity Society's application form, which was completed in May 1872, the family moved from Claremont Place to 22 Holland Street in November 1871. Miss Falkner of 34 Grand Parade made the Mendicity Society aware of the family and provided a reference. The Cards paid weekly rent of 2s 3d for two rooms and were 6s 9d in arrears. James Card was earning five shillings per week as a handchair man and Lucy Card took home three shillings per week charring. Their 12-year-old son Henry could earn four shillings per week when fully employed but was earning only 1s 4d at the time of the application. The eldest son, Thomas, was not working and was described as 'of weak intellect' by the charity's agent.

The census of 1881 shows James, Lucy and Thomas Card at 17 Richmond Buildings in 1881. James was employed as a bricklayer and Thomas was, in the language of the day, marked as an imbecile. By 1891 both James and Lucy were enumerated at Brighton Workhouse. Lucy Card's death was registered in Brighton in the September quarter of 1892.[685] *James Card continued living at Brighton Workhouse and was enumerated there in 1901. His death was registered in Brighton in the September quarter of 1907.*[686]

18 May 1872
Statement: Lucy Card wants a little relief. She states her husband only earns but a very little. It is not enough to keep them.
Report: I made enquiries respecting this case and find this man is a handchair man. I believe the least a man with a chair would earn is 10s at least. Inspector Terry states hand chairmen can earn good wages at this time of the year. The wife goes charring and generally gets plenty of work. I am informed they are both little given to drink. The oldest son is of weak intellect; he is not able to earn anything. The other goes serving plasterers. The home is in a passable state. Miss Falkner states she has relieved them on several occasions. They are known to the parish authorities having received relief on several occasions. WC [William Collingham]
Ineligible, R P Hooper, chairman

17 July 1885
Mrs Card, who has been homeless during the last three weeks was sent by the Reverend R Hamilton and applied at the office on Thursday for some assistance. Her husband earns a trifle by washing flys and sleeps in a stable. Applicant suffers from a very bad leg and is quite past work. The son Thomas is in the Union [workhouse]. Henry is married and not in a position to help his parents. They are well known to the parish authorities and have recently been offered an order for the workhouse. WC [William Collingham]
Referred to parish, R P Hooper

[685] Death of Lucy Card registered Q3 1892 Brighton 2b 124.
[686] Death of James Card registered Q3 1907 Brighton 2b 106.

12 January 1891
Mrs Card applied at the office on Saturday for some assistance. She took her discharge from the workhouse a week ago but is totally unable to earn her own living and is still addicted to drink. Her husband is in the Union. The son Henry is giving her shelter and she is subsisting on charity. WC [William Collingham]
Refer to parish, E Eager [?]

180 SARAH MILLER, 59, CHARWOMAN, 20 SUN STREET, BRIGHTON

Sarah Miller was born in Brighton in about 1813. In 1861 she was enumerated at 20 Sun Street: she had already been widowed and was living with her two sons, John and Henry, and a 75-year-old charwoman named Jane Figg, who may have been her mother. Nothing is known of Sarah Miller's late husband but the eldest of their sons was born in about 1843.

When Sarah Miller's case was forwarded to the Mendicity Society by Mrs Peters of 16 York Road in May 1872 she was still living at 20 Sun Street and claimed to have been living there since 1846. She was working as a charwoman, earning 3s 6d per week and paying rent of 2s 6d per week: she was five shillings in arrears.

She was enumerated again at 20 Sun Street in 1881 when she was living with her daughter Jane and son-in-law Alfred Baker. Sarah Miller's death was registered in Brighton in the December quarter of 1882.[687]

20 May 1872
Statement: Sarah Miller wants a little assistance. The little money she earns is not enough to keep her.
Report: I made enquiries respecting this case and find this woman gets her living by charring. Mrs Peters states she has worked for her a long time. She gave her a good character and states she believes it to be a very deserving case for a little temporary relief. Mr Jones, the town missionary, gave her a good character and states he believes this to be a deserving case. She applied to the parish in December last but refused to go in the [work]house. The home is in a passable state. WC [William Collingham]
Consideration deferred, communication to be made to Mrs Peters, R P Hooper, chairman. Relieved with grant of 3s 6d, R P Hooper, chairman. Entered, RJ [Robert Johnson, secretary]

687 Death of Sarah Miller registered Q4 1882 Brighton 2b 151.

181 JULIA BRAY, 24, CHARWOMAN, 41 WOOD STREET, BRIGHTON

Julia Bray (née Diplock) married Trayton Bray in Lewes in the March quarter of 1869. She was baptised at Holy Cross, Uckfield, on 21 November 1847, the daughter of Henry Diplock, a gardener of Ridgewood, Uckfield, and his wife, Georgiana.[688] *The family were enumererated in Uckfield in 1851 and in Framfield in 1861. Trayton Bray was born in Ringmer in the March quarter of 1849 and was enumerated at Moor Lane, Ringmer in 1851 and Spring Cottage, Ringmer, in 1861.*[689]

By 1871 Trayton and Julia Bray were living at Spring Gardens, Brighton, with their infant son, George, and Julia's widowed mother, Sarah. The Mendicity Society's application form completed in May 1872 states that they had been living in Brighton for two months and that their previous addrresses had been Malling Street, Lewes, and 11 Marine Parade, Eastbourne, suggesting that they had moved from Brighton to Eastbourne to Lewes and then back to Brighton in the space of 13 months. However, the family led a peripatetic life in the years to follow so this is quite likely to be an accurate record of their movements.

When Julia Bray approached the Mendicity Society for relief, Trayton Bray had moved to St Helens, Lancashire, to find work. She was renting two rooms at 41 Wood Street, which she shared with her son, also named Trayton though referred to as George on the census return. She paid weekly rent of 3s 6d and had an income of 16 shillings: she earned six shillings per week charring for Mrs Woodard of 44 Norfolk Square and her husband sent home ten shillings. The Mendicity Society offered to loan Trayton Bray the train fare to St Helens for Julia Bray and her young son but she wanted to go via Uckfield to visit her mother. The charity did not wish to honour this request and Bray did not receive the money.

In 1881 the family were enumerated at Hobden Court, Southwick, when Trayton Bray was employed as a fireman on the SS Brighton operating from Newhaven. This census return suggests that Julia Bray manged to make the journey to St Helens as the couple had two children born in Flintshire in about 1875 and 1877. Another child was born in Southwick in about 1880. The owner of the SS Brighton, William Watson Harvey, engaged Bray on 18 July 1881 and paid him £1 8s.[690] *Bray resigned on 6 August 1881: his conduct and ability were both recorded as 'good'.*[691]

In 1891 the family, without Trayton, were enumerated at 17 West Road, Southwick, but by 1901 Julia and Trayton Bray had moved to 49 Glen Street, South Shields, where they lived with their daughter Rosa, her husband and three boarders. Trayton Bray was employed as a marine engineer and his son-in-law, William Goodman, was a lance corporal in the Royal Engineers.

688 ESRO: PAR 496/1/2/2/27.

689 No record of Trayton Bray's baptism could be found in Ringmer parish records but successive census returns record his place of birth as Ringmer.

690 ESRO: RSS/1/587/1.

691 ESRO: RSS/1/589/1.

Trayton and Julia Bray stayed in South Shields and were enumerated at number 82 Glen Street in 1911 when Trayton, now 63, was employed as a labourer at the chemical works. His death was registered in South Shields in the September quarter of 1915.[692] *Julia Bray's death, aged 81, was recorded in South Shields in the September quarter of 1931.*[693]

21 May 1872
Statement: Julia Bray wants a little assistance to help her get to St Helens, Lancashire, where she states her husband has got work. I find St Helens is 198 miles beyond London. She states the fare will be about 25s.
Report: I made enquiries respecting this case and find this woman bears a good character. Mrs Woodard, 44 Norfolk Square, states she worked for her about a fortnight and would willingly assist her if she had the means. The home is in a passable state. This woman showed me part of a letter that she received from her husband to show me he was at St Helens. WC [William Collingham]
Advance of 10s on condition that the remainder is forthcoming. To be repaid by husband in weekly instalments. R P Hooper, chairman. Entered, RJ [Robert Johnson, secretary]

Letter from Mrs Woodard, 44 Norfolk Square, Brighton, [May 1872]
Mrs Woodard, 44 Norfolk Square, having had Mrs Bray recommended as a respectable, industrious charwoman, has been well satisfied during the time she has employed her. Mrs Bray is most anxious to join her husband in Lancashire and would be truly thankful if she could accompany her relative now about starting with her children had she sufficient means to pay her journey and her husband's earnings are not sufficient to enable her to do so [sic]. She therefore solicits the aid of some kind friends to forward her wishes now that she feels herself equal to the long journey.

Letter from J Whiteside, Inspector, St Helens [Lancashire], 28 May 1872
Sir, in answer to yours of the 25th instant I am directed by Mr Superintendent Ludlam to inform you that the husband of Julia Bray is not known to the police here but from inquiry I have made [sic] he appears to be a sober man. He is at present working for Mr Gamble, charcoal manufacturer here, and in receipt of 16s per week wages. He seems wishful to have his wife with him and states that if any money were advanced to assist in her removal he would willingly pay it back by weekly installments of one and two shillings. I am sir your obedient servant, J Whiteside, Inspector

Letter from David Gamble, Gerard's Bridge, St Helens [Lancashire], 31 May 1872

692 Death of Trayton Bray registered Q3 1915 South Shields 10a 872.
693 Death of Julia Bray registered Q3 1931 South Shields 10a 680.

Sir, in reply to yours of yesterday. I shall be glad to forward the money paid to me as you request. Yours truly, David Gamble

10 June 1872
Further information respecting this case: Mrs Bray called at the office last Thursday and stated that before she went to St Helens she wants to go to Uckfield to see her mother and then start from Uckfield to St Helens and when I informed her that she could not have the 10s and that I must see her off by the train, she then stated she thought it was very hard not to have it as it was a loan. She also stated if I did not hear from her on Friday I was to think she was gone. I have not heard from her since.
Dismissed, R P Hooper, chairman. NB woman did not call for the money allowed

182 JANE MANDER, 36, NEEDLEWOMAN, 12 DERBY PLACE, BRIGHTON[694]

The date and place of Jane and Matthew Mander's wedding is not known but in her application to the Mendicity Society Jane Mander stated that she was born in Thame, Oxfordshire. Census returns corroborate this information and show her husband's place of birth as Beckley, Oxfordshire. The Mendicity Society form states that the Manders came to Brighton in about 1861 and had been living at 12 Derby Place with their three-year-old daughter Mary Ann for four months and previously at 40 Nelson Street where they were enumerated in 1871.

When Jane Mander approached the Mendicity Society in May 1872 the family were paying weekly rent of 4s 6d and were nine shillings in arrears. Matthew Mander claimed to have been working at Hove gas works until being laid off a month previously. He stated that he was earning 15 shillings per week when in full employment and Jane Mander stated that she took home four shillings per week as a needlewoman, consequently their combined wages were reduced from 19 shillings per week to four shillings. Their daughter, Mary Ann, attended Dorset Street School.

In 1881 the Manders, now with their three-year-old son Charles, were enumerated at 3 Carlton Street, an address they shared with the Field and Hedges families. Matthew Mander was employed as a bricklayer's labourer and Jane was still working as a needlewoman.

22 May 1872
Statement: Jane Mander wants a little assistance till her husband gets work.
Report: I made enquiries respecting this case and find this man's statement is false. I saw the clerk this morning at the Hove gas works. He looked through

[694] The surname is given as Marnder by the charity's agent, William Collingham, but in census returns spelled Mander.

their books in my presence and the name of Mander is not there and I find the lowest wage they pay is 18s per week. Mr Toye the scripture reader states he cannot recommend this case for relief. The house is in a passable state. Dismissed, undeserving, R P Hooper, chairman. Entered, RJ [Robert Johnson, secretary]

183 MARIA SKINNER, 31, WIFE OF A GARDENER, 8 KEW STREET, BRIGHTON

Maria Staples married John Skinner, a labourer of St Alban's, Cheapside, London, at St Nicholas, Brighton, on 6 April 1863.[695] *Maria Staples was born in Walthamstow, Essex, in about 1840 and John Skinner was born in about 1841: different census returns give his place of birth as either East Grinstead or Lewes.*[696]

When Mr Alfred Larking of 18 Clifton Terrace contacted the Mendicity Society about the Skinner family in May 1872 they had been living at 8 Kew Street for three months and had previously been living at 19 Kew Street. They were enumerated at that address in 1871 along with their six-year-old daughter, Annie, and four-month-old son, Arthur. The Skinners paid six shillings per week rent for the entire house and were one week's rent in arrears. When in full employment John Skinner expected to earn 18 shillings per week as a gardener but he had been unwell and unable to work for two weeks. He had been a subscriber to the Manchester Unity Fund but had left in about 1866 so could not expect any assistance from them, but the parish had been providing weekly relief of 3s 3d.

In 1881 the Skinner family, now with a seven-year-old son named James, were still living at 8 Kew Street with a lodger named Henry Budd, a 21-year-old carriage cleaner from Alfriston, who married Annie Skinner in the September quarter of 1883. In 1891 they were enumerated at 39 West Hill Street, Brighton. John Staples was still making a living as a gardener and they shared the house with Maria Skinner's sister, Eliza Staples, a cook also born in Walthamstow. John and Maria Skinner were enumerated at this address in 1901 and 1911. By 1911 their daughter Annie Budd, now a widow, and grandson Albert Budd were living with them along with their son Arthur Skinner, a labourer in the railway company wheel shop.

The death of a 73-year-old woman named Maria Skinner was registered in Hove in the September quarter of 1913.[697]

Letter from Mr Larking, 18 Clifton Terrace to the committee of the Mendicity Society, [May 1872]

[695] ESRO: PAR 255/1/3/36.

[696] There are two possible candidates: John Skinner whose birth was registered at Lewes in the March quarter of 1840 and another child born in East Grinstead in December 1841.

[697] Death of Maria Skinner registered Q3 1913 Steyning 2b 309.

Skinner, a very honest industrious man when not mentally incapacitated. Mrs Skinner, hard-working, honest and industrious but just now needing assistance. Reference, Mr Larking or Miss Jay, 18 Clifton Terrace

22 May 1872
Statement: Maria Skinner wants a little assistance till her husband gets better.
Report: I made enquiries respecting this case and find the man is sick, suffering from a heavy cold. Mr Larking, 18 Clifton Terrace, states he has employed him several times and believes him to be a very respectable man. I have known him for this last eight years and believe him to be a sober hard-working man. The home is in a passable state. They received relief at the rate of 3s 3d and the relieving officer states if the wife applies again on Saturday there is no doubt she will have the same again. WC [William Collingham]. Referred to parish, R P Hooper, chairman. Entered, RJ [Robert Johnson, secretary]

184 WILLIAM MARCUTT, AGE AND OCCUPATION NOT KNOWN, PREVIOUSLY OF 2 SUDELEY PLACE, BRIGHTON

The facts regarding William Marcutt supplied by both the Brighton Mendicity Society and the Paddington Committee for Organising Charitable Relief and Repressing Mendicity are so scant it has been impossible to find out anything certain about him. We know that he worked for a Mr Wilson of Royal Mews, possibly Royal Crescent Mews, for about 12 months but no one by the name of Marcutt could be found in Brighton on the 1871 census. The census of that year carries two entries that may refer to this man: a William Henry Marcutt, house painter, of 7 Meeting House Lane, Camberwell, and, more probably, a William Murcutt, a coachman born in Penrith, Cumberland, living with his wife Letitia at 16 Conduit Place, Paddington.[698]

Letter from R Court, Paddington Committee for Organising Charitable Relief and Repressing Mendicity, 3 Leinster Street, London, 21 May 1872
Sir, a man of the name of William Marcutt and family resided a for months since [sic] at 2 Sudeley Place, St George's Road, Brighton, and he was employed by Mr Wilson, Royal Mews, Marine Parade. Will you kindly cause some enquiries to be made respecting him and inform me the result to oblige. Sir, yours truly, R Court

23 May 1872
Report: I made enquiries respecting this case and find this man's statement is correct. I saw Mr Gun, the foreman for Mr Wilson, at the Royal Mews. He states Marcutt worked for Mr Wilson about twelve months and during that time his conduct was good. Cause of leaving employ a dispute with another man in the

[698] Marriage of William Murcutt and Letitia Campbell registered Q2 1869 Lambeth 1d 498.

yard. I saw the woman they lodged with, she states they went away in her debt and also the bakers and when he was in work he used to stay out drinking about till one and two o'clock in the morning.
Entered, RJ [Robert Johnson, secretary]

185 MRS G WAITE VERNON, AGE NOT RECORDED, PROFESSOR OF PIANO AND SINGING, 16 BEDFORD STREET, BRIGHTON

The Mendicity Society's form gives little biographical information about this woman. William Collingham, the agent of the Mendicity Society, recorded this applicant's name as Mrs G Waite Vernon but she was enumerated as Elizabeth Waite Vernon on the census of 1871 when she was living at 13 Osborne Street, Hove, with her eight-year-old grandson, Arthur G Waite. The census records that she was born in Middlesex in about 1817 and that she was a professor of singing and music. Arthur Waite was born in Lewes in about 1863.

Elizabeth Waite Vernon was also known as Elizabeth Waite and it was under this name that she appeared amongst the list of insolvents published in the Brighton Guardian on 6 March 1861. The newspaper stated that 'Elizabeth Waite, formerly of Ebury Street, Pimlico, Middlesex; afterwards of Victoria Place, Dover, Kent; afterwards of Kennington Road, Middlesex; afterwards of Ponsonby Terrace, Vauxhaul, Surrey; afterwards of Upper North Street, then of Manchester Street, then of Dorset Gardens, all in Brighton, Sussex; then of Stanley Street, Brompton, Middlesex; then of Norman Road, West Street, St Leonard's-on-Sea, Sussex; then of 6 Montpelier Street, then of Russell Square, then of Hampton Place, then of 49 York Road, then of Clarence Square, then of Queen's Road, West Hill Street, and now of 44 St George's Road, Brighton, Sussex, professor of music and singing, sometimes known as Mrs G Waite Vernon, came up for her first examination, supported by Mr Goodman. Insolvent's schedule showed debts to the amount of £547 12s 11½d, assets nil. There was no opposition and insolvent passed.'[699] The report of her insolvency in the Brighton Gazette went on to state that, 'The schedule contained the names of upwards of 200 creditors of almost every description.'[700]

Elizabeth Waite Vernon's case was forwarded to the Mendicity Society by the Reverend Snowden Smith, formerly vicar of All Souls, Eastern Road, and the names of Mrs Beaumont of 19 Brunswick Square and Mrs Davidson of 7 Lansdowne Terrace were supplied as references. She had previously been resident at Marlborough Place but had been living at 19 Bedford Street for two months, where she paid weekly rent of five shillings for one room. She was £1 in arrears and was earning 3s 6d per week as a music teacher.

[699] Brighton Guardian, 6 March 1861.
[700] Brighton Gazette, 7 March 1871.

The death of a 59-year-old woman named Elizabeth Waite was registered in Brighton in the June quarter of 1875.[701]

25 May 1872
Statement: Mrs G Waite Vernon. I have not got one penny in the world. What to do I don't know. If I go to London I cannot stand the noise of the streets.
Report: this woman states she has been ill ever since last October and that she has only got one pupil to teach at present. She also states if it had not been for some kind ladies that assisted her during the winter she believes she would have been starved. The Reverend Mr Snowden Smith states what he wants is a little quiet enquiry made to see what can be done for her. He states he has assisted her on one or two occasions. I asked her if she could not do better in London than what she could here. She stated she could not stand the noise of the streets there. Captain Davidson states he has known applicant a long time and that she is a very respectable person. He also states they have assisted her several times but cannot continue to do so. Mrs Beaumont states applicant is not fit for teaching. She has assisted her on two or three occasions but cannot continue to do so. I am informed applicant has a daughter in very comfortable circumstances but she refused to give her address and said she would sooner starve in the streets than anyone should go to her daughter.
Ineligible. Result of enquiry to be communicated to Reverend Snowden Smith, R P Hooper, chairman. Entered, RJ [Robert Johnson, secretary]

186 EMILY WELLS, 26, IRONER, 3 CARLTON PLACE, BRIGHTON

Emily Howell and William Wells, both of 6 Blackman Street, married at St Nicholas, Brighton, on 7 June 1870.[702] *They were both born in Brighton, in about 1844 and 1845 respectively.*[703] *In May 1872 the family's case was forwarded to the Mendicity Society by G Duddell of Queens Park. William was training with the Chichester militia while Emily remained at 3 Carlton Place with her two young sons aged five and one. She had been working as an ironer for Mrs Mills of 17 Marine View and would usually expect to earn ten shillings per week, but had been unable to work for a week due to sickness. They paid weekly rent of two shillings for one room and were two shillings in arrears. Emily Wells did not approach the charity in person but sent another woman named Howell who was probably her mother or sister.*

By 1881 the family, now with five children, were living at 47 Spa Street. William Wells was employed as a bricklayer and their eldest son, Frederick, was working as an errand

[701] Death of Elizabeth Waite registered Q2 1875 Brighton 2b 145.

[702] ESRO: PAR 255/1/3/44.

[703] Birth of Emily Charlotte Howell Q2 1846 Brighton 7 318; birth of William Wells Q2 1847 Brighton 7 306.

boy. In 1891 the family were enumerated at 25 Chesterfield Street, Brighton, when William was still working as a bricklayer and Emily employed as a laundress.

27 May 1872
Statement: Emily Wells wants a little assistance till she gets better.
Report: I made enquiries respecting this case and find this woman's husband is a bricklayer. He is now up training in the Chichester militia. The wife I find works for Mrs Mills, laundress, 17 Marine View, and bears a good character. I find she was sick last week but she is gone to work today. I have not seen the home. When I called she was out. They are not known to the relieving officer.
Applicant did not apply herself but sent a woman named Howell.
Ineligible, R P Hooper, chairman; GDR [George Dudley Ryder]. Entered, RJ [Robert Johnson, secretary]

187 CAROLINE DEIGHTON, NO AGE GIVEN, IRONER, 21 CIRCUS STREET, BRIGHTON

Little is known about Caroline Deighton: no obvious match could be found for her on census returns, in local newspapers or on databases and there is scant information about her on the Mendicity Society's application form.

The case was forwarded to the charity by Miss S E Crisp of 15 Norfolk Terrace who had recently been in touch with the Mendicity Society regarding another family. S E Crisp is thought to be Susan Eliza Crisp who was born in Waltham Abbey, Essex, in about 1817 and was enumerated at 34 Park Crescent as a visitor in 1871.

The chairman of the Mendicity Society, Robert Poole Hooper, questioned whether Caroline Deighton might be an alias for another applicant called Caroline Tester (case 129) who was also an ironer. This theory is quite possible: Caroline Tester was also employed as an ironer and when admitted to the Sussex County Lunatic Asylum in July 1872 had recently undergone surgery for breast cancer.

Letter from Miss S E Crisp, 15 Norfolk Terrace, Brighton, [May 1872]
Gentleman, will you kindly investigate the enclosed for me – I am much obliged for your letter respecting Soughtons – I hope we shall get them out in about 10 days. I will call and pay in my subscription to your institution. I think it most excellent. Yours truly, S E Crisp, 15 Norfolk Terrace[704]

Letter [to Miss S E Crisp, 15 Norfolk Terrace, Brighton] from Caroline Deighton, 21 Circus Street, 23 May 1872

[704] Miss S E Crisp was in the process of helping the Soughton family (case 72) when this letter regarding Caroline Deighton was written.

Madam, I trust you will pardon the liberty I have taken in addressing you but having recently undergone an operation of having my right breast taken off for cancer from which I suffered five years which I can assure you madame has reduced me to my present condition being an ironer and is present unabled [sic] to work. If madame you could kindly assist me a little I should indeed be truly thankful.
Your humble servant, Caroline Deighton

27 May 1872
Statement: no statement made
Report: I have seen Miss Crisp. She states a woman came to her and asked for a little assistance and stated she was an ironer but had not been able to work for some time on account of a cancer in her breast. Miss Crisp, not knowing her, gave her sixpence and told her she had better apply to the Mendicity Society. She stated that was no use – they would not assist her. I made enquiries in Circus Street but cannot find no such party - at 21 the name is Carden.
Case to be investigated as opportunity affords. Is this the same person as in record book No 129? R P Hooper, chairman. Entered, RJ [Robert Johnson, secretary]

188 MARGARET JOHNSON, 51, NEEDLEWOMAN, 54 HEREFORD STREET, BRIGHTON

Little is known of Margaret Johnson and her husband John. John Johnson was born in about 1808 and earned his living as a hawker, Margaret Johnson was born in about 1821 but neither of their places of birth are known. According to the Mendicity Society application form they came to Brighton in about September 1871 and had previously been living in Portsmouth and London.

They rented one second floor room at 54 Hereford Street for which they paid weekly rent of 1s 6d. When in full employment they both earned seven shillings per week and were up to date with rent payments, but John Johnson had been unable to work recently due to infirmity. The Reverend Richard Snowden Smith, vicar of All Souls, Eastern Road, Brighton, supplied a reference for the couple.

29 May 1872
Statement: Margaret Johnson wants a little assistance. Her husband is not able to go hawking
Report: I made enquiries respecting this case and find this man is not fit for hawking. He is infirm from old age and has lost the sight of one eye. The wife does plain and fancy needlework but seems to get a very poor living. The Reverend Snowden Smith used to employ and relieve her but has ceased to do so. In consequence of improper conversation overheard between her and one of

the servants Mr Smith cannot recommend the case to this society. The home is in a destitute state. They are not known to the relieving officer.
Undeserving, R P Hooper, chairman. Entered, RJ [Robert Johnson, secretary]

189 UNKNOWN FRENCH WOMAN THOUGHT TO BE CALLED LE BAS

No clear matches for anyone by the name of Le Bas could be found in census returns or newspaper articles.

Letter from [the Reverend] Edmund Grindle, 9 Clarence Square, Brighton, 27 May 1872[705]
Gentlemen, there is a case which has recently come under my notice which I should be glad to suggest to you for investigation. It is that of a French woman (name, I think, Le Bas) who professes to have been deserted by her husband (an Englishman) at Newhaven on their arrival from France and to be perfectly destitute. She gives as her address 17 Cavendish Place (or street). She has made three applications to me for relief, if her story is true she is no doubt in a sad plight, if not true she must be a great humbug. I commend her to your notice if you will allow me to do so and remain your obedient servant, Edmund S Grindle

29 May 1872
Report: I made enquiries respecting this letter and find at 17 Cavendish Street, there is no such party but I believe the right party is at 18 Cumberland Place. There is a French man and his wife lodging there. They have been there about six weeks. They were accompanied by another French man who I am informed has left the town. They answer the same description as the party that went to the Reverend Mr Grindle. I believe them to be regular imposters. Mr Grindle states altogether he has given them about 7s, he also states if the committee wish this case brought forward he will attend and give evidence against them but he would not consent to my taking immediate action. WC [William Collingham]

30 May 1872
Further information: on going to the house this morning I found that since my last visit the party had left the town.
Case to be recorded and communicated to Mr Grindle, R P Hooper, chairman; GDR [George Dudley Ryder]. Entered, RJ [Robert Johnson, secretary]

[705] Edmund Grindle was curate of St Paul's, West Street, Brighton.

190 ELIZABETH KING, 30, NO OCCUPATION, 84 GEORGE STREET, HOVE

Elizabeth King (née Bates) was, according to her record on the 1861 census, born in Newick in about 1844.[706] *She married Harry King, a dairyman, at St Andrew's, Hove, on 9 February 1868.*[707] *Harry King had been baptised at that church on 23 June 1844.*[708] *The King family were enumerated at 7 Church Street, Hove, in 1861: Harry King lived with his parents John King, a pork butcher and greengrocer from Westham, Suffolk, his mother Jane, a laundress born in Coombes, and five siblings. On 14 September 1870 a 25-year-old man named Harry King, was admitted to the Sussex County Hospital with softening of the brain.*[709] *He was discharged as an out-patient on 16 November 1870.*

In 1871 the couple were enumerated at 84 George Street, Hove: Harry King was recorded as a milkman and Elizabeth King was employed as a cook. They lived with a 52-year-old widow named Ruth Bates who was also born in Newick.

The family's case was forwarded to the Mendicity Society by Mrs Bennett of 16 Ventnor Villas, Hove. The society's application form states that they had lived at 84 George Street for 12 months and previously were resident at 22 George Street. They paid weekly rent of 2s 9d for one room and were not in arrears.

Harry King died aged 31 and was buried at St Andrew's, Hove, 26 July 1875.[710]

31 May 1872
Statement: Elizabeth King would be thankful for a little assistance.
Report: I made enquiries respecting this case and find this man did work for Mr Horton, dairyman, Hove, but he has not been able to work for this last two years and for eighteen months he has been bedridden. He belongs to the London Unity of Odd Fellows, from that he gets 2s 6d per week. His father allows him 1s per week, Mrs Bennett allows him 2s per week, the parish allow 3s 6d per week, total 9s. The wife having to be in constant attendance on her husband she is not able to earn anything. The home is in a passable state. The Reverend Mr Kelly states he has assisted them on one or two occasions, and he hopes the committee will take a favourable view of their case for he can assure them it's a deserving one. Mrs Bennett stated she would like this case investigated and afterwards know the result.
Referred to parish authorities, R P Hooper, chairman

706 A girl named Elizabeth Bates was baptised at Newick on 7 March 1844 (PAR 428/1/2/1) but her parents were recorded as Henry and Barbara Bates: her father's name was recorded as Benjamin Bates in the marriage register.

707 ESRO: PAR 386/1/3/6.

708 ESRO: PAR 386/1/2/1.

709 ESRO: HB 35/3/1870-4926.

710 ESRO: PAR 386/1/5/3.

191 ESTHER WILSON, 43, NURSE, 12 UPPER NORTH STREET, BRIGHTON

The case of Esther Wilson and her family was forwarded to the Mendicity Society by John Cordy Burrows, former Mayor of Brighton. She was born in Warbleton in about 1824 and married Thomas Wilson, a traveller, in Brighton in 1851.[711] .

In 1861 Esther Wilson, a widow, was enumerated at 3 Lea Bridge Road, Hackney, Middlesex, where she lived with her daughters Esther, Mary and Elizabeth who were all born in Clapton, Middlesex, between 1853 and 1860. The death of a man named Thomas Wilson was registered at Bethnal Green in the June quarter of 1859.

The Mendicity Society's application form states that Esther Wilson moved to Brighton in 1869: initially to 3 Vine Place but by 2 April 1871 she was living with her three daughters at 8 Upper North Street and it was from this address that she came in to contact with the charity in May 1872. The application form also stated that she had been living in the parish for 39 years, which was clearly not true. She was paying weekly rent of 2s 6d for one first-floor room and was ten shillings in arrears. When fully employed, Esther Wilson stated that she could expect to earn 21 shillings per week but recently had only been taking home 2s 6d. Her 18-year-old daughter Esther earned nine shillings per week dressmaking for Mrs Biggs of St Nicholas Road; the youngest daughter, Elizabeth, attended a nursing college so did not contribute to the household income. John Cordy Burrows and Mr Beal, a subscriber to the Mendicity Society, supplied references for Esther Wilson.

Esther Wilson senior was enumerated in 1881 at 13 Elm Grove, where she lived with her daughter Esther Emma, her son-in-law Charles Wright who was a coach maker, their two children and her youngest daughter Elizabeth, a mantle maker.[712] *She was still living with the Wright family in 1891 when they were enumerated at 50 Elm Grove. The death of a woman named Esther Wilson was registered at Brighton in the September quarter of 1893.*[713]

1 May 1872
Statement: Esther Wilson wants a little assistance to help pay her arrears in rent and also to help pay a loan that she is in arrears with.
Report: I made enquiries respecting this case and find this woman is an invalid nurse and when she has not got nursing to do she does a little needlework. She receives parish relief at the rate of 3s per week. The daughter works for Mrs Biggs, dressmaker, St Nicholas Road. Her wages is 9s per week. The landlady stated instead of the arrears in rent being only 10s it's over £3. The home is in a destitute state. I have not seen Cordy Burrows esq. I called twice and on both

[711] Marriage of Esther Standen and Thomas Wilson registered Q4 1851 Brighton 7 500.

[712] Thomas Wilson, traveller, is named as the late father of Emma Esther Wilson who married Charles Sapey Wright at St Peter, Preston, on 17 May 1877 (PAR 452/1/3/4).

[713] Death of Esther Wilson registered Q3 1893 Brighton 2b 141.

occasions he was out. The servant stated applicant came there begging and believes Mr Burrows does not know her.
Referred for further enquiry, R P Hooper, chairman

3 June 1872
Further information respecting this case: Cordy Burrows states he has known applicant a long time. He believes her to be a respectable person. Mr Beal states he has known applicant a long time and that she is always in the same destitute state and that she borrowed £2 of which she has paid off 8s and is in arrears as to 12s of the £3 claimed by the landlady for. £2 10s 0d are for a shop formerly rented – 10s being the sum remaining for applicant's present lodging.
Ineligible, R P Hooper

Letter from R Johnson, secretary, Brighton Mendicity Society, to W J Standen, 11 July 1872
Sir, Mrs Wilson of this town has applied to us for assistance to enable her to send her daughter Mary to you for the benefit of country air, she having been lately discharged from the infirmary cured from a mild attack of smallpox. Before granting the help required we wish to learn from you whether the statement as to your willingness to receive the poor girl is true. I may add for your satisfaction that the authorities of the infirmary never discharge a patient until every chance of infection is gone and the clothes belonging to the party are thoroughly purified. An early answer will oblige, yours faithfully, R Johnson

Reverse of above letter, 26 July 1872
Mr Muggeridge, 36 Cobden Road, the uncle of the girls called to say that W J Standen will have nothing further further to do with the party having frequently relieved the mother and daughter in vain. The girls' father has on more than one occasion taken charge of the girls but the mother took her away and sold the clothes provided for her

192 BARBARA COOK, 50, WIFE OF A CLERK, 56 CLARENCE SQUARE, BRIGHTON

Barbara Cook was born in Lewes in about 1822. In 1871 she was enumerated at 191 High Street, Lewes, earning her living as a schoolmistress. Her husband Thomas Cook, a solicitor's clerk, was not listed at the address: the only other residents were two pupils named Catherine and Sarah Shuttleworth from Gainsborough, Lincolnshire. At the time of the application on 1 June 1872 the Cooks had been living at 56 Clarence Square for two months where they paid eight shillings per week rent. They had been living in Brighton for 12 months and were previously resident at 9 Great College Street. Thomas Cook earned

15 shillings per week working for Charles Sharood, solicitor of 74 Ship Street but was 16 shillings in debt at the time of the application.[714]

The census of 1881 contains an entry for a 59-year-old woman named Barbara Cooke [sic] who was enumerated at 9 Boyces Street, Brighton, living with a man named Walkinson Cooke, a general law clerk and photographer. In 1891 a 73-year-old widow named Barbara Cook was enumerated at 174 Eastern Road where she lodged with the Hay family and earned her living as a needlewoman.

Barbara Cook was admitted to the Sussex County Lunatic Asylum at Haywards Heath on 10 May 1895 suffering with senile dementia.[715] *She had still been working as a needlewoman but had come to the asylum from Brighton Workhouse and died on 18 December 1895.*

Letter from John Cordy Burrows, Mayor of Brighton, 62 Old Steine, Brighton 31 May 1872

My dear Mr Hayes, I believe the woman to be worthy of the aid of our society, will you kindly give her case attention and oblige. Yours truly, Cordy Burrows, Mayor[716]

1 June 1872

Statement: Barbara Cook wants a little assistance to help get some furniture so that she might be able to open a small school but she does <not> want her husband to know anything about it.

Report: I made enquiries respecting this case and find this man is a clerk. He has been of intemperate habits but lately he has been a little better. He was clerk for Mr Hillman, solicitor, Malling Street, Lewes, for a long time but was discharged through drink and after that he had no regular employment for two years until 3 months ago Mr Sharood took him <on> merely out of charity. Mr Sharood states he has nothing to say against him any more than he is a poor, easy going man and easily led away into drink. During the time they were in Lewes the wife kept a small school until her husband was discharged from his situation. The home is in a destitute state and to do the applicant any good towards starting a school she would require £10 at least for furniture.

Ineligible. Referred to private sources, R P H[ooper] chairman

Letter from Miss Butler, Lee House [12 Dyke Road], Brighton, 17 October 1876

Miss Butler begs the secretary will enquire about Mrs Cooke [sic] – 3 Saunders Building, Black Lion Street. She has an invalid husband (bath chairman) and has

714 Sharood was a solicitor of some standing and had served as Brighton's first town clerk in the 1850s.

715 ESRO: HC 24/7524.

716 G S Hayes, member of the council of the Charity Organisation Society.

been a sick nurse, has also let lodgings and lost by her lodgers – Miss B wishes to learn if the story is likely to be true as she knows nothing of the woman

18 October 1876
Further information: Miss Butler requests a report of this case. The husband, who draws a handchair is not an invalid but a great drunkard. His wife, who goes out nursing, is also given to drink. Their present weekly rent is 5s and they have one lodger. When they lived at 10 Portland Street they took in several lodgers and they left that neighbourhood very much in debt. WC [William Collingham]
Report sent to Miss Butler, HAD

February c1880 [information missing due to paper damage]
This woman went to Mr H Johnston begging on Monday and said that the Lord had sent her, she then gave two false address, after which Mr Johnstone took her to the Hove Town Hall. She was brought before the Bench this morning and at the request of Mr Johnston I attended to give evidence that I had known her as a beggar since June 1872. At the police station the sum of 9s 4½d was found on her and she was sentenced to seven days imprisonment. WC [William Collingham]
Undeserving. To be recorded. GDT [G D Turnbull]

18 May 1888
Mrs George Woodhouse of 8 Percival Terrace requests a report of this case. Mrs Cook has recently been begging at the lady's house and stated in answer to questions that she was taking charge of a house on the Marine Parade but at present I have not succeeded in tracing her. WC [William Collingham]
Report to Mrs Woodhouse, R P Hooper chairman

12 December 1888
Mrs George Woodhouse called at [the] office on Tuesday and stated that Mrs Cook had applied to her for assistance but before relieving her the lady wishes for a report of the case. Cook is taking charge of a house at 85 Marine Parade for Mr Stride and has no regular employment. His wife who takes in needlework continues to beg and upon the whole they seem unsatisfactory people. GC [George Collingham]
Report sent to Mrs Woodhouse

193 WILLIAM SAXBY, 25, CHAIR BOTTOMER, 11 WHICHELO PLACE, BRIGHTON

William Saxby was baptised at St Nicholas, Brighton, on 21 March 1847.[717] *His parents were William Saxby, a plumber born in Lewes in 1824, and Mary Ann Chapman born in Brighton in about 1819 and they were living at Middle Street at the time of their son's baptism. The couple were married at St Nicholas, Brighton, on 9 April 1843.*[718]

In 1851 the Saxby family were enumerated at 3 Paradise Street and in 1861 at Bedford Cottage, Brighton. William Saxby senior was emlpoyed as a plumber, his eldest daughter, also Mary Ann, was employed as a milliner and the remaining six children were all scholars. By 1871 they had moved to 14 Whichelo Place and William Saxby junior was employed as a cane worker. William Saxby senior was referred to in the application of Matilda Sharp, who applied to the Mendicity Society in January 1872 and whose husband George Sharp was employed by Saxby in late 1871 (see case 36).

When William Saxby junior's case was forwarded to the Mendicity Society in June 1872 he was living at 11 Whichelo Place and had apparently been living there for five years, though this does not tally with the entry on the 1871 census. He stated that before that he was living at 65 Hereford Street. Whilst at this address William Saxby was summoned before the Bench for permitting nuisances at 60-65 Hereford Street (Brighton Guardian 16 May 1866). It is not clear from the article as to why Saxby was held accountable but Francis Gifford, head sanitary inspector, stated that 'the houses were in a most filthy condition. Forty-seven persons lived in them, and the four privies were as dirty as could be imagined. A quantity of decaying vegetable matter was in the yards. The water supply - there was no water butt, was also defective; there were no dustbins. Mr Sewell, surgeon, said he considered the houses unfit for habitation. Mr Black [town clerk] said he perhaps ought to ask for the houses to be closed till they were rendered habitable, but as considerable inconvenience might be caused if such an order were made, he would merely ask for an order for the removal of the causes of nuisance. This order was made.' No charge was made against William Saxby.

Saxby's sister Catherine appeared in court seven months later on Monday 6 December 1866 as the prosecutrix in a case brought against Elvina Scott, who was charged with stealing Saxby's cloak.[719] *Catherine Saxby was employed at Hanningtons, North Street, as a mantle maker and found her cloak stolen whilst preparing to go home at the end of the working day. Scott, who was heavily pregnant, admitted to her misdemeanour and Catherine Saxby's mother stated that she had no desire to see the prisoner charged and asked that the Bench would take a lenient view of the case. In spite of this intervention the Bench 'were disposed to take a merciful view of the case, and considering her present condition, he should pass upon her a very light sentence, namely, a fortnight's*

[717] ESRO: PAR 255/1/2/14.

[718] ESRO: PAR 255 1/3/14; Marriage of Mary Ann Chapman and William Saxby registered Q2 1843 Brighton 7 362.

[719] Brighton Gazette: 6 December 1866.

imprisonment without hard labour.' William Saxby junior's case was forwarded to the Mendicity Society by George Dudley Ryder, who was on the board of the charity. Saxby was earning ten shillings per week as a chair bottomer. It was stated that he had been convicted of indecent assault some years earlier, but details of this case have not been found.

3 June 1872
Statement: William Saxby wants a licence to hawk and a little stock of cane to give him a start.
Report: I have known this young man a long time but I never knew any good of him. He was convicted some time ago at the Brighton Borough Bench for an indecent assault upon a child on the beach and sentenced to three months imprisonment with hard labour. He occasionally does a little chair bottoming. His father is a respectable man. He works for his father Mr Saxby, builder, 31/32 Upper St James Street. His wages is 33s per week besides overtime. G D Ryder esq states this man begged of him on Saturday and he not knowing him he gave him a ticket to have his case investigated. He is known to the relieving officer having been in the workhouse on one or two occasions.
Undeserving, R P Hooper, chairman

194 ARCHIBALD STEVENS, 38, CARTER, 47 SPA STREET, BRIGHTON

Archibald Stevens, son of Edward and Harriet Stevens of Hereford Street, was baptised at St Nicholas, Brighton on 4 May 1834.[720] *In July 1850 a 15-year-old labourer named Archibald Stevens was charged with stealing a pair of trousers and other articles from James Richardson, and five candlesticks and other articles from John Hunt. Stevens and his accomplice James Whiting were sentenced to three months hard labour, except three weeks which were served in solitary confinement.*[721] *In December 1856 a 23-year-old trunk maker named Archibald Stevens was indicted for stealing a sack from Joseph Hallet.*[722] *The recorder stated that Stevens had been convicted three times before but 'as the offence was a light one, he would not convict him to four years penal servitude this time, which he might do, but he would sentence him to twelve months imprisonment to hard labour; and if he came there again he would have ten years penal servitude.'*
Stevens, who was described in the parish register as a marine stove dealer, married Jane Brown at St Nicholas, Brighton, on 24 April 1859.[723] *In 1861 the couple were enumerated at 12 Paradise Street and Archibald Stevens was described as a trunk maker. By 1871 they were living at 47 Spa Street, where they lived with Stevens' niece, Martha Hart.*

[720] ESRO: PAR 255/1/2/9.
[721] Brighton Gazette: 4 July 1850.
[722] Brighton Gazette: 25 December 1856.
[723] ESRO: PAR 255/1/3/31.

In June 1872 Jane Mohun of 8 Dorset Gardens wrote to the Mendicity Society alerting them to Archibald and Jane Stevens's plight. The couple were still living at 47 Spa Street, where they stated they had lived for six years; previously they had lived at 8 Spa Street. They paid weekly rent of seven shillings for the entire house but had rent arrears of 21 shillings. Stevens was working for Edward Spary, nurseryman, florist and seedsman of 43 and 44 Park Street, where he earned 30 shillings per week.

Letter from Jane Mohun, Dorset Gardens, Brighton, 3 June 1872
Gentleman, I feel anxious to bring to your notice the case of a man of the name of Stevens residing at 47 Spa Street. He is a very industrious man and brings his earnings to his wife whom I have known from a child. Stevens is a carter and has long worked for Mr Spary but has had the misfortune to lose one horse about 10 weeks ago and the other has been ill ever since and now totally unfit for use which has thrown them into great distress. It struck me it was a case that your society would search into and assist. Believe me, yours truly, Jane Mohun

4 June 1872
Statement: Archibald Stevens wants a little assistance to help buy a horse. He states he had two horses and ten weeks ago one died. He then collected £3 to help buy another horse and then the one he has now fell sick and he was obliged to spend that which he had collected.
Report: I made enquiries respecting this case and find this man did have two horses and two carts but one died 10 weeks ago. He then collected £3 to help buy another and then then the other horse fell sick and then he states he was obliged to spend the £3 he had collected. He states it will cost about £18 to buy another horse and out of that he has got £4 what he got for one of his carts he sold. The home is in a passable state. Miss Mohun, 8 Dorset Gardens, states she has known applicant a long time and believes him to be a very respectable man. The Reverend Snowden Smith states he has known applicant a long time and believes him to be a very respectable man, he also states he has assisted him and that he can recommend this case to the committee as a deserving one. Mrs Spary states applicant has worked for Mr Spary on several occasions and she believes him to be a respectable man.
WC [William Collingham]
Referred for particular enquiry, R P Hooper, chairman

7 June 1872
Further information respecting this case: Mr Spary states he has employed applicant on several occasions and he believes him to be a respectable man. Applicant has sold the sick horse for £1 17s 6d and has got a horse on trial for

which he has to pay £10 in case it suits. Since the horse died he has tried to get his living by firing[724] and also by using his other horse for light jobs.
Recommended to Provident District Society for loan, R P Hooper, chairman

195 ALBERT DRAYCOT, 30, SHOEMAKER, 2 THOMAS STREET, BRIGHTON

When Albert Draycot applied to the Mendicity Society on 7 June 1872 he had been living in Brighton for one day. He was born in America but had come with his wife Elizabeth and four children from Gateshead, where he had been working as a shoemaker for a Mr Hall.

When fully employed he expected to earn 21 shillings per week but had been unable to work for two weeks due to sickness. They lived in one room at a lodging house at 2 Thomas Street for which they paid 3s 6d. It is not clear how or why the Draycot family came to Brighton.

7 June 1872
Statement: Albert Draycot would be thankful for a little assistance to help him over tonight and tomorrow morning. He expects to go to work for Mr Lulham, 130 Queens Road, tomorrow.

Report: I made enquiries at Mr Lulham's, 130 Queens Road, and find this man's statement is correct. I afterwards went and saw the Reverend Mr Hooper and stated the case and he very kindly gave me half a crown. With that I bought some bread, tea, sugar, butter and paid their lodgings which they were very thankful for. WC [William Collingham]
Case to be entered in record book. Relieved by member of the committee, R P Hooper, chairman

196 JAMES DAVIES, 76, NO OCCUPATION, 58 GLOUCESTER ROAD, BRIGHTON

Little is known of James Davies or James Davey as he is sometimes referred to. He did not cooperate with the Mendicity Society when Mr Holford Stevens of 96 Western Road approached the charity on his behalf.

Letter from W Holford Stevens, 96 Western Road, Brighton, 8 June 1872
Sir, George Davey [sic] of Old Providence Place, London Road, appeals for relief. On my referring him to the society he tells me he has been refused help because he receives a small sum from the parish and that in consequence of his blindness

[724] Presumably making his living by selling firewood.

this is not enough to keep him from great distress. I told him that I would make an enquiry of you as to his statement and I shall be glad to learn your opinion of his case. I am sir, your obedient servant, W Holford Stevens

10 June 1872
Statement: I do not want anything to do with your society. I went to Mr Stevens and I am sorry for it.
Report: I made enquiries respecting this case and find this is the man that went to Mr Stevens and when I asked him what he meant by giving a false name and address. He stated he did not want this society to know anything about it. I am informed applicant's sons and daughters are in very comfortable circumstances and that one daughter allows him 2s per week, and one 1s per week. The relieving officer states applicant receives relief at the rate of 5s per week. He also states if the committee wish it, he will bring this case under the notice of the Board of Guardians. The home is in a passable state. Applicant is nearly blind and I believe he has been in the habit of begging for a long time. I made enquiries in Providence Place but cannot find anyone by the name of Davey there.
Ineligible, R P Hooper, chairman. Entered, RJ [Robert Johnson, secretary]

197 EDMUND WALTERS, 17, LABOURER, 2 THOMAS STREET, BRIGHTON

Edmund Walters, or Waters, was born in Hastings in about 1855. His case was forwarded to the Mendicity Society by Mr Harrington Balfour of 104 Lansdowne Place on 12 June 1872. He had been living in Brighton for three weeks and had previously been resident in Portsmouth and Byfleet Industrial School, Surrey. 2 Thomas Street appears to have been a well-used lodging house and was also home to Albert Draycot, applicant 195, who applied to the Mendicity Society on 7 June 1872. William North, applicant 120, lived at that address in 1880. Walters paid rent of 1s 9d per week and was not in arrears.
In 1891 a married man named Edmund Waters, who was born in Hastings in about 1855, was enumerated boarding at East Ham District Shipping Federation Shed 37 where he was employed as a general labourer.

Letter from E P Gibson, Bridge House, Wandsworth, Surrey, 24 May 1872
To Mr H Balfour. Edmund Waters was an inmate of the school at Wandsworth of which I was the master. I cannot remember the date of his leaving but have no doubt his account is correct. He bore a very good character while in the school and left with the same. As far as I can judge I believe him to be deserving of a helping hand and should be very glad to hear of his welfare. Mr John Leyland of Byfleet is the principal of the school and I know that he would concur in giving the lad a good character. Yours respectfully, E P Gibson

12 June 1872
Statement: I would willingly work if I could get work to do.
Report: this boy states that when he was twelve years old his mother died in Hastings and then him and another boy tramped the country for three years and then got locked up at Croydon for begging. They were taken before the magistrates and then sent to Byfleet Industrial School for two years and was discharged about six months ago. He then went to Portsmouth and tried to join the navy but the doctor would not pass him on account of heart disease. Since that, applicant has been getting his living by begging. Mr Harrington Balfour states he would like this case investigated and see if something could be done to get him employment. He also states applicant begged of him a few days ago and he took his name and address and wrote to Mr Gibson the school master respecting his character and had in reply a very favourable report. The police give him a good character. WC [William Collingham]
Adjourned for further investigation, R P Hooper, chairman. Further information: I find this boy left the town on Thursday and I believe he is gone to London in the chance of employ with Mr Avenell, tailor, New Road, to whom I was to have taken him for inspection this morning. Case to be recorded, R P Hooper, chairman

198 ALICE SAMS, 37, MATTRESS MAKER, 50 SPRING GARDENS, BRIGHTON

Alice Guy was born in Ridgewood, Uckfield, in about 1835. In 1841 she was enumerated at Piltdown Cottages, Fletching, where she lived with her parents and sister. She married Francis Sams, upholsterer, of 7 Hampton Place at St Nicholas, Brighton, on 4 May 1862.[725]

Francis Sams was born in Lewes in about 1836 and was enumerated at Park Cottages, Lewes, on the census of 1841. In 1851 the family were living at Edward Street, Lewes, and Francis was employed as a plough boy. It is unknown when Sams took up upholstery as his livelihood, but he died in Brighton in the September quarter of 1870.[726]

When Alice Sams applied to the Mendicity Society in June 1872 she claimed to have been living in Brighton for 20 years and at Spring Gardens for two weeks: she had previously been living at 13 Upper Gardner Street. Sams paid weekly rent of two shillings and earned three shillings per week as a mattress maker working for Mrs Trille at Mott and Co, steam bedding factory, 126 Queens Road. She was suffering from consumption

[725] ESRO: PAR 255/1/3/35.
[726] Death of Francis Sams registered Q3 1870 Brighton 2b 143.

when she applied to the charity; her death was registered at Brighton in the December quarter of 1872.[727]

Letter from F Trille, Mott and Co Steam Bedding Factory, 126 Queens Road, Brighton, [June 1872]
If you can put this poor woman's case before the committee I think you will find it really a sad, deserving case. She is a widow of a mattress maker and is in the last stage of consumption, has worked for some little time but now, poor thing, has so little strength left that it is impossible she can gain her livelihood any longer. She is industrious and sober and we shall be pleased to give any further information concerning her.

12 June 1872
Statement: Alice Sams would be thankful for a little assistance.
Report: I made enquiries respecting this case and find applicant works for Mrs Trill[e], 126 Queens Road, but suffering with consumption she is not able to earn but a very little. The most she earns is 3s per week. She did have her brother's children to look after till a fortnight ago when he got married again. The brother getting married and taking his children home is the cause of applicant being in great distress. Before her husband died two years ago they received parish relief but since his death she has not applied for it. Mrs Trill[e] gave her a good character. I have known applicant for a long time and believe her to be a very respectable woman. The home is in a destitute state. WC [William Collingham]
Relieved with a dispensary letter and 3s, R P Hooper. Entered, RJ [Robert Johnson, secretary]

199 FREDERICK PEPPER, 65, NO OCCUPATION, 78 HANOVER STREET, BRIGHTON

Frederick Pepper was born in Brentford, Middlesex, on 30 April 1809 and baptised at St Lawrence, Brentford, on 26 May 1809.[728] *In the October session of 1827 a 19-year-old man named Frederick Pepper was sentenced to one month's imprisonment for larceny at the Old Bailey.*[729] *The Globe described the events leading up to the trial, 'A genteel looking youth, named Frederick Pepper, whose friends are in respectable circumstances, was charged with having robbed his master, Mr Robert Whittaker, a linen draper of 1 New Cavendish Street. Mr Whittaker, having reason to suspect the prisoner, accused him of having stoled [sic] goods to a large amount, and he then acknowledged having robbed Mr W to the amount of £30. Mr W on that occasion merely dismissed the prisoner, and he*

727 Death of Alice Sams registered Q4 1872 Brighton 2b [14]1.
728 London Metropolitan Archive: DRO/058/005.
729 The National Archives: HO 26; Piece 33; page 173.

returned to his friends at Knightsbridge; but in consequence of further information, that the prisoner had been living at the rate of £3 a week, and had supplied some of his relatives with money to pay their rent, he procured a search warrant, and on his apartments being examined a velvet waistcoat, a French box, and some ribbons were found, which Mr Whittaker identified as his property, and produced the piece of velvet from which the waistcoat was made. The prisoner was fully committed; but his solicitor requested that he might remain in the New Prison until the sessions. Mr Whittaker declared that the prisoner was not entitled to the slightest indulgence for he must have robbed him to the extent of a thousand pounds.' [730]

Pepper claimed to have come to Brighton in about 1836, and in 1841 he was enumerated at Tidy Street, where he lived with his wife Elizabeth and three young children. In 1851 he was employed as a clerk and lived with his family at 55 William Street. By 1861 the family had moved to 29 South Street, Worthing, and Frederick was employed as a railway clerk. Elizabeth Pepper died in Worthing in the June quarter of 1866 agaed 48 and after her death Frederick Pepper moved to 5 Bedford Buildings, Brighton, where he was enumerated in 1871 lodging with his daughter, Caroline, and her husband.

When Pepper's case was forwarded to the Mendicity Society in June 1872 by John Scarborow, the owner of a china and glass warehouse at 135 North Street he had no income but did not pay rent as he was living with his son. The application form states that he had a relative, also named Pepper, who lived at 2 Gilbert Road, Kennington, who may have been able to provide financial support.

He died in January in the June quarter of 1876.[731]

13 June 1872
Statement: Frederick Pepper would be thankful for a little assistance.
Report: I made enquiries respecting this man and find he lives with his son. The son has got a wife and three children. He works for Mr Sutton, carrier, Market Street, his wages is £1 per week. Applicant did work for Mr Pickford, carrier, North Street, but left four years ago. Since that he has not had any regular employment, only a few light jobs. The cause of leaving Mr Pickford was he was getting too old for heavy work. Mr Scarborow states he applied to him for assistance and he gave him the ticket, he also states he has known this man a long time and he believes him to be a respectable man. The relieving officer states he received parish relief for a long time till June 1871 when they gave an order for the [work]house which he refused. Applicant has given a false address, but he did live there a few weeks ago.
Dismissed, ineligible, R P Hooper, chairman

[730] The Globe, 11 October 1827.
[731] Death of Frederick Pepper registered Q2 1876 Brighton 2b 130.

200 ELLEN SPARKS OR SPARKES, 41, WIFE OF A RAILWAY LABOURER, 29 ST MARY MAGDALENE STREET, BRIGHTON

Ellen Caiger married James Sparkes at New Shoreham on 19 January 1862.[732] *James Sparkes worked for the London Brighton South Coast Railway and was employed as a carter between November 1858 and 2 December 1859.*[733] *He was recommended by the Reverend E J Richards and earned a weekly salary of 16 shillings. His name appears in the railway company's register again in 1871 when he was employed as a carman earning 18 shillings per week.*[734]

The couple were enumerated at Buckingham Street, New Shoreham, on the 1871 census: James Sparkes was described as 33 years of age, born in Emsworth, Hampshire; Ellen Sparkes was born in Bognor in about 1832 and their children were born in Whitstable, Kent, in 1858; Pimlico, 1862[735] *and Shoreham in 1864, 1865 and 1868.*

When Ellen Sparkes approached the Mendicity Society in June 1872 the family had been living in Brighton for three years and at 29 Mary Magdalene Street for the past five months; they had previously lodged at 17 Elder Row. They paid weekly rent of three shillings for three rooms and were not in arrears. James Sparkes still earned 18 shillings per week working for the railway company and the eldest son, Edward, worked as a labourer for Mr Rigden of Hove earning four shillings per week. The couple's only daughter, Sarah, was born in about 1862 and attended Providence Street School.

The death of a 46-year-old woman named Ellen Sparkes was registered in Brighton in the June quarter of 1877 and the death of a 40-year-old man named James Sparkes was registered, also in Brighton, in the March quarter of 1878.

13 June 1872
Statement: Ellen Sparks wants a dispensary letter for her son George.
Report: I made enquiries respecting this case and find this man works at the railway and bears a good character. The home is in a passable state. They lost one child six weeks ago. The Reverend Mr Salmon states applicant did not ask for relief: all she wanted was the dispensary letter. He believes this to be a deserving case. WC [William Collingham]
Dispensary letter granter, R P Hooper, chairman

[732] Ancestry.com England, select marriages 1538-1973.
[733] UK Railway Employment Book RAIL414; Piece 770.
[734] UK Railway Employment Book RAIL414; Piece 763.
[735] It is assumed that this refers to the area of London known as Pimlico. However, there was a street named Pimlico in the North Laine area of Brighton at this time.

INDEX OF NAMES

Notes:
References are to *Case Numbers*, not pages.
Names recorded as, for example, Mrs Smith or Mr Jones are indexed simply as Smith or Jones as appropriate, unless they can be clearly associated with more specific entries.
Searches of different name variants are advised.
Five principal officers of the Society, who names occur very frequently, are excluded from this index. These are Sir Orfeur Cavenagh, William Collingham, Robert Poole Hooper, Robert Johnson and George Dudley Ryder